Scandal and Reputation at the Court of Catherine de Medici

Scandal and Reputation at the Court of Catherine de Medici explores Catherine de Medici's 'flying squadron', the legendary ladies-in-waiting of the sixteenth-century French queen mother who were alleged to have been ordered to seduce politically influential men for their mistress's own Machiavellian purposes. Branded a 'cabal of cuckoldry' by a contemporary critic, these women were involved in scandals that have encouraged a perception, which continues in much academic literature, of the late Valois court as debauched and corrupt.

Rather than trying to establish the guilt or innocence of the accused, Una McIlvenna here focuses on representations of the scandals in popular culture and print, and on the collective portrayal of the women in the libelous and often pornographic literature that circulated information about the court. She traces the origins of this material to the all-male intellectual elite of the parlementaires: lawyers and magistrates who expressed their disapproval of Catherine's political and religious decisions through misogynist pamphlets and verse that targeted the women of her entourage.

Scandal and Reputation at the Court of Catherine de Medici reveals accusations of poisoning and incest to be literary tropes within a tradition of female defamation dating to classical times that encouraged a collective and universalizing notion of women as sexually voracious, duplicitous and, ultimately, dangerous. In its focus on manuscript and early print culture, and on the transition from a world of orality to one dominated by literacy and textuality, this study has relevance for scholars of literary history, particularly those interested in pamphlet and libel culture.

Una McIlvenna is Lecturer in Early Modern Literature at the University of Kent, Canterbury, UK.

Women and Gender in the Early Modern World
Series Editors: Allyson Poska and Abby Zanger

The study of women and gender offers some of the most vital and innovative challenges to current scholarship on the early modern period. For more than a decade now, Women and Gender in the Early Modern World has served as a forum for presenting fresh ideas and original approaches to the field. Interdisciplinary and multidisciplinary in scope, this Ashgate series strives to reach beyond geographical limitations to explore the experiences of early modern women and the nature of gender in Europe, the Americas, Asia and Africa. We welcome proposals for both single-author volumes and edited collections which expand and develop this continually evolving field of study.

Recent titles in the series:

Gender and Song in Early Modern England
Leslie C. Dunn and Katherine R. Larson

Autobiographical Writing by Early Modern Hispanic Women
Elizabeth Teresa Howe

Menstruation and Procreation in Early Modern France
Cathy McClive

Baptist Women's Writings in Revolutionary Culture, 1640–1680
Rachel Adcock

Men and Women Making Friends in Early Modern France
Lewis C. Seifert and Rebecca M. Wilkin

Rethinking Gaspara Stampa in the Canon of Renaissance Poetry
Unn Falkeid and Aileen A. Feng

Maternity and Romance Narratives in Early Modern England
Karen Bamford and Naomi J. Miller

Devout Laywomen in the Early Modern World
Alison Weber

Anna Maria van Schurman, 'The Star of Utrecht'
Anne R. Larsen

Scandal and Reputation at the Court of Catherine de Medici

Una McIlvenna
University of Kent

LONDON AND NEW YORK

First published 2016
by Routledge
2 Park Square, Milton Park, Abingdon, Oxon OX14 4RN

and by Routledge
711 Third Avenue, New York, NY 10017

Routledge is an imprint of the Taylor & Francis Group, an informa business

© 2016 Una McIlvenna

The right of Una McIlvenna to be identified as author of this work has been asserted by her in accordance with sections 77 and 78 of the Copyright, Designs and Patents Act 1988.

All rights reserved. No part of this book may be reprinted or reproduced or utilised in any form or by any electronic, mechanical, or other means, now known or hereafter invented, including photocopying and recording, or in any information storage or retrieval system, without permission in writing from the publishers.

Trademark notice: Product or corporate names may be trademarks or registered trademarks, and are used only for identification and explanation without intent to infringe.

British Library Cataloguing in Publication Data
A catalogue record for this book is available from the British Library

Library of Congress Cataloging-in-Publication Data
Names: McIlvenna, Una, author.
Title: Scandal and reputation at the court of Catherine de Medici / by Una McIlvenna.
Description: Farnham, Surrey, England ; Ashgate Publishing Limited : Burlington, VT : Ashgate Publishing Company, 2016. | Series: Women and gender in the early modern world | Includes bibliographical references and index.
Identifiers: LCCN 2015040011 | ISBN 9781472428219 (hardcover : alk. paper)
Subjects: LCSH: French literature—16th century—History and criticism. | Scandals in literature. | Catherine de Médicis, Queen, consort of Henry II, King of France, 1519–1589—In literature. | Courts and courtiers in literature. | Women in literature. | Sex discrimination—France—History—16th century. | Women's rights—France—History—16th century. | Reputation—France—History—16th century.
Classification: LCC PQ239 .M45 2016 | DDC 840.9/35844028—dc23
LC record available at http://lccn.loc.gov/2015040011

ISBN: 978-1-4724-2821-9 (hbk)
ISBN: 978-1-3156-0767-2 (ebk)

Typeset in Times New Roman
by Apex CoVantage, LLC

Contents

List of Illustrations vi
Acknowledgements vii
Abbreviations ix

1 Introduction: Catherine de Medici and the Myth of the 'Flying Squadron' 1

2 Court Life and Its Critics: The Rise in Satirical Literature 36

3 The Dissemination of Scandal: News Culture in Early Modern France 61

4 Venomous Rumours: The Scandal of Isabelle de Limeuil 102

5 Word of Honour: Françoise de Rohan versus the Duke of Nemours 131

6 The Triumph of the Matriarch: Anne d'Este, Duchesse de Guise, Duchesse de Nemours 155

7 Conclusion: A Re-assessment of Scandal 187

Bibliography 197
Index 215

Illustrations

Cover. François Clouet, *Catherine de Medici*. © BnF Estampes et photographie Réserve NA-22–4

1.1 François Clouet, *Charlotte de Beaune, dame de Sauve, dame de Fizes, marquise de Noirmoutier*. © BnF Estampes et photographie Réserve NA-22–19   16

2.1 François Clouet, *Claude-Catherine de Clermont, maréchale de Retz*. © BnF Estampes et photographie Réserve NA-22–21   39

3.1 'Comme les deux Princes estans mort sont mis sur une table avec la remonstrance de Madame de Nemours', in Pierre de L'Estoile, *Les Belles Figures et Drolleries de la Ligue*. © BnF Tolbiac Réserve LA25–6   72

3.2 Map of Paris in the sixteenth century, showing places where edicts were to be cried. © Lance Greene   73

3.3 Engraving of a colporteur, *Les cris de Paris*. © BnF Arsenal Estampes Rés. 264, f. 1r.   78

3.4 'La bibliothèque de madame de Montpensier'. BnF MS Fr 15592, f. 117 [author's own photo]   86

3.5 François Clouet, *Jeanne de Halluin, baronne d'Alluye* [Jeanne de Piennes]. © RMN-Grand Palais (domaine de Chantilly)   90

4.1 Benjamin Foulon, *Madame de Sardiny* [Isabelle de Limeuil]. © RMN-Grand Palais (musée du Louvre)   103

4.2 *Louis de Bourbon, Ier prince de Condé*. © RMN-Grand Palais (Château de Versailles)   105

5.1 François Clouet, *Jacques de Savoie, duc de Nemours*. © The Trustees of the British Museum 1910,0212.61   132

5.2 Autograph letter from Françoise de Rohan to Jacques de Savoie, duc de Nemours. BnF MS Fr 3397, f. 70v. [author's own photo]   139

6.1 François Clouet, *Anne d'Este, duchesse de Guise, duchesse de Nemours*. © BnF Réserve NA-22–19   156

6.2 'Le Tableau de Madame de Montpensier' or 'Briefue description des diverses cruautez que les catholiques endurent en Angleterre pour la foy', in Pierre de L'Estoile, *Les Belles Figures et Drolleries de la Ligue . . .* © BnF Tolbiac Rés. LA25–6   174

Acknowledgements

This book is not simply about the stories of scandalous women, but rather about the realities that lie behind those stories, the realities of women trying to make their lives a success despite the obstacles. As this book will show, often it was their networks of support that were the decisive factor in that outcome. In my own attempts to be successful, I have been blessed with a network that provided both intellectual and practical support to make all the obstacles seem small.

Both during my postgraduate time and years later when I returned as a faculty member, I have had the great fortune to be surrounded by the warm and generous group of scholars in the English department at Queen Mary University of London. Lisa Jardine routinely – and hilariously – demystified the secret world of academia and, knowing I had a baby on the way at the beginning of my doctorate, ensured that I was financially secure. Her recent passing has been hard to accept, but I hope that this book plays a tiny part in demonstrating her immense legacy. Evelyn Welch was, and continues to be, an exemplary mentor: encouraging, inspiring, supportive and eternally patient with a student who continually presented her with challenges, rather than readable work. She taught me that anything is possible. Warren Boutcher has been a continual source of friendship, encouragement and last-minute Latin/French/Italian translation. His advice at an early stage of this research was pivotal in guiding my argument. Jerry Brotton and Colin Jones have also offered crucial help and guidance. I am also grateful to the faculty and students of the Centre for Editing Lives and Letters, then at Queen Mary, now at UCL, among them Robyn Adams, Matt Symonds, Jan Broadway, Tom Parkinson, Karen Hardman and especially Kath Diamond, who has been an inspirational companion.

My three years as a postdoctoral research fellow with the Australian Research Council's Centre for the History of Emotions allowed me the time to rethink my work in an atmosphere full of positivity, intellectual rigour and true friendship. I am particularly grateful to Susan Broomhall, who has supported this project from its early stages, and me personally from the moment of my arrival in Australia. Colleagues at the University of Sydney provided immensely useful, practical advice and a wonderful working environment. In particular, my research mentor Lee Wallace was instrumental in getting this book to publication stage. My supervisor Juanita Ruys read and improved upon my work and wrote superlative references. I also benefited from the support and advice of Annamarie Jagose, Nicola Parsons, Huw Griffiths, Liam Semler, Jennifer Milam and the members of the postdoc writing group: Helen Young, Christina Alt and Hannah Burrows. And at Sydney I was blessed with the best officemate in the world, Rebecca Fields McNamara, who made our adventure Down Under a delight with her Southern hospitality and Tex-Mex cooking.

Many people have helped me by sharing their own work, reading mine or offering expertise. Of these, special thanks go to Caroline Zum Kolk, Rosa Salzberg, Sarah Bercusson, Stephen Brogan, Emily Butterworth, Alan Bryson, Elizabeth Horodowich, Filippo de Vivo, Nadine Akkerman, Birgit Houben and the other contributors to *The Politics of Female Households*, Claire Walker, Heather Kerr, Raphaële Garrod, Sheila ffolliott, Kate van Orden, Kathleen Wilson-Chevalier and Joanna Milstein. I am also especially grateful to Julian Swann and Cathy McClive, my PhD examiners who continue to offer excellent advice and support. Thanks also go to Lance Greene for the map.

Material from Chapter 2 is discussed in 'A Stable of Whores? The "Flying Squadron" of Catherine de Medici' in *The Politics of Female Households: Ladies-in-Waiting across Early Modern Europe*, eds. Nadine Akkerman and Birgit Houben (Leiden: Brill, 2014), 181–208. Material in Chapter 4 appeared in an earlier form in 'Poison, Pregnancy and Protestants: Gossip and Scandal at the Early Modern French Court' in *Fama and Her Sisters: Gossip and Rumour in Early Modern Europe*, eds. Claire Walker and Heather Kerr (Turnhout: Brepols, 2015), 137–60, and some of Chapter 5 as 'Word versus Honor: The Case of Françoise de Rohan vs. Jacques de Savoie', *Journal of Early Modern History* 16, nos. 4–5 (2012): 315–34. I would like to thank Brill and Brepols for their permission to reuse this material.

This research was made possible by a doctoral award from the Arts and Humanities Research Council. I am also grateful to the AHRC and to the Central London Research Fund for travel grants that allowed me to do research in Paris. I am also grateful to the staff of the Bibliothèque nationale de France and the Bibliothèque historique de la ville de Paris, and in London, the British Library, Senate House, the Warburg Institute and the Institute for Historical Research.

Being able to write a book is about far more than intellectual inspiration, and my practical support network has been just as crucial. I am grateful to Christine Mackley and Cara Flatley for looking after my children during my research for this book. Of my immense family, I would like to single out certain siblings for their support: Stephen McIlvenna, for making Paris more wonderful than it already is; Teresa McIlvenna, for everything; and in particular, Noeleen McIlvenna, for endless proofreading at short notice, for her sound professional advice and – above all – for blazing a trail. My parents Maeve and Hugh inspired in me a lifelong love of learning, and a questioning of injustice wherever it is found.

If I have been successful it is because of the encouragement and example of Aaron Pidgeon, who urged me to fulfil my potential and aim for the stars. Along the way he has taken on the peculiar demands of having a partner in academia (multiple international moves with small children in tow) with enthusiasm and good spirit. I am forever in his debt.

Finally, my thanks go to Annie and Aidan, for providing the most delightful distraction from all of this. I look forward to the day when you are allowed to read this book.

Abbreviations

AN	Archives nationales, Paris
BnF	Bibliothèque nationale de France, Paris
MS Fr	Manuscrits, Fonds français
Rés.	Réserve des livres rares
NA	National Archives, London
Brantôme	Pierre de Bourdeille, abbé de Brantôme, *Recueil des dames, poésies et tombeaux*, ed. Etienne Vaucheret (Paris: Gallimard, 1991).
Castelnau	*Les mémoires de messire Michel de Castelnau, seigneur de Mauvissiere; illustrez et augmentez de plusieurs commentaires & manuscrits, tant lettres, instructions, traittez, qu'autres pieces secretes & originalles, servants à donner la verité de l'histoire des regnes de François II., Charles IX & Henry III. & de la regence & du gouvernement de Catherine de Médicis; avec les eloges des rois, reynes, princes & autres personnes illustres de l'une & de l'autre réligion sous ces trois regnes . . . par J. Le Laboureur.* (Paris: Pierre Lamy, 1659).
CSPF	Calendar of State Papers, Foreign Series, of the reign of Elizabeth, ed. Joseph Stevenson (London: Longman & Co., 1870).
Discours merveilleux	Discours merveilleux de la vie, actions et deportements de Catherine de Médicis, royne-mère, ed. Nicole Cazauran (Genève: Droz, 1995).
L'Estoile	Pierre de L'Estoile, *Registre-Journal du règne de Henri III*, 6 vols., eds. Madeleine Lazard and Gilbert Schrenck (Genève: Droz, 1992).
Lettres	*Lettres de Catherine de Médicis*, 11 vols., eds. Hector de la Ferrière, G. Baguenault de la Puchesse (Paris: Imprimerie nationale, 1880–1909).
JHIV	Pierre de L'Estoile, *Journal de L'Estoile pour le règne de Henri IV*, 2 vols. (Paris: Gallimard, 1948).
Zum Kolk	Caroline Zum Kolk, 'Catherine de Médicis et sa maison. La fonction politique de l'hôtel de la reine au XVIe siècle' (unpublished doctoral thesis, Université Paris VIII, 2006).
n.d.	no date
n.p.	no publisher

1 Introduction
Catherine de Medici and the Myth of the 'Flying Squadron'

In September 1577, in the château of Poitiers, René de Villequier, chief adviser to the French king Henri III, stabbed to death his pregnant wife Françoise de La Marck, a lady-in-waiting to the queen mother Catherine de Medici. He did so after supposedly discovering a letter written to her by her lover, the seigneur Barbizi, in which the latter claimed to be the father of her unborn child. In his entry for that month, the Parisian diarist Pierre de L'Estoile described the public reaction to the murder, its protagonists and the pardon that Villequier subsequently received from his master:

> ... it was said that Villequier had discovered a plot of his wife to poison him, just as the said Barbizi had already poisoned his wife, so that they could marry each other afterwards; and that he [Villequier] had found in his wife's belongings the mixture or paste with which he was to be poisoned.
> This murder was thought to be cruel, committed as it was on a woman who was pregnant with two children; and odd, committed as it was in the King's lodgings where His Majesty was, and more so at court, where whoring is publicly and notoriously practised among the ladies, who hold it to be a virtue. But the granting and ease of the grace and pardon which Villequier obtained, without any difficulty, led some to believe that there was behind this a secret commandment or tacit consent of the King, who hated this woman (even though he had been sleeping with her for a long time, so it was said, with the co-operation of her husband who acted as her pimp), because of a report that had been made to him saying that she had spoken ill of His Majesty in public.[1]

It is a splendidly lurid account of a real event, but L'Estoile's version of this scandal is more than scurrilous gossip. It introduces several important themes around the representation of the court and its female members that this book will discuss. First, in this early modern version of an honour killing, a male courtier kills his wife because of her alleged adultery and intent to poison him. Second, L'Estoile refers to the wider reputation of the ladies of the court as notorious whores. The court acts as a site of prostitution, with the king as an active participant. Lastly, the many references to public opinion ('so it was said', 'murder was thought to be cruel', 'a report that had been made to him', 'she had spoken ill of His Majesty in public') highlight the very publicised nature of the intimate domestic life of courtiers.[2]

The scandal of the murder of Françoise de La Marck produced a torrent of literary output in the form of verse libels. L'Estoile mentioned 'many and diverse sorts of poems and epitaphs' on the subject, and copied 12 into his journal 'which', he claimed, 'fell into my hands'.[3] That the information about an early modern scandal was disseminated, discussed and analysed almost exclusively in the form of verse, with several written in Latin, is a historically specific phenomenon within the development of early modern news culture that has important consequences for historiography. The rationale behind the choice of verse, its stylistic features and its ramifications for our understanding of court scandal will be discussed in detail in Chapter 2. For now, what the La Marck verses reveal is an extraordinary knowledge beyond the court of the most intimate details of the affair: two refer to Barbizi, one mentioning his letter, several mention La Marck's pregnancy, all discuss her promiscuity and her husband's tolerance of it, and L'Estoile himself related the detail that her servant was also stabbed as she helped her mistress dress. What is also striking is the diversity of opinion within the poems, with some portraying La Marck as an innocent victim of her own beauty and her husband's jealousy, while others view the noblewoman simply as a whore: one verse, a mock epitaph, reads 'I received the death, Passerby, which my life merited'.[4] It seemed that everyone in Paris had an opinion about the intimate life of Françoise de La Marck.

Whatever their perspective, however, most of the verses assume the debauched environment of the court, as indicated in the following verse written in the voice of La Marck herself:

> If it is a fault that would offend the gods,
> Blame this court where I was raised.
> Trained by the head of an infinite troupe
> Following the slender firebrands of Cupid,
> Many lovers were rewarded by me.
> If it is a common evil, why should I be punished?[5]

The reference to 'an infinite troupe' trained by its leader to follow Cupid and reward lovers is a direct reference to the female household of Catherine de Medici, of which La Marck was a member. It was a household whose negative collective reputation is the focus of this study. Catherine's role as queen mother and regent-governor of France in the sixteenth century has traditionally been depicted as dependent on her inherently 'Italian' and 'female' skills of manipulation, deception and corruption, culminating in the legend of the wicked Italian queen that reached its zenith in the nineteenth century with Michelet's famous description of Catherine as the 'maggot born in Italy's tomb'.[6] The attacks on her rule were present much earlier: a poem in the 1573 Huguenot polemical pamphlet *Reveille-Matin des François et de leurs voisins* called Catherine 'that high born whore, /

The blood infected with the buggers of Italy, / Nursed by the milk of a horrible fury'.[7] Here, xenophobic stereotypes of sexual deviance were employed to attack Catherine's political skills. Explicit Italophobia was common in sixteenth-century France, inspired by the large numbers of Italian immigrants, many fleeing the upheaval caused by the Franco-Italian wars, who found a haven in the court of the Medici queen. Anti-Italian polemic depicted them as sexually deviant and prone to underhanded means of acquiring power, particularly the use of poison to kill enemies. These stereotypes were extended to describe Catherine's manipulative exploitation of her ladies-in-waiting, known colloquially by later historians as her *escadron volant* (flying squadron). She allegedly ordered these women to seduce and spy on influential noblemen, and some were eventually involved in scandals around poisoning, adultery, incest and illegitimate births. The scandals have been collectively used to discredit Catherine's abilities as both a negotiator and a leader, and to depict the Valois court as a hotbed of debauchery and corrupted morality, where Catherine used any means necessary to further her own selfish ambitions. This study explores how these stereotypes of Machiavellian corruption and deviance were deployed to construct a myth about the dangers of women in power at the early modern French court, and why such a myth would endure for so long.

Although she was the daughter of a French princess and had lived in France since the age of fourteen, Catherine was unable to avoid attacks on her Italian heritage. But Italians were not the only source of discontent for sixteenth-century critics of the crown. The inexorable rise of the Reformed faith in France, supported by French Calvinist exiles in Geneva, found followers at the highest levels of the nobility, tearing apart families both aristocrat and peasant and causing an endless series of crises through which Catherine attempted to steer a tolerant middle path. The massacre of Huguenot worshippers by the troops of the duke of Guise at Wassy in 1562, only three years after the death of Henri II had left Catherine as regent for her young sons François II and Charles IX, sparked almost four decades of bitter civil and religious war.[8] Catherine's responses to the new religion inevitably met with severe criticism from parties on all sides of the conflict, but particularly from those who sought to capitalise on the power vacuum left by a young king ruled by his mother. The religious conflict infiltrated every level of society: Each of the scandalous cases explored in this study hinged on the discord caused by the differing confessional beliefs of the nobles involved, and the threat of violent clashes that such differences engendered. While those who attacked the queen mother may have had sincere and profound complaint with her approach to the political and religious issues she faced, they regularly expressed their dissatisfaction through attacks on her household and on the reputations, both individual and collective, of her ladies-in-waiting.

These attacks on Catherine's household were given greater impetus by the behaviour of Henri III, Catherine's son, who ascended the throne in 1574 and promptly began to restrict court offices and favours to a select group of his close companions, known as his *mignons*, to the detriment of many of the leading families of the kingdom. His simultaneous introduction of formal measures designed to prevent access to the person of the monarch also provoked great resentment among leading nobles, many of whom left the court in protest. Much of the resentment expressed itself in attacks on Henri and his *mignons*, whose increasingly flamboyant appearance was read as a sign of their effeminacy and possible homosexuality.[9] Henri's inability to produce an heir not only confirmed his critics' suspicions, but also created a succession crisis, as the next in line for the throne was his Protestant cousin, Henri de Navarre. As Henri III refused to nullify Navarre's claim on the basis of his religion, the Catholic League, created to prevent a heretic on the French throne, offered its own candidate, and its supporters began to produce a wave of polemical literature depicting Henri III and his *mignons* as perverse and depraved.[10] The court was depicted as a locus of sexual deviance, where the monarch's power and authority had been usurped. There occurred a simultaneous rise in satirical literature portraying the ladies of the court as equally debauched, the women in Catherine's entourage acting as the female counterparts to the despised *mignons*, cuckolding their husbands and engaging in deviant sexual behaviour. For example, the *Pasquil Courtizan* of 1581 opens with a criticism of the excessive amounts spent on the recent wedding of the king's favourite, the duke of Joyeuse, but eventually evolves into a litany of the adulterous escapades of the women of the court.[11] Simultaneously, the anti-monarchical bent of the League literature provoked a backlash, and L'Estoile's journal thus abounds with verses satirising League partisans, some of whom were high-profile women of the court. Although it is at times difficult to discern the political leanings of the authors, both sides combined criticism of the men of Henri's household with attacks on Catherine and her household. The result was a tide of satirical literature that portrayed the women of the court as licentious and scandalous.

While recent research has begun to rehabilitate Catherine's reputation by revealing her tolerance, commitment to peace and compromise on religious matters, as well as her neo-Platonic aspirations and contribution to the arts, no study has yet explored the recurrent image of her 'flying squadron' and the lascivious and scandalous reputation of the women of the Valois court.[12] This study therefore may be the final act in Catherine's historiographical rehabilitation, but it is more than the simple revelation that she was an effective ruler. Rather, I use the case of a small but significant group of elite women in the early modern period to draw conclusions in two different but overlapping fields: women's studies and literary history. One thread of this study examines the image of the 'scandalous woman' and exposes it in all its varied and multiplicitous appearances, while the other thread concerns the literary, intellectual nature of scandal. This book tracks the negative historiography about Catherine de Medici, showing how the libellous attacks on her and her ladies coalesced into a myth about her ability to govern. Out of dissatisfaction with Catherine's attempts to appease both sides of the confessional divide, critics both Catholic and Protestant produced satire of courtiers that relied upon tropes of debauchery and the occult. This book reveals how their satirical representations came to be treated as genuine descriptions of life at court by historians; in other words, how satirical fiction became historical 'fact' at the expense of Catherine's reputation.

'Scandalous Women' and the Gendered Nature of Scandal

Through the use of three case studies, I explore how both individual and collective reputations were constructed, attacked and defended at the early modern court. By investigating scandal as it affected these women, one can discern a gendering of accusations to discredit high-profile figures. While their male counterparts could be mocked as cuckolds, women were regularly accused of poisoning, and allegations made about their promiscuity and infidelity, with none of these accusations necessarily based on anything more than scurrilous hearsay. This study demonstrates that such accusations were traditional literary tropes employed against women whose political influence, public profile or superior education made them socially transgressive. From Cleopatra to Anne Boleyn to Catherine the Great to Marie-Antoinette, throughout history powerful women have been attacked in terms of their sexuality, usually depicted as deviant and/or promiscuous.[13] Powerful women have also been regularly represented as dangerous, with poison a perennially popular choice of feminine murder weapon, and this study looks at how these ostensibly unrelated accusations were often closely linked.

For 'scandalous women' were rarely accused of only a single misdemeanour. Therefore, this book looks at the multiplicity of scandal: how one accusation or attack on her reputation could make a woman vulnerable to other allegations. Through an analysis of this layering of indictments, and an examination of the reactions of accused women and those closest to them when faced with such harmful allegations, I reveal a 'hierarchy of scandal': the idea that certain accusations were perceived as more damaging than others. That such perceptions could change over time, such as in the case of illegitimate births which were considered to be more shameful to eighteenth- and nineteenth-century historians than to sixteenth-century commentators, is proof that it is time for a re-assessment of the historical contingency of scandal in early modern France. Such a re-assessment has been carried out for scandals involving the English aristocracy of the seventeenth century: Alastair Bellany's study of the Overbury scandal under James I's reign and Cynthia Herrup's investigation of the Castlehaven scandal under his son Charles I's reign.[14] Avoiding straightforward conclusions about the guilt or innocence of the protagonists, both authors instead explore the social, political, literary and legal aspects of each case. Herrup's interpretation of the Castlehaven case, which involved charges of rape and sodomy and resulted in the execution of a peer, investigates early modern anxieties around aristocratic behaviour and sexual deviance, themes that are addressed repeatedly in this study. Bellany's study builds on his pioneering work on the study of pamphlet and libel culture to reconstruct the news culture by which the Overbury poisoning scandal circulated among the early Stuart 'public', an approach that will also be used in this book.[15] Both Bellany and Herrup examine the impact of the scandals on the reigning monarch and discuss what measures were taken to limit that impact, stressing the political significance of court scandal. By following the changing representations of each case over several centuries and the shifting political contexts in which their stories were told, both readings offer an analysis of contemporary and long-term perceptions of the monarch and court.

It is important to stress that this study is not only about the short-term reputations of individuals, but also about the long-term reputation of a group of women. In her study of American university fraternity 'little sisters', Mindy Stombler explored the vulnerability of women to being labelled with a 'collective sexual reputation' and examined how each woman would interpret such a label and resist it to protect her own individual sexual reputation.[16] She also identified how the brothers of the fraternity would contribute by sexually objectifying and commodifying them. This phenomenon can also be witnessed in the sixteenth century in the pamphlet literature and verse libels, in general composed by the educated, male legal fraternity, that targeted the women of the court. While one may be surprised at the degree to which individual women in this study demonstrated their resistance to attempts made to slander their personal honour, there was little they could do to prevent the development of a posthumous collective sexual reputation.[17] This book will therefore examine the phenomenon of the 'collective reputation', looking at its origins in the classical literary tradition of the enumeration and cataloguing of women. This satirical tradition was a reductive, literary trope that nevertheless has serious, long-term repercussions for the historiography of the women of the early modern French court and, I would argue, for women in history more broadly.

Honour and Reputation in Sixteenth-Century France

In the turmoil that defined the French Wars of Religion, sexual libels, accusations and poetic attacks on the nobility were serious in both political and military terms. In his seminal work on the early modern aristocracy, Lawrence Stone comments, 'One of the most characteristic features of the age was its hyper-sensitive insistence upon the overriding importance of reputation'.[18] Based on the notion of personal honour, 'that most precious of early modern possessions', noble reputations were an unstable commodity that required constant care to maintain and enrich.[19] Kristen Neuschel's work on noble culture in sixteenth-century France explains how elites maintained and developed reputation, status and honour through the judicious combination of land rights, violence and favour, exploring how family relationships could be mobilised both to strengthen claims to favour and to resolve disputes.[20] However, Neuschel's study, like most case studies of honour and reputation among the nobility, tends to discuss it almost exclusively from a masculine perspective.[21] While there have been numerous studies of defamation and slander among working-class women, their elite counterparts have received far less attention.[22] Meanwhile, Sharon Kettering's valuable work on the patronage and household service of early modern French noblewomen is concerned more with the practical side of the patron-client relationship and how women established and maintained careers at court than it is with issues of honour and defamation.[23] Female honour among the nobility was, however, a matter of much debate in the early modern period. The vast literature on female honour and deportment produced by the *querelle des femmes* was given new inspiration by the publication in France in 1540 of Baldessare Castiglione's *Il Cortegiano*.[24] The subsequent *querelle des amyes* debated the behaviour of courtly women, specifically, how their sexual deportment could affect their reputations.[25] As the case studies in this book will show, the individual reputations of the ladies at court were extremely vulnerable to attacks on their sexual honour. But they also demonstrate the surprisingly varied nature of what was deemed scandalous for a woman at court. The scandals explored in this book allow us to understand more about the anxieties around female behaviour in the early modern period, and they reveal – in a way that the prescriptive literature of the period such as conduct books cannot – how those who had access to information about the court reacted to news of scandalous behaviour, and the 'unwritten' rules governing moral transgression.

Similarly, the case studies demonstrate the agency a courtly woman had to protect her public image – her connections to those more powerful – which was often the deciding factor in a female courtier's struggle to protect her reputation. In each case, the women show tenacity in the fight to rehabilitate their good names, and often reveal a savvy understanding of how the law courts could help them achieve this goal. While at times they also employed methods in their campaigns that could be seen as typically 'feminine', such as correspondence, tears or choice of clothing, they often did this in conjunction with a deployment of the physical presence of the military might of their male relatives. What becomes clear is that, while women may have been the subject of attacks which were of a different nature to men (such as slanders on their chastity), honour was an entity shared by all members of the wider kin group, and so we regularly come across male relatives employing tactics to preserve or restore the good name of their female relative.

Literary Scandal and the Circulation of Information

The other thread of this study concerns the literary, intellectual nature of scandal and the means by which scandalous events, both real and imagined, could leave the domestic confines of the court to be disseminated into the wider public sphere. It is thus vital to be clear about what is meant in this study by the word 'court', for it was simultaneously the residential quarters of the royal family and the site of royal power in a more abstract sense. Each senior member of the royal family, the king, the queen, princes, princesses, as well as the queen mother, had their own household. This was made up of aristocratic office holders who performed various domestic tasks and made up the entourage that contributed to the royal member's prestige, as well as non-noble members of staff, who performed more arduous and menial tasks such as laundry and dressmaking. While the court was a residential and domestic space where the intimate, day-to-day lives of royalty and nobles were carried out, courtiers could not, and did not, expect to encounter the kind of privacy we today expect in a family home. Events and acts that might in other places and situations be considered private were there considered to be appropriate for common knowledge. Because of the significance of the body of the monarch and the importance given to the reproduction of heirs, not only in the royal family but also in the noble families that surrounded and served it, information and knowledge of sexual acts, childbirth and medical conditions were shared openly and in a manner that can at times be surprising to a modern observer. This does not mean, however, that courtiers did not at times attempt to keep certain matters secret; indeed, it is usually these moments, when the exposed nature of courtly life is met with attempts to silence it, that we discover scandalous events.

The French court of the sixteenth century was an itinerant one, moving regularly from one château to another, and all members of the household tended to travel as a group. Given that each senior member was allocated his or her own household, these households could travel independently, and thus Catherine's household could at times be distinct from the king's, for example. These châteaux were mostly in the Loire valley and the Île-de-France, although when not in Paris, the court was still in constant communication with its officers there, where key decisions by the monarch needed to be registered by the Parlement, situated in the Palais de Justice right next to the Parisian royal palace, the Louvre. With a particular focus on Paris therefore, I explore the geography of news and information transmission within the urban environment of sixteenth-century France. I track the methods and means by which gossip, rumour and factual information circulated both at court and on the streets. Through close literary analysis of the verse libels and other satirical material that criticised the women of the court, the origins of much of this material can be traced to the intellectual fraternity of the Parlement of Paris, France's leading sovereign law court. The Parlements were judicial courts responsible for the registration of royal edicts as well as issuing arrêts for the policing of the city, the University and the guilds. As the sixteenth century progressed, the venality of offices in the Parlement grew, and its members increasingly purchased their offices to preserve them hereditarily. Eventually the men of the Parlement began to conceive of themselves as the *noblesse de robe* (robe nobility), an alternative nobility to the traditional, martial *noblesse d'épée* (sword nobility), and as a social class which distinguished itself by its superior intellectualism. As a result, the obscene, misogynist material they created was simultaneously highly literate, in contrast to the tabloid journalism of today that is aimed primarily at an uneducated audience.[26]

The legal profession in France in the sixteenth century was a privileged, influential fraternity that has been described by Marc Fumaroli as 'the backbone of French humanism'.[27] Its members built their individual reputations through the circulation and publication of literary works designed to entertain and impress their colleagues. In his study of their contribution to the Republic of Letters, Fumaroli depicts this elite fraternity in glowing terms: 'Through its works and its erudite patronage, through the tranquillity of its libraries, it could not help but articulate, in the interior of the Palais de Justice, an eloquence that manifested and guaranteed its religious, moral and political authority'.[28] This study presents another, less idealistic, facet of the parlementaires' literary oeuvre. Employing David LaGuardia's argument about the literary performance of gender in the French Renaissance, I argue that, rather than construct their masculinity on the battlefield, these men constructed it on the page through the denigration of women.[29] The central political role of Catherine de Medici over a sustained period, and the subsequent public role of the ladies in her entourage, threatened the patriarchal model that the parlementaires sought to establish and reinforce through the laws they passed. Their resistance to the prominence of women found expression in misogynist literature that betrayed the parlementaires' own anxieties around gender and sexuality.[30] Thus, the literary depiction of courtly women as what L'Estoile called 'the cabal of cuckoldry' became a central aspect of the subsequent negative representation of Catherine's rule.[31] The parlementaires' incessant exchange of manuscript verse, attested to by L'Estoile, allowed for this representation to circulate widely and to eventually become entrenched.

Another group of men were a key link in the distribution of scandalous information about the court: ambassadors and diplomats. Intriguingly, they were usually university-educated men themselves, also often trained in the law and always with a knowledge of Latin.[32] Ambassadors occupied a unique and often troublesome position at court: ever-present, even in moments of particular tension, they were the representatives of what were often rival courts, sometimes even those of opposing religions.[33] Their role was to acquire as much information as possible about their host, and they were known to reward informers generously for evidence that would give their superiors an advantage in diplomatic terms. As Filippo de Vivo has shown us, 'diplomacy and illicit intelligence differed in acceptability and lawfulness, but were mutually necessary activities, and the growth of the former entailed an increase in the latter'.[34] As modern scholars, we are grateful for ambassadors: given that their role was to acquire information for their superiors at home, their dispatches are often full of social and political interactions that their host was trying to keep secret or would not have deemed interesting, given that they were the details of everyday life at court. We are therefore able to piece together not only the international perception of scandals at court but also their day-to-day unfolding. Ambassadors were as interested as we are in how scandals were being perceived by their contemporaries, and so enclosed with dispatches one finds libellous verses, and reports of graffiti or public arguments that not only documented information about scandalous events but which in so doing also spread that information – often slanderous opinion – more widely. If an informer (such as Gaspar Barchino whom we shall meet in Chapter 4) felt that Catherine was exploiting her ladies for political advantage, such a portrayal would spread quickly to those who were willing to pay for that viewpoint. I will therefore discuss the origins of that portrayal, how the myth of the 'flying squadron' helped to construct – and was itself given strength by – Catherine's own negative reputation, and how the legend developed within historiography to become 'factual' evidence of Catherine's underhanded political methods.

The Reputation of Catherine de Medici

Nicola Sutherland's historiographical summary of the legend of the 'Wicked Italian Queen' charts the evolution of Catherine's sinister image at the hands of historians.[35] Locating contemporary negative depictions of Catherine exclusively among Protestant polemical writers after the massacre of St. Bartholomew's Day in 1572, Sutherland says, 'It is notable, however, that no resentment against Catherine is expressed in the *Histoire ecclésiastique des églises réformées de France*, first published in Geneva in 1580', a sign that moderate Protestants did not share the extreme opinions of Catherine expressed in the pamphlet literature.[36] While moderate reformers may have been reserved in their criticism of Catherine, pamphleteers were eager to re-deploy vicious themes that had been effective against earlier foreign-born queens of France. By the end of the sixteenth century, notes Caroline Zum Kolk, 'the criticisms addressed to Catherine de Medici reutilised motifs already encountered in descriptions of Isabeau de Bavière: the foreign woman who delivers up the kingdom to its enemies, the unnatural mother, hungry for power . . . the repetition of arguments is striking. The archetype of the wicked queen had taken shape'.[37]

That Catherine was one of a succession of foreign-born queens of France was due in large part to an alleged statute within Salic law that defined all authority to govern, in both the French political state and the marital household, as fundamentally masculine in nature. French-born princesses could never inherit the throne in the same way as Elizabeth I of England, and so French queens were consorts: almost always foreign-born princesses of European royal families who had married into the French royal family and who suffered the same xenophobic criticism down the centuries. Its fraudulence notwithstanding, the existence of Salic Law gave jurists and pamphleteers a legal basis from which to attack Catherine's access to power, citing it as unnatural and anti-Gallican.[38] The fact that this law was not enough to stop Catherine assuming power was bemoaned by the vitriolic and highly influential 1574 pamphlet *Discours merveilleux de la vie, actions et deportements de Catherine de Médicis, royne-mère*:

> notwithstanding the opposition of several of the deputies of the Estates based on the authority of our Salic law, and the bad fortunes of the government of women in this kingdom . . . the government was deferred to the Queen.[39]

Written in response to the recent St. Bartholomew's Day Massacre in which several thousand Protestants had been slaughtered, the pamphlet was determined to blame Catherine not only for the massacre but for all the ills of the kingdom.[40]

With the seventeenth-century Bourbon dynasty's desire to establish itself as the kingdom's rightful rulers at the expense of the extinct Valois, the theme of Catherine's unnatural ambition would begin to recur even among serious historians, developing into a legend of monstrous proportions among historians of the nineteenth century, who blamed her not only for masterminding the massacre but for the entire period of the civil wars. This argument would be deployed particularly against Catherine's numerous regencies, especially during the minority or absence of her sons, moments that were portrayed as manifestations of her unnatural ambition. Katherine Crawford has demonstrated how Catherine constructed her entitlement to the regency based on her status as devoted mother, both to the king and to the kingdom, but notes that this left Catherine vulnerable.[41] Her critics thus depicted the queen mother as a bad or unnatural mother, surrounding her children with a licentious court. The *Discours merveilleux* claimed that Catherine supplied prostitutes for her son Charles IX when he was underage, and had introduced her sons to cockfighting in order to make them cruel.[42] The subsequent image of her children as sexually deviant would develop over time, culminating in Patrice Chéreau's 1994 film adaptation of the Dumas novel *La Reine Margot*, in which Catherine and her children are portrayed as incestuous.[43] Incest was a recurring accusation against members of the early modern nobility, including members of Catherine's own retinue, which Chapter 6 of this study will examine in more detail, and current popular culture continues to perpetuate the myth of the later Valois court as one of sexual depravity, overseen by its morally suspect queen mother.

Catherine's Medici origins would also work against her with rampant xenophobia targeting the large numbers of Italians who had found a new home in France after the turbulence of the Italian wars.[44] Ignoring Catherine's quasi-royal French inheritance through her mother, Madeleine de La Tour d'Auvergne, the *Discours merveilleux* claimed that, true to her Medici ancestors who came from obscure origins to achieve unprecedented and ultimately tyrannical power in Florence, Catherine used dissimulation to gain influence in order to eventually control and destroy the kingdom of France:

> Amongst the nations, Italy takes the prize for cunning and shrewdness; in Italy, Tuscany; and in Tuscany, the city of Florence . . . Now, when a person without a conscience has the art of deception, as often seen in that country, imagine how much evil you can expect. And besides, Catherine comes from the house of Médicis.[45]

As an Italian, she was also credited with introducing the art of poisoning to her new country. The author of the 1579 libel *Le Tocsain, contre les massacreurs* [Alarm bell against the massacrers] claimed that, until Catherine arrived, poison was unknown to France:

> For there you have the artifices that we have newly learned; how, by secret poison, to cleverly get rid of those which the fury of an open war could not have achieved with the sword; which was unknown to us before, until this Italy vomited upon us an infinite scum of *fuoriusciti* [Florentine exiles] which this woman has favourised and enriched with the treasures of France.[46]

The accusation of poisoning would also be levelled at the women of her entourage. Poisoning has traditionally been viewed as a 'female' crime due to both a woman's lack of physical strength and her responsibilities for preparing or serving food and drink, or supervising the feeding of the household. The secretive nature of the crime meant that little evidence was needed to make the accusation believable, rumour and gossip playing a vital role in slandering the reputation of the accused. Whether baseless or not, it was a powerful and damaging allegation which is examined in depth in the case of Isabelle de Limeuil in Chapter 4.

12 Introduction

Depicting Catherine as a mistress notorious for – indeed, as an Italian woman, naturally inclined to – political scheming, sexual deviance and poisoning, Catherine's black legend would extend to her manipulative exploitation of her ladies-in-waiting, the so-called 'flying squadron'. Although the details vary from one historian to the next, there has been general agreement that Catherine employed hundreds of women as her ladies-in-waiting, eighty of whom she had handpicked for their sexual attractiveness. She would command these 'sexual Machiavels' to seduce courtiers for her own ends, often getting them to accompany her on delicate political missions around the kingdom.[47]

The Origins of the Term 'Flying Squadron'

The first use of the term *escadron volant* to describe the ladies of Catherine's court is found in the 1695 *Les amours de Henri IV, roi de France*, an anonymous chronicle written almost a century after the events it purports to describe:[48]

> This princess [Catherine], who thought of nothing but her ambition, and who held modesty and religion to be of no value, had always a Flying Squadron, if I am permitted to speak in such a manner, composed of the most beautiful women of the court, whom she used by any means to amuse princes and lords, and to discover their most secret thoughts.[49]

The inspiration for the term 'flying squadron' can be traced to several sources: the first, and perhaps most obvious, is what LaGuardia calls 'the metaphorical register of warfare' that is used to describe heterosexual relationships in the early modern period.[50] The Petrarchan discourse of 'unassailable' women who are the source of despair for their weary, 'battled-hardened' suitors is a cliché for us now, but a constant of the literature of the period. The court memoirist Brantôme, for example, habitually refers to women who must 'defend' the 'fortress' of their bodies from the 'assault' or 'siege' of the amorous males he calls 'brave and determined soldiers'.[51] Thus a group of women could be regularly referred to in a romantic context as a 'squadron', 'troupe', or 'little army'. In the example of the 'flying squadron', the passivity of the female submitting to the male Petrarchan gaze is subverted, with the women given the active roles of lusty pursuers. This is a subversion that also fits, however, with the stereotypical depiction of women as lusty in the early modern period. This figurative trope of women as a squadron could be assimilated into another literary *topos*, that of a beautiful woman as Muse, inspiring the writer. The maréchale de Retz, Claude-Catherine de Clermont, one of Catherine's ladies-in-waiting, kept an album of the poetic output by the invitees to her salon, several of whom use the metaphor of the 'squadron' or 'troupe' of Muses to describe Retz's female companions.[52] One verse refers to the 'immortal band of these nine sisters', while another conflates their beauty with military terminology:

> In this sole squadron is the flower of Europe
> In that we can see in this beautiful troupe
> The elite of beauty, and the most gentle regards.[53]

The term 'squadron' with its military connotations was thus regularly employed in the praise of the ability of women's beauty to inspire the poet.

Related to this is the use of military terminology to describe the dancers in Catherine de Medici's celebrated *ballets de cour*. Introduced at the pageants she produced during the Wars of Religion with the aim of encouraging harmony and diverting aggression among the fractious nobility, this earliest form of ballet in France was performed by selected members of Catherine's entourage. At the pageant for the Polish ambassadors in 1573, sixteen of her ladies-in-waiting performed the 'Balet des provinces' that incorporated intricate movements, turns and interweavings of geometric precision that dazzled spectators. Brantôme described them as a 'petit bataillon' and the choreographer of the 1581 *Balet comique de la Royne*, Balthasar Beaujoyeulx, called it a 'bataille'.[54] As Kate van Orden points out, 'Given that the dancers made entrées to *airs de guerre*, marched, and fell into various formations, it would seem that the creators of *ballets de cour* fully intended them as some sort of military display'.[55] Ronsard's forty-ninth sonnet likened the dancers to cranes in flight, using the term 'squadron' to denote their geometrical formation as they moved:

> Now it [the ballet] was round, now long, now narrow
> Now in a point, in a triangle as one sees
> The squadron of the crane escaping the cold[56]

This theory also explains the reference to 'flying' in the nickname. The term 'squadron' would become a lasting expression to describe the queen's entourage in this context. Henri IV used the term 'squadron' to refer to his wife Marie de Medici's ladies-in-waiting who danced in the ballet she choreographed in 1602:

> From the distance which the King saw them, he turned to the papal nuncio, who was slightly apart, with the other ambassadors, and asked him what it seemed like to him, and if such a squadron was not beautiful; '*Bellissime*', answered the nuncio, 'and very perilous. So many beauties were powerful enough to acquire another empire for love. So many virtues were strong enough to destroy and crush all the designs of love'.[57]

It would appear that the term 'squadron' had become a standard metaphor employed to sing the praises of the beauty and sexual allure of the queen's entourage. In as much as the entourage existed as an essential visual component of the queen's dignity, a phenomenon identified by Monique Chatenet as occurring since the reign of Anne of Brittany, it is understandable that the women would be praised for their aesthetically pleasing qualities.[58] But we can also observe here the 'Petrarchan gaze' in which the female members of court are reduced to a two-dimensional image of monolithic and unrealistic beauty.

This romanticisation of the women of the court found its negative representation in what David LaGuardia has identified as the 'masculinist literature' of the early modern period: the exchange and transmission of stories by men of women's insatiable sexuality and men's limitless virility. A crucial aspect of this masculinist discourse, he argues, is the enumeration of female sexual voracity:

> These authors thus seem to have been obligated to recount, to give an account of, or simply to *count* the myriad faces and facets of their (often phantasmic) relations with women within the confines of marriage. Given these necessities, the idea of number is fundamental to the complex of themes and motifs that constitute cuckoldry, and hence to this comic face of masculinity.[59]

This drive to enumerate the apparently limitless capacity of women's sexual desire makes the development of the myth of the flying squadron easier to understand: a group of women with voracious sexual appetites, who were numerous, but locatable and identifiable.[60] The satirical literature attacking them also has its origins in this desire to control them numerically, with lists and catalogues of their vices. The cataloguing of women, both for their vices and for their virtues, has been a perennially popular tradition. In her study of nineteenth-century collective biographies of women, Alison Booth notes that this urge to catalogue women can be found 'in contexts ranging from classical Latin, Chinese, and Arabic, to medieval and early-modern Italian and French, to Victorian and contemporary British and North American'.[61] The classical literary tradition that used the catalogue of women as a misogynist rhetorical device can be found in Juvenal's *Satire 6* on the adultery of wives, and Semonides of Amorgos's catalogue of women, in which they are compared to a sow, a bitch, a vixen, a donkey and a mare. The rhetorical education of early modern authors, such as the university-educated men in this study, encouraged the emulation of classical models.[62] The difference between the classical antecedents and early modern misogynist catalogues is that the sixteenth-century literature, rather than attack goddesses or historical figures, instead targets specific, contemporary, identifiable women whose reputations could be destroyed in their own lifetime. The catalogue of the adulterous ladies-in-waiting in *The Library of Madame de Montpensier*, the catalogue of women in the *Manifesto of the Ladies of the Court* who plead forgiveness for the repeated cuckolding of their husbands, or the numerous verse libels inspired by the murder of Françoise de La Marck that paint the court as a hotbed of prostitution – all these forms participate in a long-standing tradition: the construction of a masculinist homosocial discourse which LaGuardia describes as 'the intertextual practice of telling stories, expressing opinions, and transcribing examples concerning adultery, cuckoldry, and "women's wiles", which men are called upon to share with one another'.[63] Taken together, they also operate to form a collective depiction of the court as a glorified brothel in which sexually voracious women are grouped together, their sexuality on demand yet controllable – in this case by their mistress. This portrayal of Catherine's entourage as one of her weapons of underhanded political negotiation was to become an integral aspect of her black legend. This depiction of Catherine's use of sex as a political strategy is one model of the recurrent stereotype of the politically active, highly educated or otherwise transgressive woman portrayed as sexually deviant and/or promiscuous. Like their ancient and medieval counterparts, early modern writers seemed to have found it impossible to describe a publicly prominent woman in terms that did not employ sexual imagery, a handicap that later writers reproduced and expanded upon.[64] However, Catherine's self-presentation as both devoted mother and grieving widow, dressed always in black widow's weeds since her husband Henri II's death in 1559, made it difficult to represent her as lustful. Instead, that sexuality was transferred to her ladies, who became the 'seducers by proxy' of the men whom Catherine was trying to seduce politically.

A key source for the origins of the myth of the flying squadron are the memoirs of Pierre de Bourdeille, abbé de Brantôme, a Périgord nobleman who frequented the Valois court.[65] Although most of Brantôme's oeuvre contains works describing men and warfare, his two-part *Recueil des dames* is his most well-known work. The first section of the book describes the lives of the country's most celebrated women, such as Catherine de Medici. Her household practices are described at length, including a list of eighty-six women whom he remembered as serving at the court. The second section of the book, which has been known almost ever since as 'Les dames galantes', opens with a large chapter entitled 'On Ladies who make love and their cuckolded husbands' ('*Les Dames qui font l'amour et leurs maris cocus*').[66] LaGuardia situates Brantôme's work within a tradition of literature by men for men, in which an early modern version of masculinity is constructed through the telling of stories in which women, unable to control their overwhelming sexual desires, constantly break the rules of marriage to seek other partners, resulting in irate husbands who are transformed into cuckolds.[67] Accordingly, this section of Brantôme's *Recueil des dames*, dedicated to the king's younger brother, the duke of Alençon, is a long succession of voyeuristic, titillating and sometimes pornographic anecdotes detailing the sexual exploits of women at court. Juxtaposed as it is with the entry for Catherine's court, described by Brantôme as 'a true paradise on earth' where 'ordinarily more than three hundred women were present', the section on the 'cuckolding wives' creates the impression that Catherine's household was populated primarily by sexually voracious, adulterous women. The literary construct of a large group of scandalous, promiscuous women under the command of a Machiavellian mistress has thus been allied to the legend of the wicked Italian queen to construct a gendered representation of Catherine's – and indeed, all female – rule as inherently sexual, manipulative and corrupt.

The Evolution of the Myth of the Flying Squadron

If there was one woman who, in the minds of her critics, exemplified the *modus operandi* of the flying squadron, it was Charlotte de Beaune, Madame de Sauve (Figure 1.1). She figures large in the memoirs of Catherine's daughter, Marguerite de Valois, who bitterly describes Sauve's apparently irresistible appeal to both Marguerite's husband, Henri of Navarre, and her favourite brother, the duc d'Alençon (known as Monsieur).[68] Claiming that Sauve consciously played the love rivals off each other during the volatile period in 1574–5 when both men

Figure 1.1 François Clouet, *Charlotte de Beaune, dame de Sauve, dame de Fizes, marquise de Noirmoutier*

Source: BnF, Estampes et photographie Réserve NA-22–19

were under house arrest at court, Marguerite says that Sauve did so because she was in the service of Le Guast, one of Henri III's *mignons*. In a satirical verse ten years later, however, the blame had shifted to Catherine, with the claim that she used Sauve as a negotiating tool during these difficult times:

> Madame de Sauve is good for it:
> Her cunt is always for peace.
> That's why you never see
> Catin [Catherine] without her by her side.
> When the late Monsieur was quarrelling
> With the king, Catin
> Brought her along to make accords.
> For the peace she was fucked.
> Catin led her totally naked
> To the king of Navarre, and with that
> Made the war go away.[. . .]
> Catin, you are fortunate
> To have a stable of whores![69]

The metaphor of Catherine's entourage as a stable (*haras* translates directly as 'stud farm') of women from whom she could choose the most suitable to seduce unsuspecting men was adopted unquestioningly by later writers and seems to have reached its zenith in the nineteenth century among both historians and fiction writers. An 1836 novel by the baron de Bazancourt, *L'Escadron volant de la reine* was followed by Alexandre Dumas's much more successful novel *La Reine Margot* in 1845; followed in turn in 1880 by a three-act comic-opera, *L'escadron volant de la reine* by Litolff, d'Ennery & Brésil, all of which portray Catherine as a Machiavellian schemer, commanding her ladies to seduce politically significant men.[70]

Meanwhile, nineteenth-century historians of the religious wars rarely failed to mention the flying squadron, with each one surpassing the other in attempts to both elaborate on the military metaphor and exaggerate Catherine's reliance on the women as an integral part of her negotiating strategy. For example, in his 1885 study of three scandalous women at court, the editor of Catherine's correspondence, Hector de La Ferrière, provides a good example of the then current viewpoint: 'But Catherine would not, could not, do without her flying squadron, that battle-hardened militia of love'.[71] By the early twentieth century the myth of the flying squadron was firmly entrenched. In his contribution to the *Histoire de France*, Jean-Hippolyte Mariéjol situates the women in a 'court of delights', claiming that Catherine 'used them to discover a secret, to remove a scruple, to initiate a conviction. The flying squadron, as they were called, made many conquests'.[72] In his 1920 biography of Catherine, Mariéjol continues with the military metaphor, noting that among the eighty women 'there were some favourites whom she brought with her on her holidays and her diplomatic riding trips. It was the famous flying squadron whom she relied upon to attack in her own way and subdue party leaders'.[73] As the metaphor became more developed, the literary imagination of some writers introduced the element of witchcraft into the women's power over men. Jean Héritier's 1959 biography of Catherine makes allusions to Armide, the sorceress from Torquato Tasso's *Gerusalemme liberata*, who falls in love with the Crusader Renaud, her sworn enemy: 'She [Catherine] chose the prettiest of her followers in order to turn them into Armides, who would disarm the Renauds who threatened the State'.[74] Héritier explains Catherine's reliance on her female entourage by introducing the other recurrent theme of Catherine's wicked reputation, her unnatural ambition: 'A passion too despotic had taken over her, which left her neither the free time, nor the least taste, for the frivolities of love and sensual pleasure: the passion for power'.[75]

By the late twentieth century, historians felt able to invent stories about specific members of Catherine's entourage. In a 1979 essay in which he identified each character in Shakespeare's *Love's Labour's Lost* with a real French historical figure, Hugh Richmond could state about Catherine:

> Having failed to entrap Henri de Navarre by his marriage with her own skilfully trained daughter, she succeeded in entangling him with another of her *escadron*, Madame de Sauve, whose sexual proficiency (at times refreshed by systematic instruction from professional prostitutes) sufficed for a time to neutralise Henri as a moral and political force: 'an early instance of that employment of affairs of gallantry as a political instrument which the Queen Mother was to develop into a fine art'. Only after some years did Henri manage to escape from the court of this Renaissance Circe.[76]

Leaving aside the invention of 'systematic instruction from professional prostitutes', Richmond paints Catherine's negotiations to marry her daughter Marguerite to the Protestant Henri de Navarre, a difficult task aimed at uniting the warring parties on either side of the confessional divide, as a 'trap' and transforms it into a motif of bewitchment by calling her a 'Renaissance Circe'.[77] Henri de Navarre is thereby depicted as the Odyssean hero with the women around him reliant on witchcraft to further their own political designs. Catherine's beliefs in astrology, superstitions and the abilities of fortune-tellers such as Cosimo Ruggieri and Nostradamus, beliefs that were widespread in the sixteenth century, were exaggerated by later writers who portrayed them as an obsession with diabolical acts of necromancy and black magic. One nineteenth-century author even claimed that she kidnapped and sacrificed a Jewish boy in a black mass in order to restore the health of the ailing Charles IX.[78] Her reliance on her women was portrayed as another manifestation of her sinister, malevolent plotting to further her own ambitions.

Later historians who attempted to rehabilitate Catherine's image by presenting her as a ceaseless negotiator for peace, thereby erasing the elements of wickedness and witchcraft from the legend, nevertheless could not restrain themselves from depicting her as creating a homogenous, young, female retinue specifically for the purpose of sexual attraction. Thus Simone Bertière could recently write:

> The court was above all women, a swarm of ladies and maidens of quality whom she had chosen for their beauty, their charm, their conversational

talents, to sing, to dance [...] Catherine wanted to keep the warriors permanently at court. It was not by allowing her girls to succumb too quickly that she would achieve it: they would be much more successful by being desirable and desired for a long time.[79]

Even the respected historian Robert Knecht, in his 1998 biography of Catherine, did not question the role of Catherine's female household, repeating the idea that they 'were allegedly used by her to seduce courtiers for political ends'.[80] As late as 2003, Jean-François Solnon would state with similar confidence:

> The flying squadron is not a myth. The queen did not disdain the collaboration of the ladies of her household in order to accelerate or complete political negotiations. She placed several beautiful girls in the path of her son François d'Anjou – who had fled the Louvre in September 1575 – and of his entourage, so much did the alliance of the Huguenots with the Malcontents, of which he was the leader, threaten the kingdom.[81]

Only Denis Crouzet, in his 2005 biography of Catherine, would finally question the idea of a brothel-like environment at court, with a reference from Mark Franko's history of dance:

> Rather than suggest a female group ordered to sexually seduce courtiers to encourage them to fall under the control of the queen mother, the term 'flying squadron', which was used to denote certain ladies and maidens of Catherine de Medici's household, should have been associated with their harmonious execution of ballet formations . . . It is unlikely that Catherine de Medici would have encouraged, in addition, the development of a court culture charged with carnal seduction for which satirical texts gave her credit. On the contrary, under the reign of Henri II, she seems to have undertaken a course of reformation of the court in terms of moral austerity.[82]

Crouzet's claims have been strengthened by Caroline Zum Kolk's 2006 doctoral dissertation on the political function of Catherine de Medici's household.[83] While Zum Kolk's prosopographical study of the dynamics of the queen's household disproves the existence of a 'flying squadron' and of Catherine's reliance on the sexual attractions of her ladies as a tool of government, there has still been no study of how such a reputation came to exist and persist. The collective depiction of courtly ladies as licentious is a trope that would be repeated, for example, in the portrayal of the noblewomen of Charles II's court in England. Now known collectively as the 'Windsor Beauties' after the series of paintings by Sir Peter Lely, discussion of these women (who included mistresses of the king as well as members of the queen's household) has been inextricably linked to the alleged moral laxity and lasciviousness of the Restoration court. As the curators of the exhibition of the paintings note, 'It is impossible to extricate fully the women

20 *Introduction*

at Charles II's court from the myths that have grown up around them'.[84] This study aims to show that much of the historical record concerning noblewomen is, at best, incomplete, and that we must investigate more closely the sources that inspired such a portrayal.

By comparison with the idealistic and somewhat fantastical depictions of the 'Windsor Beauties', we are fortunate to have extremely lifelike pictorial representations of many of the women who frequented the late Valois court, thanks to the efforts of Catherine de Medici, who, like her Medici foremothers, was a great patron of artists and architects.[85] As well as commissioning oil paintings which, according to the conventions of European courtly life, served as displays of dynastic lineage and power as well as representations of potential marriage partners in foreign courts, Catherine commissioned an altogether different series of portraits.[86] She amassed a collection of several hundred pencil drawings by the leading artists of the French Renaissance, predominantly François Clouet (c. 1510–1572), of her family members and officers of the court, both female and male, which she kept unbound in a personal cabinet to which entrance was forbidden to almost all. Unlike the painted portraits she also commissioned (sometimes using the drawings as a model) which would have been put on display, these highly-realistic pencil drawings seem to have comprised a strictly personal collection for Catherine's own use. Alexandra Zvereva claims that Catherine's collection differed from other, lesser-quality portrait albums collected by contemporaries in that she united in her collection both genealogical interest and a quest for artistic excellence.[87] Like a proper collector, she carefully organised and annotated many of the drawings, some of which appear in this book, leaving us not only with a wealth of information about the appearance and clothing of the late sixteenth century, but also a vivid, visual record of noblewomen at the French court – a notably valuable resource for a period in which daughters, even those of aristocratic families, were routinely omitted or glossed over in genealogies. Their realistic presence in these drawings is testament to Catherine's concern for, and interest in, her household, and gives the lie to the depiction of her court as scandalously unrestrained.

The Transmission of Scandalous Information

Controlling scandal was, and is, about controlling the flow of information. News of scandalous events, both real (as in illegitimate birth) and imagined (such as poisoning), relied heavily on rumour, gossip and hearsay. In his discussion of gossip in our modern world, Ronald Burt reminds us that, in the stories one tells of others, 'Accuracy is a nicety more than a requirement for the stories. What circulates depends on the interests of people doing the circulation, which empowers gossip with its sociologically interesting effect on reputation'.[88] This means that, then as now, one must investigate the sources of information, their motives for telling the stories, and their conduits and networks of circulation. Historians have begun to reappraise the political value of previously ignored oral communication in the form of gossip and rumour, and their efforts have demonstrated how to access and utilise that apparently ephemeral oral communication as a historical tool.[89] This book uses legal depositions, recorded speech within written correspondence, and popular libels and songs to reconstruct the oral and aural world of early modern Paris at a pivotal moment in French history when orality is being superseded (at least in law) by the written word. Networks of information transmission become more visible as attention is paid to the depositions of household servants, who unwittingly reveal the select circles of those privileged to sensitive information and how those supposedly privileged circles were themselves vulnerable to leaks. Leaks are also visible through the regular dispatches of resident or visiting ambassadors to the court, and the case studies demonstrate that ambassadorial dispatches were more likely to be filled with scurrilous rumour than the evidence-based 'gossip' of illiterate servants. Information travelled both within the palace walls and out to the wider urban setting, but its dissemination could be managed in order to mitigate the damage caused by negative publicity. Gossip made its way into print, song and preachers' tirades; but some, interestingly, did not, suggesting that there were ways of manipulating and controlling information. The success of Anne d'Este, duchess of Guise and Nemours, in protecting her own reputation from the worst of the polemic attacking her family is a model of pro-active management of information transmission, explored in Chapter 6. Likewise, the efforts undertaken by Catherine de Medici to secure and protect her ladies' reputations – or to destroy them – are here revealed for the first time. They show her to have been keenly aware of the hierarchy of scandal, tireless in managing a potentially explosive situation, and above all, dedicated to the collective reputation of her household.

So how was information about court scandal transmitted at a more public level? Given that there were no newspapers or other form of sanctioned public press in sixteenth-century France, we are reliant on collections of pamphlets, songs and other ephemera, often distributed by hand or posted in public squares, to inform us of contemporary public perceptions of court life. The best source for this material is the journals of Pierre de L'Estoile, an *audiencier* for the *Chancellerie*, one of the many institutions serving the Parlement de Paris, who collected and commented upon the hundreds of pamphlets that, as we have seen, 'fell into his hands'. In an entry for 1576, L'Estoile gave a sense of the volume of satirical material flooding Paris in his diatribe against the deportment of courtly women, using a reference to the prophet Isaiah's metaphor of Judah as a prostitute (Isaiah 3. 16–17):

> To speak the truth, that which the prophet [Isaiah] complained about, chapter III, regarding the daughters of Zion . . . could just as well be said and more in those days about the women of Paris and girls of the court. Of which one should not be surprised, if the Lord, just like the threat which he made in that place by his prophet, had their heads and their shameful parts shaved by these lascivious writers of pasquils, of which the city of Paris and the court were full. In brief, the disorder, not to mention worse, was such that the cabal of cuckoldry was one of the clearest incomes of the times.[90]

22 *Introduction*

L'Estoile's entry not only attacks the sexual honour of the women of the court, claiming that they are prostituting themselves by making an 'income' from 'the cabal of cuckoldry', but also points out that the city and court are full of pasquils, or written defamations, that shame them. He envisions the libellous literature as bodily mutilations, shaving 'their heads and their shameful parts', a violent depiction of physical punishment and public shaming through the means of satire. As we shall see, this rise in misogynist satire was largely produced within the parlementaire community who disapproved of the prominence of women during Catherine's time in power. As Tatiana Debaggi Baranova has shown, 'It [was] in these juridical and clerical microsocieties that political and religious satire [took] root'.[91] Working in the *Chancellerie*, located within the Palais de Justice, L'Estoile was ideally situated to collect the production of an intellectual fraternity whose constant exchange of satire and comment, primarily in verse, forms a large part of the primary source material for this study.

While other parlementaires kept journals in which they voiced similar opinions to L'Estoile on the nature of court life, he seems to have been the only one who systematically collected the works of others, in both manuscript and print, with a view to their importance for posterity. Another parlementaire, for example, Anne Robert, wrote of his dissatisfaction with Henri III's *mignons* and the unfair influence he felt the king's advisers were having, but there is no indication that he intended to circulate or publish this material.[92] In this he is unlike L'Estoile who, although protective of his dangerously subversive collection of verse and pamphlets, did exchange certain materials.[93] Furthermore, he was always aware of their political and historical value and passed on strict instructions about the posthumous publication of his (by that time heavily edited) journals.[94] François Rasse des Noeux, physician to Charles IX and then to Jeanne d'Albret once he had converted to Protestantism, also collected volumes of polemical manuscript verse, some of which was edited by Prosper Tarbé in 1866 as *A Collection of Calvinist Poetry*, and some of that material, often attacking members of the Guise family, is also analysed in this study.[95] In his collecting habits, it could be argued that Rasse des Noeux presents a Protestant counterpart to L'Estoile; intriguingly however, despite their religious differences, the depiction of courtiers in their collections employs the same satirical and literary tropes.

L'Estoile's collection in particular is rich in offerings of anti-court material, but this is the first comprehensive examination of the detail of the verse that targets the women of the sixteenth-century court, and the impact of such defamatory publications on the court. Unlike English historiography, where so much scholarship has been devoted to libels concerning the early Stuart court and courtiers that Alastair Bellany has edited a survey of this scholarship,[96] the study of the ephemeral literature of sixteenth-century France has been devoted mostly to the pamphleteering that concerned the confessional debates in the Wars of Religion, omitting to investigate the women who were often also the targets of satirical literature.[97] The same cannot be said for later periods; a debate rages between those who believe that the satirical libels attacking Marie-Antoinette in the eighteenth century contributed to a 'pornographic desacralisation of monarchy' that brought about the French Revolution, and

Introduction 23

those who believe that the conditions of its production precluded its having such a powerful effect.[98] This book offers a new – and earlier – perspective from which to view such a debate. While I argue that satirical libels were used to discredit powerful women through a pornographic libel culture, it was actually one of these women, the duchess of Montpensier, who turned the tables on her detractors by orchestrating a systematic propaganda campaign that resulted in the regicide of Catherine's son, Henri III. Chapter 6 examines the effect it had on her own reputation. Montpensier's exploitation of the printing press to such devastating effect stands in contrast to the medium of manuscript verse which characterises much of the anti-court material exchanged by the lawyers and attorneys of the Parlement, and this study thus offers a nuanced reading of the co-existence of print and manuscript cultures in late sixteenth-century France.

Every scandal investigated in this study involved a crime, either actual or potential, and therefore at some point came into contact with the legal system of the Ancien Régime. In sixteenth-century France, this system was a complex amalgamation of Roman law, canon law and customary law, where magistrates and jurists attempted to resolve each dispute through judicial precedent rather than royal legislation. This study highlights the bitter jurisdictional battles that could be fought between the crown and the Parlement, who each resented the other's interference in legal decisions. Despite being a royal institution, the parlementaires were generally independent and impartial. In particular, the case of Françoise de Rohan in Chapter 5 highlights how the Parlement did not necessarily accept the king's rulings as final, and how a case could be appealed to several different institutions, dragging out the dispute for decades. As that case explores the legal grey areas around clandestine marriage, it also demonstrates the ways in which not only traditional practices in the period clashed with the Vatican's Tridentine reforms around marriage and families, but also the refusal of parlementaires to recognise Rome's influence in legal matters. At issue here, and one which could profoundly exacerbate legal disputes given the Church's responsibility for judging so many kinds of cases, was the Gallican nature of the French Church. Although in France the Church had gained major independence from Rome since the Pragmatic Sanction of Bourges in 1438, François I had relinquished many of the freedoms it awarded by agreeing to the Concordat of Bologna in 1516. However, the French king retained the right to appoint his own choice of bishops who, as a result, were answerable to the king rather than the Pope, and overall, French authorities both civil and ecclesiastical defended their independence. For example, although all cases involving the sacraments initially were heard in the ecclesiastical courts, an unsuccessful plaintiff could appeal to the parlements on the grounds that the Church had no jurisdiction. Thus, the women in these cases could appeal to courts both royal and legal, both civil and ecclesiastical, all the while creating a corpus of written material that allows us to examine how notorious events were perceived in a moral, legal and social sense.

By its very nature, scandal is a public phenomenon. Since all of the scandals explored in this study resulted in some sort of legal investigation, and some involved multiple court appearances, they had the potential to provide the public with salacious details of courtiers' intimate lives. This book reveals the complex interweaving of scandal with the law courts and the public arena, and demonstrates how noblewomen actively used and exploited the legal system to defend their reputations and, in some cases, secure their rightful inheritances. Given the status of the women involved in these cases, appeals often reached the highest levels of the judiciary. As Sarah Maza has commented, 'cases that involved prominent women raised the volatile and increasingly problematic issue of the role of femininity within the public sphere'.[99] Maza's work is not only an example of how legal material can be used to analyse the elite, for whom litigation over guardianship and inheritance was a fact of daily life, but it also highlights the public literary efforts of the legal fraternity, who profited from their privileged position of knowledge to broadcast lurid details of scandalous cases. As Marie Houllemare has demonstrated, this position of knowledge was also enjoyed by the magistrature of the sixteenth century who, like their eighteenth-century counterparts, exploited it in the form of verse and other literary production.[100] Their creative output and its damaging effects on the women they targeted are the subjects of this book.

This book opened with the scandalous murder of Françoise de La Marck; the following chapter examines that event in more detail, using it as a case study to analyse how female behaviour was prescribed, envisaged and criticised in the early modern period. The verse libels that the scandal inspired reveal the recurrent themes and imagery of the literature that attacked the court: female sexual voracity, cuckoldry, poisoning and prostitution, and a portrayal of the monarch as impotent and corrupt. That depiction of the court is then compared with the day-to-day realities of life in a royal entourage, in this case, the queen mother's. Using the *états de maison de la reine* (the queen's household accounts), it explores the varied functions of court officers, the diverse backgrounds of the women chosen to serve at court, and the evolution of Catherine's household over her long time in power. As we shall see, Catherine was intimately involved in the upbringing and training of the women in her service, and profoundly concerned with the prevention of any scandalous information or event that would damage the reputation of her household. This evidence refutes the legendary notion that Catherine handpicked young, beautiful women to exploit their sexual allure for political gain. She was unsuccessful, however, in preventing all negative information circulating about the women of her court. Chapter 3 charts the rise in satirical material that targeted the women of her household, and examines that material from a literary perspective. The choice of verse over prose, and the use of Latin rather than the vernacular, point to the authors' attempts to impress their audience with their intellectual skills. I locate the origins of much of this literature in the intellectual fraternity of the legal profession, men who spent much of their time within and around the Palais de Justice, at the heart of Paris.[101] Chapter 3 therefore explores the geography and soundscape of sixteenth-century Paris, revealing how newsworthy information about scandalous events – whether real, such as an illegitimate birth, or imagined, such as poisoning – left the porous environment of the court to circulate on the streets of Paris and further afield.

The following three chapters use case studies of scandals involving high-profile women within Catherine's household, exploring how information about them did (or did not) circulate, and Catherine's role in preventing or mitigating any potential damage to the reputation of her household. Chapter 4 examines the notorious case of Isabelle de Limeuil, one of Catherine's ladies, who gave birth to an illegitimate baby rumoured to be fathered by Louis de Condé, the leader of the French Protestant movement, a situation made even more scandalous when she was subsequently imprisoned on charges of poisoning. Historians have repeatedly used the case as an example of Catherine's exploitation of her ladies for political gain, usually under the assumption that Limeuil was ordered to woo Condé to the Catholic cause and then imprisoned because she had failed. However, using never-before-analysed correspondence from within Limeuil's prison to individuals at the court, I reveal that Catherine closely managed the affair, keeping the poisoning accusation a secret in order to prevent this (apparently baseless) accusation from not only destroying Limeuil's reputation but potentially taking her life. With a discussion of the poison metaphor and its potency as an accusation against one's enemies in early modern France, this chapter reveals Catherine's manipulation of the affair, her acute awareness of the hierarchy of scandal and her concern for the women of her household.

This concern for her household could, however, override the fortunes of individual ladies. The legal battle between Françoise de Rohan and the duke of Nemours, Jacques de Savoie, discussed in Chapter 5, forced Catherine to choose between one of her ladies-in-waiting and the powerful duke, partisan of the Guise faction and lover of Catherine's close friend, Anne d'Este. Rohan claimed that she and Nemours had been clandestinely married and that a child had resulted from their relationship, claims which were denied by Nemours. Rohan's decision to air the intimate details of their relationship in a law court, thereby exposing the entire household to scandal, was for Catherine a step too far. Catherine's pro-active involvement – sometimes legitimate, at other times underhanded – in testifying against Rohan and securing Nemours' later marriage to Anne d'Este resulted in defamatory libels against her and the new couple. This episode thus also offers an opportunity to explore how public opinion manifested itself in a dispute that antagonised the confessional divisions during the religious wars, and how the dispute was eventually resolved, perhaps surprisingly, by Anne d'Este herself.

The career of Anne d'Este, duchess of Guise and duchess of Nemours, matriarch of the powerful Guise clan and *de facto* leader of the Catholic League (and of Paris) during a key moment in French history, offers a contrasting perspective on scandal and reputation. Chapter 6 looks at Este's ability, and the role of the agency she possessed as member of a powerful noble family, to control the circulation of information about her intimate and familial life. I look at early attempts to smear Este's name through the accusation of incest, and discuss the ubiquity of this accusation against the nobility in early modern libels. Like allegations of poisoning or cuckoldry, accusations of incest were often based on no more than scurrilous rumour, but were taken extremely seriously, sometimes resulting in prosecution of the accuser. Este had little agency to stop that allegation, but later accusations of adultery offer examples of Este's superlative management of potentially scandalous situations. Her strategic negotiations, along with her conformity to accepted codes of female behaviour, are contrasted with the behaviour of her daughter, Catherine-Marie de Lorraine, duchess of Montpensier. Este's traditional performance within accepted gender codes of widowhood and maternity earned her a more sympathetic treatment at the hands of pamphleteers and libellers than her daughter, whose contravention of gender norms resulted in her eventual vilification.

By investigating the facts surrounding these scandals, we can see that throughout her time in power, and especially when scandal threatened the reputations of the women at her court, Catherine appears to have been acutely aware of the potency of the accusations against her ladies, supporting some women, excluding others, and always with the collective reputation of her household as a top priority. With their personal lives the target of sexually explicit mockery by a literature that was beginning to find its way from the hands of its elite male creators into the new print culture, it could be argued that the women of Catherine de Medici's court became the model for the collective portrayal of transgressive women in pornographic material as numerous, deviant and sexually voracious. Their unprecedented role at the forefront of public life resulted in their depiction in pamphlet literature as scandalous, a collective representation that would be a model for the portrayal of later prominent women, such as Marie-Antoinette, whose negative reputations are thereby shown to warrant further investigation. This study offers new readings of some of the most notorious court scandals of sixteenth-century France, giving a fresh perspective on the slanderous accusations that have been directed at prominent women for millennia. In the end, scandal as a gendered phenomenon is revealed to be both historically contingent and temporally universal.

Notes

1 Pierre de L'Estoile, *Registre-Journal du règne de Henri III*, eds. Madeleine Lazard and Gilbert Schrenck, 6 vols. (Genève: Droz, 1992), II, 127–8: 'Et encore disait-on que ledit Villequier avait découvert une entreprise que sa femme avait fait de l'empoisonner, comme jà ledit Barbizi avait empoisonné la sienne, afin de se marier ensemble après la mort de l'un et de l'autre; et qu'il avait trouvé dans les coffres de sa femme la mixtion ou pâte dont il devait être empoisonné.

Ce meurtre fut trouvé cruel, comme commis en une femme grosse de deux enfants; et étrange, comme fait au logis du roi, Sa Majesté étant et encore en la cour où la paillardise est publiquement et notoirement pratiquée entre les dames, qui la tiennent pour vertu. Mais l'issue et la facilité de la grâce et rémission qu'en obtint Villequier, sans aucune difficulté, firent croire qu'il y avait en ce fait un secret commandement ou tacite consentement du roi, qui haïssait cette dame (encore qu'il en eût abusé longtemps, à ce qu'on disait, par l'entremise de son mari qui en était le maquereau), pour un rapport qu'on lui avait fait qu'elle avait médit de Sa Majesté en pleine compagnie'.

For more on this murder and Villequier's career, see Nicolas Le Roux, *La faveur du roi: mignons et courtisans au temps des derniers Valois* (Seyssel: Champ Vallon, 2001), in particular 269–70; Michel de Castelnau, *Les mémoires de messire Michel de Castelnau, seigneur de Mauvissiere; illustrez et augmentez de plusieurs commentaires & manuscrits* ... ed. J. Le Laboureur, 2 vols. (Paris: Chez Pierre Lamy, 1659), 2, 756–60.

2 For a discussion of the public-private nature of the royal households, see the epilogue by Jeroen Duindam to *The Politics of Female Households: Ladies-in-Waiting Across Early Modern Europe*, eds. Nadine Akkerman and Birgit Houben (Leiden: Brill, 2014), 368–9.

3 L'Estoile, II, 128: 'Sur cette mort tragique et étrange accident furent faits et divulgués plusieurs et diverses sortes de tombeaux et épitaphes entre lesquels j'ai recueilli les suivants qui sont tombés en mes mains'. There has been some good recent work on L'Estoile, especially since the publication of the scholarly Droz edition. See Florence Greffe and José Lothe, *La vie, les livres et les lectures de Pierre de l'Estoile: nouvelles recherches* (Paris: H. Champion, 2004); Gilbert Schrenck, 'Jeu et théorie du pamphlet dans le Journal du règne de Henri III (1574–1589) de Pierre de L'Estoile' in *Traditions Polémiques* (Paris: Cahiers V. L. Saulnier, 1984), 69–79; Gilbert Schrenck and Chiara Lastraïoli, 'L'Estoile, Pierre de, 1546–611' in *Dictionnaire des lettres françaises*, ed. Michel Simonin (Paris: Fayard, 2001), 739–41; Antónia Szabari, *Less Rightly Said: Scandals and Readers in Sixteenth-Century France* (Stanford: Stanford University Press, 2010).

4 L'Estoile, II, 129: 'J'ay eu la mort, Passant, que meritoit ma vie'.

5 Ibid.:

> Si c'est faute où les dieux doivent estre offensés,
> Blasmés en ceste Court où j'ai esté nourrie.
> Me formant au patron d'une trouppe infinie,
> Suivant de Cupidon les Brandons eslancés,
> Maints Amants ont esté par moi recompensés.
> Si c'est un mal commun, devois-je estre punie?

6 Jules Michelet, *Histoire de France* (Paris: Librairie Internationale, 1874), 9, 38: 'un ver, né du tombeau de l'Italie'. It did not help Catherine's image that Machiavelli's most famous work, *The Prince*, had been dedicated to her father, Lorenzo II, duke of Urbino. Niccolò Machiavelli, *The Prince*, ed. and trans. Peter Bondanella, Oxford World's Classics (Oxford: Oxford University Press, 2005).

7 *Le Réveille-Matin des François et de leurs voisins, composé par Eusèbe Philadelphe, cosmopolite, en forme de dialogues* (Edimbourg: Jaques James, 1574), 'Dialogisme sur l'effigie de la Paix. Le Polonois. La Paix Valoise'.: '. . . cette noble Putain,/Le sang infect des bougres d'Italie,/Nourry du laict d'une horrible Furie'.

8 Mack Holt, *The French Wars of Religion, 1562–1629* (Cambridge: Cambridge University Press, 1995; 2nd ed. 2005); Denis Crouzet, *Les Guerriers de Dieu. La violence au temps des troubles de religion (vers 1525–vers 1610)*, 2 vols, (Seyssel: Champ Vallon, 1990); Barbara Diefendorf, *Beneath the Cross: Catholics and Huguenots in Sixteenth-Century Paris* (Oxford: Oxford University Press, 1991); Arlette Jouanna, Jacqueline Boucher, Dominique Biloghi, Guy Thiec, *Histoire et dictionnaire des Guerres de religion* (Paris: Laffont, 1998).

9 The exact nature of Henri III's relationship with his circle of favourites is still cause for scholarly debate. See Le Roux, *La faveur du roi*; Gary Ferguson, *Queer (Re)Readings in the French Renaissance: Homosexuality, Gender, Culture* (Aldershot: Ashgate, 2008); Katherine B. Crawford, 'Love, Sodomy, and Scandal: Controlling the Sexual Reputation of Henry III', *Journal of the History of Sexuality* 12 (2003): 513–42; Jacqueline Boucher, *La cour de Henri III* (Rennes: Ouest-France, 1986).

10 Keith Cameron, *Henri III: A Maligned or Malignant King? (Aspects of the Satirical Iconography of Henri de Valois)* (Exeter: University of Exeter Press, 1978).

11 L'Estoile, III, 170–85.

12 Mark Greengrass, *Governing Passions: Peace and Reform in the French Kingdom, 1576–1585* (Oxford: Oxford University Press, 2007); Janine Garrisson, *Catherine de*

Médicis: l'impossible harmonie (Paris: Payot, 2002); Denis Crouzet, *Le haut coeur de Catherine de Médicis: une raison politique aux temps de la Saint-Barthélemy* (Paris: Albin Michel, 2005); Thierry Wanegffelen, *Catherine de Médicis: le pouvoir au féminin* (Paris: Payot, 2005).

13 Duane W. Roller, *Cleopatra: A Biography* (Oxford: Oxford University Press, 2010); Eric Ives, *The Life and Death of Anne Boleyn* (Oxford: Blackwell, 2004); John T. Alexander, *Catherine the Great: Life and Legend* (Oxford: Oxford University Press, 1989); Antonia Fraser, *Marie Antoinette: The Journey* (New York: Doubleday, 2001).

14 Cynthia Herrup, *A House in Gross Disorder: Sex, Law, and the 2nd Earl of Castlehaven* (Oxford: Oxford University Press, 1999); also, Herrup, 'To Pluck Bright Honour from the Pale Faced Moon: Gender and Honour in the Castlehaven Story', *Transactions of the Royal Historical Society*, Sixth Series, 6 (1996): 137–59; Alastair Bellany, *The Politics of Court Scandal in Early Modern England: News Culture and the Overbury Affair, 1603–1660* (Cambridge: Cambridge University Press, 2002). Another study of the Overbury scandal, which is particularly useful as it focusses on the representation of a scandalous female courtier, is David Lindley, *The Trials of Frances Howard: Fact and Fiction at the Court of King James* (London: Routledge, 1993).

15 See, for example, Alastair Bellany, '"Railing Rhymes and Vaunting Verse": Libellous Politics in Early Stuart England, 1603–28', *Culture and Politics in Early Stuart England*, eds. Kevin Sharpe and Peter Lake (Basingstoke: Macmillan, 1994), 285–10. Bellany has also produced a web-based edition of verse libels: 'Early Stuart Libels: An Edition of Poetry from Manuscript Sources', eds. Alastair Bellany and Andrew McRae, *Early Modern Literary Studies Text Series I* (2005) http://purl.oclc.org/emls/texts/libels/.

16 Mindy Stombler, '"Buddies" or "Slutties": The Collective Sexual Reputation of Fraternity Little Sisters', *Gender and Society* 8, no. 3 (Sept. 1994): 297–323. Another study of the collective sexual reputation of women is found in Victoria Goddard, 'Honour and Shame: The Control of Women's Sexuality and Group Identity in Naples', *The Cultural Construction of Sexuality*, ed. Pat Caplan (London: Tavistock, 1987), 166–92.

17 For studies of slander, see Emily Butterworth, *Poisoned Words: Slander and Satire in Early Modern France* (London: Modern Humanities Research Association and Maney Publishing, 2006); Laura Gowing, *Domestic Dangers: Women, Words and Sex in Early Modern London* (Oxford: Clarendon Press, 1996); M. Lindsay Kaplan, *The Culture of Slander in Early Modern England* (Cambridge: Cambridge University Press, 1997).

18 Lawrence Stone, *The Crisis of the Aristocracy 1558–1641* (Oxford: Clarendon Press, 1979), 42.

19 Butterworth, *Poisoned Words*, 2.

20 Kristen B. Neuschel, *Word of Honor: Interpreting Noble Culture in Sixteenth-Century France* (Ithaca: Cornell University Press, 1989).

21 Richard Cust, 'Honour and Politics in Early Stuart England: The Case of Beaumont v. Hastings', *Past and Present* 149 (November 1995): 57–94; A.J. Fletcher, 'Honour, Reputation and Local Officeholding in Elizabethan and Stuart England', *Order and Disorder in Early Modern England*, eds. Anthony Fletcher and John Stevenson (Cambridge: Cambridge University Press, 1985), 92–115; Stuart Carroll, *Noble Power During the French Wars of Religion* (Cambridge: Cambridge University Press, 1998).

22 A good selection of studies of female defamation can be found in *Women, Crime and the Courts in Early Modern England*, eds. Jenny Kermode and Garthine Walker (London: University College Press Ltd., 1994), in particular Laura Gowing, 'Language, Power, and the Law: Women's Slander Litigation in Early Modern England', 26–47.

23 Sharon Kettering, 'The Household Service of Early Modern French Noblewomen', *French Historical Studies*, 20, no. 1 (Winter 1997): 55–85; Kettering, 'The Patronage

Power of Early Modern French Noblewomen', *The Historical Journal*, 32, no. 4 (Dec 1989): 817–41. Various studies of scandal involving elite women do exist for eighteenth-century England; see Matthew J. Kinservik, *Sex, Scandal and Celebrity in Late Eighteenth-Century England* (New York: Palgrave Macmillan, 2007); Hallie Rubenhold, *Lady Worsley's Whim: An Eighteenth-Century Tale of Sex, Scandal and Divorce* (London: Chatto & Windus, 2008).

24 For a recent study of the *querelle des femmes*, see Lyndan Warner, *The Ideas of Man and Woman in Renaissance France* (Farnham: Ashgate, 2011); Baldassare Castiglione, *The Book of the Courtier*, trans. Thomas Hoby (London: Dent, 1974).

25 For a study of the 'querelle des amyes', see Pauline Smith, *The Anti-Courtier Trend in Sixteenth-century French Literature* (Genève: Droz, 1966).

26 While the clergy may also have played a crucial role in the creation and dissemination of satirical literature attacking courtly women, almost no printed Calvinist sermons from sixteenth-century France have survived, and few Catholic sermons. Of these, the sermons of the League preachers that attack Henri III do not mention the women of the court. This is unsurprising given that many of the women in the material under discussion in this study were attacked because of their involvement with the League. See Charles Labitte, *De la démocratie chez les prédicateurs de la Ligue* (Paris: Durand, 1865); Larissa Juliet Taylor, 'Dangerous Vocations: Preaching in France in the Late Middle Ages and Reformations' in *Preachers and People in the Reformations and Early Modern Period*, ed. Larissa Juliet Taylor (Leiden: Brill, 2001), 91–124.

27 Marc Fumaroli, *L'Age de l'éloquence: rhétorique et 'res literaria', de la Renaissance au seuil de l'époque classique* (Genève: Droz, 1980), 432. For more on the Parlement of Paris and the intellectual environment it fostered, see Marie Houllemare, *Politiques de la parole, le parlement de Paris au XVIe siècle* (Genève: Droz, 2011); Sylvie Daubresse, *Le Parlement de Paris ou la voix de raison* (Genève: Droz, 2005); J.H. Shennan, *The Parlement of Paris* (London: Eyre & Spottiswoode, 1968); Bailey Stone, *The French Parlements and the Crisis of the Old Regime* (Chapel Hill: UNC Press, 1986). For a more critical view of the parlementaires' activities, see Sarah Hanley, 'Engendering the State: Family Formation and State Building in Early Modern France', *French Historical Studies* 16, no. 1 (Spring 1989): 4–27. For a recent study of the parlementaires' literary activities, see Warner, *The Ideas of Man and Woman in Renaissance France*, 2011.

28 Fumaroli, *L'Age de l'éloquence*, 432: 'A ses travaux et à son mécénat érudit, dans l'*otium* de ses bibliothèques, elle ne pouvait manquer d'articuler, dans l'enceinte du Palais de Justice, une éloquence qui manifestât et garantit son autorité religieuse, morale et politique'.

29 David LaGuardia, *Intertextual Masculinity in French Renaissance Literature: Rabelais, Brantôme, and the Cent Nouvelles Nouvelles* (Aldershot: Ashgate, 2008), ch. 4.

30 In its interest in gender, patriarchy and the legal profession in early modern France, this work therefore also engages with Julie Hardwick, *Practice of Patriarchy: Gender and the Politics of Household Authority in Early Modern France* (University Park, PA: Penn State University Press, 1998). Crucially, however, Hardwick's work discusses how patriarchy informed the everyday lives of notarial families in Nantes, whereas this work examines the literary output and patriarchal *aspirations* of the legal profession.

31 L'Estoile, II, 167.

32 Garrett Mattingly, *Renaissance Diplomacy* (Baltimore: Penguin, 1964), 204–5.

33 For evidence of Catherine's dissatisfaction with her own foreign ambassadors, see Susan Broomhall, '"My Daughter, My Dear": The Correspondence of Catherine de Médicis and Elisabeth de Valois', *Women's History Review* 24/4 (2015): 548–69.

34 Filippo de Vivo, *Information and Communication in Venice: Rethinking Early Modern Politics* (Oxford: Oxford University Press, 2007), 75.

35 Nicola Sutherland, 'Catherine de Medici: The Legend of the Wicked Italian Queen', *The Sixteenth Century Journal* 9, no. 2 (1978): 45–56. Another excellent study of

30 *Introduction*

Catherine's negative reputation is by Elaine Kruse, 'The Blood-Stained Hands of Catherine de Medici', *Political Rhetoric, Power and Renaissance Women*, eds. Carole Levin, Patricia A. Sullivan (Albany: SUNY Press, 1995), 139–155. Catherine did not suffer the same negative historiography in her native land, and is instead perceived, much like her distant relative Marie de Medici, as a successful member of the Medici family who became queen of France. See the catalogue for the 2008 exhibition at the Palazzo Strozzi, *Women in Power: Caterina and Maria de' Medici: The Return to Florence of Two Queens of France*, ed. Clarice Innocenti (Firenze: Mandragora, 2008).

36 Sutherland, 'Catherine de Medici', 46.
37 Caroline Zum Kolk, 'Catherine de Médicis et sa maison. La fonction politique de l'hôtel de la reine au XVIe siècle' (unpublished doctoral thesis, Université Paris VIII, 2006), 23. 'Les critiques adressées à Catherine de Médicis reprennent des motifs déjà rencontrés dans le cas d'Isabeau de Bavière: l'étrangère qui livre le pays à ses ennemis, la mère dénaturée, avide de pouvoir . . . la répétition des arguments est frappante. L'archétype de la reine néfaste a pris forme'.
38 Sarah Hanley has written extensively on the fraudulent nature of Salic Law; see 'Engendering the State', 4–27.
39 Nicole Cazauran, ed., *Discours merveilleux de la vie, actions et deportemens de Catherine de Médicis, royne-mère* (Genève: Droz, 1995), 155: 'nonobstant les oppositions d'aucuns des deputez des estats fondées sur l'authorité de nostre loy Salique, et les mauvais succez des gouvernemens des femmes en ce roiaume . . . le gouvernement est deferé à la Roine'.
40 For the contemporary literary response to the *Discours merveilleux*, see Yvonne Roberts, 'The Regency of 1574 in the Discours Merveilleux and in the Poems of Jean-Antoine de Baïf', *Bibliothèque d'Humanisme et Renaissance* 63, no. 2 (2001): 261–75.
41 Katherine Crawford, *Perilous Performances: Gender and Regency in Early Modern France* (Cambridge, MA: Harvard University Press, 2004).
42 *Discours merveilleux*, 170.
43 *La Reine Margot*, dir. Patrice Chéreau (AMLF, 1994).
44 Jean-François Dubost, *La France italienne, XVIe–XVIIe siècle* (Paris: Aubier, 1997).
45 *Discours merveilleux*, 130: 'Entre les nations, l'Italie emporte le prix de finesse et subtilité: en Italie la Toscane, en Toscane la ville de Florence . . . Or quand ceste science de tromper tombe en personne que n'a point de conscience, comme il se voit le plus souvent és gens de ce pais-là, je laisse à penser combien de maux on en doit attendre. En après elle est de la maison de Médicis'.
46 *Le Tocsain, contre les massacreurs et auteurs des confusions en France. Par lequel la source et origine de tous les maux, qui de long temps travaillent la France, est descouverte, etc.* (Reims, 1577), 65r: 'Car voilà les artifices qu'on avoit appris de nouveau, de se deffaire dextrement par secrette poison de ceux que la furie d'une guerre ouverte n'avoit peu attaindre avec le glaive; ce qui nous avoit esté incogneu auparavant, jusques à ce que l'Italie nous a eu vomi une racaille infinie de foruscis que cest femme a favorisé et enrichi des trésors de la France'. *Fuoriusciti* was the name given to Italian (usually Florentine) political exiles who sought refuge in France during the upheavals of the Italian wars.
47 The term 'sexual Machiavels' is found in Hugh Richmond, 'Shakespeare's Navarre', *The Huntington Library Quarterly* 42, no. 3 (Summer, 1979): 36.
48 I have found two roughly contemporary uses of the term 'flying squadron'. The first relates to the army of Alessandro Farnese, duke of Parma, in whose Spanish-style army a group of cavalry were employed to ride off at short notice at the captain's command, and because of this were known as the 'flying squadron'. See Léon van der Essen, *Alexandre Farnèse, prince de Parme, gouverneur général des Pays-Bas* (Bruxelles: Librairie nationale d'art et d'histoire, 1934), 2 (1578–1582), 24. The second reference, much later, relates to the papal conclaves of the mid-seventeenth century in which a group of cardinals, who were unaligned to either of the main

factions and would move from one to the other, were known as the 'flying squadron'. See Antoine Furetière, *Dictionnaire universel: contenant généralement tous les mots françois*, ed. Jean Baptiste Brutel de la Rivière (Hildesheim: Georg Olms, 1972).
49 *Les amours de Henri IV. Roy de France, avec ses lettres galantes & les réponses de ses Maîtresses* (Cologne, 1695), 20: 'Cette Princesse qui n'avoit que son ambition en tête, & qui ne comptoit pour rien la pudeur & la Religion, avoit toûjours un Escadron Volant, s'il m'est permis de parler ainsi, composé des plus belles femmes de la Cour, dont elle se servoit à toutes mains pour amuser les Princes & les Seigneurs, & pour découvrir leur plus secrettes pensées'.
50 LaGuardia, *Intertextual Masculinity*, 189.
51 Pierre de Bourdeille, abbé de Brantôme, *Recueil des dames, poésies et tombeaux*, ed. Etienne Vaucheret (Paris: Gallimard, 1991), 45. All further references to this work will be cited as 'Brantôme'.
52 BnF MS Fr 25455. Catherine de Clermont, Maréchale de Retz, *Album de poésies (Manuscrit français 25455 de la BnF)*, eds. Colette H. Winn and François Rouget (Paris: Honoré Champion, 2004).
53 BnF MS Fr 25455:

'En ce seul Escadron est la fleur de l'Europe,
Aussi bien que lon voit en ceste belle troppe
L'eslite des beautez, & de plus doux regars'.

54 Brantôme, 54; Kate van Orden, *Music, Discipline and Arms in Early Modern France* (Chicago: University of Chicago Press, 2005), 5.
55 Van Orden, *Music, Discipline and Arms*, 5.
56 Pierre de Ronsard, *Oeuvres complètes*, ed. Paul Laumonier, 20 vols (Paris: Marcel Didier, 1946):

'Ores il [le ballet] estoit rond, ores long, or'estroit
Or' en pointe, en triangle en la façon qu'on voit
L'escadron de la Gruë evitant la froidure'

57 Claude Malingre, *Les Annales générales de la ville de Paris* (Paris: Pierre Rocolet, Cardin Besongne, Henry Le Gras, and La Vefve Nicolas Trabovilliet, 1640), 481: 'De loin que le Roy les vid, il se tourna deuers le Nonce du Pape, qui estoit vn peu à quartier, auec les autres Ambassadeurs, & luy demanda ce qu'il luy en sembloit, & si vn tel escadron n'estoit pas beau; Bellissime, respond le Nonce, & bien perilleux. Tant de beautez estoient assez puissantes pour acquerir vn autre Empire à l'Amour. Tant de vertus estoie[n]t assez fortes pour destruire & desesperer tous les desseins de l'Amour'. I am grateful to Melinda Gough for this reference.
58 Monique Chatenet, *La Cour de France au XVIe siècle: Vie sociale et architecture* (Paris: Picard, 2002), 27.
59 LaGuardia, 184.
60 This phenomenon has also been identified by Antónia Szabari, *Less Rightly Said*, 198. She discusses 'L'Estoile's efforts to gather, select and catalogue the licentious words that circulated in the public space'.
61 Alison Booth, 'The Lessons of the Medusa: Anna Jameson and Collective Biographies of Women', *Victorian Studies* 42, no. 2 (Winter, 1999-Winter 2000): 257–88, 258.
62 Juvenal, *The Satires*, trans. Niall Rudd, ed. William Barr (Oxford: Clarendon Press, 1991); Susanna H. Braund, 'Juvenal – Misogynist or Misogamist?', *The Journal of Roman Studies*, 82 (1992), 71–86; Hugh Lloyd-Jones, *Females of the Species: Semonides on Women* (London: Duckworth, 1975).
63 LaGuardia, *Intertextual Masculinity*, 8. The libels/pamphlets mentioned are all found in L'Estoile, and each will be discussed in detail in the following chapters.
64 For an anthology of misogynist writings in both the ancient and medieval worlds, see *Woman Defamed and Woman Defended: An Anthology of Medieval Texts*, ed. Alcuin

32 *Introduction*

Blamires, with Karen Pratt and C. W. Marx (Oxford: Clarendon Press, 2002). A possible exception to this statement could be made in the case of Elizabeth I, for whom there are some positive dialogues regarding female rule. However, Elizabeth's choice to present herself as the 'Virgin Queen' demonstrates the centrality of sexuality to discussion of female rulers.

65 For an overview of Brantôme's career and publications, see Dora Polachek, 'A la recherche du spirituel: l'Italie et les Dames galantes de Brantôme', *Romanic Review* 94, nos. 1–2 (2003): 227–43.

66 In the Vaucheret edition, the section on Catherine de Medici's court is 26–70 and the second section on 'les dames galantes' is 233–722.

67 LaGuardia, *Intertextual Masculinity*.

68 *Mémoires et lettres de Marguerite de Valois*, ed. M.F. Guessard (Paris: Renouard, 1842).

69 L'Estoile, V, 139–40:

> Madame de Sauve y est bonne:
> Son con est tousjours pour la paix.
> C'est pourquoi l'on ne void jamais
> Que Catin ne l'ait auprès d'elle.
> Quand feu Monsieur fut en querelle
> Contre le Roy, Katin alors
> Lui mena faire les accords.
> Pour la paix elle fut foutue.
> Catin la mena toute nue
> Au Roy de Navarre, et de là
> Feit que la guerre s'en alla.[. . .]
> Catin, vous estes fortunée
> D'avoir un haras de putains!

The word 'catin' translates in modern French as 'whore', and such a definition can be traced back to this period. For a discussion of the word as used to describe Catherine de Medici, see Stephen Murphy, 'Catherine, Cybele, & Ronsard's Witnesses', *High Anxiety: Masculinity in Crisis in Early Modern France*, ed. Kathleen Long (Kirksville: Truman State University Press, 2002), 55–70, in particular 60.

70 César de Bazancourt, *L'Escadron volant de la reine. 1560* (Paris, 1836); Henry Charles Litolff, Adolphe d'Ennery and Jules Brésil, *L'Escadron volant de la reine. Opera-comique en trois actes, etc.* (Paris, Châtillon-sur-Seine, 1888); Alexandre Dumas, *La Reine Margot* (Oxford: Oxford University Press, 1997). Litolff was also the musical composer of a three-act comic-opera about the medieval story of Héloïse and Abélard, suggesting a vogue for the licentious representation of French historical figures; cf. Charlotte Charrier, *Héloïse dans l'histoire et dans la légende* (Genève: Slatkine Reprints, 1977), 557–63.

71 Comte Hector de La Ferrière, *Trois amoureuses au XVIè siècle: Françoise de Rohan, Isabelle de Limeuil, La reine Margot* (Paris: Calmann Levy, 1885), 71: 'Mais Catherine ne voulait pas, ne pouvait pas se passer de son escadron volant, cette milice galante si aguerrie'.

72 Jean-Hippolyte Mariéjol, *Histoire de France, t. VI: La Reforme et la Ligue. L'edit de Nantes 1559–1598*, ed. Ernest Lavisse (Paris, 1904), 88: 'Elle se servait d'elles pour découvrir un secret, lever un scrupule, entamer une conviction. L'escadron volant, comme on l'appelait, faisait bien des conquêtes'.

73 Mariéjol, *Catherine de Médicis 1519–1589* (Paris: Jules Tallandier, 1979, originally written 1920), 216–21: 'Parmi ces dames et ces demoiselles, il y en avait de plus favorites qu'elle emmenait dans ses villégiatures et ses chevauchées diplomatiques. C'est le fameux escadron volant dont elle se serait servie pour assaillir à sa façon et reduire les chefs de partis'.

74 Jean Héritier, *Catherine de Medici* (London: George Allen & Unwin, 1963), 310: 'Elle choisit les plus jolies de ses suivantes, afin d'en faire des Armides, qui désarment les Renauds, dangereux pour l'Etat'; Torquato Tasso, *The Liberation of Jerusalem (Gerusalemme Liberata)* (Oxford: Oxford University Press, 2009).
75 Héritier, *Catherine de Medici*, 310: 'Une passion trop despotique s'était emparée d'elle, et qui ne lui laissait le moindre loisir, ni le moindre goût, pour les frivolités du coeur et des sens: la passion du pouvoir'.
76 Hugh M. Richmond, 'Shakespeare's Navarre', 200–1. Richmond's quote is from *Cambridge Modern History*, ed. A.W. Ward (Cambridge: University of Cambridge Press, 1904), III, 27.
77 For a discussion of the tortuous negotiations that lay behind the marriage of Marguerite de Valois and Henri de Navarre, see Nancy Lyman Roelker, *Queen of Navarre: Jeanne d'Albret 1528–1572* (Cambridge MA: Harvard University Press, 1968).
78 Eugène Defrance, *Catherine de Médicis, ses astrologues et ses magiciens-envoûteurs: documents inédits sur la diplomatie et les sciences occultes du XVIe siècle* (Paris: Mercure de France, 1911).
79 Simone Bertière, *Les Reines de France au temps des Valois 2*. 'Les années sanglantes' (Paris: Fallois, 1994), 101–2: 'La cour, ce sont d'abord des femmes, un essaim de dames et de demoiselles de qualité qu'elle a choisies pour leur beauté, leur charme, leur talent à deviser, à chanter, à danser . . . Catherine veut fixer durablement les guerriers à la cour. Ce n'est pas en laissant ses filles succomber trop vite qu'elle y parviendra: désirables et longuement désirées, elles seront beaucoup plus efficaces'.
80 Robert J. Knecht, *Catherine de' Medici* (London: Longman, 1998), 235.
81 Jean-François Solnon, *Catherine de Médicis* (Paris: Perrin, 2003), 327–28: 'L' 'escadron volant' n'est pas un mythe. Catherine n'a pas dédaigné la collaboration de dames de sa Maison pour accélérer ou parfaire des négociations politiques. Elle plaça ainsi quelques belles filles sur le chemin de son fils François d'Anjou – enfui du Louvre en septembre 1575 – et de son entourage, tant l'alliance des huguenots avec les malcontents dont il était le chef était une menace pour le royaume'. Solnon gives no evidence or reference for this claim.
82 Crouzet, *Le haut coeur de Catherine de Médicis*, 110–11: 'Plutôt que de suggérer un groupe féminin chargé de séduire sexuellement les courtisans pour mieux les faire tomber sous la coupe de la reine-mère, le terme 'escadron volant', qui fut employé pour désigner certaines des dames et des damoiselles de la maison de Catherine de Medici, aurait été associé à leur exécution harmonique de figures de ballet . . . Un sonnet de Ronsard, dans cette optique, remémore un ballet mimant 'l'escadron de la Gruë évitant la froidure' . . . Il est peu probable que Catherine de Medici ait encouragé, en outre, l'essor d'une culture de cour chargée de séduction charnelle telle que les textes satiriques lui en attribuèrent la responsabilité. Bien au contraire, sous le règne de Henri II, elle paraît avoir engagé une action de réformation de la cour dans le sens d'une austerité morale'. See also Mark Franko, *Dance as Text: Ideologies of the Baroque Body* (Cambridge: Cambridge University Press, 1993), 24.
83 Zum Kolk, 'The Household of the Queen of France in the Sixteenth Century', *The Court Historian* 14, no. 1, (June 2009).
84 *Painted Ladies: Women at the Court of Charles II*, eds. Catharine MacLeod and Julia Marciari Alexander (London: National Portrait Gallery, 2001), 206. See also *Politics, Transgression, and Representation at the Court of Charles II*, eds. Catharine MacLeod and Julia Marciari Alexander (New Haven: Yale University Press, 2007).
85 Sheryl E. Reiss, 'Widow, Mother, Patron of Art: Alfonsina Orsini de' Medici', *Beyond Isabella: Secular Women Patrons of Art in Renaissance Italy* (Kirksville: Truman State University Press, 2001), 125–8; Sheila ffolliott, 'The Italian "Training" of Catherine de Medici: Portraits as Dynastic Narrative', *The Court Historian* 10/1 (October 2005), special issue: *Queens and the Transmission of Political Culture: The Case of Early Modern France*, eds. Melinda Gough and Malcolm Smuts: 37–54.

34 *Introduction*

86 Sheila ffolliott, 'Portraying Queens: The International Language of Court Portraiture in the Sixteenth Century', *Elizabeth I: Then and Now*, ed. Georgianna Ziegler (Washington, DC: The Folger Shakespeare Library, 2003), 164–75.
87 Alexandra Zvereva, *Les Clouet de Catherine de Médicis: chefs-d'oeuvre graphiques du musée Condé* (Paris: Somogy, 2002), 7. See also Zvereva, *Portraits dessinés de la cour de Valois: Les Clouet de Catherine de Médicis* (Paris: Arthena, 2011).
88 Ronald Burt, 'Gossip and Reputation', *Management et réseaux sociaux: ressources pour l'action ou outil de gestion?*, eds. Marc Lecoutre and Lievre Pascal (Paris: Hermès sciences publications, 2008), 27–42.
89 For studies of oral culture in early modern Italy, see De Vivo, *Information and Communication in Venice*; Elizabeth Horodowich, 'The Gossiping Tongue: Oral Networks, Public Life and Political Culture in Early Modern Venice', *Renaissance Studies* 19 (2005): 22–45. The close links between gossip, scandal and print culture are explored in Nicola Parsons, *Reading Gossip in Early Eighteenth-Century England* (Basingstoke: Palgrave Macmillan, 2009). An excellent introduction to the historical uses and definitions of gossip is found in Chris Wickham, 'Gossip and Resistance among the Medieval Peasantry', *Past & Present* 160 (1998): 3–24; see also *Fama: The Politics of Talk and Reputation in Medieval Europe*, eds. Thelma Fenster and Daniel Lord Smail (Ithaca: Cornell University Press, 2003). From a literary perspective, see Patricia Meyer Spacks, *Gossip* (New York: Alfred A. Knopf, 1985). From an anthropological perspective, see Max Gluckman, 'Papers in Honor of Melville J. Herskovits: Gossip and Scandal', *Current Anthropology* 4 (1963): 307–16.
90 L'Estoile, II, 167: 'Pour parler à la vérité, ce dont se plaint le prophète Jérémie [L'Estoile is mistaken; the passage he refers to is in Isaiah], chapitre IIIe, des filles de Sion qui étaient élevées, cheminant le col étendu et les yeux affettés, se guindant et branlant, et faisant résonner leurs pas, se pouvait à aussi bon titre et meilleur, dire en ce temps des femmes de Paris et filles de la cour. Dont ne se faut ébahir, se le Seigneur, selon la menace qu'il en fait au lieu même par son prophète, déchevelait leurs têtes et leurs parties honteuses par ces folâtres faiseurs de pasquils, dont la ville de Paris et la cour étaient remplies. Bref, le débordement, sans parler de pis, était tel que la cabale du cocuage était un des plus clairs revenus de ce temps'.
91 Tatiana Debbagi Baranova, 'Poésie officielle, poésie partisane pendant les guerres de Religion', *Terrain* 41 | 2003, URL: http://terrain.revues.org/1610; DOI: 10.4000/terrain.1610, accessed 17/05/2013. ['C'est dans ces microsociétés juridiques et cléricales que la satire politique et religieuse prend racine'.] For a more in-depth discussion of libellous verse during the Wars of Religion see Baranova, *À coups de libelles: une culture politique au temps des guerres de religion (1562–1598)* (Genève: Droz, 2012).
92 Marie Houllemare, *Politiques de la parole: le Parlement de Paris au XVIe siècle* (Genève: Droz, 2011), 275–6.
93 On 24 June and 8 July 1607 he loaned his good friend Pierre Dupuy his collections *Les Bigarrures Folastres* and *Drôleries de la Ligue*, respectively, *JHIV*, 251 and 257.
94 For L'Estoile's editorial decisions, see Fanny Marin, 'La fortune éditoriale des *Registres journaux des règnes de Henri III et Henri IV* de Pierre de L'Estoile', *Nouvelle Revue du XVIe siècle* 20/2 (2002), 87–108.
95 The original collection is found in BnF MS Anciens petits fonds français, 22560–22565, *Recueil de pièces de vers, chansons, sonnets, triolets, sur les guerres de religion, formé par le chirurgien protestant Rasse des Noeux. XVIe siècle*. Prosper Tarbé, *Recueil de poésies calvinistes* (Reims: P. Dubois, 1866). On Rasse des Noeux, see Jeanne Veyrin-Forrer, 'Un collectionneur peu connu, François Rasse Des Neux [sic], chirurgien parisien', *La Lettre et le Texte* (Paris: ENS Jeunes Filles, 1987), 423–77; Françoise Charpentier, 'Formes de l'esprit pamphlétaire: quelques questions autour du manuscrit Rasse des Nœux', in *Traditions Polémiques* (Paris: ENS Jeunes Filles,

1985). Rasse des Noeux also collected printed epitaphs; see also by Veyrin-Forrer, 'François Rasse des Neux [sic] et ses tombeaux poétiques' in *Le poète et son oeuvre de la composition à la publication: actes du colloque de Valenciennes (20–21 mai 1999)*, ed. Jean-Eudes Girot (Genève: Droz, 2004), 37–46.

96 Alastair Bellany, 'Railing Rhymes Revisited: Libels, Scandals, and Early Stuart Politics', *History Compass* 5, no. 4 (2007): 1136–79.

97 Luc Racaut, *Hatred in Print: Catholic Propaganda and Protestant Identity during the French Wars of Religion* (Aldershot: Ashgate, 2002). One exception is the study of pamphlet literature *Traditions Polémiques*, ed. Nicole Cazauran (Paris: ENS Jeunes Filles, 1985) which contains chapters by Gilbert Schrenck on the journal of Pierre de L'Estoile and by Mireille Huchon on the *Discours merveilleux* (although the latter focusses on its translation techniques rather than the subject matter of the pamphlet).

98 The first theory is found in Robert Darnton, *The Literary Underground of the Old Regime* (Cambridge, MA: Harvard University Press, 1982); the second theory is found in Simon Burrows, *Blackmail, Scandal and Revolution: London's French Libellistes, 1758–1792* (Manchester University Press, 2006). See also Lynn Hunt, 'The Many Bodies of Marie-Antoinette: Political Pornography and the Problem of the Feminine in the French Revolution', *Marie-Antoinette: Writings on the Body of a Queen*, ed. Dena Goodman (New York: Routledge, 2003).

99 Sarah Maza, *Private Lives and Public Affairs: The Causes Célèbres of Prerevolutionary France* (Berkeley: University of California Press, 1993), 15.

100 Houllemare, *Politiques de la parole*.

101 A recent study that situates the marketplace inside the Palais de Justice as a key locus for the exchange and circulation of information in this period is Warner, *The Ideas of Man and Woman in Renaissance France*.

2 Court Life and Its Critics
The Rise in Satirical Literature

In his memoirs, Pierre de Bourdeille, seigneur de Brantôme, recalled how Catherine de Medici reacted to the news of libellous material that attacked the women of her household:

> Moreover, the queen mother took a firm hand in supporting her ladies and girls, and gave a good hiding to these detractors and libellers, once they were discovered, even though she herself was no more spared than were her ladies; but she didn't worry as much for herself as for the others in as much as, she said, she felt her soul and her conscience to be pure and clean, which says enough for her, and the majority of the time laughed and made fun of these critical writers and libellers. 'Let them torment, she'd say, and go to the trouble for nothing', but when she found them out, she really let them have it.[1]

Brantôme's memories of Catherine de Medici's anger at libels specifically targeting her entourage show that this type of satirical literature was both substantial and injurious to the reputation of her household. These 'detractors and libellers' who believed it to be their duty to publicly shame women who they felt had become debauched originated for the most part in the legal profession, the body of men from the educated bourgeoisie and robe nobility who staffed the increasingly bureaucratic Parlement of Paris and its associated courts and corporate bodies. This chapter looks at the origins of this increase in written and oral attack on court women, exploring how L'Estoile's colleagues constructed and reinforced their own social and political status by portraying the queen's household as a site of debauchery and prostitution. By way of contrast, it then compares that representation with the realities of life in the queen's entourage, demonstrating how specific changes in Catherine's status could affect the portrayal of the women of her household in the pamphlet literature that circulated in Paris and beyond.

Sarah Hanley has demonstrated how the sixteenth-century parlementaires, heavily invested in the venal system which allowed them to consolidate a power base through the inheritance of offices and intermarriage with other allied families, began to construct a social framework through the means of law that would support and reinforce their familial power structures. First, they promoted the superiority of French judicial expertise and sought national status as a supreme court for the Parlement of Paris. Then, 'as the authors of individual reputations', Hanley argues,

> the legists sought professional fame through scholarly erudition and the practice of law. They vied for the attention of the elite – kings and royal councils, scholars and intellectuals – by publishing legal commentaries, political tracts, and historical works. More important here, they competed with colleagues for public attention by publishing and peddling broadsheets, pamphlets and books that lauded their own legal prowess.[2]

Marie Houllemare has demonstrated how the legists of the sixteenth century exploited the printing press and pamphlet literature for their own intellectual reputations.[3] To take one example, the magistrate Anne Robert published a version of his argument (*plaidoyer*) of 1577 against an empiric, in which he exhibited his knowledge of Latin and Greek, and deployed examples from the Old Testament, St. Bernard, Epicurus and Virgil.[4] Lastly, parlementaires promulgated what Hanley calls a 'Family-State compact', 'which was designed to bring family formation under parental (that is, patriarchal) control in the first instance and under the magisterial control of the Parlement of Paris in the second'.[5]

With the introduction of laws that made increasing inroads into women's freedoms through greater control by fathers and husbands over marriage, pregnancies and inheritance, the parlementaires attempted to create a society in which women's roles were less public and more domestic. This patriarchal tendency subsequently found expression in public literary efforts which promoted their world-view. Susan Broomhall points to the disproportionate influence these men enjoyed:

> it was a small, socially privileged, wealthy and educated minority of men who most influenced the cultural, theological and intellectual practices of early modern France. Furthermore, in literary discourse, this learned subset most affected the criteria of what was to be written and accepted. Literary discourse was produced by, and in turn reproduced, the power and authority of those men who defined it.[6]

This power and authority was threatened – at least, in the eyes of the parlementaires – by the political prominence of Catherine de Medici and the increasingly public role of the women of her household.

There had been periods in the recent past when women had held the title of queen or regent and/or exercised legitimate political power: Anne de Beaujeu was regent during her brother Charles VIII's minority from 1483 to 1491, during which time she made the Treaty d'Etaples, ending the Hundred Years War, and married her brother to Anne de Bretagne, thereby annexing the powerful duchy of Brittany to the French crown; Anne de Bretagne herself was twice queen of France (she also married Charles's successor Louis XII) from 1491 to 1514 and duchess of Brittany during her second reign, and successfully defended the independence of the duchy during this time; Louise de Savoie, raised in Anne de Beaujeu's household, would go on to act as regent three times for her son François I during his absences because of the Italian wars, and was the principal negotiator, along with her sister-in-law Margaret of Austria, of the Treaty of Cambrai in 1529, known as 'The Ladies' Peace'. Eliane Viennot has remarked that during the sixteenth century, women became involved 'at all levels of public life, to an extent never before seen in Western history, [an extent] which would then decrease after the Fronde'.[7] What made the situation different in the second half of the century to this earlier period was not only the predominance of women in seats of power but also the religious struggles which saw women play key roles on all sides of the conflict. Among others, Jeanne d'Albret, queen of Navarre was the figurehead for the Reform movement, the Guise women were pro-active on the pro-Catholic front, and Catherine de Medici took a middle, *politique* path. Moreover, as Viennot has demonstrated, women were active in all aspects of the religious wars: not only did they actively engage in plots, act as spies, spread propaganda and negotiate for peace, they even fought, defending cities and castles.[8] As Michel de Waele notes, 'the disorders that emerged during the second half of the sixteenth century had the distinction that they placed women, for the first time, completely centre stage, and therefore at the forefront of political discourse'.[9] This ironically occurred as parlementaires sought more than ever to prop up the legitimacy of the fraudulent Salic Law that prevented women from holding power.

To add to this, the protracted nature of Catherine's political prominence – almost 30 years spent as regent, *gouvernante* of France or as chief adviser to Henri III – ushered in an era where women's roles at court became steadily more visible, due to her ever-expanding household.[10] The humanist education given to the royal children (their tutor was Jacques Amyot, translator of Plutarch) resulted in Charles IX founding, in 1570, the first *Académie française* in the style of the famous Florentine academy of Marsilio Ficino.[11] Although Charles' death four years later ended the academy, Henri III restarted it, renaming it the *Académie du Palais*, and holding it twice a week for nine years in his own cabinet, to which were invited well-known poets such as Pierre de Ronsard, Jean-Antoine de Baïf and Philippe Desportes, as well as men of science, doctors, diplomats and – significantly – his sister Marguerite de Valois, Henriette de Clèves, duchesse de Nevers and Catherine's close friend, Claude-Catherine de Clermont-Dampierre, maréchale de Retz[12] (Figure 2.1). This invitation would not have seemed surprising given that since 1570 the maréchale had been hosting her own salon in her hôtel in the faubourg Saint-Honoré in winter, or her château of Noisy-le-Roi in the summer.[13]

Long before her great-niece, the marquise de Rambouillet, would begin her celebrated salon in 1607, Retz and her female friends were at the centre of a network of literary and artistic creation. The learned maréchale, familiar with classical languages (she was chosen as Latin interpreter for the visit by the Polish ambassadors to the French court in 1573) as well as Italian and Spanish, was an expert player of the lute, and kept an album full of encomiastic works written in her honour by renowned poets and writers, addressed to her literary name of

Figure 2.1 François Clouet, *Claude-Catherine de Clermont, maréchale de Retz*
Source: BnF Estampes et photographie Réserve NA-22–21

Dictynne.[14] The 'cabinet vert' of the rue Saint-Honoré became celebrated as a Parnassus, inspiring writers such as the celebrated barrister and poet Estienne Pasquier, the Huguenot writer Agrippa d'Aubigné, the court poet Philippe Desportes and the anti-League writer and magistrate Nicolas Rapin, but also welcoming women of the court who, like the maréchale herself, would write anonymously. In the opinion of the bibliographer La Croix du Maine, the maréchale merited 'to be placed in the ranks of the most learned and most well-versed, as much in poetry and oratory art as in philosophy, mathematics, history and other sciences, from which she knows well how to profit [from] those whom she feels worthy of these learned discourses. She has still not brought to light any of her works or compositions'.[15] D'Aubigné claimed that 'the maréchale de Retz . . . has given me a great work in her own hand which I would very much like to bring forth from secrecy into the public domain'.[16] The poet Jean Dorat sang her praises in an epigram in which he compared her to Virgil's heroine Camilla:

> To the noble, skilled in arts, studious
> Heroine Camilla, Countess of Retz.
> The poetess and female warrior Camilla
> Merited the praise of Virgil, and men have imitated the work of Virgil.
> She would be more praised by poets if she lived like you,
> Learned woman who disputes with learned men.[17]

Dorat's comparison of Retz to the warrior Camilla highlights Retz's involvement in literary debates, implying that she could more than hold her own against the university-educated men she invited.

This direct participation by women in literary inspiration, creation and debate (as opposed to a Petrarchan discourse in which the woman is the passive object of the male gaze) resulted in their being celebrated for their literary attributes. But it had other, less welcome, consequences. The presence of writers such as Pasquier, Rapin and d'Aubigné in the homes of noblewomen such as Retz gave them first-hand knowledge of the intimate, domestic lives of courtiers which provided ample material for satire. Pasquier, for example, was one of the authors of the La Marck verses that L'Estoile copied into his journal, and d'Aubigné's oeuvre abounds with vitriol attacking the allegedly debauched domestic arrangements of the women of the court. Similarly, the anonymous writer of the 1587 *Manifesto of the Ladies of the Court* would eventually paint the maréchale de Retz as an adulterous wife, waiting for her husband to die so she could marry her lover Charles de Balsac, baron de Dunes, known as '*le bel Entraguet*':

> Madame de Rets, speaking to Monsr de Lyon.
> I know, Sir, that if the compromise that I have made with Antraguet, to marry him after the death of my base husband, does not excuse me before you, that I will have to admit that I am a dishonest and infamous woman even though the good man is not unaware of my scam. But, Sir, Long Live the League![18]

Retz's personal life – in particular her alleged love for Henri III's *mignon* Entraguet – was the regular subject of satirical libels in the 1580s which pictured the intellectually dominant (and thus transgressive) Retz as cuckolding her husband, Albert de Gondi-Retz, maréchal de France. As early as 1581, L'Estoile included verses alluding to a sexual relationship between Retz and Entraguet: 'The maréchale de Retz gets on well with Entraguet./She was wise, if only she hadn't been so foolish as to give him her jewels'.[19]

The theme of cuckoldry was an ever-present motif in the satirisation of politically or intellectually active women: women who transgressed gender boundaries in this way could not be trusted, their unnatural public roles betraying an uncontrollable sexuality. This suggests that artistic patronage could be problematic for courtly women: writers who depended on their favour in order to make a living would sing their praises but could live a literary 'double life', penning anonymous polemical literature according to their confessional beliefs or attacking what they saw as an increasingly debauched court.[20] For example, d'Aubigné would write several polemical works, *la Confession du Sieur de Sancy*, *Les Aventures du baron de Faeneste* and *Les Tragiques*, all of which portray the court and its ladies as depraved and often perverse. In *Les Tragiques*, under the section 'Les Princes', d'Aubigné describes courtly women as filthy whores, cuckolding their husbands with their servants: 'One counts the loves of our dirty princesses,/Whores of their valets, sometimes their mistresses'.[21] Nowhere can this phenomenon be better witnessed than in the flurry of verse libels L'Estoile collected on the murder of Françoise de La Marck by her husband René de Villequier in 1577 which was briefly discussed in the introduction.

The Murder of Françoise de La Marck

With its themes of adultery, homicide and alleged poison and prostitution, La Marck's murder was fertile ground for the authors of anti-court literature. The sheer number (as previously mentioned, L'Estoile chose 12 of the 'many and diverse sorts of *tombeaux* and *épitaphes*' to include in his journal) is evidence of the fascination this particular scandal inspired among writers.[22] These 'tombeaux' or 'épitaphes' were mocking verses that subverted the notion of the traditional tribute to the dead with its elevated register, respectful tone and celebration of the life and accomplishments of the deceased. The humour and irony of the epitaph results from the thwarting of such high expectations, achieved in the La Marck verses by descriptions of debauchery, prostitution, murder, adultery and sodomy. The epitaph form demands some type of summary of the deceased's life which, in this case, results in an anti-eulogy in which the moral failings of La Marck, her husband and the entire court are enumerated.

For example, Verse I in L'Estoile's collection is a sonnet in La Marck's voice.[23] It attempts to apportion blame for the murder, locating the origin of her immoral lifestyle in the licentious environment of the court where she was raised. As part of the 'infinite troupe/Following the slender firebrands of Cupid', she is less culpable because she is surrounded by this 'common evil'. Thus the collective sexual reputation of the women of court is tarnished, the military theme conjured by the term 'troupe', like the term 'squadron', implying that strategic planning is behind the sexual libertinage. The octave ends with the rhetorical question: 'should I be punished?' 'No' replies the sestet, which claims that Villequier's sexual frustration led him to train his wife as a whore ('he made me so'). His lack of virtue, claims the poet, meant that he became a pimp, choosing to offer his wife's body to 'his master' the king to win his favour, 'Trafficking his credit at the price of [his wife's] honour'. The denigration of the court to a mere brothel (also alluded to in Verses VI, VIII and X) that boasts the king Henri III as a client creates the sense that the moral turpitude reaches – or originates from – the highest power in the land. The theme of prostitution is a regular feature of most cuckold literature of the early modern period which rests on the premise that wives, their libidos out of control, are constantly tricking their husbands with the help of other clever women.[24] By contrast, in these poems Villequier is depicted as the pimp of his own wife, thereby doubly shaming himself by not only becoming a cuckold, but also by sourcing sexual partners for her. His double shame is then compounded by his homicide which, ironically, was meant to save his honour.

This concept of honour killing, with its themes of guilt and punishment, reveals the patriarchal concerns of the epitaphs' authors. Although only one epitaph is attributed to Estienne Pasquier, the origins of many of the anonymous verses are clearly among the literary fraternity of the legal profession. Three are in Latin, and another verse, again in La Marck's voice, debates the legal status of the parties involved:

> Should I not feel the madness
> At the hands of a husband, for a life such as mine,
> Who, to soil his bed, gave me counsel,
> Guilty like me in the eyes of the Julian law?[25]

The author's legal training would explain the desire to apportion guilt, and the various arguments put forward within the poem for one party's responsibility over another. Julian law (a subsection of Roman law) dictated that women were under the permanent tutelage of their fathers until they were married, at which point their husbands took over this responsibility. Thus, explains the poem, Villequier was duty-bound to behave the way he did:

> Having no parents, nor father in any place,
> My husband, the nearest, was inspired by God,
> To serve the need of parents and father.[26]

Punishment of women is thus figured as part of the patriarchal role, here enacted to its full extent by the husband.

Given parlementaires' concern with patriarchal control, it is unsurprising that another verse warns husbands to treat their wives violently, taking them 'by the ears', as they are most likely already cuckolding them. Within the patriarchal model, however, the husband carried the burden of his wife's sexual honour and was expected to keep his wife and household under control. Villequier is therefore blamed for not exerting due control over his wife.[27] In the one verse in his voice, Villequier bemoans the irony that the killing of his adulterous wife which should have restored honour to him has backfired, and has exposed his inability to perform his patriarchal responsibilities:

> For, thinking to achieve glory through my shame,
> Now I am seen as a murderer, as cruel, and a cuckold.[28]

Honour killing is therefore presented as a lose/lose situation for the husband: as the head of the patriarchal household he must punish his wife for her infidelity but, ironically, by that action he is exposed as unable to keep control of his household in the first place. As Cynthia Herrup notes, 'Anarchic households were particularly abhorrent because the household was the emulative structure that at once illustrated and legitimated the benefits of monarchy'.[29] The verses criticising Villequier therefore reflected on the royal household as well, portraying it as anarchic, with the queen mother unable to control the actions of her courtiers.

The Queen's Household

But what constituted Catherine de Medici's court and who were her courtiers? How did they become so vulnerable to attacks such as those generated by La Marck's death? This chapter now charts the evolution of Catherine's household, demonstrating how it evolved as her own status changed. The royal household was a multi-functional environment. Much more than a residential space, the royal household also performed as a marker of prestige for the head of each household and could be used as a political tool. Studies of early modern royal households are becoming steadily more frequent, although there are far more investigations into the households of kings and princes than of female members of the royal household.[30] Within France, while studies of Versailles are numerous, there has been comparatively less research done on earlier courts.[31] Such studies of the sixteenth-century French court have until recently only concentrated on male households, such as Nicolas Le Roux's exhaustive 2001 work on Catherine's son Henri III and his *mignons*, as well as Mack Holt's study of the household of Henri III's younger brother, the duc d'Anjou.[32] Le Roux's study is particularly enlightening as he uncovers the complex backgrounds of courtiers who, because they were the victims of criticisms directed at a newly absolutist monarchy, are often dismissed by other historians with the overly simplistic label of corrupt and debauched sycophants. It has until now been Sharon Kettering's work on French nobility, in particular the patronage systems and household service of early modern French noblewomen, that has been most helpful for learning how positions for women in noble and royal households were obtained and how noblewomen's careers developed.[33]

Prosopographical studies of royal households are an invaluable tool; as Guido Guerzoni and Guido Alfani state, 'Prosopographical analysis can prove an excellent test of historiographical hypotheses, especially in the field of socio-political relationships and political patronage'.[34] But, as Jeroen Duindam reminds us, 'we miss the point if we fail to add other dimensions, such as the daily routines of the household: the intimacy of the ruler and his entourage; or the interactions of household and government'.[35] Such a rounded prosopographical approach has been undertaken for Catherine de Medici's household by Caroline Zum Kolk in her 2006 *thèse de doctorat* in which she used the *états de maison de la reine*, or queen's household accounts, along with Catherine's own voluminous correspondence to determine exact numbers and identities of persons in the queen's employment and the logistics by which they entered and left service in the royal households.[36] She charts the evolution of Catherine's household as she progressed through the several stages of her career, from princess to dauphine to queen, a period when control over the appointment of offices to her household was exercised mostly by her father-in-law François I or her husband Henri II, through her later positions, after her husband's death in 1559, of regent, *gouvernante* and queen mother, when she had total control over appointments not only to her own household but to those of other royal households. Her work benefits also from the pioneering work done by Monique Chatenet on the architecture and social structure of the French royal households in the sixteenth century.[37] Both authors reveal that, while Catherine's household never attained the exaggerated numbers of women referred to by Brantôme, the nature of her political involvement as queen mother meant that she usually employed larger numbers of staff than the reigning queen, both female and male. But the large numbers of female officers continued a trend that had begun with Anne de Bretagne at the beginning of the century. Chatenet concludes that 'Anne was apparently the first – at least for a long time – to conceive of her female entourage as an essential component of her dignity', a crucial element in the understanding of the large numbers of women in Catherine's court during her years of political involvement.[38]

The introduction of large numbers of women into what had been an almost exclusively male French court by Anne de Bretagne in the 1490s has led to much speculation on the impact their presence had on the men and the court in general. Inevitably, this speculation becomes a discussion of sexual attraction, and morality and scandal are always mentioned whenever the women of the court are discussed. For example, Jean-François Solnon's study of the French court concludes:

> The delicacy with which Catherine de Medici's female entourage refined manners was admirable. Glamorous, friendly, the queen's maids were charming hostesses who demanded in return praise and respect from their friends at the Louvre . . . The court helped in the promotion of an elite feminine corps which, in return, policed the court.[39]

While Solnon's appraisal attempts to cast the female household in a positive light, it not only depicts the women of the court as a uniform, monolithic group, but also places the burden of sexual honour and morality on them, leaving them vulnerable to criticism.

What, then, was the role of the women of the queen's household? Studies have begun to appear which deal with the specific nature of women's roles and functions at court, both as queens and princesses and as ladies-in-waiting, i.e., the women who serve those queens and princesses.[40] These studies reveal that Catherine's appointments fell within a distinctly French tradition, one that she expressed her admiration for in a letter to her son Charles IX on the occasion of his majority.[41] In it, she repeatedly evokes the traditions set by 'the Kings your father and grandfather', and particularly hopes that her son will take up the practice of his 'ancestor King Louis XII', keeping tight control over appointments of offices 'to avoid the importunities and the throng at court, and to let everyone know that it is only you who grants properties and honours'. Catherine's admiration for the traditions of the French court where she had grown up under François I stand in contrast to the criticisms made against her allegedly 'Italian' style of manipulation.[42]

Richard Cook, an Englishman who visited the French court in the 1580s, distinguished three groups of noblewomen there: 'princesses, ladies affectioned to live in Court, ordinarie maides of honour'. Of these, princesses (by which he meant women related to the royal family) 'be not compelled to be in Court nor to attend one the Queene, but at great solempnities & ceremonies'. The women in Catherine's service, however, 'because there charge is allwaies to accompanye the Quene, & have therefore & for theire paynes their table in Court & twentie pounde a yere pention, they be constrayned to be allwaies there'. However, the other group, 'ladies affectioned to the Court', would attend 'when theire owne desires & fances move them'.[43] Therefore one could find women at court who were not directly employed by the queen. This explains Brantôme's list of 86 women whom he claimed frequented the court, many of whom do not appear in the *états de maison* detailing those in Catherine's service, and can explain his claims of over three hundred women at court at any one time. This figure has been misinterpreted by historians as an indicator of the numbers of women employed by Catherine, leading to a portrayal of her retinue as an excessive number of women from whom she would choose the most attractive. The reality is that when she was finally able to exercise real political power as regent upon the accession of her underage son Charles IX in 1560, Catherine took steps to ensure a household of experienced, respected and politically moderate members, both male and female. Her role towards her servants also evolved as her own political status and involvement developed, and this chapter will explore each stage in turn as she moved from young bride to elderly widow.

Establishing the Household

Catherine was born in Florence in April 1519 to Madeleine de La Tour d'Auvergne and Lorenzo II de Medici, and was niece to Pope Leo X. While her Florentine and papal familial ties have been the focus of most attention ever since, it was through her French maternal aunt that in 1524, Catherine became heiress to one of the last great independent fiefs of France. It was an inheritance which François I was keen to bring under control of the French crown, and he made strenuous attempts to have the newly-orphaned Catherine raised in France. Although his efforts were foiled by the ambitions of the new pope, Catherine's self-styled 'uncle' Clement VII, François would eventually secure Catherine's arrival in France by promising her the hand of his second-born son, Henri. Upon her arrival in October 1533, the 14-year-old Catherine was assimilated into the household of Henri's sisters Marguerite and Madeleine, along with at least 10 Italian women who had arrived with her, and who were permitted to remain in her service [état 1534–36]. From this point until August 1536, appointments to the household of the young princess were controlled by the king. She had received a good humanist education during her formative years in Florence, and in the Renaissance court of François I, where the Italian influence was very welcome, her ability to speak French and her love of hunting meant that she assimilated well.

However, the untimely death on 10 August 1536 of the dauphin catapulted Catherine as the new dauphine to second rank behind the queen. She was swiftly awarded her own household along with its own retinue of personnel. Along with this new-found prestige came other more pressing matters: suddenly, her duty as progenitrix of heirs to the throne became of primary importance and the 10 years of barrenness which she would face from the year of her marriage until 1543 encouraged arguments for her repudiation. Luckily, in 1543, Catherine found herself pregnant for the first time, and the birth of her first child Claude was followed, in rapid succession, by the births of nine more children, seven of whom would survive until adulthood. Zum Kolk notes that in 1543, the year that Catherine was first pregnant, the household of the queen, Eléonore d'Autriche, witnessed a purge: 80 women, many from the kingdom's most high-ranking families, left her household; in 1547, the first year for which there are records for Catherine's household, many of them re-appear there. It is likely that they were transferred to the dauphine's house in 1543, which would imply that her new-found maternity gave her greater prestige at court, resulting in a greater number of higher status women in her service.[44]

On 31 March 1547, François I died and was succeeded by Catherine's husband, Henri II. As the new queen of France, Catherine found herself with a vastly increased household of 353 staff, of whom 40 were women: one *dame d'honneur*, 22 *dames*, and 15 *demoiselles* supervised by two *gouvernantes*.[45] A closer look at the wages of the women in her employment, however, reveals that control over the appointments to the queen's household were still in the hands of the king, her husband. Four women received double the salary of the other ladies: Diane de Poitiers; her daughter Louise de Brezé; Madeleine de Savoie, the wife of the constable Anne de Montmorency; and Marguerite de Lustrac, wife of Jacques d'Albon de Saint-André. The first two ladies were the king's mistress and her daughter, and the latter two were the spouses of the king's favourites. Furthermore, the chief position among the women of the household, the *dame d'honneur*, a post that received 1200 *livres* in wages, and whose role was to command and govern the ladies and to be constantly by the queen's side, assisting her on all occasions, was held by Diane's other daughter Françoise de Brezé. While these appointments favouring the king's mistress may have been interpreted as damaging to Catherine's reputation as the royal consort, the possible ignominy of the loss of patronage may have been mitigated by Henri's increasing recognition of Catherine's political abilities: he would appoint her regent on three separate occasions, in 1548, 1552 and 1553, while he fought in the Italian campaigns against Emperor Charles V. Catherine's duties included responsibility for overseeing supplies to the army, gaining subsidies and dealing with administration and justice. While the roles were limited, they provided good training and experience, and she performed impeccably.

The training would stand her in good stead when Henri II was accidentally killed in a jousting accident on 10 July 1559, leaving her as the widowed queen mother of the new king François II. His 15-year-old bride Marie Stuart, otherwise known as Mary, Queen of Scots, was now Queen of France, but Catherine's continuing political involvement meant that she did not mourn for the traditional month. It was the right of the leading noblewomen of the kingdom to serve the reigning queen, and so many women transferred from Catherine's household to the household of the new queen.[46] Although this transfer was purely a matter of etiquette and prestige, it does seem that this arrangement would nonetheless have given Catherine significant knowledge of Marie's household and perhaps thereby the political machinations of Marie's uncles, the powerful Guise brothers.[47] Much has been made of the seizure of power by the Guise, but whatever power they wielded did not last for long. The sickly François died 16 months later in December 1560, and his successor, Charles IX, was a 10-year-old boy. During François's illness Catherine had already moved to secure herself the regency for her underage son, bringing with it huge political power. France had a history of mothers of underage kings assuming responsibility for their care, but not for the administration of the kingdom as well. Catherine managed it by obtaining the consent of the first 'Prince of the Blood' (a member of the royal lineage with a claim to the throne), Antoine de Bourbon, king of Navarre, whose younger brother Louis de Bourbon, prince of Condé, had been involved in the Conspiracy of Amboise (17 March 1560) and was awaiting judgment. Catherine accused Antoine of involvement in the conspiracy, so he relinquished claims to the regency to demonstrate his good faith. Although neither the Parlement nor the Estates General that met in December 1560 voiced any opposition to Catherine's assumption of the regency, claims of manipulation were put forward by the author of the 1574 *Discours merveilleux*, which attempted to blame Catherine for all the nation's misfortunes by recasting past events. The pamphlet would thus allege that Antoine's relinquishing of his claim was directly due to Catherine's manipulation of one of her ladies, Louise de la Beraudière, known as 'la belle Rouet', with whom Antoine had been having an affair:

> she commanded her thus to seduce him and to please him in any way she could, so that, forgetting his own affairs he upset many people . . . Indeed, she did it so well that notwithstanding the oppositions of some of the deputies of the Estates based on the authority of our Salic Law, and the bad fortunes of the government of women in this kingdom, the king of Navarre agreed to it out of nonchalance . . .[48]

Although this pamphlet appeared in 1574, 14 years after the events it describes, it is clear that the motif of Catherine's exploitations of her ladies' sexual allure as a political tool was already being employed by critics during her lifetime.

Even in 1563 when Charles IX reached 14, the age of majority for a king, Catherine's political status did not wane: At a formal ceremony Charles decreed that 'he wants to be regarded as an adult in all things and everywhere, and in every place as having strength, except towards the queen his mother, to whom he reserves the power to command'.[49] Now that she was in full control of the kingdom, she was also in control of appointments to her household. However, what becomes clear from study of the *états de maison* for this period is a sense of exceptional stability when it came to the personnel of the queen's household. Many of the officers who had served Marie Stuart while she was queen simply transferred back into Catherine's employment on the death of François II. As Zum Kolk remarks, 'the queen's household seems to have become a stable institution that was transmitted from one reign to the next'.[50] Perhaps even more remarkable is that one of the women who transferred from Marie Stuart's household was Françoise de Brezé, Diane de Poitier's daughter and Catherine's former *dame d'honneur*.[51] She had lost her status as *dame d'honneur* on the death of Henri II, but Catherine invited her to return to her household on the death of François II, along with several of her close relatives, a testament to the enduring friendship that was shared between the two women, and a challenge to writers who have attempted to portray Catherine's relationship with her late husband's mistress as motivated by bitterness and jealousy.[52] Françoise de Brezé would remain in Catherine's household until four years before her death, aged 52, in 1570.

Catherine's new appointments would reflect the experience and stability she intended to implement throughout her reign: her new *dame d'honneur* was Jacqueline de Longwy, duchesse de Montpensier (born before 1524–1561), one of her oldest friends.[53] Aged at least 36, Longwy had been at court since 1533, and had been instrumental in the negotiations to encourage Antoine de Bourbon to relinquish his claims to the regency. Although she would die prematurely in August 1561, Longwy's replacement was another old friend: Philippe de Montespedon, princesse de La Roche-sur-Yon.[54] Her role as overseer of discipline among the female household was related by the English ambassador who noted in April 1565, that

> Orders are also taken in the Court that no gentleman shall talk with the Queen's maids, except it is in the Queen's presence, or in that of Madame la Princess de Roche-sur-Yon, except he be married; and if they sit upon a form or stool he may sit by her, and if she sits on the ground he may kneel by her, but not lie long, as the fashion was in this Court.[55]

This position of moral arbiter meant that Philippe played an important role in the scandal of Isabelle de Limeuil, discussed in Chapter 4. However, by 1587 such discipline was being openly mocked in the anonymously-penned libel *The Manifesto of the Ladies of the Court*, an imaginary group confession by leading women of the court of their various sins and debaucheries.[56] Among them, Christine of Lorraine, about to become Grand Duchess of Tuscany, begs for forgiveness for her affair with the duc de Joyeuse, blaming it on the 'liberal upbringing of [her] grandmother [Catherine de Medici] and governess' as well as her 'ancient' bloodlines which are 'subject to wanton love'.[57] The implication that the Grand Duke of Tuscany was about to marry a woman whose sexual liaisons were public knowledge was a highly provocative slur. Such allegations were explicitly directed at Catherine, whose alleged inability to control the ladies of her household was indicative of her inability to run the kingdom. Claiming that she was actively training her young ladies in whoredom, the libel implied that Catherine's Machiavellian exploitation of her entourage had backfired, resulting in a royal household rife with sleaze.

But if Catherine did not consciously select attractive women as part of an alleged sexual master plan, how did women join the queen's household? As we have seen, large numbers of women transferred from one royal household to another upon the death of the monarch, often serving a succession of queens. Madeleine de Savoie (along with 18 other women) left Catherine's household on the death of Henri II in 1559 to serve in the house of the new queen, Marie Stuart, only to return on the death of the young king François II a year later.[58] The elite families of the kingdom could expect patronage at the royal level for many of their members, and would often move from the household of one royal family member to another. Service to a royal would also usually result in rewards for one's family members. Thus, Catherine's first major change to her household after assuming the regency was the appointment as *chevalier d'honneur* of Antoine de Crussol, husband of her closest friend and lady-in-waiting since 1547, Louise de Clermont-Tonnerre, duchesse d'Uzès.[59] Yet even the stability of the queen mother's household could be material for satire: the death of the duchesse d'Uzès at approximately 94 years of age, after most of her life spent in the queen's service, was satirised in one version of the 1587 *Library of madame de Montpensier* with the imaginary title *Lexicon de fouterie de la mort par Madame la duchesse duzez* (which roughly translates as *Lexicon of Telling Death to Fuck Off*).[60]

Like Uzès's husband, women could also find a position in Catherine's household as a reward for service by their spouses. When the king's ambassador in Spain, Monsieur de Fourquevaux, asked for a place for his wife at court in 1571, Catherine honoured him by giving his wife a position as *dame* in her own household.[61] Catherine's correspondence from her earliest days in France demonstrates her concern with patronage, which operated across borders. In a letter to her distant relative Cosimo de Medici, the duke of Florence, in 1546, she asks that his wife the duchess take into her own household the daughter of Jean Baptiste Boni, ruined by a legal suit. One of his relatives, Marie Boni, was already a *demoiselle* in her service and Catherine claimed that she would have employed the girl herself, were it not that 'it is very far away, and also she is not accustomed to this land'.[62] This international traffic in household officers could be employed for strategic purposes too: when tensions began to rise between two of the ladies-in-waiting to Catherine's daughter Elisabeth de Valois, consort of Philip II of Spain,

Catherine chose to have one of them, Louise de Bretagne-Avaugour, madame de Clermont, return to her household in France. Aware of how the dispute could result in negative gossip about Elisabeth's ability to manage her household, Catherine reassured her daughter that by employing Clermont in her own household, 'everyone will know how agreeable I have found the service that she has done for you'.[63] In these matters, Catherine was in no way different to other elite women of the time, whose correspondence was regularly devoted to the concerns of servants and the logistics of clientage.

Another way in which she participated in traditions of aristocratic culture was by ensuring that young women were placed in her household to train them in the expectations of noble society. Thus, a letter to Louis de Bourbon, prince of Condé, shortly after the death of his wife in 1564 mentions the case of Anne du Chastel, heiress to her parents' estate in Brittany, whose parents had placed her under the care of his late wife. Catherine felt that 'while my said cousin lived I did not want that she was removed from there, but since she has left this world and since she [du Chastel] is from a good enough place to be raised close to me, I ask you to send her to me'.[64] Catherine clearly felt a duty of care to the younger women of her entourage, known as *demoiselles*, employing a *gouvernante des filles* to oversee their good behaviour and education. In 1547, she employed not only two *gouvernantes* but also *sous-gouvernantes*.[65] The Venetian ambassador also noted in 1550 that she allowed three of her youngest *demoiselles* to eat at her table, the 11-year-old Diane de France, bastard child of her husband, along with Jeanne de Savoie, sister of the duke of Nemours and Françoise de Rohan, both 15 years old.[66] While this would have been seen as a great honour, it is noteworthy that the women chosen would have been among the youngest in her entourage. The queen had a responsibility to oversee the upbringing of her younger ladies, ensuring that they were prepared for the demands that would be placed on them as married noblewomen: diplomacy, the running of estates and the management of their own households. Her status as *gouvernante* of France increased the scope of her activity in this sphere, as the significance of marriage alliances to the aristocratic society meant that negotiations were often overseen and approved by the monarch.

In her role as *gouvernante* the task of arranging and/or assisting with the marriages of the ladies of the court was now undertaken by Catherine in negotiation with their own relations, such as the marriage in 1564 of Henriette de Clèves, duchess of Nevers and countess of Rethel, to Louis de Gonzague, the brother of the duke of Mantua. In her letter to the duke, Catherine speaks of Henriette as being 'raised by my own hand', an indication of how closely involved she felt herself to be in the upbringing of the young women of her household.[67] Accordingly, those who arranged marriages without her knowledge were reprimanded. Imbert de la Platière, lieutenant general in Piedmont, who married Françoise de Birague in 1561 without consulting Catherine first was told, 'I would have desired that, before you had done it, that you had written me a little letter, because loving you as I do, I would have taken great pleasure in counselling you and in having been able to help arrange the marriage'.[68] In a comparable study of the illicit affairs of noble men and women at Elizabeth I's court, Johanna Rickman argues that in order to assert her authority as an unmarried female sovereign, Elizabeth needed to be able to control the sexual activity of the members of her court.[69] Similarly, Paul Hammer, in his article on Elizabeth I's attempts to control scandalous acts by her own courtiers, dismisses the long-held notion of Elizabeth's 'sexual jealousy' when confronted with her courtiers' secret marriages.[70] Rather, he argues that a queen's responsibility to her maids was to secure them successful and lucrative marriages, and that Elizabeth's well-documented rage at illicit weddings (often accompanied by a punishment of imprisonment) was the typical response that the couple would have expected from their own parents. Thus Catherine's interest in overseeing the details of aristocratic marriages and preventing unauthorised ones was explained by the ramifications of unsuitable clandestine marriages, such as the scandal caused by the secret marriage agreement between her *demoiselle* Françoise de Rohan and the duke of Nemours, Jacques de Savoie, which is discussed in detail in Chapter 4.

However, there appears to have been a diversity of expectations of behaviour for various members of the household: while younger, unmarried women were closely supervised, the case was very different for the women within her household who had already found marriage partners. Invariably, due to their status, they found themselves as heads of their own large estates, with households and female entourages of their own. They would be absent from court for numerous reasons, often to oversee the management of their estates, especially when their husbands were absent because of war. Claude-Catherine de Clermont, duchesse de Retz, corresponded with Estienne Pasquier about the military strategies of her husband, and during the struggle with the Catholic League in the early 1590s, she successfully defended her land from League forces by assembling her own group of soldiers.[71] Women could also be absent from court for political reasons, such as, in the case of Anne d'Este, the large gatherings of the Guise clan at Joinville in the 1560s. They might also point to sickness, both their own and of family members, and pregnancies, as it was generally felt to be unsafe to travel, as reasons for avoiding court. In the case of these absences, Catherine would regularly write to the women, enjoining them to return to her service as soon as possible. Numerous such letters exist, mostly for Anne d'Este, Madeleine de Savoie and Diane de France (Henri II's natural daughter).

The political power exercised by these higher ranked ladies-in-waiting is slowly being investigated. Unlike the majority of earlier studies that tend to focus on mistresses, concubines, consorts and ex-wives, and thus link female power in a courtly setting to sexual access to the king, the essays in *The Politics of Female Households* focus on female officers of the household and the influence they derived from their proximity to the queen.[72] In his summary of the essays that cover the Habsburg courts in Vienna and the Netherlands, the English Tudor and Stuart courts, and the French and Swedish courts, Jeroen Duindam states, 'these women used trust and proximity to further their own dynastic interests, to intervene in favour of their family, friends, or clients, and at times to influence major policy decisions'.[73] Similarly, in another study of aristocratic women at the Tudor court, Barbara Harris states, 'Since the family was the ultimate source of power among the aristocracy, their activities inevitably affected the political influence and effectiveness of their spouses and children'.[74] Thus, the recent scholarly biography of Anne d'Este, duchess of Guise, by Christiane Coester is a welcome study of such an influential political figure whose power and reputation as the matriarch of the Guise clan will be further explored in Chapter 6.[75] Este's close relationship with Catherine was crucial to her success: Natalie Mears' essay on the political involvement of Elizabeth I's ladies-in-waiting demonstrates that the politics of the Privy Chamber was dependent upon an effective working relationship being developed with the women who served the queen.[76] In times of political controversy, the women of her household acted as intermediaries between Catherine and their own male relatives, such as Catherine's request to Madeleine de Savoie to act as appeaser in 1560 when her husband was stripped of his position as grand-maître in favour of the Guises.[77] The women from Protestant families also acted as intermediaries during the Wars of Religion, such as Eléonore de Roye, who arranged negotiations between Catherine and her husband, Louis, prince de Condé. Zum Kolk's thesis explores the political function of her entourage, although its reliance on Catherine's correspondence as its main source does not permit a broader investigation of her ladies' activities in this sphere. Even in its limited scope, however, it quickly dispenses with the 'caricatural image of the flying squadron' as an invention of pamphleteers and those hostile to the later Valois dynasty.[78]

The women of her household also functioned as a marker of prestige for the queen mother. In keeping with tradition, Catherine's household as queen mother was larger than those of the reigning queens, her sons' consorts, Elisabeth d'Autriche, wife of Charles IX, and Louise de Lorraine, wife of Henri III. This elevation in numbers is also due to Catherine's political importance, even in her reduced status under Henri III. As well as in sheer numbers of women, one of the ways in which Catherine displayed this prestige was in the royal festivals, pageants and ballets that she organised, in which her ladies played a highly visible role. In the letter to Charles IX on his majority, Catherine outlined her views on the need to offer activities that would distract the restless nobility from aggressive behaviour. She reminded him that

> in times gone by, the garrisons of soldiers would station in the provinces, where all the nobility of the area would exercise in running at the ring, or any other honest exercise, and other than when they served the security of the country, they restrained their desire to make trouble.[79]

Her celebrated pageants at Fontainebleau in 1564, in Bayonne in 1565 and the spectacular reception for the Polish ambassadors in 1573 featured either mock tournaments or ballets where the women had leading roles. Denis Crouzet has interpreted these pageants as part of Catherine's attempts to create a neo-Platonic harmony in a kingdom divided by the wars of religion.[80] Catherine, he argues, employed her entourage to represent the ideal state, and the spectacles and pageants that she devised operated simultaneously as political programme and spiritual education. While for the queen mother these functions served to present a vision of the kingdom as united, others were quick to denounce them as examples of reckless expenditure and depraved morality. Thus the queen mother's banquet at Chenonceaux on 15 May 1577, in celebration of her son the duke of Anjou's victory at the siege of Plessis-les-Tours, was sarcastically described by Pierre de L'Estoile as an occasion of debauchery: 'At this lovely banquet, the most beautiful and charming [*honnêtes*] women of the court were employed as serving-ladies, being half naked with their hair down loose like brides'.[81] Although L'Estoile was not present at the function, and his description of the women as 'half-naked' is vague enough to be ambiguous, this episode has been regularly recounted, with the noblewomen in her entourage specified as topless, to discredit Catherine's efforts at peacemaking as lewd excesses. However, in her study of masquing at the English Jacobean court, Clare McManus discusses the tradition and courtly ideal of exposed (or only partially covered) female breasts within the performance as part of a discourse of eroticism that was intelligible only to a courtly audience:

> Defined by both gender and class, courtly women were required to conform to the demands of female chastity, while simultaneously displaying their bodies in a manner which would have brought condemnation upon the non-courtly.[82]

L'Estoile's criticism of the women's actions as debauchery therefore expose him as a non-elite, ignorant of what McManus calls the 'shared European discourse of courtly dance' of the late sixteenth and early seventeenth centuries.[83]

As the quote from L'Estoile intimates, it was during this later period of Catherine's life that criticisms of her household became most vociferous. Under the reign of Henri III, the numbers of women in Catherine's household rose progressively from 1573 to reach 160 (including laundresses and chambermaids) by 1583. To put this in perspective, however, in the king's house, the numbers of *gentilshommes de la chambre* rose from 48 under Charles IX to 128 in 1575, and to 380 in 1583. The rise in numbers, Zum Kolk argues, is directly due to the political functions of the queen mother, and to Henri III's courtly reforms. At the time of his accession, Henri III found himself with a household filled primarily with servants loyal to his mother. While Catherine, anxious to create a politically moderate court, had formed a religiously heterogeneous household in which many of the established families of the aristocracy were represented, Henri had different ideas about patronage. He preferred what Nicolas Le Roux calls 'a selective policy of grace as opposed to the generalised liberality of the queen mother', which resulted in a select group of favoured courtiers receiving honours and benefices to the detriment of other noble families.[84] L'Estoile's journal abounds with verses denouncing or ridiculing the *mignons*, especially their sexual activities, and many of the longer verses combine criticism of the men of his household with attacks on the women of Catherine's. For example, the *Pasquil Courtizan* (a recurrent title of several verse libels that circulated) in December 1581 begins with satirical descriptions of the homosexual activities of the *mignons* and evolves into an enumeration of the alleged extra-marital affairs of many of the women in Catherine's entourage, such as Charlotte de Beaune, dame de Sauve and Claude-Catherine de Clermont, maréchale de Retz.[85] Although Catherine was unable to control her son's appointments, and found many of the appointments she had made to the king's household under Charles IX overturned, Henri III made no attempt to control the makeup of her household. Nonetheless, criticisms of his courtiers, couched in terms of sexual deviance, were applied to the ladies of her entourage as well.

Henri III's rejection of the itinerant traditions of the French court also had ramifications for his mother. The onus of travelling for the purposes of negotiation now fell to her, even in her advanced years. Even here, when she put herself at risk to travel long distances into hostile enemy territory to successfully negotiate with enemies of the crown, Catherine's political skills were denigrated by historians. Ivan Cloulas, in his 1979 biography, thus described Catherine's negotiations for the 1576 Peace of Monsieur, a peace treaty which would bring to an end the fifth War of Religion in France:

> Tireless, the queen mother travelled to Sens to negotiate with the confederates. Faced with their army of 20,000 men, Catherine manoeuvred by lining up the charms of a bevy of attractive ladies: Mme de Sauve; Mlles d'Estrées, de Brétèche; Mme de Kernevenoy, the mistress of Fervaques; Mme de Villequier, whose jealous husband would stab her the following year; Mme de Montpensier, the future Leaguer; and, queen of Beauty, the gallant queen of Navarre. Truly was this the flying squadron in its entirety. With these beautiful ladies, who served as a screen to severe negotiators, the queen mother's men of confidence, like Pomponne de Bellièvre, Catherine moved from abbey to chateau. With Alençon, Condé and Navarre were exchanged precise memorandi from councillors at the same time as amorous glances. The king would apostille the projects. Finally an accord was concluded.[86]

In this reductive depiction, Catherine is given a secondary role, leaving her 'severe . . . men of confidence' to negotiate, while she brings with her a select group of her ladies-in-waiting to act as a 'screen' of distracting beauty. Cloulas names specific women along with evidence of other sexual scandal with which they were involved (Mme de Kernevenoy is listed as 'the mistress of Fervaques', while Mme de Villequier was otherwise better known as Françoise de la Marck). It is true that Catherine regularly chose some of these women to accompany her on longer trips, but this was standard behaviour – for a royal to appear unaccompanied by his or her entourage would have been an unimaginable breach of protocol and decorum. These negotiations were also the perfect opportunity for Catherine to give her officers experience in the demands of political negotiation and the appropriate decorum in antagonistic conditions. Indeed, the 'gallant queen of Navarre' was Catherine's own daughter, Marguerite de Valois and 'Mme de Montpensier' was Catherine-Marie de Lorraine, the daughter of Anne d'Este, duchess of Guise. These were women chosen not for youth or beauty but because of their rank or personal relationship with the queen mother.

We can therefore see a development of the scandalous reputation of Catherine's ladies as her own political role and household evolved. As Catherine's political power increased, numbers of officers within her household grew, in keeping with traditions already set by former queens of France. The makeup of her retinue was varied in age, rank and experience, although she was keen to award more influential positions to experienced, moderate servants who were loyal to the crown. As her role towards her ladies adapted depending on their age and status, so they served various functions for Catherine: some as political intermediaries and informers, some as companions, but all as a marker of prestige in her role as queen, queen mother or *gouvernante*. While Protestant polemical authors accused Catherine of exploiting her ladies to serve her own political ends, other writers within the intellectual fraternity of the Parlement frowned upon the increasingly visible role of the women supporting Catherine's ever-growing political status, and attacked them directly for having loose morals. Both strands of criticism were taken up by historians, who portrayed the women in her service as one of Catherine's arsenal of manipulative tools to sexually distract men who stood in the way of her overweening ambition. In the following chapter, I examine the origins of the pamphlet literature that created this myth and the methods by which stories of scandal were disseminated amongst the wider public.

Notes

1 Brantôme, 484: 'De plus, la reine mère y tenoit fort la main pour soustenir ses dames et filles, et le bien faire sentir à ces détracteurs et pasquineurs, quand ils estoyent une fois descouverts, encor qu'elle-mesme n'y aye esté espargnée non plus que ses dames; mais ne s'en soucioit pas tant d'elle comme des autres, d'autant, disoit-elle, qu'elle sentoit son âme et sa conscience pure et nette, qui parloit assez pour soy: et la pluspart du temps se rioit et se mocquoit de ces médisans escrivains et pasquineurs. "Laissez-les tourmenter, disoit-elle, et prendre de la peine pour rien;" mais quand elle les descouvroit, elle leur faisoit bien sentir'.
2 Sarah Hanley, 'Engendering the State', 7.
3 Houllemare, *Politiques de la parole*. For the same activity in the eighteenth century, see Maza, *Private Lives and Public Affairs*.
4 Houllemare, *Politiques de la parole*, 281–4.
5 Hanley, 'Engendering the State', 8.
6 Broomhall, *Women and the Book Trade in Sixteenth-Century France* (Aldershot: Ashgate, 2002), 10.
7 Eliane Viennot, 'Des "femmes d'Etat" au XVIe siècle: Les princesses de la Ligue et l'écriture de l'histoire', *Femmes et pouvoirs sous l'Ancien Régime*, eds. Danielle Hasse-Dubosc and Eliane Viennot (Paris: Rivages, 1991), 77–97, 78: 'à tous les niveaux de la vie publique, dans une mesure jusque-là jamais vue dans l'histoire de l'Occident, et qui ne fera que décroître après la Fronde'
8 Viennot, 'Les femmes dans les "troubles" du XVIe siècle', *Clio. Histoire, femmes et sociétés* 5 (1997), accessed 13 July 2015. URL: http://clio.revues.org/409; DOI: 10.4000/clio.409
9 Michel de Waele, 'La fin des guerres de Religion et l'exclusion des femmes de la vie politique française', *French Historical Studies* 29, no. 2 (Spring 2006): 199–230, 209–10: 'les désordres qui émergent durant la seconde moitié du seizième siècle eurent ceci de particulier qu'ils placèrent les femmes, pour la première fois, complètement à l'avant-plan de la scène, et donc du discours politique.'

10 For Ivan Cloulas, *Diane de Poitiers* (Paris: Fayard, 1997); Adrien Thierry, *Diane de Poitiers* (Paris: La Palatine, 1955); Sheila ffolliott, 'Casting a Rival into the Shade: Catherine de' Medici and Diane de Poitiers', *Art Journal*, 48 (1989): 138–43.

11 Jean Pierre Babelon, *Paris au XVIe siècle*, Nouvelle histoire de Paris (Paris: Diffusion Hachette, 1986), 94.

12 The Venetian ambassador Morosini would write to the Signory on 3 February 1576, 'For the last few days his Majesty has taken his pleasure by retiring into a small apartment which has no window, and where in order to see, candles must be burnt all day, and to this apartment his Majesty summons four or five youths of this city who follow the profession of poets and light literature, and to meet these people his Majesty invites the Duke of Nevers, the Grand Prior, Mons. de Biragues, Mons. de Souré, the Queen of Navarre, his sister, Madame de Nevers, and the Maréchale de Retz, all of whom profess to delight in poetry'. 'Venice: January 1576', in *Calendar of State Papers Relating to English Affairs in the Archives of Venice, Volume 7, 1558–1580*, ed. Rawdon Brown and G. Cavendish Bentinck (London, 1890), pp. 542–4 http://www.british-history.ac.uk/cal-state-papers/venice/vol7/pp542–544 [accessed 4 August 2015]. Henri III's academy would become the target of vicious polemic: René de Lucinge described it in 1586 as 'a true seraglio of all lechery and debauchery, a school for sodomy' ['un vray sarail de toute lubricité et paillardise, un'escole de Sodomie'], cited in Ferguson, *Queer (Re)Readings in the French Renaissance*, 181.

13 Babelon, *Paris au XVIe siècle*, 96.

14 Maréchale de Retz, *Album de poésies*. For more on the life of the maréchale de Retz, see Joanna Milstein, *The Gondi: Family Strategy and Survival in Early Modern France* (Farnham: Ashgate, 2014), 182–4.

15 François Grudé, sieur de La Croix du Maine, *Les bibliothéques françoises de La Croix du Maine et de Du Verdier* (Paris: Saillant & Noyon, 1773) I, 99: 'elle mérite d'être mise au rang des plus doctes et mieux versées, tant en la poésie et art oratoire qu'en philosophie, mathématiques, histoire et autres sciences, desquelles elle sait bien faire son profit entre tous ceux qu'elle sent dignes de ces doctes discours. Elle n'a encore rien mis en lumière de ses oeuvres et compositions'.

16 Théodore Agrippa d'Aubigné, *Oeuvres complètes*, ed. Reaume et Caussade (Genève: Slatkine, 1967), I, 447: 'm'a communicqué un grand oeuvre de sa façon que je voudrois bien arracher du secret au public'.

17 Jean Dorat, 'Ad bonarum artium studiosissimam Heroïnam Camillam Comitissam de Retz', as cited in Castelnau, *Les mémoires*, 2, 104:

> Ad bonarum artium studiosissimam
> Heroïnam Camillam Comitissam de Retz.
> Virgilio meruit celebrari Vate Camilla
> Bellatrix, & opus Virgo imitata virûm.
> Te plus laudaret Vates si viveret idem,
> Quae certas doctis femina docta viris.

18 L'Estoile, V, 347.

> 'Madame de Rets, parlant à Monsr de Lyon.
> Je sçai, Monsieur, que si le compromis que j'ai fait avec Antraguet, de l'espouser apres la mort de mon vilain mari, ne m'excuse devant vous, qu'il faut que je m'accuse comme femme peu honneste et infâme; encores que le bon homme n'ignore pas ma brigue. Mais, Monsieur, Vive la Ligue!'

19 L'Estoile, III, 175.

> 'La mareschalle de Rets
> Se contente du bon mesnage
> De Dantraguet.
> Elle etait sage,

> S'elle n'eust fait cest folie
> De lui donner ses pierreries'.

For more on this incident, and how Agrippa d'Aubigné would use it in his criticisms of Catherine's daughter, Marguerite de Valois, see Eliane Viennot, 'Marguerite de Valois et le Divorce satyrique', *Albineana – Cahiers d'Aubigné* 7 (1996): 111–129, 4. Viennot also identifies the ways in which d'Aubigné used his connections and time at court to pen highly misogynistic literature against courtly women.

20 The same phenomenon can be witnessed in Venetian writers' accounts of courtesans. See Courtney Quaintance, 'Defaming the Courtesan: Satire and Invective in Sixteenth-Century Italy', *The Courtesan's Arts: Cross-Cultural Perspectives* (New York: Oxford University Press, 2006).

21 Agrippa d'Aubigné, *Les Tragiques*, Textes de la Renaissance 6 (Paris: H. Champion, 1995), 109,

> 'L'un conte les amours de nos salles princesses,
> Garces de leurs valets, autrefois leurs maistresses'.

22 L'Estoile, II, 128: 'plusieurs et diverses sortes de Tombeaux et Epitaphes'.
23 Ibid., 129.
24 LaGuardia, *Intertextual Masculinity*.
25 L'Estoile, II, 129:

> 'Si ne devois-je point ressentir la folie
> Par les mains d'un mari, à ma vie pareil,
> Qui, pour souiller son lict, me servoit de conseil,
> Coulpable comme moi fait par la loy Julie?'

26 Ibid., 130:

> 'N'aiant point de Parens, ni Pere en aucun lieu,
> Mon mari, plus prochain, fut inspiré de Dieu,
> Pour servir au besoin de Parents et de Pere'.

27 Charles de Secondat Montesquieu, *De l'esprit des lois*, 1 (Paris, 1834), 14–15: 'On pouvoit craindre qu'un malhonnête homme, piqué des mépris d'une femme, indigné de ses refus, outré de sa vertu même, ne formât le dessein de la perdre. La loi Juli ordonna qu'on ne pourroit accuser une femme d'adultère qu'après avoir accusé son mari de favoriser ses dérèglements, ce qui restrignit beaucoup cette accusation, et l'anéantit pour ainsi dire'.

28 L'Estoile, II, 133:

> 'Car, pensant acquerir de ma honte une Gloire,
> Lors je suis veu meurtrier, et cruel, et coquu'.

29 Herrup, *A House in Gross Disorder*, 70.
30 Both Kevin Sharpe, 'The Image of Virtue: The Court and Household of Charles I, 1625–1642)', *The English Court from the Wars of the Roses to the Civil War*, eds. Starkey et al. (Harlow: Addison Wesley Longman, 1987), 226–60, and in the same collection, Pam Wright, 'A Change in Direction: The Ramifications of a Female Household, 1558–1603)', 147–72, explore the political and personal ramifications of appointments to the monarch's household after a new succession.
31 A recent work on Versailles which does refer to Catherine's court is Frédérique Leferme-Falguières, *Les courtisans: une societe de spectacle sous l'Ancien Regime* (Paris: Presses Universitaires de France, 2007).
32 Boucher, *La cour de Henri III*; also, Boucher, *Société et mentalités autour de Henri III*, 4 vols. (Paris: Honoré Champion, 1981); Le Roux, *La faveur du roi*. See Mack Holt, 'Patterns of Clientele and Economic Opportunity at Court during the Wars of

Religion: The Household of François, Duke of Anjou', *French Historical Studies* 13, no. 3 (Spring, 1984), 305–22.
33 Kettering, 'The Household Service of Early Modern French Noblewomen'; 'The Patronage Power of Early Modern French Noblewomen'; 'Patronage in Early Modern France', *French Historical Studies* 20, no. 4 (1992): 839–62; 'Clientage During the French Wars of Religion', *The Sixteenth Century Journal* 20 (1989): 221–39.
34 Guido Guerzoni and Guido Alfani, 'Court History and Career Analysis: A Prosopographic Approach to the Court of Renaissance Ferrara', *The Court Historian* 12, 1 (June 2007), 1–34, 3.
35 Jeroen Duindam, 'Rival Courts in Dynastic Europe: Vienna and Versailles 1550–1790', *The Court Historian* 7, 2 (December 2002), 75–92, 75.
36 Zum Kolk; *Lettres*.
37 Chatenet, *La cour de France au XVIe siècle*; also, 'Les logis des femmes à la cour des derniers Valois', *Das Frauenzimmer. Die Frau bei Hofe in Spätmittelalter und früher Neuzeit. 6. Symposium der Residenzen-Kommission der Akademie der Wissenschaften in Göttingen*, eds. Jan Hirschbiegel, Werner Paravicini (Stuttgart: Thorbecke, 2000), 175–92.
38 Monique Chatenet, 'Les logis des femmes à la cour des derniers Valois', 177: 'Anne est apparement la première – en tout cas depuis longtemps – à concevoir son entourage féminin comme une composante essentielle de sa dignité'.
39 Jean-François Solnon, *La cour de France* (Paris: Fayard, 1987), 27: 'On a admiré aussi la délicatesse avec laquelle l'entourage féminin de Catherine de Medici a affiné les manières. Parées, aimables, les filles de la reine ont été de charmantes hôtesses qui exigeaient en retour égards et respect des familiers du Louvre. ... La cour a aidé à la promotion d'une élite féminine qui, en retour, l'a policée'.
40 *The Politics of Female Households: Ladies-in-Waiting Across Early Modern Europe*, eds. Nadine Akkerman and Birgit Houben (Leiden: Brill, 2014); *Femmes et pouvoir politique: les princesses d'Europe XVe–XVIIIe siècle*, eds. Isabelle Poutrin and Marie-Karine Schaub (Rosny-sur-Bois: Bréal, 2007).
41 *Lettres*, II, Catherine de Medici 'Au Roy Monsieur mon fils', 18 September 1563.
42 To put Catherine's appointments into the context of French traditions, see Caroline zum Kolk, 'The Household of the Queen of France in the Sixteenth Century': 3–22.
43 David Potter, R. Roberts, 'An Englishman's View of the Court of Henri III, 1584–1585: Richard Cook's "Description of the Court of France"', *French History*, 2:3 (1988), 312–44, 342–3.
44 Zum Kolk, 164.
45 Zum Kolk, 173.
46 Rosalind K. Marshall, *Queen Mary's Women: Female Relatives, Servants, Friends and Enemies of Mary, Queen of Scots* (Edinburgh: John Donald, 2006), 60.
47 See the chapters in Akkerman and Houben, eds., *The Politics of Female Households* by Sara Wolfson and Oliver Mallick for the political motivations behind the appointments by Marie de Medici to the households of both her daughter, Henrietta Maria, and daughter-in-law, Anne of Austria, and then by Anne to her son Louis XIV's household: Sara J. Wolfson, 'The Female Bedchamber of Queen Henrietta Maria: Politics, Familial Networks and Policy, 1626–40', *The Politics of Female Households*, 311–41; Oliver Mallick, 'Clients and Friends: The Ladies-in-Waiting at the Court of Anne of Austria', *The Politics of Female Households*, 231–64.
48 *Discours merveilleux*, 154: 'elle luy commande donc de l'entretenir et luy complaire en ce qu'elle pourroit, afin qu'oubliant les affaires de soy-mesme il mecontentast un chacun, comme de fait elle en vint à bout par ce moyen. En somme elle fait si bien que nonobstant les oppositions d'aucuns des deputez des estats fondees sur l'authorité de nostre loy Salique, et les mauvais succez des gouvernemens des femmes en ce roiaume, le Roy de Navarre y condescent par nonchalance'. For a balanced account of this episode, see Katherine Crawford, 'Catherine de Medici and the Performance of Political Motherhood', *Sixteenth Century Journal* 31, no. 3 (Autumn, 2000): 643–73.

49 Crawford, 'Catherine de Medici', 669.
50 Zum Kolk, 197.
51 Ibid., 176.
52 A more nuanced version of the relationship is found in Kathleen Wellman, *Queens and Mistresses of Renaissance France* (New Haven: Yale University Press, 2013), 208–14.
53 Zum Kolk, 191.
54 Ibid., 191.
55 *CSPF*, 11 April 1565, no. 1091, 'Occurrences in France'.
56 L'Estoile, V, 344–9, 'Le Manifeste des dames de la Court'.
57 Ibid., 344–9, 'Hé! mon Dieu! puisque je suis de race antique, subjecte à l'amour impudique, excuse l'horoscope de ma nativité, et libre nourriture de ma grand'mere et de ma gouvernante'.
58 Zum Kolk, 197.
59 Ibid., 187.
60 BN MS fr 15592 f. 117–119, *La Bibliotheque de Madame de Montpensier*.
61 *Lettres*, IV, 25: Catherine de Medici to M. De Fourquevaux, 8 January 1571.
62 Ibid., I, 17: Catherine de Medici to Cosimo de Medici, 20 December 1546.
63 Broomhall, 'The Correspondence of Catherine de Médicis and Elisabeth de Valois', 550–2: 'tout le mont conestra coment je ay agréable le servyse qu'ele vous ha fayst'.
64 *Lettres*, II, 234, 16–30 November 1564, Catherine de Medici to Louis de Bourbon, prince de Condé: 'pendant que madicte cousine a vescu je n'ay poinct voulu qu'elle en fust ostée; mais puisqu'elle est allée de vie à trespas et qu'elle est d'assez bon lieu pour estre nourrie auprès de moy, je vous prie me l'envoyer'.
65 Zum Kolk, 124.
66 Chatenet, *La cour de France au XVIe siècle*, 189: 'Elle fait très grand honneur à sa table où mange presque toujours la fille bâtarde du roi qui s'appelle Diane et est âgée de 11 ans; y mangent aussi la soeur du duc de Murs (Nemours – Jeanne de Savoie) et Mlle de Rohan, toutes deux mangeant loin de S. M. au bout de la table'.
67 *Lettres*, II, 214, Catherine de Medici to the duke of Mantua, 17 August 1564.
68 *Ibid.*, I, 196: Catherine de Medici to M. De Bourdillon, 20 May 1561.
69 Johanna Rickman, *Love, Lust, and License in Early Modern England: Illicit Sex and the Nobility* (Aldershot: Ashgate, 2008), 27–68.
70 Paul Hammer, 'Sex and the Virgin Queen: Aristocratic Concupiscence and the Court of Elizabeth I', *Sixteenth Century Journal* 31, no. 1, *Special Edition: Gender in Early Modern Europe* (Spring 2000): 77–97.
71 Milstein, *The Gondi*, 184.
72 Akkerman and Houben, eds, *The Politics of Female Households*.
73 Jeroen Duindam, 'Epilogue', *The Politics of Female Households*, 367.
74 Barbara Harris, 'Sisterhood, Friendship and the Power of English Aristocratic Women, 1450–1550', *Women and Politics in Early Modern England*, ed. James Daybell (Aldershot: Ashgate, 2004), 43.
75 Christiane Coester, *Schön wie Venus, mutig wie Mars. Anna d'Este, Herzogin von Guise und von Nemours* (1531–1607), (München: Oldenbourg, 2006).
76 Natalie Mears, 'Politics in the Elizabethan Privy Chamber: Lady Mary Sidney and Kat Ashley', *Women and Politics in Early Modern England*, 67–82.
77 *Lettres*, I, 144, Catherine de Medici to Madeleine de Savoie, 15 August 1560.
78 Zum Kolk, 270.
79 *Lettres*, II, Catherine de Medici 'Au Roy Monsieur mon fils', 18 September 1563.
80 Denis Crouzet, *Le haut coeur de Catherine de Médicis*. See also Crouzet, 'Catherine de Médicis actrice d'une mutation dans l'imaginaire politique (1578–1579)', *Chrétiens et sociétés. Documents et mémoires* 9 (2009): 17–50, Special Issue: 'La coexistence confessionnelle à l'épreuve. Etudes sur les relations entre protestants et catholiques dans la France moderne'.

81 L'Estoile, II, 112–13: 'En ce beau banquet, les dames les plus belles et honnêtes de la cour, étant à moitié nues et ayant leurs cheveux épars comme épousées, furent employées à faire le service'.

82 Clare McManus, *Women on the Renaissance Stage: Anna of Denmark and Female Masquing in the Stuart Court (1590–1619)* (Manchester: Manchester University Press, 2002), 127–31; 130.

83 Ibid., 22.

84 Nicolas Le Roux, *La Faveur du Roi*, 123.

85 L'Estoile, III, 170–80.

86 Ivan Cloulas, *Catherine de Medici* (Paris: Fayard, 1979), 389: 'Infatigable, la reine-mère se rendit à Sens pour négocier avec les confédérés. Face aux 20 000 hommes de leur armée, Catherine manoeuvra en alignant les grâces d'un parterre de dames attirantes, Mme de Sauve, Mlles d'Estrées, de Brétèche, Mme de Kernevenoy, la maîtresse de Fervaques, Mme de Villequier que son mari jaloux poignardera l'année suivante, Mme de Montpensier la future ligueuse et, reine de Beauté, la galante reine de Navarre. C'était bien cette fois l'escadron volant au complet. Avec ces belles dames, qui servent de paravent à des négociateurs sévères, hommes de confiance de la reine, comme Pomponne de Bellièvre, Catherine se déplace d'abbayes en châteaux. On échange avec Alençon, Condé et Navarre, les mémoires précis des conseillers en même temps que les oeillades amoureuses. Le roi apostille les projets. Enfin un accord est conclu . . .'.

3 The Dissemination of Scandal
News Culture in Early Modern France

In December 1581, L'Estoile transcribed the following verses into his journal which he said had been 'dispersed around the court' ['fust semé à la Cour']:

> Madame de Châteauvillain
> Having left there her knave
> Chases Monsieur de Guise, with great might;
> Madame de Sauve tries very hard
> To content all of her valets [. . .]
> As for madame de Nemours
> Pibrac turns her round the wrong way
> While his good wife
> Goes off to sing her wares somewhere else.[1]

These lines are a small excerpt from the *Pasquil Courtizan* which runs to over 200 lines, almost all of which mock the sexual exploits of the women of the court.[2] The libel depicts Antoinette, comtesse de Châteauvillain, conducting an affair with a peasant and then chasing the duc de Guise; as a result his erstwhile companion Charlotte de Beaune, dame de Sauve, accordingly becomes the voracious seducer of all of her servants; Anne d'Este, duchesse de Nemours, conducts an adulterous, sodomitical affair with Pibrac, whose wife meanwhile seeks partners elsewhere. Written in octosyllabic couplets, a highly memorable and popular form in the late sixteenth century and one associated with farce, the long verse succeeds in satirising scores of courtiers, and its themes of cross-class promiscuity, cuckoldry and sodomy are omnipresent themes in the late sixteenth-century satires of court ladies.[3] Whether the verses referred to genuine affairs or imagined misdeeds is not the central issue here. Instead, having established how Catherine appointed her ladies-in-waiting in the previous chapter, this section explores the multiplicity of forms in which they were attacked, highlighting salient features, such as the use of verse over prose, and the use of Latin rather than French. The investigation of literary form provides hints as to authorship and audience. For example, the fact that the verses above are followed by a 'Suitte' – a response to the original verses – points to their circulation, most likely in manuscript. One centre of manuscript circulation of verse was the Palais de Justice, where parlementaires regularly disseminated, exchanged and amended manuscript verse.[4] As we will see, many of these parlementaires were engaged in paradoxical behaviour, composing verse both in praise of and ridiculing courtly women. Most of the attacks took the form of verse, handwritten like those above or printed on cheap broadsheets. These could be distributed either openly throughout the city of Paris by being handed out or sold by colporteurs who cried out their wares for sale. For those that sought a more clandestine option, libels could be left lying around or pasted on walls in squares, crossroads and other areas of high traffic, or passed secretly from one person to another. Songs could be composed and sung, then memorised and passed on, distributing news of scandalous events throughout the country.[5]

This chapter therefore also discusses the methods by which news of the court, whether in pamphlet, verse or song form, was distributed. These methods of circulation, described in more detail by L'Estoile in his journal of the reign of Henri IV, reveal much about the identities of those responsible for creating the works and their relationship to the court.[6] In order to gain a better picture of this distribution, I recreate the geography of sixteenth-century Paris: the location of the royal court in relation to the law courts and the university, with their large body of educated magistrates and clerks; the main thoroughfares through which thousands of Parisians passed each day, which served as sites of news distribution; and the various locations of pamphlet distribution and public spectacle.[7] But newsworthy events were not only publicised in written form: sixteenth-century Paris was a noisy city, full of the sounds of town criers, itinerant vendors, singing charlatans and other street performers who all earned their daily living by informing a populace eager to hear about salacious events regarding the elite of the court. This chapter thus attempts to recreate the soundscape of Paris in the early modern period, and the songs and cries that would have spread the news of court scandal.

A striking aspect of the thousands of pieces of satirical and libellous material that mocked the court is the diversity of forms in which they appeared. L'Estoile himself made a distinction between two categories: first, 'libelles d'Etat', which were texts in prose of varying length and which targeted, in a polemical style, those in power, such as the *Epistre envoiee au Tigre de la France* which attacked Charles, cardinal de Lorraine (discussed in more detail in Chapter 6), and the *Discours merveilleux de la vie, actions et deportemens de la Royne-mere*, the invective against Catherine de Medici we are already familiar with; and second, 'ramas' (short for *ramassés* – 'gathered' or 'collected'), a diverse group of satirical works, often in verse, which at the time were known as 'pasquils' or 'pasquins'.[8] In this latter category, a myriad poetic forms could be used, from couplets to quatrains to dixains; epigrams and sonnets; songs and *chansons* and mock epitaphs, designed to mock the memory of the deceased. There was also considerable diversity in length: anagrams of the names of public figures were very popular, and implied that a person's name carried within itself clues about the true nature of that person's character. These could be positive, such as those found in the album belonging to the maréchale de Retz, in which writers invited to her salon created anagrams based on various spellings of her name:

CATHERINE DE CLAIRMONT
RICHEMENT A LA DOCTRINE[9]

This tradition could be subverted to make the anagram libellous, however, such as the following which implied that Catherine de Medici was the embodiment of hate and discord, and was a new Circe, a treacherous poisoner leading the country to Hell:

CATHERINE DE MEDICIS, ROINE DE FRANCE
HAINE ET DISCORD CIRCE D'ENFER AMEINE[10]

By contrast, long verses such as the *Pasquil Courtizan* (L'Estoile includes several verses with this title) of 1579 and 1581 had over two hundred lines, and an untitled 'pasquin' in 1586 runs to 486 lines. These long verses could thereby ridicule scores of courtiers and public figures. Literary genres could even be combined: one of the most famous pamphlets of the period was the *Satyre Ménippée*, a mixture of satirical prose and verse by a collective of lawyer-authors that first appeared in 1594 and which attracted more verse with each subsequent re-edition.[11] The literary environment which fostered this enormous rise in anti-court literature resulted in the satirical treatment of other literary productions: while the imaginary *Library of Madame de Montpensier* of 1587 was based on Rabelais' imaginary library of Saint-Victor in *Pantagruel*, the Manifesto of Peronne, put forward by the newly-formed Catholic League in 1585, may have been the inspiration for the spoof *Manifesto of the Ladies of the Court*.[12]

Literary Forms and the Use of Verse

The choice of verse over prose had its origins in the medieval traditions of oral performance which informed, entertained and educated a largely illiterate population: verse aided in the memorisation of long tracts of material, particularly if it employed a simple rhyme scheme.[13] Some of the verses that mention the women of Catherine's entourage were actually lyrics set to the tune of a well-known song, a phenomenon known as a 'contrafact' which I will explore in more detail below.[14] Thus they could operate on a performative level in the way that a long prose pamphlet could not, and melody, rhythm and rhyme would help with the memorisation of the lyrics. Not all verse libels were designed to be memorised in full – the *Pasquil Courtizan* form as we have seen generally had more than two hundred lines – but those which were could be disseminated to a wide audience, both literate and illiterate alike. An example of this is the verse included by L'Estoile in January 1580 on the occasion of the marriage of Robert Combaut, Henri III's *premier maître d'hôtel* to one of Catherine's ladies-in-waiting, Louise de la Beraudière, also known as 'La Belle Rouet', notorious for her earlier scandalous affair with Antoine de Bourbon, king of Navarre which had resulted in the birth of a son. 'La Rouet's' dowry of the Breton bishopric of Cornouailles (Cornwall) was mocked in a sixain (six-line verse) which employed the imagery of *cornes* (horns) to imply that Combaut would wear the cuckold's horns in his marriage to one who had already had such a high-profile liaison with another man:

> By marrying Rouet to get a bishopric,
> Hasn't Combaut sinned sacreligiously

> For which the people murmur and the Church sighs?
> But when the name Cornwall is heard said,
> The gift is thought to be worthy of the marriage,
> And instead of crying, everyone just laughs.[15]

The sixain was a fashionable form among the writers of the Pléiade, and although its alexandrine meter distinguishes this verse from less elevated material, its overall brevity and tripartite rhyme scheme (aabccb) means that it could be easily memorised or copied and passed on, resulting in the mockery of Beraudière's sexual honour being disseminated among a wide audience.[16]

In his study of English verse libels, Alastair Bellany notes, 'Verse libels took many different forms, and the form of the verse often, but not always, determined the means of circulation and the potential audience.'[17] Thus more 'literary' forms of verse, such as the sonnet or epigram, lend themselves more to written works than performance. Over a third of the verses in L'Estoile's journal are sonnets, the choice of this demanding poetic form revealing the artistic and intellectual ambition of the authors.[18] Du Bellay was the first to utilise the genre as a satirical device, with the humour of the satire produced by the inversion of the genre's normal form and function.[19] The particular qualities of the French sonnet, closing with two tercets rather than one sestet as in the English style, allow for a greater freedom of themes in the final six lines.[20] An example of this can be observed in the celebrated *Dialogue du jeune de La Bourdaisière et sa soeur* (*Dialogue of the young La Bourdaisière and his sister*) of 1576, which turns the traditional love poem on its head when, at the volta, it is revealed to be an obscene attack on the sexual activities of specific courtiers. The sonnet opens as a charming dialogue between a brother and a sister, Georges Babou de La Bourdaisière, *premier gentilhomme* to the duc d'Alençon, and his sister, Françoise.[21] In the first tercet, however, Georges attacks his sister for her affair with Louis Béranger le Guast, one of Henri III's most-favoured *mignons*:

> Ok, to make it quick, they tell me that Le Guast
> Has made of your honour a marvellous spoil;
> That you are the page where he often composes.

The shock of the change in theme after the volta is increased by Françoise's enumeration in the second tercet of other courtiers involved in adultery (including their mother, Françoise Robertet) and even more so by the revelation that the king is having sodomitical relations with Georges.[22]

> Go on, little brat, they say just as much
> About my mother and Clermont, and of you even more:
> Because they say the king does the same to you.[23]

The speakers of the sonnet, far from being a young couple in love as the traditions of the genre lead the reader to expect, are a sexually promiscuous, and in his case deviant, couple of sibling courtiers who do not appear to resent the fact that the debauchery of their entire family is the stuff of everyday gossip. The two tercets unfold as a steady accumulation of sexual deviance culminating in the final line presenting the king as a sodomite.

As exotic as it may seem, verse was considered to be part of news dissemination: it was a means of transmitting information, and of gauging public opinion.[24] In May 1566, when the English ambassador Sir Thomas Hoby claimed that the recent controversial marriage of the duke of Nemours was 'leeke to breed great trouble in fraunce' he included two verse libels with his ambassadorial dispatch as evidence. Similarly, when Isabelle de Limeuil scandalously gave birth to an illegitimate child while the court was in Dijon in July 1564, information about the event was transmitted back to Paris in the form of over a hundred lines of Latin rhyming couplets. Therefore we must be wary: verse, in this period as in any other, draws attention to the creative skills of its author; it is designed to impress the reader with the writer's technical and imaginative talents. It is no surprise, then, that verse proved to be by far the most popular format for libels in L'Estoile's journal, given that he was surrounded by an intellectual elite that was concerned about its own literary reputation. The circulation of finely crafted, satirical verse was a regular activity of the men of the Palais who sought to dazzle their colleagues through literary pyrotechnics. Writers who are concerned with rhyme and meter will sacrifice accuracy for their art, however, and therefore the information contained within verse libels must be scrutinised rather than taken at face value. If the audience for many of the verse libels about women at court was intended to be exclusively male, its function was often to titillate rather than to inform.

Use of Latin

In her biography of the acclaimed barrister and author Estienne Pasquier, Dorothy Thickett remarks that all sixteenth-century barristers could write verse with equal facility in both French and Latin, and this is attested to by the proportion of Latin verses L'Estoile included in his journal.[25] The use of Latin indicates both an educated author and reader: although it was widely used in legal and scholastic milieux, it was a language accessible only to those who had been to school, and therefore unavailable to a large majority of the population, such as women and members of the lower social groups. Thus, the audience for verse in Latin was a remarkably restricted one. However, the fact that nearly a third of the verses included by L'Estoile are in Latin indicates an avid readership among those groups to whom it was accessible, such as faculty and students of the university, poets and other *lettrés*, and L'Estoile's own colleagues, the members of the magistrature.[26]

Pasquier claimed to write verse rather than play cards or bowls, and from an early age composed Latin epigrams on the spur of the moment as intellectual exercise.[27] Similarly, as we have just seen, one of his colleagues in July 1564 composed 124 lines (although Jean Le Laboureur, the publisher of the verse,

66 *The Dissemination of Scandal*

implies there were more) of 'news in prosaic rhyme' (*nouvelles en rime Prosaïques*) 'addressed under the name of John Philoglutius, doctor of the Sorbonne, to *maître* Pandolphus Verunculius, *bachelier*, July 9 1564'.[28] The news, written in octosyllabic Latin rhyming couplets, is of the grand tour of the kingdom by Catherine de Medici and her son the king, Charles IX, during which Isabelle de Limeuil famously gave birth to an illegitimate child, reputed to be fathered by the prince de Condé. This short excerpt demonstrates how news of the court, along with its rumour and gossip, could be transmitted to the capital even when the court was on tour:

> This noble maiden
> Who was so lovely
> Committed adultery
> And created a child,
> But they say the queen mother
> In this played Lucina
> And permitted this
> To profit from the prince.[29]

The verse is an example of the verbal gymnastics that the intellectual elite would perform to impress their colleagues. As Marie Houllemare notes, Latin allowed the parlementaire 'to distinguish himself, to present himself as more knowledgeable than his adversary'.[30] Rather than simply writing a newsy letter to one's colleague, the author of these *nouvelles* chose instead to write hundreds of lines of short rhyming verse in Latin, an exercise in erudition and artistry which could only boost his intellectual reputation. Latin allowed creators of verse to show off their education through the use of puns and word-play. Thus, Limeuil's future husband, Scipion Sardini, one of the Italian financiers who had profited so greatly under Catherine de Medici's protection, found himself vilified in Latin verse. In August 1574, L'Estoile included the following distique, which played on the names of Sardini ('sardine') and Ludovic Adjacet ('caete' = 'whale'), another Italian banker:

> Qui modo Sardini, jam nunc sunt grandia caete,
> Sic alit Italicos Gallia pisciculos.
>
> Just like sardines, which have now turned into huge whales,
> So France feeds the Italian small bait.

The distique (a two-line verse employing hexameter in the first line and pentameter in the second) was the form *par excellence* of the Greek and Latin elegy of Antiquity, and its use provided further evidence of the writer's classical learning. The very next day a French version appeared:

> Quand ces bougres poltrons en France sont venus,
> Ils étaient élancés, maigres comme sardaines,

Mais par leurs gros impôts, ils sont tous devenus
Enflés et bien refaits, aussi gros que baleines![31]

When these cowardly rascals came to France
They were slender, thin as sardines,
But by their huge taxes they have all become
Swollen and well recovered, as big as whales!

That the Latin version had been translated into French within a day demonstrates the active participation in manuscript poetry circulation and manipulation in intellectual circles, and furthermore allowed the poem to move beyond its original audience among an intellectual minority to reach a much wider audience.

Importantly, the use of Latin by a writer of satire or criticism would alert the target of that satire to the fact that their behaviour was being commented upon by a member of one of the learned, intellectual elite – a cleric or a magistrate, perhaps – and should therefore be taken seriously, rather than a bawdy *chanson*, for example, which could be attributed to the peasant classes whose opinion could be deemed insignificant. Criticism from such an influential group would have greater repercussions, an aspect of which the writers were also aware, using their attacks on individuals as a platform to make grander statements about the society or court. Thus, the writer of the anonymous 1566 verse libel *In nuptias Ducis de Nemours* ('On the Marriage of the duke of Nemours') could portray the corruption behind the duke's recent marriage to Anne d'Este as representative of the systemic corruption destroying the kingdom:

A cloak encourages and presides/is matron of honour over this wedding.
An unclean, extravagant and grasping cloak, a chasm and abyss,
This kingdom formerly of substance and widely vigorous,
Moreover threatens to lie fallen in complete destruction and rot.[32]

With its choice of Latin hinting at its origins within the magistrature, it is unsurprising that this poem attacks the corruption in a court case which found the Parlement repeatedly opposed to the will of the king and queen mother.

The language could also explain the violently misogynistic terms used to describe Anne d'Este, duchess of Guise, a public figure who usually inspired respect among commentators, but who in this verse is referred to as an 'obscene, withered,/ Putrid, worn-out harlot.' It is possible that the writer of the verse felt able to express something in Latin that he could not write in French. Latin created a closed environment, a kind of 'members-only' club, in which the language itself included select men to the exclusion of others. Educated men could revel in their intellectual superiority on the one hand, showing off their linguistic skills and creative flair, while engaging in an erotic, anti-female, pornographic discourse on the other. The literature exchanged in Latin, I argue, worked to construct a masculinity that was defined by the language's ability to exclude those who were being discussed, i.e., women.[33] This is not to say that these writers used Latin consciously to conduct a secret misogynistic discourse – as we have seen, Latin was the language they used every day at work, and would not have seemed out of the ordinary – rather, it created an environment populated almost entirely by learned men for whom masculinity could not be displayed on the battlefield, but instead through words. Thus a literature written by men, for men, was created in which women were the impotent victims of the language being used. Latin became an effective weapon of misogynistic literature because it was a weapon unavailable to most women. That Anne d'Este had received an exemplary humanist education in Ferrara and could therefore read and write Latin does not diminish the fact that this poem was most likely intended for other men within an intellectual circle that disapproved of the legal corruption in the case, and which expressed its disapproval in misogynistic language.

If Latin permitted the circulation of misogynistic tropes, the return to a 'classical' form of Latin by Renaissance humanists went hand-in-hand with a return to the misogynistic poetry of classical writers, such as Juvenal's *Satire 6*, which depicted women as lust-crazed and marriage as nothing but inescapable, relentless cuckoldry. It contains lines such as 'If you are honestly uxorious, and devoted to one woman, then bow your head and submit your neck to the yoke'.[34] It also presents the familiar threat of wives cheating on their husbands with lower-class servants, so common in the satirical material in this study:

> I hear all this time the advice of my old friends – keep your women at home, and put them under lock and key. Yes, but who will watch the warders? Wives are crafty and will begin with them.[35]

Renaissance humanism also encouraged a return to the classical themes of mythology, and here there was no shortage of powerful women committing perverse acts. While the story of Circe could be employed to praise the attractive charms of a woman whose beauty could lead men astray, her poisonous tricks could also be used to denigrate a woman seen as using deception to achieve her ends. It was Medea, however, the poisoner who killed her own children, who was the mythological figure of choice for those hoping to criticise the queen mother. That Medea, Medici and medicine all appeared to be formed from the same root word was entirely convenient for the writer of this 1574 Latin pasquil, whom L'Estoile described as 'one of the premier and most learned poets of our century':

> What shall I call this, what shall I say about that particular witch?
> Once the heroic physician maiden,
> She has used medicines, so that she should bear fruit well.
> And thus, the potent juice blessed her with an abundant progeny,
> by means of its medical virtue,
> And thus the blessed woman had nine children.
> Yet Fame has it that once her labours were done,
> the children she had brought forth with medicine,
> she ruined by means of medicine.
> They used medicine in such ways in sacred Tuscany,
> That it turned the one who was once the physician maiden into Medea.[36]

The verse plays on the orthographical similarities beween Medici, medicine and Medea to accuse Catherine de Medici of using poison initially to conceive her children and then using poison to kill them. As such, the Medici has gone from her roots in medicine (the alleged original occupation of her ancestral family) to become Medea, the legendary murderer of her own children. L'Estoile's colleagues thus displayed their classical education through verses written in Latin with themes drawn from classical mythology chosen for their negative portrayal of the female.

The Production of Satirical Material: Manuscript and Print

Given the quantity and sophistication of attacks on Catherine, her son and their respective courts, how were these poems produced and circulated? When trying to ascertain the extent of production and dissemination of libels and pamphlets in the sixteenth century, it is always tempting to look for answers in the output of printing presses. However, while the presses certainly played a major role in the publicisation of court scandal, printing must be understood in the context of the still-active manuscript circulation which occurred around poetry and libel composition, especially where potentially treasonable material was concerned.[37] L'Estoile's own journals testify to the scribal culture within which he operated: his two journals in the Bibliothèque nationale in Paris are large collections of his own hand-written copies of the pamphlets, verses and libels he collected, rather than the original documents themselves.[38] While L'Estoile was conscious of the material form of these political writings, often noting for printed material the size of paper or the choice of type ('*imprimée en gros canon*') he continued to copy them out by hand.[39] He was also careful to note their manuscript status: in December 1589 he noted that there was 'published secretly in Paris a writing by hand that was not printed, composed by M. de Villeroi'.[40] There appears to have been an active participation among the legal profession in the interception and transcription of others' letters: in July 1590 he says he was 'shown a copy of an intercepted letter' belonging to the Spanish ambassador, which 'was secretly doing the rounds of Paris.'[41] Similarly, he describes being 'loaned' a letter by M. de Sermoise, *maître des requêtes*, which had been written to him by M. d'Espesse, *avocat du roi*.[42] In another example, Estienne Pasquier's verses on the La Marck scandal were copied out by an admirer who then took them to Venice where another friend copied them out again. Printing figures, then, give scant indication of the extraordinary amount of material that was handwritten and retranscribed: even a cursory glance in the archives will reveal handwritten copies of poems found elsewhere.

The co-existence of print and manuscript material was mutually self-sustaining. Certainly, L'Estoile's journals reveal that the printing presses were producing thousands of pieces of cheap print in the late sixteenth century. Nicolas Le Roux estimates that 'about a thousand' different pamphlets were published in Paris between 1585 and 1594, the years of League ascendancy, although French historians define a 'pamphlet' as a short book or broadsheet in prose, and this therefore gives no indication of the vast numbers of *ramas* or verse libels also circulating.[43] To add to this, Henri IV's repeated commands in the 1590s to destroy all League-related documents in order to erase the collective memory of his enemies' propaganda means that only a fraction of the material printed then still exists.[44] Although heretical literature was the main target of all ordinances against printing, the new laws were also intended to put an end to attacks on public figures. The Edict of Romorantin of May 1560 outlawed 'placards, broadsheets and defamatory books, which can only stir people to sedition, and also printers, sellers and distributors thereof, who are enemies of us and of public repose and guilty of lesemajesty'.[45] The Edict of Moulins in February 1566 similarly forbade anyone from 'writing, printing or displaying for sale any defamatory ... books, libels or writings.'[46] In 1571 a fairly comprehensive ordinance regulating the printing industry was enacted in which two master printers and four of the 20 master booksellers officially recognized by the University of Paris were to supervise the 'community' to ensure that heretical, inflammatory and libelous material not be printed.[47] But the leaders of the publishing community were neither willing nor able to police their colleagues effectively, and, in any case, the legislation was only concerned with printing, rather than handwritten material.

Distributing Satirical Material

In accordance with the diversity of forms in which these satirical and political writings appeared, they were also distributed in a variety of ways. A large proportion of the *ramas* were posted on walls, sold or exchanged, whether clandestinely or openly, in the streets and squares of Paris. L'Estoile claimed a certain pro-League pasquin in March 1588 was 'dispersed (*semé*) in large quantities at the Palais, at the Louvre, thrown under doors and on nearly all the corners and streets of Paris.'[48] L'Estoile would collect them while walking around the city, rip them off the walls at crossroads ('*arrachait aux carrefours*'), copy them out where he found them or learn them by heart. He relied on friends, colleagues, family members and those who owed him a debt of obligation to supply him with ones that they had found. He even had some sent to him in a 'paquet' from Italy and Germany. His entry for August 1576 is a typical example: 'On Sunday the 19th of this month, were displayed (*affichée*) in the crossroads and dispersed in the streets of Paris the following twaddle (*fadeze*) printed in large characters. ... The next day and the following days it was again thrown (*jeté*), and I collected one on my way to the Palais.'[49] L'Estoile noted that the pamphlet was printed, the type that was used, that it was distributed over several days, that it could be found either stuck on the walls at the busy crossroads or lying in large numbers on the streets as if thrown, and that he collected a copy on his way to work in the Palais de Justice, where he could presumably show it to his colleagues.

Graffiti was another method of distributing short pieces of political writing, and the location seems to have been directly related to the issue at stake. To decry Henri III's recent penchant for nightime processions of self-flagellating penitents in 1583, coal was used to write a quatrain against the king on the wall of the 'chapelle des Battus ['Chapel of the Beaten'], aux Augustins'.[50] Similarly, L'Estoile recorded an eight-line verse 'written with coal on the Porte Saint Antoine' which decried the starvation that the people were suffering during the siege of Paris in 1590, the location of the verse on the walls of the besieged city adding to its poignancy.[51] The same entry records graffiti written on 'the awnings of the butchers at the gate of Paris', which read *Haec sunt munera pro iis qui vitam pro Philippo profuderunt* ['Here are the offerings for they who squander their lives for Philip']. This anti-League message in Latin – a criticism of those who supported Philip II of Spain's involvement in French affairs – demonstrates that graffiti was destined for the eyes of the educated and politically involved as well as the uneducated peasant.

For the illiterate there were other forms of satire which did not rely on verbal expression. Woodcuts could be printed onto a pamphlet as an accompaniment to the written text alongside it. After the murders of the two Guise brothers in 1588, for example, a series of pamphlets recounted the assassinations in verse, with large woodcuts showing several events in the same picture. In one of the series, Anne d'Este, duchess of Nemours, the mother of the two murdered men, stands over their corpses, with Henri III next to her (Figure 3.1). The verses below recount the mother's grief at the murders and her anger with the king, but a viewer with only basic literacy could read the name NEMOVRS underneath the woman's image and be able to guess at the message in the text. Similarly, murals could be painted on city walls to mock public figures. L'Estoile recounted:

> This Friday, the last day of August was found at the lodging of Marc Antoine, in the faubourg Saint-Germain, a pleasant joke, but common, painted on a wall: which was a naked woman showing her uncovered nature, and a large mule next to her, with its big thing (*talcas*), which was mounting her, and above the woman was written: madame de Montpensier, and above the ass: monsieur the legate.[52]

While L'Estoile does not give any hint of how long the image was allowed to remain on the wall, the implications of the attack did not require any special skill to understand its meaning.

Location of Distribution

We have seen the diverse forms which literary attacks could take, and how they might have been distributed; now we will look at the locations where they would have been disseminated. Paris in the sixteenth century retained the same tripartite layout it had had since the Middle Ages. The central island, the île de la Cité, was the heart of the city where royal and religious power were located in Notre-Dame Cathedral and in the ancient royal Palais, since known as the Palais de Justice, home of the kingdom's highest sovereign court, the Parlement of Paris. The Right Bank to the north had become the commercial centre, where the city's business and trading was carried out, and the Left Bank to the south, with its celebrated

72 *The Dissemination of Scandal*

Figure 3.1 'Comme les deux Princes estans mort sont mis sur une table avec la remonstrance de Madame de Nemours'

Source: Pierre de L'Estoile, *Les Belles Figures et Drolleries de la Ligue*, BnF Tolbiac Réserve LA25–6

university, as well as several monastic centres, was associated with teaching and learning.[53] To understand how news was disseminated throughout these areas it is essential to understand the medieval tradition in which royal edicts and proclamations were published orally as well as scribally. For more than two centuries after the advent of printing, edicts were still cried in the street (*a la criée*) and

The Dissemination of Scandal 73

announced at the sound of trumpets (*a son des trompes*), and many edicts contained the words 'to be cried in all the usual places.'[54] In an edict of 1556, the places in which it was to be proclaimed (accompanied by the royal trumpeters) were listed as follows (see Figure 3.2):

> before the main gate of the Palace [1]; at the apport of Paris in front of Châtelet [2]; at the cross of Trehoir at the Halles [3]; at the apport Baudoyer [4]; the place de Grève in front of the Hôtel de Ville [5]; at the Saint Séverin crossroads [6]; at the place Maubert near the cross of the Carmelites [7]; at the Mount Saint Genevieve crossroads near the well [8]; Rue Saint Jacques in front of the Jacobins [9]; and at the end of the Saint Michel bridge. [10][55]

To help us understand where each of these areas would have been, each has been given a number which corresponds to the map below.

Figure 3.2 Map of Paris in the sixteenth century, showing places where edicts were to be cried (nos. 1–10)

Source: Lance Greene

The listing of these places takes the crier on a somewhat circuitous route, unsurprisingly beginning with the location, the Palais de Justice, where the edict itself would have been written. From there, the crier would move to the Right Bank and to the main business districts of Paris, where the following four posts – the apport de Paris, les Halles, the apport Baudoyer and the place de Grève – were all major ports or markets serving the city.[56] The crier would thereby target a large number of merchants and their customers as the main places of unloading, distribution and consumption of goods. From there, it would move across the île de la Cité to the Left Bank south of the river, where the following posts targeted the intellectual élite in the university quarter: the Saint-Séverin crossroads was close to the Petit Pont, a site of public intellectual debates, the place Maubert was the customary site of execution for those accused of 'thought crimes' such as heresy (which is why the first printer to be executed met his end there), the mont Saint-Genevieve was the location of the one of the seats of the university, and the rue Saint-Jacques was home to all of the main printing houses and over 160 booksellers crammed into 80 houses, the location *par excellence* of the literate classes.[57] From there the crier would move back again, to the pont Saint-Michel and the crowds crossing the bridge to return once more to the Palais. Pamphlet and libel distribution simply slotted into these pre-existing traditions and trajectories of news distribution. Those in the business of selling news carried on this idea of news as vocal and performative, especially the colporteurs and charlatans, who would perform in these locations to attract consumers. Paris was overcrowded in the sixteenth century: the small number of bridges connecting the tripartite city meant that regular bottlenecks occurred where people became passive audiences for any performer to exploit, and where consumers were targeted by the vocal charms of those in the business of selling.[58]

The Role of Parlementaires in the Circulation of Information

One key area for the distribution and exchange of news was the Palais de Justice itself, home of the kingdom's pre-eminent sovereign court, the Parlement of Paris. The Parlement was made up of three essential components: the Grand Chambre, the Chambre des Enquêtes and the Chambre des Requêtes, supported by the criminal court, the Tournelle. These were supplemented by other courts: the Chambre des Vacations and the Chambre des Marées, among others.[59] Other sovereign courts also meeting under the same roof of the Palais de Justice were the Chambre des Comptes, the Cour des Aides and the Cour des Monnaies.[60] The magistrates in all these courts and chambers were served by a host of barristers, solicitors, clerks, ushers and notaries, who all formed part of what J.H. Shennan has called 'the parlementaire world'.[61] Since the introduction of venality for public offices by François I, this 'parlementaire world' made up a sizable minority of the city's population. As we have seen, L'Estoile himself was an *audiencier de la Chancellerie*, the Chancellerie serving as the link between the royal council and the Parlement, just one of the many legal institutions and corporate bodies also located in the Palais de Justice. The Parlement issued arrêts for the policing of the city, the University and the guilds, but more importantly, was responsible for registering royal legislation, and presenting remonstrances to the king when the legislation was deemed to be unsuitable.[62] Based in the old Capetian royal palace on the Ile de la Cité, a few minutes walk away from the Louvre and right in the heart of the city, the Palais regularly swarmed with enormous numbers of judges, counsellors, lawyers, solicitors, bailiffs, sergeants and other clerks along with litigants, defendants and all the other thousands of people attracted by the judicial work carried on there.[63] Henri-Jean Martin describes how in this city that buzzed with news ('*une ville bruissante de nouvelles*'), where information circulated quickly and by many channels, parlementaires were at the hub of the action.[64] From the passionate discussions in the halls of the Palais where the well-informed legists took positions on political and moral decisions, to the book burnings on the steps of the Palais, to the processions that filled the streets, parlementaires could hear the sermons of preachers, witness tortures and executions, hear news announced with trumpets and buy publications sold '*a la criée*'.

There were even figures who were reknowned for their ease in moving between the Parlement and the royal court, such as Guy du Faur de Pibrac, the 'model magistrate' who was chosen to represent France at the Council of Trent, who accompanied the future Henri III when he went to be crowned in Poland in 1573, and who became a member of the king's Académie royale. Other men also illustrated and strengthened the links between the Palais and the court, such as Jean Bodin, Robert Garnier, Barnabé Brisson and Nicolas Rapin (of whom we will speak shortly), and as Marie Houllemare demonstrates, they shared not only the physical space of the two institutions, but a rhetorical space as well.[65] This proximity between the two courts encouraged a shared linguistic style, which championed a Ciceronian model of 'suave and gentle eloquence', a model described by the Premier Président, Pierre II Séguier, in a speech on the opening of the Palais in 1581 as a 'vision of eloquence that completely refuses vehemence or fury' and which aims only to please 'without virulent reproaches'.[66] As we shall see, of course, these ideals were often abandoned when it came to the satirical verse about the members of the royal households.

Unsurprisingly, parlementaires were by far the most literate group in society, more so even than the clergy. Of 186 personal libraries inventoried between 1500 and 1560, 109 belonged to men of law and royal officers while the clergy possessed only 29.[67] As we have seen in the previous chapter, the members of the magistrature were keenly aware of their individual intellectual reputations and were active in the business of circulating, printing and publishing their own works, and of collecting the works of others. In this they were served by the thriving commercial centre which had developed within the Palais itself. Vendors had set up shop in the gallery opening onto the main steps and in the great hall, and also in stalls attached to the walls of the palace and the church of Sainte-Chapelle within it, selling books and other printed matter, as well as clothing and other related services.[68] Thus parlementaires found themselves surrounded, both inside and outside the Palais, by those in the business of selling newsworthy information.

76 *The Dissemination of Scandal*

They represented an intellectual, literary and cultivated group of men whose daily work meant they were perfectly located to hear news from the royal palace, to learn about cases from the legal courts, and to purchase books, pamphlets and other printed goods. Their key geographical position, combined with their learning and literacy, meant that the men of the Palais were an unrivalled source of commentary, criticism and argument about the political events of their day.

The Selling of Scandal: Colporteurs, Peddlers, Charlatans

Their location meant that the parlementaires also regularly listened to the *chansons* and declamations of the ambulant vendors, charlatans, street-criers, colporteurs, ballad singers and other street performers located in the area. A few minutes walk away from the Palais was the Petit Pont, the bridge leading from Notre-Dame to the south bank of the river. It was a bottleneck exploited by ambulant peddlers of every kind of product, and the noise of the gossiping fishwives plying their trade there was celebrated by François Villon in his *Ballade des femmes de Paris*:

> Bretons and Swiss are mere beginners,
> Like Gascons and Toulousains;
> Two jabberers on the Petit Pont
> Would silence them and Lorrainers too,
> And women from England and from Calais
> (I've named a lot of places, eh?),
> From Picardy and Valencienne . . .
> There's no tongue like a Parisian one.
>
> Prince, to the ladies of Paris
> Present the prize for fine chatter;
> Whatever is said of Italians,
> There's no tongue like a Parisian one.[69]

The traditional link between gossiping and women is strengthened here by the fact that 'harangere' means both a female seller of herrings and a gossip or jabberer. The sound of the same fishwives as well as other vendors on the Petit Pont was also evoked by the poem 'Les laudes et complainctes de Petit Pont' in which the bridge itself complains about the noise it has to put up with everyday. Amid the din of traversing pack mules, raucous students and the cries of vegetable sellers, fishwives and bakers is heard: '. . . a boy who cries out "new books: New farce, prognostication!"'[70] This cry was the sound of news and other kinds of literature being sold by colporteurs in the area.[71] Colporteurs were itinerant vendors who frequented the main streets, thoroughfares, squares and public places of the city selling goods usually from a tray suspended around their neck (*col* = neck, *porte* = carry), advertising their wares by singing aloud. L'Estoile called them 'contre-porteaux' (a bastardisation of colporteurs) or 'port-paniers' (basket-carriers). As well as selling all sorts of trinkets and various mercery, such as ribbons, tape, mirrors, gloves and other odds and ends, colporteurs were known for their sale of cheap print.[72] Books of hours, abc's, almanacs, romances, indexed literature and *canards* with their stories of gruesome and/or fantastical events (crimes and executions, two-headed dogs, armies fighting in the sky) were the regular stock-in-trade of the colporteur, as they represented the kinds of literature that would appeal to a broad, semi-literate market.[73] Printed pamphlets satirising or commenting upon the court and its denizens were very much a part of the literature of the colporteur, who would advertise by crying out the scandalous details within. L'Estoile talked about the 'defamatory libels against His Majesty, coloured with all the most atrocious insults ... printed in Paris and cried publicly in the streets.'[74] Court scandal was thereby broadcast in aural as well as written form.

This vocal marketing meant that the cry of the colporteur, 'beaulx abc, belles heures', made up one of the already famous 'cris de Paris', the sounds of vendors hawking their wares through the capital's streets that by the sixteenth century had already been immortalised in a series of engravings (Figure 3.3) as well as in a polyphonic song by the composer Clément Janequin.[75] As well as pamphlets, colporteurs sold single song-sheets or cheap *recueils de chansons* (song collections) with the lyrics of newly-composed songs set to the tune of familiar ballads or dance tunes, which often had ladies of the court and their amorous relationships as their subject. As Kate van Orden points out:

> singing and peddling cheap print went hand in hand, as songs pitched the sale of the print to those who paused to listen – hence the bounty of rhetorical hooks used in the songs, opening formulae such as 'Who would like to hear a little song ...' or 'Listen, ladies, listen to the story. ...'.[76]

Courtly women, such as Jeanne de Piennes and Isabelle de Limeuil who were the subject of popular songs of the day, could thus find details of their personal lives being performed by poor, itinerant peddlers for the entertainment of the illiterate masses.

To add to the musical marketing of the colporteurs, the citizens of Paris would also be courted by the street theatre of charlatans who, along with dubious medical remedies, also peddled cheap print. Charlatans or mountebanks (so-called because, originating in Italy, charlatans often mounted benches or *banchi*) were performing peddlers who used songs, jokes and persuasive banter to sell an array of goods, usually to gullible spectators.[77] The outer courtyard of the Palais de Justice played host to the Italian charlatan Hieronimo di Bolonia in June 1601. According to L'Estoile, Hieronimo used stones, unguents and herbs to cure toothache and migraines, but also had 'a certain oil which within a day cured a number of wounds, as he himself demonstrated by experimenting on his own person'.[78] In roughly the same space a few years later – by then the newly-created Place Dauphine – the most famous of the French charlatans, Tabarin, had developed and perfected this art of semi-improvised street theatre, with a running banter of topical allusions and bawdy jokes that eventually won him entry to Henri IV's court. Charlatans thus bridged the gap between the palace and the public arena. Like

Figure 3.3 Engraving of a colporteur
Source: *Les cris de Paris*, BnF Arsenal Estampes Rés. 264, f. 1

the Florentine poet-singer L'Altissimo, who dedicated poems to the king and was rewarded with invitations to perform at court, charlatans and the newly-arrived *commedia dell'arte* performers eventually began to earn an income by selling printed versions of their poems, songs and performances.[79] In sixteenth-century Venice, reported Thomas Coryate, mountebanks sold 'oyles, soveraigne waters, amorous songs printed, Apothecary drugs, and a Commonweale of other trifles'.[80] These 'amorous songs printed' are the same song-sheets or *recueils de chansons* sold by the colporteurs which, as I will explore further, often publicised news of the private lives of courtly ladies in a very public location.

The close relationship between charlatans and the production and distribution of cheap print has been demonstrated by Rosa Salzberg for sixteenth-century Venice, and their role in the cycle of information distribution in France is highlighted by the prominence given them in what is arguably the most celebrated pamphlet of the period: the *Satyre Ménippée*.[81] Printed in 1594 after circulating in manuscript for about a year, the pamphlet is a combination of verse and prose ridiculing the vices, cruelty and pro-Spanish pretensions of the League and its followers. Its full title is *The Menippean Satire of the Virtue of the Spanish Catholicon and of the Holding of the Estates of Paris* (*Satyre Ménippée de la Vertu du Catholicon d'Espagne et de la tenue des Estats de Paris*), and its preface introduces two charlatans, one Spanish, one from Lorraine, who, established in the court of the Louvre, sell to passersby an extraordinary new panacea, 'Catholicon', which will pardon all one's faults. By employing the irreverent and dubious figure of the charlatan in the preface, the pamphlet immediately alerts the reader not only to the dangers of trusting the Lorraine-Guises' support of the Spanish, but also to expect the satirical mockery of prominent figures of the League. The pamphlet's depiction of two of the leaders of the League in a mock procession, Anne d'Este, duchess of Nemours and her daugher Catherine-Marie de Lorraine, duchess of Montpensier, linked them with the falsehoods promoted by the charlatan figure and painted their supporters as gullible.

The Performance of Scandal: Joyous Societies and the Commedia dell'arte

There was a close link between the performance of political news and satire and the intellectual world of the Left Bank. Since medieval times, the area around the Petit Pont at the foot of the rue Saint-Jacques had become, notes Colin Jones, 'a special place for students to come and listen to teachers engaging in intellectual jousting in open-air settings which gave the site the atmosphere of 'a sort of amphitheatre'. The name of the Rue du Fouarre ('Straw Street') evokes the bales on which clerics would sit to enjoy the heady intellectual atmosphere.[82] This theatrical atmosphere found expression within the Parlement itself: from the time of Philippe le Bel in the early fourteenth century, the *clercs de la Basoche* were a confraternity of young apprentice-clerks, numbering up to ten thousand by the sixteenth century, who trained in their future career by holding mock hearings and staging farces that would form a large part of the comic repertoire of the medieval period.[83] As the sixteenth century progressed, they merged with the societies of laymen known as the *Enfants-Sans-Souci* (led by the *Prince des Sots*, the 'Prince of Fools') who specialised in 'sottie': drama which used bitter laughter to provoke thought and political action.[84] Carnival celebrations and fairs would find them performing on trestles for large crowds, exploiting the impunity of the fool to criticise public figures. From the medieval period onwards, the *clercs de la Basoche*, the *Enfants-Sans-Souci* and other joyous confraternities based within the legal profession revelled in the public performance of mocking theatre, fostering a tradition of satire of prominent figures.[85]

Their popularity would eventually be threatened by a new kind of satirical performance: the *commedia dell'arte*, whose irreverent style would so influence later French theatre, most famously in the work of Molière, were a new phenomenon in France in the late sixteenth century.[86] The famous troupe *I Gelosi* first played in France in 1571 for the celebrations of the wedding of Charles IX, invited by Louis de Gonzague, duc de Nevers. Henri III, who had enjoyed their work in Venice, invited them to return, and their performance on 19 May 1577 was so popular, claimed L'Estoile, that 'they had better attendance than the four best preachers of Paris combined!'[87] The Parlement of Paris did not approve of this new theatre that celebrated adultery and debauchery, but their complaints to the king went unheard. With their unscripted yet predictable plots, and stock characters, the *commedia dell'arte* represented a less intellectual, more generic form of satirical theatre, aimed less at specific public figures, but rather at standard figures of fun like the cuckold or the eccentric servant. It is little wonder that Henri III, targeted so regularly by the satirical writers and performers originating from the educated legal milieux, chose to welcome this less barbed form of theatre. Significantly, along with charlatans, poet-singers and other performers, the *commedia dell'arte* troupes had access to the palace interior and the homes of wealthy nobles, giving them privileged insight into the domestic situations of the king and courtiers. That all these performers played a prominent role in the creation, production and dissemination of information explains how permeable the palace walls could be when it came to scandalous news that could be sold to an interested public.

Authorship and the 'Double Life' of Writers

Traditional songs, charlatan performances and other long-standing verbal and visual forms could be updated with contemporary satirical references. But where did the new poems come from? Who wrote or adapted them? Attempts to attribute authorship to verse libels and other satirical pamphlets inevitably run into problems with anonymity. The common method of leaving pamphlets in the street points to a central concern to avoid identification as either the author or the distributer of potentially treasonous material. Often, pamphlets were printed with misleading title pages, such as the *Réveille-Matin des François, et de leurs voisins* [*Wake-Up Call for the French and their Neighbours*] which claimed to have been written by 'Eusèbe Philadelphe' and printed in 'Edimbourg', although it was actually printed in Basel, and its author was Nicolas Barnaud, a noted Huguenot.[88]

Brantôme was of the opinion that a large part of the new fashion for libelling court women came from within the court itself:

> During his [Charles IX] reign, the great libellers began however to come into fashion, and even certain very gallant gentlemen of the court, whom I will not name, who strangely criticised the ladies, both in general and as individuals, even the grandest.[89]

These 'gallant gentlemen' rightly feared the wrath of their targets, however, and concealed their identity most commonly through simple denial. Brantôme recalled a group of men at court who disapproved of the impending marriage of 'a certain prince' and wrote verses comparing the potential bride to

> five or six great whores, ancient, famous, really lecherous, and that she surpassed all four [sic]. They themselves who had written the pasquin presented it to him, saying however that it had come from others, and that it had been given to them.'[90]

Anonymity could be sought in other ways, however. L'Estoile wrote that

> in this month of July (1586), was brought a letter to brother Maurice Poncet, curé of Saint Pierre des Arsis, which in his absence was delivered to his man (servant), by an individual dressed in a long robe and a wimple (*cornette*), who could not be recognised or identified. . . . This letter, delivered to the Chancellor, was found to have been written in the same hand that had written certain placards, around the middle of June last year, pasted up on the Louvre and other places in the city of Paris.[91]

Such concern with anonymity became less obvious as the century progressed, and the League's promoters began to produce enormous quantities of polemic denouncing 'Henry de Valois', as its supporters called Henri III. L'Estoile claimed that these pamphlets, which depicted Henri III as a tyrant and called for regicide, were 'cried publicly in the streets'.[92] However, the League's fanaticism and intolerance was generally despised by parlementaires, who viewed the attacks on the king as tantamount to treason, and who, in response, produced a simultaneous torrent of anti-League libels and pamphlets. The *Satyre Ménippée* was the most celebrated of these, and its authorship was a collaborative effort involving Nicolas Rapin, Florent Chrestien, Gilles Durant, Pierre Pithou and Jean Passerat, all members of the magistrature. Among these, Nicolas Rapin, a soldier, poet and lawyer, is generally most celebrated for his satirical verse, and all the Latin verse in the *Satyre Ménippée* is attributed to him.[93] He was, however, an invitee to the maréchale de Retz's salon and, like all the other guests, wrote encomiastic verse of the maréchale and her female companions in the maréchale's album of poetry:

> Happy place which brings
> A thousand deities together [. . .]

But over all the group
A Diane commands,
Of the noble blood of the Gondis,
Aggrandized by their valour,
Who in this divine temple
Serves as conduct and example.[94]

Presenting the maréchale as the goddess Diana chastely supervising her nymph-goddess companions, Rapin employs a repeated metaphor in the album: that of the women of the court as Muses inspiring the creative process, one of the origins, I argue, of the image of the 'flying squadron'. As we have seen, the male invitees to the salon make repeated references to the 'immortal band of nine sisters', 'deities' or 'nymphs' so beautifully adorned that France and the court 'burn in the rays' of their light.[95]

But, as suggested in Chapter 2, the role women played in inspiring and nurturing writers could backfire as the religious struggles became entangled in intellectual disputes. For example, Rapin's collaborator on the *Satyre Ménippée*, Florent Chrestien, would become involved in an argument in 1563 over Ronsard's praise for the Protestant prince de Condé. Ronsard expressed his praise by means of encomiastic sonnets dedicated to Condé's lover, Isabelle de Limeuil. As we shall see in the following chapter, Chrestien mocked Ronsard's hypocrisy in seeking patronage from a prince he felt was unsuitable because of his heretical beliefs, although Ronsard could make the claim that he was simply participating in the clientage relationship that characterised most writers' careers in the period. But while Ronsard was creating these encomiastic works, he was also simultaneously engaged in composing violently obscene verse criticising Henri III and his *mignons* for their effeminacy and homosexual activity. In April 1578, L'Estoile copied into his journal three obscene, satirical sonnets attributed to Ronsard, which attack the king for his sodomitical practices with his favourites. The third sonnet, for example, ends:

The king doesn't like me because I've too much beard:
He likes to sew his seed in a grassless field,
And like the beaver to mount from behind:
When he fucks arses, which are tightened cunts,
He follows the nature of the Medicis,
When he takes the front, he acts like his father.[96]

Gary Ferguson has made a sustained and learned exploration of the pederastic and homosexual discourse operating within these sonnets.[97] For the purpose of this study, however, what is interesting is the one aspect Ferguson does not examine: the reference to 'the nature of the Médicis' as being closely linked with sodomy. Juxtaposed with the last line which claims that Henri's father preferred sex 'from the front', i.e., heterosexual sex, this is a direct reference to his mother, Catherine de Medici, and her Italian familial background, suggesting that, although her gender does not allow her to actively engage in sodomy, Catherine has transferred an Italian predisposition towards homosexuality to her son (what the French would have termed 'les plaisirs ultramontains'). Ferguson explains that we need to situate these works 'in the context of a late sixteenth-century libertinism' in which even the most celebrated court poets were involved in obscene literature satirising the court.[98] In her study of the satirical literature attacking Venetian courtesans, Courtney Quaintance finds a similarly paradoxical behaviour at work:

> Sixteenth-century literary responses to courtesans – and to women in general – tended to be radically polarized, consisting at one extreme of highly idealized images of angelically chaste femininity and at the other of grotesque caricatures of mercenary, deceitful whores with voracious sexual appetites. Paradoxically, many writers even indulged in both tropes simultaneously.[99]

Similarly in France, such dichotomous behaviour, seeking patronage and protection from noble women while simultaneously engaged in a violently misogynistic discourse, can be witnessed in some of the better-known satirical writers.

Another name that can be linked with Rapin and Chrestien is that of François Viète, the celebrated lawyer and mathematician.[100] In his role as lawyer, he was best known for his work with Huguenot families, and in particular, for his support of Françoise de Rohan in her 21 year lawsuit against Jacques de Savoie, duc de Nemours (the subject of Chapter 5). His unswerving devotion to Rohan brought him into conflict with his old friend Nicolas Rapin who, in 1581, was attempting to prosecute her for harbouring Protestants on her lands. What Viète is less well known for, however, is his authorship of one of the most virulent anti-League verse libels, the *Prosa cleri Parisiensis ad ducem de Mena* or *Letter of the clergy of Paris to the duke of Mayenne*, which attributes the assassination of Henri III by Jacques Clément, a Dominican friar, to the encouragement given him in the form of sexual favours by the duke's sister, Catherine-Marie de Lorraine, duchess of Montpensier.[101] Viète's attack on Montpensier thereby links him with Rapin and Chrestien in their attacks on the excesses of the League, and also highlights the multiple roles played by these lawyer-writers in the lives of aristocratic women – simultaneously the defender of Rohan and the slanderer of Montpensier, Viète is representative of the parlementaires who employed their intellectual creativity in the scandals that were often the product of both sides of the confessional divide.

Another example of this literary behaviour is the verse of Estienne Pasquier, *avocat-général* at the Cour des Comptes, a close friend of the maréchale de Retz and a regular at her salon.[102] Despite this close connection to high-ranking courtiers (or perhaps because of it) Pasquier did not hesitate to criticise the court in verse. He composed a Latin verse on the notorious 1577 murder of Françoise de La Marck by her husband.[103] Written in La Marck's voice, it plays on the similarity in Latin between *thalamus* (marital bed) and *tumulus* (tomb) to highlight how La Marck's adultery (in the marital bed, it is implied) led to her death. Thus, she experienced both pleasure and death in the same place. The final couplet,

84 *The Dissemination of Scandal*

however, serves as a warning to her colleagues, the 'Venuses' at the court of the prince, who are referred to as an 'impudent crowd'. The women of the court are described collectively both as having loose morals and as luring men to the court with divine trickery, a theme returned to repeatedly by composers of anti-courtier verse libels. This verse in particular made its way to Venice where Pasquier's friend Nicolas Audebert copied it, unaware of its author. He praised it to Pasquier upon his return, telling him how much it had been admired there, his comments revealing the geographical extent to which news of this scandal had travelled.[104]

Writers based within the robe nobility occupied a position which provided them with the education and stimulating intellectual environment within which to create literary works, and with the material to inspire them. At the hub of news emanating from the royal court and the legal courts, and at the crossroads of the performance and distribution of news, parlementaires revelled in the creation of countless genres of literature that commented upon and criticised society at large. Operating within a literary fraternity which simultaneously celebrated and vilified the women of the court, they exchanged and circulated a variety of libels about those women that functioned to construct an image of (in)appropriate female behaviour. Having discussed the authorship and distribution of libels, we move to two specific genres – imaginary libraries and songs – to reveal the particular qualities that made them so effective when discussing scandalous women.

Imaginary Libraries

If, as LaGuardia suggests, masculinity in the early modern period was constructed through the circulation and exchange among men of stories of women's sexual voracity and eternal infidelity, then there is probably no better example of such a tradition than the 1587 *Library of the Duchess of Montpensier*.[105] This is a list of imaginary book titles said to belong to Catherine-Marie de Lorraine, duchess of Montpensier, the spiritual figurehead of the Catholic League in Paris. She was a well-known vocal and visible opponent of both the Protestant pretender to the French throne, Henri of Navarre, and of the king himself, Henri III. Based on Rabelais' imaginary library of Saint-Victor in *Pantagruel* which mocked the scholasticism of the late medieval world, this list of books is a satirical attack on the members of the French court and supporters of the League with a firm emphasis on the sexual transgressions of the women of the court. One entry reads *Inventory of the Proportions of French Cocks, with the Great Balls of Lorraine, by Madame de Nermoutier*, a reference to the infamous exploits of Charlotte de Beaune, dame de Sauve and marquise de Noirmoutier, whose extra-marital liaisons included, it was alleged, Henri, duke of Guise; Henri, king of Navarre; and the king's brother, the duke of Alençon. More than just a list of bawdy jokes, however, the imaginary library was a tool of satire that was perfectly suited for the exchange, circulation and transmission of stories that depicted women as sexually voracious.

A manuscript copy of the *Library* can be found in the Bibliothèque nationale in Paris (see Fig. 3.4) and two published versions of L'Estoile's journal contain the *Library*, but with substantial differences both to each other and to the manuscript version.[106] While a large number of titles are the same, many titles are missing and new titles have been added, while some of the titles have been amended. The three different versions point to a tradition of manuscript circulation in which the libel was re-worked and re-invented. It typifies Jason Scott-Warren's description of manuscript poetry circulation: 'a poem which circulated widely will tend to appear in many different versions, varying in verbal details or bearing witness to wholesale revision'.[107] That the three lists contain most of the same titles but with significant differences such as varying running order and the addition or subtraction of certain words in each title, and the addition in each version of completely new titles, demonstrates that the libel was probably circulated in manuscript, memorised in large part upon reading and rewritten at a later time. Thus the more memorable titles remain constant, albeit with small refinements, from version to version.

These more memorable and repeated titles are those which refer to women's sexual infidelity, cuckoldry of their husbands, prostitution or their fraudulent claims to chastity. In this genre, women's sexual voracity is compounded by their attempts to deceive men, a state of affairs which the writers circulating the manuscript versions felt impelled to express numerically by listing these deceptions. As LaGuardia argues, 'men were interpellated as men in this historical context by the necessity of taking and giving accounts of women's tricks, containing them within limits, and even simply of counting them'.[108] Even the titles, which claim to be genuine books while making allusions to secret affairs, operate as one of these 'women's tricks'.

In Montpensier's imaginary library, the duchess herself is mocked in sexual terms, with the title: *The Method of Working/Getting One's Leg Over with a Limp with All Comers, by Madame de Montpensier* (*Le Moien de besongner à clochepied à tous venans, par Madame de Montpensier*). Not satisfied with simply mocking her physical disability, a limp, the term 'besogner', meaning 'to work', also had connotations of a sexual nature which would have been well understood by readers.[109] Other titles refer to specific women alleged to be cuckolding their husbands, such as *The Diverse Plates of Love, translated from Spanish into French, by Madame the Maréchale of Retz, to the Seigneur of Dunes* (*Les Diverses assiettes d'amour, traduites d'espagnol en françois, par Madame la mareschale de Rets, au seigneur de Dunes*) which alludes to the maréchale's alleged affair with Charles de Balsac, baron de Dunes, known as 'le bel Entraguet' (in his marginal notes L'Estoile refers to Dunes as her 'equerry', i.e., someone who 'rides' her). Similarly, *The Manner of Quickly Surveying Great Fields, by Madame de Nevers* (*La Maniere d'arpanter brieufvement les grands prés, par Madame de Nevers*) refers to Henriette de Clèves, duchess of Nevers's alleged affair with someone named Grandpré. L'Estoile's note in the margin explains that 'Grandpré' also refers to her 'equerry', and is thus a reference to her lover, presumably one of the Joyeuse family who owned the lands of Grandpré. Importantly, L'Estoile's use of the term 'equerry' depicts the women both as bestial and as under the control of lower-ranked servants.

Other titles are less specific, describing female insatiability in more hyperbolic terms: *The Spinning Wheel of Cuckoldry, by Combaud, First Master of the*

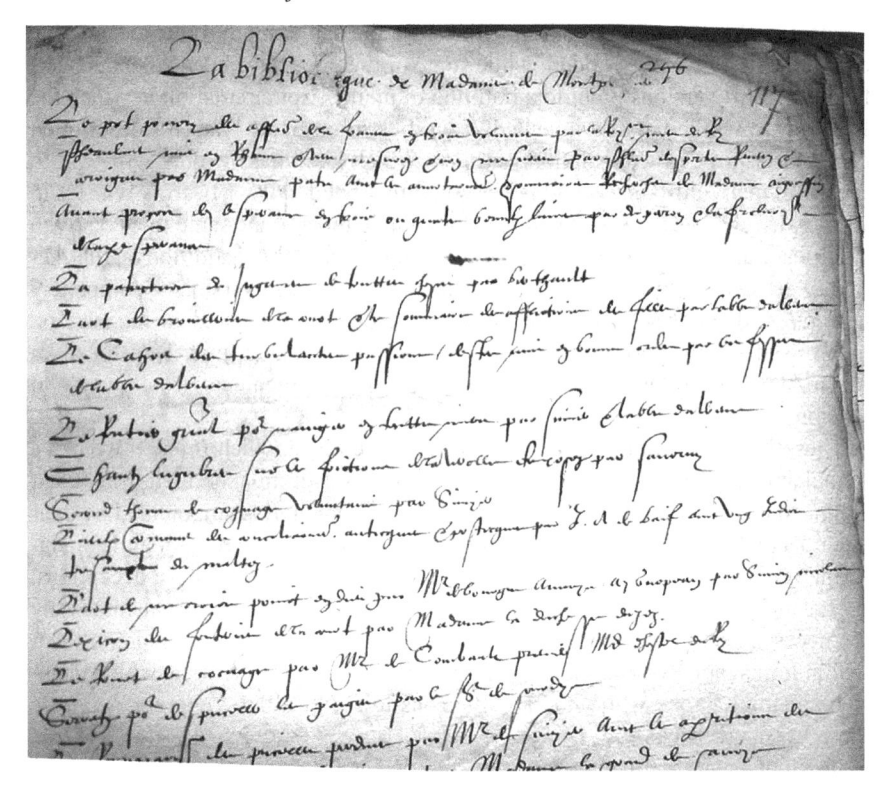

Figure 3.4 'La bibliothèque de madame de Montpensier'
Source: BnF MS Fr 15592, f. 117

King's Hotel (*Le Rouet de cocuage, par Combaud, premier maistre d'hostel du Roy*) implies that not only will the infidelity of Robert Combaut's wife ('La Belle Rouet') be a never-ending wheel of torture, but also that he is the author of his own misfortune. Less imaginatively, *The Lexicon of Fucking, by the Duchess of Uzès* (*Lexicon de Fouterie, par la duchesse d'Uzès*), depicts the sexual experience and knowledge of the duchess as so vast that it even has its own language. In a consistent motif of cuckold literature in which women are constantly deceiving their husbands with the help of other clever women, several titles paint the court as a site of prostitution, such as *The Rhetoric of Pimps, by Madame de la Chastre* (*La Rethorique des maquerelles, par Madame de la Chastre*). Another topos of cuckold literature that LaGuardia has identified is the display of virginity and the tricks women play to present themselves as virgins on their wedding day, represented in titles such as *The History of Jane the Virgin, by Madamoiselle de Bourdeille* (*L'histoire de Jeanne la Pucelle, par Madamoiselle de Bourdeille*), which utilises the nickname of Joan of Arc, known as 'La Pucelle d'Orléans' ('The Maid of Orleans') to satirise one woman's attempt to present herself as a virgin. The word histoire with its double meaning of 'history' and 'story' implies that Madeleine de Bourdeille's virginity is perhaps a fiction as well.

The imaginary library was a genre that would prove exceptionally popular because of its flexibility, its ability to be updated with new names or crimes: every subsequent reign would inspire its own satirical library.[110] For example, *The Inventory of Books Found in the Library of Master Guillaume* (*Inventaire des livres trouvés en la bibliothèque de maître Guillaume*) was the title of a satirical pamphlet under Henri IV, its attribution to Guillaume, the king's fool, allowing its writer the same impunity enjoyed by that figure. A few years later another mock inventory would appear, this time alleged to have been discovered 'in the chests of M. le chevalier de Guise' also mocking the members of Henri IV's court. Under Louis XIII's reign a list of imagined books was credited to Pierre de Montmaur, professor of Greek at the Collège de France, whose vanity and rise to fame created many enemies, and Louis XIV would find his court attacked in the *Bibliothèque du roi Guillemot*, a reference to William III, prince of Orange. In each of these cases the alleged owner of the library is either a vilified figure, like the duchess of Montpensier, or like Guillaume, a useful cover of anonymity.

In addition to its criticisms of female courtiers, the imaginary library's satirical target was also the literate classes and the contemporary rise in the number of personal libraries predominantly found, as we have seen, in the homes of the magistrature. That this anti-League libel was circulated and amended in manuscript, and that at least two different versions made their way into the hands of L'Estoile, is strong evidence for its origins among the parlementaires. This literate group of men, engaged as they were in the publishing trade and in the purchase and collection of printed material, would have appreciated the humour in the spoof book titles and the clever manipulation of typical early modern publishing details. The imaginary library performs as a self-parody of the literary fraternity in tandem with the parody of public figures, and serves both as evidence for the parlementaires' involvement in misogynistic satire as well as an example of the recurrent themes of sexual deviance employed against women in that satire.

Music and Songs

If imaginary libraries remained the preserve of a small group of male readers and writers, the women of the court could expect newsworthy events in their lives to be transmitted quickly into the much wider public domain not only through the medium of written text but also through song. Poems composed in their honour by court poets such as Ronsard and Desportes were regularly transformed into lyrics by composers including the work Ronsard dedicated to Isabelle de Limeuil, *Quand ce beau printemps je voy*.

> When I see this beautiful spring
> I perceive
> The earth and the sea become young again

88 *The Dissemination of Scandal*

>And it seems to me that the day
>And love
>Like infants are born unto the world.
>
>Quand ce beau Printemps je voy,
>J'apperçoy,
>Rajeunir la terre et l'onde,
>Et me semble que le jour,
>Et l'Amour,
>Comme enfans naissent au monde.[111]

Written around the time of her scandalous relationship with the prince of Condé in 1563 (described in the following chapter), it was set to music in 1576 by the composer Jehan Chardavoine. Ladies of the court could thus find their praises being sung in a literal sense and indeed all of Ronsard's love poetry would eventually be set to music.[112] The popularity of *Quand ce beau printemps je voy* resulted in its being used as the melody for 'contrafacts': new song texts written to the tune and rhythm of familiar songs. These *chansons nouvelles* (new songs) used the details of current affairs to create songs on well-known tunes and, because they required no musical literacy, nor prodigious musical talent, were extremely popular.[113] Given that the lyrics used already well-known tunes and thus required no costly musical notation, they were published in extraordinarily large numbers by printers eager to produce inexpensive *recueils de chansons*. The *recueils* cost approximately one sou (the cost of a pound of beef or a week's worth of wine in Lyon in 1580), while *canards* and single sheets only cost a denier or two like the penny ballad sheets sold in London.[114] Although the contrafacts set to *Quand ce beau printemps je voy* were usually love songs as befitting the original written for Limeuil, the version in the 1580 recueil *Le rosier des chansons nouvelles* subverted the traditional themes of love to bemoan the state of the kingdom after years of bloody civil war. The 'beautiful springtime' of the original has become for the author a time of misery and hardship:

>When I see this hard springtime
>I know
>All the unhappiness in the world
>I see nothing but disorder
>And horror
>Pouring just like a wave.[115]

The song catalogues the infinite ways in which the kingdom has been turned upside down, one stanza in particular decrying the sort of woman the original song had been written for:

>We see women talking
>Getting mixed up

In an abundance of affairs,
And wearing big hair
Powdered
To be attractive to the world.[116]

The song for Isabelle de Limeuil had, in the space of four years, been transformed from an encomiastic courtly love song to an invective against noble women's worldly vanity and their propensity to implicate themselves in business inappropriate to their sex.

One could argue that the *chanson*, which only mentions Limeuil in the written version, could therefore have been performed with any woman in mind. By contrast, the 1556 *Deux chansons sur les amours de M. de Montmorency et de Mademoiselle de Pienne, fille d'honneur de la reine Catherine de Médicis* are unambiguous about their subject matter, demonstrating not only that court scandal reached a wide public audience but also highlighting the link between the classical tradition of courtly lyric production and popular street songs.[117] In October 1556, the constable, Anne de Montmorency, arranged for his eldest son François to marry Henri II's legitimated daughter, Diane de France. The father's satisfaction at this confirmation of his unrivalled favour in the king's eyes was quickly dispelled when his son informed him that he had secretly married his sweetheart, Jeanne de Halluin de Piennes, and had consummated the marriage. The enraged father had Piennes imprisoned in the Filles-Dieu convent where she would remain for seven months, while François was sent to Rome to seek an annulment from the Pope.[118] The public outcry at the treatment of the young lovers, in particular that of Jeanne de Piennes (Figure 3.5), imprisoned and eventually betrayed by her husband who saw his inheritance as ultimately more important than her, found expression in the above-mentioned *chansons*.

The *chansons* are set to the tune of '*Laissez la verde couleur*', a composition known as a 'complainte': a lament, usually in a woman's voice, that was popular as a courtly genre in the early part of the sixteenth century, but which had become, in the years of the religious wars, a song of lament for the working people.[119] *Laissez la verde couleur* was composed by the court poet Mellin de Saint-Gelais and recounts Venus's mourning at the death of Adonis (itself based on the famous lament of Venus by Bion of Smyrna); Kate van Orden describes it as 'the most famous female lament of its time'.[120] *Laissez la verde couleur* was printed many times and its melody became the basis for countless contrafacts, printed into the inexpensive *recueils de chansons* described above. It was in one of these that the *chanson* about Piennes and Montmorency would have been printed. Its verse is short with a simple rhyme scheme, making it easy to learn and memorise. The song is in two parts, opening with Montmorency lamenting the anger of his father and disapproval of the king:

The king, my sovereign master,
Has made
My heart feel great pain;

Figure 3.5 François Clouet, *Jeanne de Halluin de Piennes, baronne d'Alluye*
Source: BnF Réserve NA-22

> And the fury of my father
> Too bitter
> Comes from too great rigour[121]

The response by Piennes reveals her punishment, imprisonment in a convent, while her lover must depart:

> You go off to Italy
> But the Compline [night prayers]
> Meanwhile I will sing
> In a convent unhappy,
> Very pitiful
> Where I will lament you.[122]

The popularity of the Saint-Gelais original on the topic of Venus and Adonis meant that those who read, sang or heard the Montmorency/Piennes version would have been aware of the classical associations of the song. The cross-fertilization of themes (classical mythology with contemporary scandal) and of media (street song with courtly *complainte*) remind us of the blurred boundary between an educated, courtly audience and an urban, lower class audience. The format and low price of the *recueils* in which the Piennes song would have been printed made them affordable to members of every level of society, who could then pass on their contents via reading or singing to others whose illiteracy may have prevented them from doing so. Having one's personal life set to the tune of such a popular song meant that the details of one's scandal were accessible even to the poorest and least literate citizen. This crossover between cheap print and aural reception of news has been explored by Natalie Zemon Davis who says, 'The addition of printed pamphlets to traditional methods for spreading news (rumour, street song, private letters, town criers, fireworks displays, bell-ringing, and penitential processions) increased the *menu peuple*'s stock of detailed information about national events.'[123] Moreover, the popularity of the song is attested to by the fact that other *recueils*, printed for the most part in Lyon, include new song texts written 'to the tune of the Piennes song' (*sur le chant de Pienne*), evidence that Mlle de Piennes had become a household name, and her scandalous story was known throughout the kingdom.[124]

Although the Piennes song takes the form of a *complainte*, and is therefore sympathetic to its subjects and their situation, mocking songs that satirised members of the court functioned instead to shame those embroiled in scandal. As Alastair Bellany explains,

> Originally part of the charivari rituals against those who had violated local sexual norms, mocking rhymes were often sung to the tunes of popular ballads or pinned up in public places. . . . Verses and mocking songs on national personalities may thus have seemed a natural extension of a traditional local genre.[125]

92 *The Dissemination of Scandal*

The collective reputation of the women of the court was mocked in *The Dance of the Court* (*Le Triory de la Cour*), which portrayed them as prostitutes, cuckolding their husbands in order to gain money:

> The women of Fontainebleau,
> The women of Fontainebleau,
> They like to drink wine without water,
> And for the love of ecus
> They make lots of men cuckolds
> Those from Saint Germain en l'Aix
> Were ridden like relays,
> Treating their apron
> To the common people of the Chateau.[126]

In this example we can find what are by now familiar *topoi* of the literature surrounding women in the early modern period: women's unbounded sexual appetite, their deception and cuckolding of their husbands, their sexuality expressed in animalistic, usually equine, terms ('ridden like relays') and prostitution. That this song goes on to refer to each royal château in turn is another example of the enumeration of this paradoxically insatiable sexual desire of the female.

Conclusion

Information circulated in diverse ways in early modern society. The transmission of news in sixteenth-century France was at times performative, employing theatre, music, song and poetry to entertain as well as inform. Its dissemination relied on street criers, singers, actors and poets, and its subject matter included such diverse items as two-headed babies, foreign military conquests and the sexual transgressions of courtiers.[127] It was also non-centralised and therefore disorganised, subject to the various demands of time, weather and most importantly, the marketplace. News was often conceived in terms of what would sell, and was only one aspect of performances by colporteurs and charlatans who sold pamphlets along with a variety of other goods. The term 'pamphlet' itself usually denotes printed material, while news about the court – in particular, libellous or treasonous material – was regularly circulated in manuscript form, copied and disseminated without ever being printed. We must also therefore reconsider the 'hegemony' of the printing press when we discuss court scandal, as this kind of news usually was libellous and therefore often circulated secretly. Authorship of a large body of material about court scandal originated in the legal and intellectual milieux of the Parlement, as its members were strategically located to witness the domestic lives of courtiers, to have access to the legal cases concerning them and to hear the rumours and gossip from the palace. The traditions of their common university background resulted in an incessant exchange and circulation of verse and prose, in both French and Latin, that served to establish their individual reputations as intellectual elites and to construct a masculinity that found expression in written material rather than in military combat. This historically-contingent version of masculinity was defined by the exchange and circulation of stories of women's exaggerated sexuality, resulting in a portrayal of the court and its women as scandalous. It is to the story of one of these women that we will turn in the following chapter, to learn what was deemed scandalous at court, how information about that scandal was disseminated and what agency a noblewoman had when accused of crimes both real and imagined.

Notes

1 L'Estoile, III: 170–185.

> 'Madame de Chasteauvilain
> Aiant là laissé son vilain
> Court Monsieur de Guise, à force;
> Madame de Sauve s'efforce
> A contenter tous ses vallets. [. . .]
> Quant à madame de Nemours
> Pibrac la renverse à rebours
> Cependant que sa bonne femme
> Va chanter autre part sa gamme.'

2 Compare this libel of courtly women with the 1636 libel 'A health to my Lady Duchess' which sexually slanders the women of Charles I's court: http://www.earlystuartlibels.net/htdocs/misc_section/R6.html, accessed 15/05/2013. 'Early Stuart Libels: An Edition of Poetry from Manuscript Sources', eds. Alastair Bellany and Andrew McRae, *Early Modern Literary Studies Text Series I* (2005).

3 Madeleine Lazard, *Le théâtre en France au XVIe siècle* (Paris: Presses Universitaires de France, 1980), 69.

4 The 'Suitte' is found directly after the original poem, L'Estoile, III, 180–185. As a locus for the circulation of manuscript verse, the Parlement de Paris is in many ways similar to the English Inns of Court, where student lawyers spent much of their time composing and exchanging verse. See Jayne Elisabeth Archer, Elizabeth Goldring and Sarah Knight, eds., *The Intellectual and Cultural Worlds of the Early Modern Inns of Court* (Manchester: Manchester University Press, 2011).

5 Some good studies of pamphleteering during the Wars of Religion are Debaggi-Baranova, *À coups de libelles*; Racaut, *Hatred in Print*; Crouzet, *Les Guerriers de Dieu*; *Le pamphlet en France au 16e siècle* (Paris: Centre National des Lettres, 1983); Gilbert Schrenck, 'Jeu et théorie du pamphlet dans le *Journal de règne de Henri III (1574–1589)* de Pierre de L'Estoile', in *Traditions Polémiques* (Paris: Cahiers V. L. Saunier, 1984), 69–79. Other works tend to be simply catalogues of pamphlets. See Robert O. Lindsay and John Neu, *French Political Pamphlets, 1547–1648: a Catalog of Major Collections in American Libraries* (Madison: University of Wisconsin Press, 1969); Denis Pallier, *Recherches sur l'imprimerie à Paris pendant la Ligue (1585–1594)* (Genève: Libraire Droz, 1975). Research on pamphlets and pamphleteering in France is more extensive for the seventeenth century and the Mazarinades that appeared during and after the Fronde. See Jeffrey K. Sawyer, *Printed Poison: Pamphlet Propaganda, Faction Politics, and the Public Sphere in Early Seventeenth-Century France* (Berkeley: University of California Press, 1990). An excellent overview of the European book trade that examines the flow of seditious works into France is Robert Darnton, *The Forbidden Best-Sellers of Pre-Revolutionary France* (London: Harper Collins, 1996). The work on English and British pamphleteering is, by comparison, enormous. See, for example, Joad Raymond, *Pamphlets*

94 *The Dissemination of Scandal*

    and Pamphleteering in Early Modern Britain (Cambridge: Cambridge University Press, 2003); Alexandra Halasz, *The Marketplace of Print: Pamphlets and the Public Sphere in Early Modern England* (Cambridge: Cambridge University Press, 1997); Marcus Nevitt, *Women and the Pamphlet Culture of Revolutionary England, 1640–1660* (Aldershot: Ashgate, 2006); Paul J. Voss, *Elizabethan News Pamphlets: Shakespeare, Spenser, Marlowe and the Birth of Journalism* (Pittsburgh: Duquesne University Press, 2001).

6 L'Estoile, *JHIV*, 2 vols. (Paris: Gallimard, 1948).
7 This geographical approach to early modern information transmission is also found in de Vivo, *Information and Communication in Venice*, and in Rosa Salzberg, *Ephemeral City: Cheap Print and Urban Culture in Renaissance Venice* (Manchester: Manchester University Press, 2014).
8 M. Charles Read, *Le Tigre de 1560* (Paris: Académie des Bibliophiles, 1875); *Discours merveilleux*.
9 BnF MS Fr 25455: 'Album of Claude-Catherine de Clermont-Dampierre, maréchale de Retz', f. 8 v°.
10 L'Estoile, I, 192.
11 *Satyre Ménippée: de la vertu du catholicon d'Espagne et de la tenue des estats de Paris*, ed. Martin Martial, Textes de la Renaissance 117 (Paris: Champion, 2007). For another study of the *Satyre Ménippée* see *Études sur la* Satyre Ménippée, eds. Franck Lestringant and Daniel Ménager (Genève: Droz, 1987).
12 *Catalogue de la Bibliothèque de l'Abbaye de Saint-Victor au seizième siècle rédigé par François Rabelais, commenté par le Bibliophile Jacob [i.e. Paul Lacroix] et suivi d'un essai sur les bibliothèques imaginaires par G. Brunet*, ed. Paul L. Jacob (Paris, 1862).
13 Lazard, *Le théâtre en France au XVIe siècle*.
14 Kate van Orden, 'Cheap Print and Street Song following the Saint Bartholomew's Massacres of 1572', *Music and the Cultures of Print*, ed. Kate van Orden (New York: Garland, 2000), 271–323; Van Orden, 'Female "*Complaintes*": Laments of Venus, Queens, and City Women in Late Sixteenth-Century France', *Renaissance Quarterly* 54, 3 (Autumn, 2001): 801–45.
15 L'Estoile, III, 92.

    'Pour épouser Rouet avoir un évêché,
    N'est-ce pas à Combaut sacrilège péché
    Dont le peuple murmure et l'Eglise soupire?
    Mais quand de Cornouaille on oit dire le nom,
    Digne du mariage on estime le don,
    Et au lieu d'en pleurer, chacun n'en fait que rire.'

16 A helpful introduction into the particular traditions and qualities of early modern French verse is David Hunter, *Understanding French Verse: A Guide for Singers* (New York: Oxford University Press, 2005).
17 Bellany, '"Railing Rhymes and Vaunting Verse": Libellous Politics in Early Stuart England, 1603–28', 288.
18 Of the 572 verses included by L'Estoile, 202 are sonnets.
19 Joachim Du Bellay, *Les antiquitez de Rome; Les regrets*, GF-Flammarion 245 (Paris: Flammarion, 1994).
20 'Sonnet' in *Dictionnaire des lettres françaises*, ed. Georges Grente (Paris: Fayard, 1964).
21 L'Estoile, I, 166:

    'Donc, pour le faire court, on m'a dit que Le Guast
    A fait de votre honneur un merveilleux degast,
    Que vous estes la carte où souvent il compose.'

22 Françoise Robertet had five daughters by her first marriage to Jacques Babou de la Bourdaisière; one of these daughters, also called Françoise, was the mother of

Gabrielle d'Estrées, mistress to Henri IV. Upon d'Estrées's untimely death in 1599 the following mock epitaph appeared, attacking her entire female family:

> Passerby, here lies a Venus,
> Who passed away suddenly;
> She was the Queen of all Whores,
> And her husband was the King of all Cuckolds.
> She who was recently a whore,
> All her sisters stinking whores,
> Her grandmother and all her aunts,
> Except for madame de Sourdis.

> 'Passant, cy gît une Venus,
> Qui trépassa de mort soudaine;
> Elle étoit des Putains la Reine,
> Et son Mari Roy des Cocus.
> Elle qui fut putain jadis,
> Toutes ses soeurs putains putantes,
> Sa Grand-mere & toutes ses Tantes,
> Fors que Madame de Sourdis.'

Madame de Sourdis was her aunt Isabelle Babou de la Bourdaisière; it is unknown why the author chose to make an exception of her.

23 L'Estoile, I, 166:

> 'Allez, petit fascheus, on en dit bien autant
> De ma mere et Clermont, et de vous plus avant:
> Car on dit que le Roi vous fait la mesme chose.'

24 And news travelled quickly: within a few days the citizens of Lyon or Rouen could read of events that had occurred in Paris and by the end of the century, according to L'Estoile, one could read news from the Netherlands within a week, and within twelve days for the Mediterranean, *Histoire générale de la presse française, I: Des origines à 1814*, ed. Claude Bellanger, (Paris: Presses Universitaires de France, 1969), 33.

25 Dorothy Thickett, *Estienne Pasquier (1529–1615) The Versatile Barrister of Sixteenth-Century France* (London: Regency Press, 1979), 77.

26 Out of the 572 verses in L'Estoile's collection, 166 (29%) are in Latin.

27 Thickett, *Estienne Pasquier*, 77.

28 Castelnau, II, 369–71.

29 Ibid., 369–71.

> Puella illa nobilis
> Quae erat tàm amabilis
> Commisit adulterium
> Et nuper fecit filium,
> Sed dicunt matrem reginam
> Illi fuisse Lucinam
> Et quod hoc patiebatur
> Ut principem lucraretur.

30 Houllemare, *Politiques de la parole*, 291.

31 L'Estoile, I, 75.

32 NA SP 70/84 f. 356.

> Huius coniugii hortatrix et pronuba laena est.
> Laena impura, profusa, rapax, barathrũ atq' vorago
> Regni huius quondã śtantis latéq' viventis,
> At mine funditus cuersi putrisq' iacentis.

96   *The Dissemination of Scandal*

33 For a discussion of the restriction of obscene satirical material to an elite male audience since Antiquity, see Joan E. DeJean, *The Reinvention of Obscenity: Sex, Lies, and Tabloids in Early Modern France* (Chicago: University of Chicago Press, 2002).
34 Juvenal, *The Satires*.
35 Juvenal, *The Satires*.
36 L'Estoile, I, 74–5: 'ung des premiers et plus doctes Poëtes de nostre siecle'. I would like to thank Raphaële Garrod for help with this translation.

> De quadam Maga
> Esse quid hoc dicam? Quondam Medicaea virago,
> Usa fuit Medicis, ut bene foeta foret.
> Sicque virum medicè numerosa prole beavit,
> Sicque fuit natis illa beata novem.
> Hanc tamen effoetam, Medicè quos edidit ante,
> E medio Medicè tollere fama refert.
> Utitur et tantum Thusco Medicamine sacro,
> Ut Medaea fiat, quae Medicaea fuit.

37 A recent study of manuscript circulation in Italy that examines the relationships between manuscript and print, and between manuscript and the spoken or sung performance of verse is Brian Richardson, *Manuscript Culture in Renaissance Italy* (Cambridge: Cambridge University Press, 2009). There is also a good deal of research that has been done on manuscript circulation of Renaissance verse in English. See *Print, Manuscript, and Performance: The Changing Relations of the Media in Early Modern England*, eds. Arthur F. Marotti and Michael D. Bristol, (Columbus: Ohio State University Press, 2000); Arthur F. Marotti, *Manuscript, Print, and the English Renaissance Lyric* (Ithaca, N.Y: Cornell University Press, 1995); H.R Woudhuysen, *Sir Philip Sidney and the Circulation of Manuscripts, 1558–1640* (Oxford: Clarendon Press, 1996); Jason Scott-Warren, 'Reconstructing Manuscript Networks: The Textual Transactions of Sir Stephen Powle', *Communities in Early Modern England: Networks, Place, Rhetoric* (Manchester: Manchester University Press, 2000), 18–37. I have been unable to find any studies devoted to manuscript circulation in early modern France.
38 As mentioned above, he did keep a number of League-related pamphlets bound in a separate scrapbook entitled *Les belles figures et drolleries de la Ligue*, BnF Rés. f. La 25.6.
39 L'Estoile, III, 124–5.
40 L'Estoile, *JHIV*, I, 31: 'fut publié secrètement à Paris un écrit à la main qui n'a été imprimé, composé par M. de Villeroi.'
41 Ibid., 60: 'Ce jour, me fut montrée une copie de lettre interceptée qu'on écrivait de Rome au seigneur de Mendoza, ambassadeur d'Espagne, qui était lors à Paris. Elle était datée du 21 avril 1590 et courait à Paris secrètement, il y avait un mois et plus.'
42 Ibid., 35.
43 LeRoux, *La faveur du roi*, 649.
44 Although not all material was destroyed: a large part of the Parlement of Paris's archive regarding the League was preserved by Pierre Pithou; see Sylvie Daubresse, with Bertrand Haan, *Actes du Parlement de Paris et documents du temps de la Ligue (1588–1594)* (Paris: Champion, 2012).
45 Donald R. Kelley, *The Beginning of Ideology: Consciousness and Society in the French Reformation* (Cambridge: Cambridge University Press, 1981), 244.
46 *Recueil général des anciennes lois françaises, depuis l'an 420 jusqu'à la révolution de 1789*, 29 vols, eds. Isambert et al. (Paris, 1822–23), 27.
47 Sawyer, *Printed Poison*, 24–5.
48 L'Estoile, VI, 17: 'en fust semé quantité au Palais, au Louvre, jetté dessous les portes, et quasi par tous les coins et rues de Paris.'

49 Ibid., II, 52: 'Le Dimanche XIXe, fust affichée par les quarrefours et semée par les rues de Paris la fadeze suivant imprimée en gros canon . . . Le lendemain et les jours suivants, il en fust encore jetté, et en ramassai un, allant au Palais.'
50 Ibid., IV, 83–4.
51 Ibid., *JHIV*, I, 63.
52 Ibid., I, 72: 'Ce vendredi dernier aout, on trouva au logis de Marc Antoine, au faubourg Saint-Germain, une plaisante drôlerie, mais vilaine, peinte contre une muraille: à savoir une femme nue montrant sa nature découverte, et un grand mulet auprès, avec son grand cas, qui montait dessus; et y avait au-dessus de la femme écrit: madame de Montpensier; et au-dessus de l'âne: monsieur le légat.'
53 Colin Jones, *Paris: Biography of a City* (London: Penguin, 2006), 37.
54 For an account of the difference between town criers in the provinces who used drums and those from Paris who used trumpets, see Amand-Alexis Monteil, *Histoire des Français des divers états aux cinq derniers siècles*, 5 vols. (Paris, 1853), III, 5–10.
55 *Ordonnance du Roy & de sa Court des Monnoyes, contenant les prix & poix, tant des monnoyes de France qu'estrangeres, d'Or & d'Argent, ausquelles ledict Seigneur à do'né cours en son royaume, pays, terres & seigneuries de son obeissance* [Lyon, du Rosne, 1556]. Avignon BM: 8o 14528, in Andrew Pettegree, *The French Book and the European Book World* (Leiden: Brill, 2007), 21n:
    devant la principale porte du Palais; a l'apport de Paris devant Chastelet; a la croix du Trehoir aux Halles; a l'apport Baudoyer; place de Greve devant l'hostel de la ville; au Carrefour sainct Severin; a la place Maubert pres la crois des Carmes; au carrefour du mont saincte Geneviefve pres le puis; rue sainct Jacques devant les Jacobins, & au bout du pont sainct Michel
56 Jones, *Paris: Biography of a City*, 56.
57 Babelon, *Paris au XVIe siècle*, 106. The first printer to be executed was Antoine Augereau, burned on the place Maubert in 1534. Etienne Dolet, another printer famously burned for printing heretical books met his end there in 1544.
58 Babelon, 223; Jones, *Paris: Biography of a City*, 60.
59 Shennan, *The Parlement of Paris*, 40–2.
60 Ibid., 79–80.
61 Ibid., 45.
62 Ibid., 3–4.
63 Babelon, *Paris au XVIe siècle*, 222.
64 Greffe and Lothe, *La vie, les livres et les lectures de Pierre de l'Estoile*, 13–14.
65 Houllemare, *Politiques de la parole*, 311.
66 Ibid., 311–2.
67 Babelon, *Paris au XVIe siècle*, 105.
68 Ibid., 222.
69 The Villon verse is found Hunter, *Understanding French Verse*, 52.

> 'Brettes, Suysses, n'y sçavent guères,
> Ne Gasconnes et Tholouzaines;
> Du Petit Pont deux harangères
> Les concluront, et les Lorraines,
> Angleshces ou Callaisiennes,
> (Ay-je beaucoup de lieux compris?)
> Picardes, de Valenciennes . . .
> Il n'est bon bec que de Paris.
> Prince, aux dames parisiennes,
> De bien parler donner le prix;
> Quoy qu'on dit d'Italiennes,
> Il n'est bon bec que de Paris.'

98 *The Dissemination of Scandal*

For the musical cacophony created by the cries of ambulant vendors in Paris, see Victor Fournel, *Les cris de Paris: Types et physionomies d'autrefois* (Paris: Les Editions de Paris, 2003); Georges Kastner, *Les voix de Paris: Essai d'une histoire littéraire et musicale* (Paris: Brandus, Dufour et Co., 1857). For similar examples of the musicality of the cries of ambulant vendors in Italy, see the poem by the sixteenth- and seventeenth-century Bolognese poet Guilio Cesare Croce, 'The chatterings on the business and bargains that happen everyday on the Square in Bologna', quoted in Evelyn Welch, *Shopping in the Renaissance* (London: Yale University Press, 2005), 29.

70 Jean Babelon, 'Les Laudes et Complainctes de Petit Pont', *Mélanges offerts à Émile Picot*, 2 vols, (Paris: Damascène Morgand, 1913), I, 83–89: 'Puis un garson qui crie livres nouveaulx: Farce nouvelle, prenostication!'

Original (printed) was found in library of Ferdinand Columbo, with note written *Este libro cost 2 dineros en leon por otubre de 1535 y el ducado vale 570 dineros*. The author is Jo. le Ha (found both in title and in last line) which Babelon claims refers to Jean le Happère.

71 The literature on colportage throughout Europe and France is vast. See *Colportage et lecture populaire: imprimés de large circulation en Europe, XVIe–XIXe siècles: Actes du colloque des 21–24 Avril 1991, Wolfenbüttel*, eds. Roger Chartier and Hans-Jürgen Lüsebrink, Collection 'In Octavo' (Paris: IMEC éditions, Institut mémoires de l'édition contemporaine, 1996); *Fairs, Markets and the Itinerant Book Trade*, eds. Robin Myers, Michael Harris and Giles Mandelbrote (New Castle, DE: Oak Knoll Press, 2007); Laurence Fontaine, *Histoire du colportage en Europe: XVe–XIXe siècle* (Paris: A. Michel, 1993); Pierre Brochon, *Le livre de colportage en France depuis le XVIe siècle: Sa littérature, ses lecteurs* (Paris: Librairie Gründ, 1954).

72 Welch, *Shopping in the Renaissance*, 32–55; Fournel, *Les cris de Paris*, 42–4.

73 Van Orden, 'Cheap Print and Street Song', 284–286.

74 L'Estoile, *Les belles figures*, 1: 'libelles diffamatoires contre Sa Majesté, farcis de toutes les plus atroces injures . . . imprimés à Paris et criés publiquement par les rues'.

75 Clément Janequin, *[Voulez ouyr] Les cris de Paris[?]* (Paris: La cité des livres, 1928).

76 Van Orden, 'Cheap Print and Street Song', 284.

77 Laurence Brockliss and Colin Jones, *The Medical World of Early Modern France* (Oxford: Clarendon Press, 1997); Rosa Salzberg, 'In the Mouth of Charlatans: Street Performers and the Dissemination of Pamphlets in Renaissance Italy', *Renaissance Studies*, 24/5 (2010): 638–653; Welch, *Shopping in the Renaissance*, 60; Fournel, *Les cris de Paris*, 46. For a contemporary, negative view of charlatans, see Thomas Sonnet de Courval, *Satyre contre les Charlatans, et Pseudo-medecins Empyriques. En laquelle sont amplement descouuertes les ruses & tromperies de tous Theriacleurs, Alchimistes, Chimistes, Paracelsistes, Fondeurs d'or potable, Maistres de l'Elixir et telle pernicieuse engeance d'imposteurs. En laquelle sont refutees les erreurs, abus, et impietez des Iatromages, ou Medecins Magiciens, etc* (Paris: J. Milot, 1610), 101–11.

78 L'Estoile, *JHIV*, 30–1.

79 Welch, *Shopping in the Renaissance*, 60.

80 Salzberg, *Ephemeral City*.

81 Ibid.

82 Jones, 43.

83 Lazard, *Le théâtre en France au XVIe siècle*, 39–42.

84 Jean-Claude Aubailly, *Le Monologue, le dialogue et la sottie: essai sur quelques genres dramatiques de la fin du moyen âge et du début du XVIe siècle* (Paris: Honoré Champion, 1976).

85 Sara Beam, *Laughing Matters: Farce and the Making of Absolutism in France* (Ithaca, N.Y.: Cornell University Press, 2007). For the growing political involvement of the

86 *Transnational Exchange in Early Modern Theater*, eds. Robert Henke and Eric Nicholson (Aldershot: Ashgate, 2008); Robert Henke, *Performance and Literature in the Commedia dell'arte* (Cambridge: Cambridge University Press, 2002).
87 L'Estoile, II, 113: '... il y avoit un tel concours et affluence du peuple, que les quatre meilleurs predicateurs de Paris n'en avoient pas trestous ensemble autant quand ils preschoient.'
88 *Le Reveille-matin des François, et de leurs voisins. Composé par Eusebe Philadelphe Cosmopolite, en forme de dialogues* (Edimbourg: Iaques Iames, 1574).
89 Brantôme, 636: 'De son regne, les grands pasquineurs commencerent pourtant avoir vogue, et mesmes aucuns Gentilshommes bien gallants de la Cour, lesquels je nommeray point, qui detractoyent estrangement des Dames, et en general et en particulier, voire des plus Grandes.'
90 Brantôme, 637: 'cinq ou six grandes putains anciennes, fameuses, fort lubriques, et qu'elle les surpassoit toutes quatre. Ceux-mesmes qui avoyent fait le pasquin le luy présentèrent, disans pourtant qu'il venoit d'autres, et qu'on leur avoit baillé.'
91 L'Estoile, V, 197: 'En ce mois de juillet, fut apportée une lettre à frere Maurice Poncet, curé de Saint Pierre des Arsis, laqelle en son absence fut baillée à son homme, par un quidam accoustré d'une robe longue et d'une cornette, qu'on ne peust reconnoistre ne descouvrir... Ceste lettre, communiquée au Chancelier, fut trouvée escrite de la mesme main, qu'avoient esté escrits certains placcars, environ la mi juin precedent, affichés au Louvre et autres endroits de la ville de Paris...'
92 L'Estoile, *Les belles figures et drolleries de la Ligue*, 1: criés publiquement par les rues'.
93 *Satyre Ménippée*, XLIX-L; Jean Brunel, *Un Poitevin poète, humaniste et soldat à l'époque des guerres de religion: Nicolas Rapin (1539–1608): la carrière, les milieux, l'oeuvre* (Paris: H. Champion, 2002); Nicolas Rapin, *Œuvres*, eds. Jean Brunel and Emile Brethé (Genève: Droz, 1982).
94 Nicolas Rapin, *Oeuvres latines et françoises* (Paris: Olivier de Varennes, 1610):

> Séjour heureux qui assemble
> Mille deitéz ensemble [...]
> Mais dessus toute la bande
> Une Diane commande,
> Du noble sang des Gondis,
> Par leur valeur agrandis,
> Qui dedans ce divin temple
> Sert de conduite et d'exemple.

95 BnF MS Fr 25455, f. 58 'Stances aux dames parées'; Maréchale de Retz, *Album de poésies*.
96 L'Estoile, II, 185:

> Le Roi ne m'aime pour estre trop barbu:
> Il aime à semencer le champ que n'est herbu,
> Et comme le castor chevaucher le derriere:
> Lorsqu'il foute les culs qui sont cons estrecis
> Il tient du naturel de ceux de Medicis,
> Et prenant le devant il imite son pere.

97 Gary Ferguson, *Queer (Re)Readings in the French Renaissance: Homosexuality, Gender, Culture* (Aldershot, England: Ashgate, 2008), 134–40.
98 Ibid., 140.
99 Quaintance, 'Defaming the Courtesan, 199–208, 201.

100 *The Dissemination of Scandal*

100 Viète's work on early algebra made significant steps towards modern algebra and was instrumental in the later work of Descartes. *François Viète: un mathématicien sous la Renaissance*, eds. E. Barbin, Anne Boyé, and Laurence Augereau (Paris: Vuibert, 2005).
101 François Viète, 'Prosa cleri Parisiensis ad ducem de Mena, post cædem regis Henrici III. (Prose du clergé de Paris . . . traduite en françois par Pighenat, etc.)', *Recueil de poésies françoises des XVe et XVIe siècles, morales, facétieuses, historiques* (Paris, 1855). The attribution of the poem to Viète is made by Brunel, *Un Poitevin poète, humaniste et soldat à l'époque des guerres de religion*; a version of the poem in BnF MS Fr 15499 ff. 624–625 is preceded by 'Par M. Viete Me des Requestes.'
102 Thickett, *Estienne Pasquier*; Marie Henriette de Pommerol, *Albert de Gondi, Maréchal de Retz* (Genève; Lyon printed, 1953).
103 L'Estoile, II, 133–134.
104 Thickett, *Estienne Pasquier*, 82.
105 L'Estoile, V, 349–57.
106 The three different versions are found in: L'Estoile, V, 349–357; Pierre de L'Estoile, *Journal de Henri III., Roy de France et de Pologne: ou, Mémoires pour servir à l'histoire de France.* ed. Lenglet du Fresnoy, 5 vols. (Paris: La Haye, 1744), II, 45–86; BnF MS Fr 15592 f. 117–119.
107 Scott-Warren, 'Reconstructing Manuscript Networks', 18–37, 18.
108 LaGuardia, 184.
109 'Getting one's leg over' is a British term that I think combines both elements.
110 Gustave Brunet, 'Essai sur les bibliothèques imaginaires', *Catalogue de la bibliothèque de l'abbaye de Saint-Victor au seizième siècle*, ed. Le Bibliophile Jacob (Paris: Techener, 1862), 297–390.
111 Ronsard, *Oeuvres complètes*, XII, 163–70: 'Quand ce beau printemps je voy'.
112 Jeanne d'Albret, queen of Navarre also composed a song upon the scandal of Isabelle de Limeuil's love affair with the prince of Condé. *Mémoires et poésies de Jeanne d'Albret*, ed. Alphonse, baron de Ruble (Paris: Paul, Huart et Guillemin, 1893), 137–8.
113 Van Orden, 'Cheap Print and Street Song', 278.
114 Ibid., 283.
115 *Le rosier des chansons nouvelles. Tant de l'amour, que de la guerre, contenant la pluspart les heureuses victoires obtenues en Auvergne & ailleurs* (Lyon, 1580), 13:

> Quand ce dur printemps ie voy
> Ie cognoy
> Toute malheurté au monde
> Ie ne voy que tout erreur
> Et horreur
> Courir ainsi que fait l'onde.

116 Ibid., 13:

> Nous voyons femmes parler
> Se mesler
> D'une infinité d'affaires,
> Et portans de grands cheveux
> Fardineux
> Pour à ce monde complaire.

117 Found in Adrien Jean Victor Le Roux de Lincy, *Recueil de chants historiques français, 2ᵉ série: XVIe siècle* (Paris: Charles Gosselin, 1842), 204–6.
118 Alphonse, baron de Ruble, *François de Montmorency: Gouverneur de Paris et Lieutenant du Roi dans l'isle de France (1530–1579)* (Paris: Champion, 1880).
119 Van Orden, 'Female "Complaintes"'.

120 Van Orden, 'Cheap Print and Street Song', 278.
121 Le Roux de Lincy, *Recueil de chants historiques français*, 204:

> Leroy, mon souverain maistre,
> A faict mettre
> A mon coeur grande douleur;
> Et la fureur de mon pere
> Trop amère
> Vient de trop grande rigueur.

122 Ibid., 205:

> Tu t'en vas en Italie,
> Mais complie
> Ce pendant je chanterai
> En religion facheuse,
> Fort piteuse,
> Où je te regretterai.

123 Natalie Zemon Davis, 'Printing and the People', *Society and Culture in Early Modern France: Eight Essays* (Cambridge: Polity, 1987), 219.
124 Three such songs are found in *Ample recueil des chansons tant amoureuses, rustiques, musicales que autres, cōposees par plusieurs Autheurs. Ausquelles sont adioustés plusieurs Chansons nouvelles, qui n'ont encores esté imprimées.* (Lyon: Benoit Rigaud, 1582).
125 Bellany, 'Railing Rhymes and Vaunting Verse', 288.
126 *Recueil des chansons amoureuses de ce Temps. Tant Pastorelles que Musicales, propres pour danser & ioüer sur toutes sortes d'instrumens. Augmenté de plusieurs Airs de Cour non encor veus ny Imprimez* (Paris: Pierre Des-Hayes [rue de la Harpe, a l'Escu de France, proche la Roze Rouge]), Aiii[v]:

> Les femmes de Fontainebleau,
> Les femmes de Fontainebleau,
> Ils boivent bien le vin sans eau,
> Et par force d'escus
> En font d'aucuns cocus,
> Ceux la de S. Germain en l'Ays,
> Avoient posté comme relays,
> Trestant leur devanteau
> Au commun du Chasteau.

127 Jean Pierre Seguin, 'L'Information en France avant le périodique. 500 canards imprimés entre 1529 et 1631', *Arts et traditions populaires*. année 11. no. 1–3/4 (1963); *Histoire générale de la presse française*, Bellanger.

4 Venomous Rumours
The Scandal of Isabelle de Limeuil

> Bruit: m. a rumour, common tale, publike voice, fame, reputation, report, the talke of people, the speech abroad
> *Randle Cotgrave, A Dictionarie of the French and English Tongues*[1]

On 15 March 1565, the Italian informer Gaspar Barchino wrote to the Spanish ambassador to France relaying information about Huguenot proposals. The French Protestants wanted to end the relationship that their leader, the prince of Condé, was conducting with his mistress, Isabelle de Limeuil, one of Catherine de Medici's *filles damoiselles*. If negotiations encouraging Condé to end the affair failed, claimed Barchino, the Huguenots felt 'that the Limeuil woman ought to be excommunicated, cursed and rendered to Satan's power'.[2] This dramatic ultimatum, suggesting both Huguenot desperation and the international significance of the affair, forms only part of one of the most notorious scandals of sixteenth-century Europe. The rise and fall of Isabelle de Limeuil (Figure 4.1) is probably the most cited example of proof of the existence of the 'flying squadron'. Her story has been used to illustrate Catherine's ruthless treatment of her ladies-in-waiting, but this chapter will show that the public condemnation of Limeuil was limited as a direct result of Catherine's involvement. The case study of Isabelle de Limeuil allows us to study how scandalous behaviour was treated at court, the modes by which the public were informed of the events, and what measures could be taken to control the flow of information both within the court and beyond it. Above all, the Limeuil affair offers insights into early modern notions of shame, disgrace and ridicule, and demonstrates how a noblewoman's reputation could be rehabilitated after enduring a scandal of international proportions.

Two years earlier, in 1563, Limeuil had begun a relationship with the married Louis de Bourbon, first prince de Condé and leader of the French Protestant movement. The affair was tolerated at court until, in May 1564, Limeuil became ill during a solemn audience in Dijon and shortly thereafter gave birth to a son. She was immediately removed from the court and imprisoned in the Franciscan convent at Auxonne. While contemporary observers were quick to criticise the severity of her punishment, they were unaware that Limeuil had been imprisoned not simply for sexual offences but also because she had been accused of attempting to poison the

Figure 4.1 Benjamin Foulon, *Madame de Sardiny* [Isabelle de Limeuil]
Photo (C) RMN-Grand Palais (musée du Louvre) / Stéphane Maréchalle

prince de la Roche-sur-Yon. Her alleged motive was revenge: the elderly prince had taken great delight in informing Condé that the child in Limeuil's womb was probably not his, but more likely had been fathered by one of Catherine's secretaries of state, Florimond Robertet, seigneur de Fresnes. Yet despite the widespread doubts about his paternity and taunts about his potential cuckoldry, Condé pursued Limeuil during her imprisonment and eventually helped her escape in the early months of 1565. The possibility that he might then relinquish his Protestant beliefs in order to marry the Catholic Limeuil was the stuff of gossip at courts across Europe, and was the catalyst for the Huguenot ultimatum quoted above.[3]

This is a particularly 'early modern' story: while adultery and illegitimate birth are still concerns for us today, cuckoldry, heresy and poisoning would seem out of place in a modern day scandal. Given the multiplicity of scandalous factors in this case, and the historical contingency of many of those factors, the story of Isabelle de Limeuil can shed light on early modern notions of scandal, sexual morality and crime. It also provides an illuminating study of how gossip and rumour could be expressed and controlled at the early modern court. Gossip is inherent to scandal, and particularly to accusations such as poisoning and cuckoldry which often relied on rumour rather than material evidence and were thus harder to refute.[4] This chapter exposes the ubiquity of poisoning accusations against women in the early modern period, demonstrating how the charges against Limeuil were sustainable in part because of pre-existing notions of female behaviour. The accusations against Limeuil, both those based on fact and on scurrilous rumour, resulted in her exclusion, and the chapter explores possible motives for her exclusion as well as the agency available to a noblewoman faced with imprisonment. It reveals the strategies nobles employed to defend their reputations against slander based on events both real, such as an illegitimate birth, and imagined, such as poisoning. Controlling information is always key to managing a scandal, and so we shall examine how women and men exploited, controlled and managed information in order to further their causes, revealing that, in this case at least, there appears to have been a gendered approach to information management. Ultimately, the case study establishes how Catherine de Medici's apparent manipulation of information about the affair was effective at both the local and international level, preventing the revelation of the most shocking aspect of the case, and thereby allowing the rehabilitation of her lady-in-waiting after such an infamous scandal.

The case of Isabelle de Limeuil was a clear example, claimed Catherine's critics, of the 'flying squadron' in action, and the scandal has been portrayed until now as the inevitable result of a 'female' style of rule, in which sexual allure and duplicity are exploited to succeed in politics. Catherine's superlative negotiating abilities, testified to by her contemporaries, would be depicted by historians in this reductive way. She succeeded in March 1563, for example, in convincing Condé to sign the Peace of Amboise, thereby ending the first War of Religion.

It was during these negotiations that the prince, brother of Antoine de Bourbon, king of Navarre, fell in love with the Catholic Limeuil, and quickly began to neglect both his wife, Eléonore de Roye, and his Protestant faith. The Huguenot poet and historian, Agrippa d'Aubigné, would later attribute Condé's lack of concern for the atrocities being visited on his Protestant countrymen directly to his

Figure 4.2 François Clouet, *Louis de Bourbon, Ier prince de Condé*
Source: RMN-Grand Palais (Château de Versailles), BnF Réserve NA-22 (7)-BTE

affection for Limeuil: 'If such complaints managed to reach the prince of Condé, the queen's caresses and Limeuil's affections took up all his spirit'.[5]

Although the act of taking a mistress was not only acceptable but expected of noblemen in early modern France, the new reformed religion celebrated marital fidelity.[6] Rumours of Condé's behaviour travelled all the way to Geneva, attracting the attention of Calvin himself, who, along with Théodore de Bèze, his French counterpart, wrote Condé a letter in September 1563, urging the young prince to remember his role as moral example, and underlining the damage his conduct could cause to his reputation:

> You do not doubt, my lord, that we esteem not your honour as much as we desire your salvation. Yet we would be traitors if we were to hide from you the rumours that are circulating. We do not believe that evil is being committed that would directly offend God, but when we are told that you are making love to women, such a claim will seriously damage your authority and reputation. Good people will be offended by it, the wicked will make you a laughing stock. There is distraction which impedes you and prevents you from attending to your duty.[7]

Calvin was aware that *bruit*, or rumour, could be just as dangerous to the cause of reform as confirmed fact, and the court represented many of the material, earthly delights shunned by the new religion. Protestants were eager to depict the ladies of the French court as a debauched and dangerous group of sexually aggressive women, ready to relinquish their moral values at the behest of their ambitious queen. In a letter to her son, the future Henri IV, in 1572, Jeanne d'Albret, the Calvinist queen of Navarre, would describe the French court as a place where 'it is not the men who invite the women here but the women who invite the men'.[8] Limeuil's affair with Condé is thus usually described as part of Catherine's master plan to seduce the Protestant leader away from his political and religious leanings and closer to her own political goals. The vitriolic 1575 pamphlet *Discours merveilleux* claimed that 'the Prince of Condé was then in love with the young lady Limeuil, one of her girls, whom she had sent to debauch him, as she always would use very 'honest' means to succeed in her plots'.[9]

Eventually Catholic writers would also begin to perpetuate the rumours that Catherine ordered her lady-in-waiting to begin a sexual relationship with Condé as a means of retaining him at court. In 1606, for example, the historian de Thou (approximately 10 years old at the time of the events) wrote in his memoirs:

> For the Queen having perceived that his gaze often fell on one of her maids of honour, who was her relative, she counselled this girl, in order to penetrate his secrets and to enchain him at Court, to respond to his love-making, and to omit nothing that could increase his ardent passion.[10]

The affair did provide Catherine de Medici with some political advantages: having Condé at court impeded him from ordering or participating in religious militancy. That said, Catherine's relationship with Condé was an ambivalent one. His presence at court was not without its drawbacks: militant Catholics mistrusted any negotiations with the Huguenot leader and were suspicious of her motives.

Thus, rather than submitting to an order from her queen, it seems more likely that Limeuil made an independent choice to pursue a relationship with the influential prince of Condé.

Literary Scandal

Having such a high-profile partner meant that Limeuil immediately found herself at the centre of controversy, but initially it was primarily a literary debate. Already the subject of an effusive 27 sonnet sequence by Brantôme, Limeuil then found her praises sung by the poet Pierre de Ronsard.[11] In 1563, Ronsard published his *Recueil des Nouvelles Poésies* in three volumes: Book One opens with a dedicatory sonnet to 'Ysabeau de La Tour, damoiselle de Limeuil' and Book Two contains a long song, 'Chanson en faveur de Mademoiselle de Limeuil', which begins *Quand ce beau printemps je voy*.[12] As suggested in the previous chapter, the popularity of this *chanson*, set to music by Jehan Chardavoine, was so great that it resulted in its being used for contrafacts, new song texts put to familiar tunes. Published during the period of Condé's courtship of Limeuil, it is believed that the verses were commissioned by the prince as a romantic gesture.[13] However, Ronsard's compositions for Limeuil were viewed by Protestant contemporaries as political acts because of his earlier criticism of the Reform movement and, in particular, its leader Condé. In his *Remonstrance au peuple de France* written shortly before 9 December 1562, Ronsard, a staunch Catholic, had attacked the prince's Protestant inclinations and his military actions on the Huguenots' behalf.[14] But by April 1563 Ronsard's *Responce aux injures et calomnies . . .* told a different story: Condé had recently signed the Peace of Amboise, returning to favour at court, and Ronsard felt the need to praise his former adversary, 'this magnanimous Prince / This Lord of Condé'.[15] Fortunately, Condé needed his services to win over Limeuil. Thus, in a reciprocal exchange of favour, Ronsard agreed to become a 'plume-for-hire', writing verse praising Limeuil and her princely suitor. Ronsard's new approach to the Protestant leader he had so recently criticised in the *Remonstrance* angered those Huguenots who were already disgusted at Condé's rapprochement with the queen mother. In the same year, F. de la Baronie, a pseudonym for the Reformed humanist Florent Chrestien, one of the future collaborators on the famous *Satyre Ménippée*, attacked Ronsard in verse which read his transformation of Limeuil into a Petrarchan-style goddess as an inherently political action:

> So you thought that by favouring Limeuil
> You would be regarded by him with a more gracious eye:
> But you were sore mistaken; such a quarrel
> Should not be appeased by a gentlewoman.[16]

The romantic relationships of the aristocracy were a fertile ground for the poetic imaginations of writers eager to win their favour. The political decisions made by their patrons, however, especially during the volatile period of confessional wars, meant that poets could become embroiled in political controversy.

108 *Venomous Rumours*

Chrestien's lines are a reminder of the political engagement of sixteenth-century courtly poetry. To have one's praises sung by a renowned poet was certainly good for one's image, but fame can also attract negative publicity. Isabelle's union with a high-profile partner raised her political profile also, and inevitably implicated her in the ongoing religious debate.

Tour of France

If Limeuil's behaviour was already viewed as controversial by Protestant leaders and writers, it would reach a scandalous climax during the tour of France by Charles IX in 1564. Catherine de Medici decided that when her son reached 14, the age of maturity for a king, he should make a grand tour of his kingdom in order to greet his subjects first hand. So for 27 months, from 1564 to 1566, the entire court travelled across France.[17] Florimond Robertet, seigneur de Fresnes, Catherine's secretary of state, was assiduous at the court of his queen, and would nostalgically refer to this tour in his later letters to Limeuil:

> I am reminded, however, of the unfortunate places of Danestal and Fescamps, of Caen and la Chambrolle, then of the poor lady who knew nothing about it: and I would call him very fortunate who in all those places received so much happiness.[18]

The places he refers to are the towns where the court stayed during its voyage through Normandy and Picardy in July and August 1563. The 'happiness' Fresnes received in those places would become obvious when, nine months later, during the visit to Dijon in late May 1564, at 'a solemn gathering' ['*une audience solennelle*'] Limeuil became ill and was taken into the queen's wardrobe, where she gave birth to a son.[19] She was shortly thereafter (between 22 and 29 May) taken from the court and imprisoned in the Franciscan convent in Auxonne, a few miles east of the court's location. As we have seen in the previous chapter, the news of the scandalous circumstances of the birth in Dijon was disseminated on 9 July via a 'doctor of the Sorbonne' to his friend in Paris in the form of 'news in prosaic rhyme' ['*nouvelles en rime Prosaïques*']. The news, written in Latin rhyming couplets, cast doubt on Catherine's ignorance of the affair and criticised the severity of her treatment:

> Yet, faced with this, the Queen
> Reveals herself to be so full
> Of anger, and whether ignorant or not
> Of that which the maid had done
> She gives her to the guards
> Too proud and rough;
> She is thrown into a monastery
> And seeks for consolation.
> But surely for such a trivial affair,

She does not deserve such treatment
Whereas it can be somewhat explained by
Time, personality and rank.
No one exists
Who would have acted differently.[20]

Significantly, this gossip about scandalous events was transmitted via the means of verse, a genre that, as we have seen in the previous chapter, could necessitate the sacrifice of factual accuracy for the sake of metre and rhyme. It is important to note that both the writer and recipient of the verses were university-educated males, fluent in Latin, and that their status as intellectual elites in no way prevented them from trading in gossip and hearsay. While much of the verse related actual events – the birth and subsequent imprisonment in a convent – the writer was unaware of crucial mitigating details, and painted Catherine's punishment as draconian.

The Scandal of Illegitimate Births

But was this a 'trivial affair'? How damaging to one's reputation was an illegitimate birth at court? The memoirist Brantôme claimed that the commandment was clear for the ladies of Catherine's household: she demanded that 'they had the wisdom, ability and knowledge to prevent a swelling of the stomach'.[21] If a lady-in-waiting was unlucky enough to become pregnant, all possible measures were to be undertaken to cover up the scandal. Catherine's daughter Marguerite de Valois, queen of Navarre, recounted the efforts to which she and other women of the court went in 1581 to disguise the illegitimate birth of a child to her own husband's mistress, Françoise de Montmorency-Fosseux, known as 'la belle Fosseuse':

> I had her promptly taken from the girls' bedroom and put in a separate room, with my doctor and some women to serve her, and had her very well taken care of . . . Once she had been delivered, she was taken into the girls' room where, although it had been carried out with all the discretion possible, it was unavoidable that the news would spread throughout the château. The King my husband, having returned from hunting, went to see her as was his custom. She beseeched him to make me go to see her, as I was accustomed to doing whenever any of my girls were sick, hoping by this method to put an end to the gossip that was circulating.[22]

Marguerite's comments make it clear how many people would have had access to information about this birth, including servants and medical professionals. News travelled within the royal household but could be modified by the behaviour of the most senior (in this case) female member. If the queen acted in such a way as to suggest illness rather than pregnancy, there would be few who would contradict this interpretation to her face. Thus it is not surprising to find that, when in 1557 Catherine's lady-in-waiting Françoise de Rohan was discovered to be in the late stages of pregnancy with the duke of Nemours's child, Catherine immediately returned her to her family home in Brittany to give birth, a situation studied in more detail in Chapter 5. Like Limeuil, however, some women chose to hide the pregnancy and carry on as if nothing had happened. La Ferrière claims that 'the same misfortune had occurred to Mademoiselle de Vitry, but having given birth in the morning, she had had the strength and the courage to drag herself to the ball being given in the Louvre'.[23] In all these cases, it would appear that decorum was the most significant aspect; preventing the gossip of others by creating a façade – however transparent – of seemly behaviour was more important than the reality of an illegitimate conception. Limeuil's very public delivery shattered the secrecy of her pregnancy and, with it, her reputation. Her own comments, as reported by Brantôme, reveal the lengths to which the women at court were prepared to go to erase knowledge of their illegitimate pregnancies:

> What did I know to do? It shouldn't be blamed on me, nor on my fault, nor the heat of my flesh, but on my too slow foresight: because if I had been really shrewd and well advised, like the majority of my companions, who've done just as much as I have, if not worse, but who knew very well the remedies for their pregnancies and their births, I would not now be in this pain, and no one would have known anything about it.[24]

While Limeuil may not have uttered these exact words, Brantôme's account is nevertheless enlightening as to current beliefs around, and attitudes to, conception and its prevention and treatment. No explanation is given for the 'remedies for pregnancies and births' of which Limeuil is alleged to have referred, but the comments highlight the importance of secrecy and discretion when faced with an illegitimate pregnancy.

Matthew Gerber's study of bastardy in early modern France reveals the complex and contradictory nature of French law relating to illicit births in the sixteenth century. 'The history of illegitimacy in this period', he argues, 'is thus best understood as the story of an ongoing legal and political debate'.[25] The conflicts between Roman law, customary law, church law, royal statute and judicial precedent were exacerbated by the beliefs that elites could operate beyond the (already ambiguous) letter of the law. Moreover, the assumption that an illegitimate birth was automatically shameful or harmful to a woman's social rank was complicated by the status of the father involved. When, in 1551, Lady Fleming, governess to the young Marie Stuart (later Mary queen of Scots), became pregnant with Henri II's child she is alleged to have boasted publicly:

> I did as much as I could, so that, thank God, I'm pregnant by the king, for which I feel very honoured and very happy; and I'd like to say that the royal blood is a much smoother and sweeter liquor than any other, for I have never felt so well.[26]

While her alleged flaunting of the affair ruffled the feathers of Henri II's official mistress, Diane de Poitiers, and resulted in Lady Fleming's return to Scotland, her child, Henri d'Angoulême, was recognised by his father and would go on to become Grand Prieur de France. Another royal bastard, Charles IX's son Charles de Valois, duc d'Angoulême, by his long-term mistress Marie Touchet, was also legitimated and would inherit a large part of his grandmother Catherine de Medici's estate. Limeuil would have been aware of a similar event that had already occurred in 1555, when one of her colleagues, Louise de La Beraudière, aka 'la belle Rouet', the mistress of Antoine, king of Navarre, gave birth to a son who was legitimated by his father and later became Charles, Cardinal de Bourbon. Antoine de Navarre was Condé's elder brother, so it is possible to imagine that Limeuil envisaged a similar fortuitous result for her own offspring. The identity of the father of a bastard was of primary concern for the legitimation of the child, and a powerful prince such as Condé, who was so enamoured of her as to be commissioning poetry in her honour, provided Limeuil with excellent prospects of achieving respectability.[27] The diverse cases studied here demonstrate the variety of possible outcomes of an illicit birth for a woman of the court.

Limeuil, however, found herself imprisoned within days of giving birth. At the time, courtiers were critical of Limeuil's treatment, on the grounds of what they perceived as Catherine's hypocrisy. The 1564 Latin verse quoted above reveals that public rumour ['dicunt'] painted Catherine as the instigator of the relationship as part of her plan to keep Condé on her side:

> This noble maiden
> Who was so lovely
> Committed adultery
> And recently created a son.
> But they say that the queen mother
> In this was Lucina
> And permitted this
> To profit from the prince.[28]

Depicting Catherine as Lucina, the Roman goddess of childbirth, the author credits her with overseeing the whole affair for her own ends. Brantôme related how Limeuil was 'sent away from the troop by her mistress, who it was said however had commanded her to obey the will of the said prince, because she had some business with him and needed to win him over'.[29] In Brantôme's description of events we again see how rumour ['it was said'] was crucial to the development of the myth of the 'flying squadron': Limeuil was portrayed as a sexual pawn in the service of her queen, sacrificed by her mistress when she contravened the 'rules'.

The Scandal of Poisoning

As it was, those who criticized her imprisonment were remarkably ignorant of the true circumstances. Not only had Limeuil allowed herself to become pregnant, but an accusation had also been levelled at her that she had threatened to poison Charles de Bourbon, prince de la Roche-sur-Yon, an elderly Prince of the Blood.[30] Her accuser was Charles-Robert de La Marck, comte de Maulevrier. A close companion of Henri III, Maulevrier was described by Brantôme as one who 'loved to laugh, joke around, be witty and take the mickey'.[31] His fondness for pranks of a sexual nature would go on to be satirised in the 1587 *Library of Madame de Montpensier* with the imaginary title '*Singular Treatise of the Buffooneries and Pimpings/Prostitutions of the Court, by the Count of Maulevrier*' ['*Traicté singulier des bouffonneries et maquerelages de la Cour, par le comte de Maulevrier*']. In the presence of two leading bishops, Maulevrier gave two depositions, the first on 25 May 1564.[32] He claimed that Limeuil had, on several occasions, offered to help him poison la Roche-sur-Yon, with whom he had a longstanding grudge.[33] Limeuil had attempted to ally with him against la Roche-sur-Yon, he alleged, because of her own ill-treatment by the prince. The prince's wife, Philippes de Montespedon, was Catherine's close friend and *dame d'honneur*, a role which required her to oversee discipline within the royal household. La Roche-sur-Yon was evidently pressuring his wife to control the younger ladies at court. In her deposition, Limeuil admitted to feeling singled out for criticism from the couple:

> The said princess, at the behest of the said prince her husband, aside from the pains that she gave to all the maids of the Queen, seemed to have a particular animosity towards her [Limeuil] and tried to verify whether she was pregnant, often tormenting her in front of the Queen on this matter and others.[34]

In the same deposition Limeuil claimed the prince had boasted to her lover of his efforts at discipline. She claimed he had

> undertaken to do the worst that he could to the Queen's maids, as he said himself to monsieur the prince of Condé, saying that he wanted to pursue a reformation; asking him whether in faith and conscience he wished that one lived in his house in the manner one did in the Queen's household?[35]

One can only speculate as to how accurate was the prince's depiction of the court, but Limeuil's deposition reveals that it was certainly a site of conflict over morality, and of acrimonious rivalry among courtiers. Maulevrier felt it was acrimonious enough to inspire Limeuil to thoughts of murder. In his deposition, he quoted her as saying 'all he (the prince) needs is one good meal'[36] and said that she 'took from her purse a certain white powder, which was inside some paper, and gave him part of it in a little piece of paper'.[37] He then claimed that Limeuil threatened him that 'he would be found dead on a street corner' if he were to divulge any of the plot.[38]

Poisoning a Prince of the Blood was a treasonable offence. If convicted, Limeuil could expect the same treatment that would a few years later be promised to another of Catherine's ladies-in-waiting, Charlotte-Catherine de La Trémoille, widow of Henri, prince de Condé (coincidentally, Louis's son).[39] When Henri died after a painful seizure at home in March 1588 and the coroner's report claimed he had died from poisoning, suspicion immediately fell on the person closest to him. His wife, along with two of her servants, was convicted of treason and murder. One of those servants was tortured, then drawn, hanged and quartered in the town square (the other escaped before he could be arrested). La Trémoille, who was pregnant at the time, was imprisoned and told that 40 days after giving birth she too would be tortured and executed in the same way. Upon the birth of the child, however, his extraordinary resemblance to his father removed the only motive for La Trémoille's conviction, that of alleged adultery. She was then judged not to have ordered the murder, but was still believed to have had committed adultery with the escaped servant and so had her sentence commuted to life imprisonment. She would spend seven years under house arrest, and was finally pardoned in 1596. The injustice of her story becomes all the more acute when studies of the autopsy reports reveal no burns to the victim's throat, casting doubt on the verdict of poisoning and hinting at death from natural causes.[40] The similarities between La Trémoille's situation and Limeuil's are remarkable, particularly because of the specific crime of which both were accused.

In her dissertation on poisoning in early modern France, Silje Normand reveals the ubiquity of accusations of poisoning in the period, calling it a 'poison epidemic' that reached a frenzy in the Affaire des Poisons (1679–1682) which saw 44 people executed, 218 people imprisoned for life, and Louis XIV's mistress, Mme de Montespan, accused along with many other aristocratic women.[41] Poisoning is a crime that has longstanding associations with women for reasons both physical and social.[42] A woman's lack of physical strength to overcome others makes poison more attractive as a murder weapon to her, goes the theory. Moreover, women's traditional domestic status enables and encourages the use of poison: with access to the food her loved ones eat, and the medicines they take, a woman is seen to be in the perfect position to carry out such a crime. Poisoning's secretive nature was thought to appeal to women who, for centuries, were believed to be more naturally duplicitous than men. In his 1584 study of witchcraft, Reginald Scot claimed that 'women were the first inventors and the greatest practisers of poisoning and more naturallie addicted and given thereunto than men'.[43] Such a belief in the 'natural' disposition of women to the use of poisoning has encouraged the literary trope of woman as poisoner from Circe and Medea onwards, and poison histories, Normand reminds us, abound with examples of notorious female poisoners, including the French queens Frédégonde and Brunehaut.[44] Cosmetics in the early modern period, already a site of anxiety around a woman's duplicitous ability to transform or mask herself with 'false' colours, were themselves often made of potentially poisonous materials.[45] Even menstruation was believed to make women venomous, causing noxious fumes to emanate from their eyes and mouths.[46] 'The image of poison in literature', Margaret Hallissy tells us, 'is an image of fear: fear of female power to deceive and destroy men'.[47] Thus, in much the same way that Cynthia Herrup has recognized 'the social utility of sodomy as an accusation' against men in this period because of its potency as an 'organizing principle for other fears', so poisoning can be said to operate as a means of distilling fears about women into one single felony.[48]

If being a woman in the early modern period meant that one was more likely to be accused of poisoning, being foreign meant that the suspicion was doubled. The countless treatises on poisoning in the period regularly depicted venoms as bodily invaders that encroached upon a territory that was not their own.[49] This same language was also used in early modern France towards foreigners and, in particular, towards Italians. Rampant xenophobia in France in the sixteenth century vilified Italian immigrants as sly and cowardly, stopping at nothing to usurp power from its rightful owner.[50] Limeuil's mistress, Catherine de Medici, was female, Italian and regent, and therefore alleged to be usurping male power via her immature sons, with poisoning as her preferred method of dispatching enemies. 'According to popular rumour', says Normand, 'poison first made its way to France through Catherine de Medici's Italian entourage, which contained perfumers thoroughly versed in the art of poisoning, and courtiers more than willing to use it'.[51] Eventually, Catherine's name would become synonymous with poison. She was given the nickname 'Madame la Serpente' and vicious libels circulated linking her family name with venomous qualities. After a disastrously botched coup d'état in Flanders in January 1583 in which her son, the duke of Anjou, and his forces were driven from Antwerp after attacking its citizens, L'Estoile included verses that laid the blame at Catherine's door:

> It is true that all medicine
> Must be taken at the right time and season,
> Depending on the illness. A great part of the medicine
> Of the Medici is full of poison.[52]

One of her many planned assassinations, claimed the *Discours merveilleux*, was that of Jeanne d'Albret, queen of Navarre, who died shortly before the wedding of her son Henri IV in 1572: 'Meanwhile she had recourse to Master René her hired poisoner, who by selling scents and perfumed collars to the queen of Navarre, found a way to poison her that a few days later she died, which he has since boasted of . . .'[53]

Although much of Catherine's negative reputation was developed by later Huguenot polemicists, it is true that several of her ladies suffered unsubstantiated accusations of poisoning, including, of course, Françoise de La Marck. Since her husband Villequier had openly tolerated his wife's infidelities for some time, a cuckolded husband's desire for revenge would not stand up to public scrutiny as a legal defence. To portray her as a conniving poisoner, however, would evoke more sympathy for his cause. To blame an adulterous wife of conspiring to poison her husband was an almost reflexive response in this period, adultery being the motive and poison the weapon. Even when neither adultery nor poison existed, as in the case of La Trémoille, the theory was still believable because it consolidated several stereotypical notions of woman as lustful, mysterious and dangerous. 'To analyse the idea of poison as a woman's weapon', argues Hallissy, 'is to examine a variety of misogynistic notions that find a locus and a focus in an image of primitive fear of the secret enemy'.[54] The portrayal of the women of the 'flying squadron' as both duplicitous and sexually aggressive operated within a time-honoured tradition of the female as dangerous, and made accusations of poisoning against them more believable. Maulevrier's description of the private conversations he had had with Limeuil, coupled with the veiled threat to himself were he to reveal any of the plot, fit in precisely with the contemporary expectations of a woman as secretive and dangerous, and thus more likely to poison.

That Maulevrier provided no material evidence, nor even an actual victim of poisoning, was unimportant: the accusation had strength because it was directed at one whose reputation (due to her illegitimate pregnancy) was already vulnerable. In his cultural history of rumour, Hans-Joachim Neubauer reminds us that 'rumours are not lies; in fact they are stirred up when knowledge and conditions combine'.[55] As was the case with La Marck, the rumours about Limeuil's potentially damaged honour would make the allegation of her secretive plotting more believable. In addition to its debilitating effects on the reputation of the accused, the poisoning accusation also had a practical use. 'The early modern poison metaphor', says Normand, 'much like modern metaphors of pollution and disease, was used as a means of branding and exclusion'.[56] Limeuil's refusal to conform to the moral code, by conducting a relationship with a controversial political figure, becoming pregnant and then giving birth in such a public manner, created anxiety at court where the appearance of decorum was of paramount importance. Limeuil was identified as a disorderly subject, and an accusation of poisoning – with its suspiciously coincidental timing – was an effective means of removing her from the household.

Intelligence and Information

At Auxonne, Limeuil was placed in the Franciscan convent under the guard of Claude de Saulx, seigneur de Ventoux et de Torpes, the king's lieutenant and local governor. A convent was the accepted lieu of imprisonment for a noblewoman who had incurred the monarch's wrath. As we have seen, there is precedence for such an imprisonment within the ladies of Catherine's entourage. Only 12 years previously, in 1556, Jeanne de Halluin de Piennes, one of Catherine's *filles damoiselles*, was imprisoned in the Filles-Dieu convent in Paris for approximately seven months. Her crime, as described in the previous chapter, was to have become clandestinely married to her admirer of six years, François de Montmorency, son of the Constable Anne de Montmorency, Henri II's national military commander. In a fit of rage, the Constable sent his son to Rome to seek a papal annulment and had Jeanne imprisoned within the Benedictine convent of the Filles-Dieu on the rue Saint-Denis, originally a refuge for reformed prostitutes but which by the late sixteenth century was regarded as 'an acceptable placement for daughters of the lesser nobility and bourgeoisie'.[57] More comfortable than some of the more ascetic convents, and lax in its observance of the Benedictine rule, the Filles-Dieu was where many prominent families placed their daughters when marriage prospects looked bleak, a common situation for second and later born daughters of the nobility. A noblewoman imprisoned there for some infraction would thus find herself cared for by women of a similar social rank and background. Notwithstanding its more comfortable setting however,

Piennes's seven-month imprisonment, which ended only once Montmorency was safely married to Diane de France, separated her from her family and friends and made her disgrace public. Her long imprisonment also highlights the arbitrariness of the punishment that could be meted out to a woman of impeccable aristocratic standing when she threatened a man's ambitious plans for his patrilineage.

Similarly, Limeuil's lineage did not prevent her from imprisonment, not even during her recovery from childbirth. Although no mention is ever made of the baby (who would not survive infancy) or her post-partum recuperation by Limeuil or de Saulx in the letters they write, de Saulx's letters to Catherine are poignant in their description of Limeuil's emotional appearance:

> I assure you she has received no more news since the depart of my lords du Puys and de Serlan [the interrogating officers], which is the cause of the great discomfort that she is in, believing herself abandoned by all in whom she had hope, and I cannot believe that she can survive in this state for long if a woman may die of melancholy, for in seeing her face it seems to me that she must soon die. Begging you very humbly that it will please Your Majesty to have her put somewhere else, or else to have pity on her.[58]

Despite her distressed emotional state as testified to by de Saulx, Limeuil was energetic in her defence. While she admitted in her interrogation to animosity between herself and the prince de la Roche-sur-Yon, she strongly denied any involvement in a plot to poison him. She claimed 'never to have had nor seen such drugs, and often had desired to see some sublimé or Spanish white, because she had heard that there were those who used it for make-up', demonstrating her knowledge of the links between early modern cosmetics and poison.[59] After establishing her own innocence, Limeuil then went on the offensive, turning the focus of the deposition onto the count's reputation. Had she wanted to poison someone, she said, the count would have been the last person she would have confided in, since he 'was notoriously thought of by everyone as a madman and a drunk'.[60] Whether she was aware of it or not, Limeuil's response accorded with the legal doctrines of 'fama' and 'infamia': she initially established her own honour, reputation and trustworthiness, and then attacked those of her detractor.[61] Both in Roman law and in customary law (both of which operated in sixteenth-century France), individuals marked with the condition of 'infamia' due to their behaviour and reputation were prevented from testifying in court.[62] Limeuil's attack on Maulevrier's mental capacity and fondness for alcohol – in particular her use of the term 'notoirement', meaning well-known or notorious – referred to the public knowledge, or fama, of Maulevrier's behaviour and was a shrewd means of rendering his testimony redundant and inadmissible.[63]

Her deposition given, Isabelle then wrote a letter to her mistress, Catherine de Medici, to reveal her emotions at the accusations levelled against her:

> Madame, after having heard from their lordships Du Puy and Sarlan the causes which moved Your Majesty to send them to me, I have been so tormented that

without the help of God and the hope that I have in your goodness which would never accept such a calomny and false accusation, such as the one about which they interrogated me, I would have entered into the greatest despair that ever a poor creature could be in, having never been so abandoned by God as to have conceived nor put such a wickedness in my thoughts. But since it has pleased Your Majesty to have warned me of it, I beseech you most humbly to do me this grace of seeking to know the truth of it; and where it shall be found that I have thought such a wicked thought, I beseech you most humbly to seek to make such an exemplary justice that one could make of the most unfortunate woman in the world; and when it has pleased God to let you know of my innocence in this, I beseech you most humbly, for the honour of those to whom I belong, have done the same justice to the false accuser, as I would have merited, having committed such a fault. Beseeching you most humbly, Madame, to believe that I did not have, nor ever have had, the will but to do you most humble and loyal service.[64]

Rather than reply to her directly, which would have been inappropriate considering Limeuil's status as a potential traitor, Catherine chose to have one of her ladies who was also a relative of Limeuil, Charlotte de Vienne, dame de Cureton, write to her:

I pray you to console yourself and to remind yourself that the place wherein you are will help you very much. Also you must be sure to conduct yourself wisely, for all these things happen for a good reason. Given that it was commanded by such a wise princess, obeying her as you should nothing can come of this but good, and I hope that you will soon have news from your good relatives and friends: which is why I will not write you a longer letter, except to recommend myself most humbly to your good grace, praying God to give you His.[65]

Cureton's reference to the 'wise princess' who had commanded the imprisonment reveals that Catherine was using this approach as part of a larger strategy to 'help' Limeuil, although this long-term plan may not have been evident to others.

Meanwhile, Limeuil appears to have been aware that the most effective means of combating scurrilous rumours was to pro-actively disseminate verifiable intelligence. Indeed, her letters and those of her guardian, de Saulx, reveal a remarkable amount of agency on her part even when imprisoned and excluded from court. De Saulx's letters to the queen mother show that he was obeying her order to make doubles of all letters both written and received by Limeuil. Nevertheless, de Saulx felt that Limeuil was capable of bypassing these measures by exploiting the sympathies of allies on both sides of the confessional divide:

I fear only one thing which is, given her religion, the walls are here in several places very low, and having won over all the Franciscans, as she has done, she will just throw the letters over the said wall or that they will be thrown over to her; . . . Or even that one night someone will throw her some kind of ladder to escape over the said walls, and afterwards hide her in the house of some Huguenot of this town: I do not say this without cause, because I was warned about it by my soldiers, that the said basque [Condé's servant] spoke to two or three of the most prominent Huguenots of this said town . . .[66]

Limeuil had, through force of personality, provoked sympathy among the Catholic nuns who were, ironically, allowing her to exploit the poor defences of the convent to communicate with Condé's Huguenot allies. Her intelligencing activities did not stop there: even as Limeuil was moved around from Auxonne to Mâcon, Lyon and Vienne – all towns situated along the Rhône – as the court moved around the south-east on its tour of the country, she kept Condé informed with crucial details that would help him to find her and help her escape: 'I am writing this letter to you while en route to Mâcon: but from there I do not know where they will take me. My driver is a valet of the queen's chamber called Gentil; you know him well'.[67]

She also regularly petitioned Condé to mobilise influential nobility on her behalf, asking him to write not only to the queen, but also to the maréchal de Bourdillon, Imbert de la Platière, and the duchess of Savoy, Marguerite de France, who had come to Lyon to visit her nephew the king.[68] Limeuil's actions demonstrate both a remarkable knowledge of the visitors to court – information probably gleaned from the bearers of the numerous letters – and initiative in exploiting her ties to such prestigious members of the nobility who could plead her case with the queen.

Gossip and Cuckoldry

Limeuil's ability to send and receive factual and reliable intelligence even while imprisoned stands in contrast to Condé's regular complaints to her of his ignorance of her whereabouts, and of his suffering due to slanderous gossip. Back at court, Fresnes was evidently exploiting his privileged position as secretary of state to taunt Condé with his access to sensitive information:

> Monsieur du Fresne tells me very often that you write to him of your news, but I am unable to find out where you have been sent. I find it very surprising, since you have the means to write to certain people, that I am unable to receive your letters also, for you know that there is not a man in the world who is as aggrieved at your pains as I.[69]

Although his emotions could be staged for dramatic effect rather than genuine, Condé's letters to Limeuil reveal his jealousy of Fresnes's relationship with her, particularly because it threatened him with the abhorrent label of cuckold, the most shaming of labels for a man in the early modern period. His resentment of Fresnes was a longstanding one; Brantôme related an anecdote in which Fresnes, in the presence of Condé, mocked a courtier for only having had sexual intercourse five times on his wedding night: 'My God! I had a dozen rides in 24 hours on the most beautiful mount that could be found here, or anywhere else in France'. The lord [Condé] was dismayed, claimed Brantôme,

> because with that he learned what he had feared for a long time; and given how much in love he was with this princess, he was really angry for what he had chased for such a long time in this way without ever taking anything, and the other had been so happy in his hunt and in his taking.[70]

That Fresnes's claims of sexual performance seem hyperbolic and therefore untrue did not appear to be an issue for either Brantôme or Condé. Male reputation in the early modern period was based on claims of virility, however much those claims were falsified. David LaGuardia argues that these claims make up 'the foundations of cuckold literature: the fantasy of masculine virility, which works in combination with the myth of women's insatiability; the idea that writing about eternally virile men and equally receptive women is potentially infinite'.[71] Cuckoldry anxiety, ubiquitous in the period, was a fear rooted in this homosocial male activity of boasting of one's sexual exploits, whether factual or fantastical.[72] As an activity that relied entirely on hearsay (at least on sexual matters), male-only gossip was thus competitive and damaging by its very nature, deliberately attempting to create jealousy in the listener.

Condé did not hide his fear of having been deceived from Limeuil: 'For I assure you, my love, that it annoys me greatly that one can find in your actions to say: 'To whom belongs this child?', as if two persons had been there'.[73] After having originally been put in the care of a local woman, the baby was now in the arms of its proud alleged father, who viewed it as a physical manifestation of the loyalty Isabelle had shown to him: 'I assure you that our son is a beautiful and strong cord to tie us together forever'.[74] Condé, perhaps disingenuously, claimed ignorance of a matter that was clearly common knowledge at court. The prince de la Roche-sur-Yon's earlier comments, that Condé 'was well fooled if he thought that if she were pregnant it was by him, and that no one else had had a part in it' would have added to Condé's fear of being reputed as a cuckold.[75] The public nature of the birth, however, would catapult those rumours from within the palace walls to the wider public arena. Condé's cuckolded state was also alluded to in the Latin news verses sent to Paris which punned on the word '*secretis*' to refer to Fresnes's position as secretary of state:

> But many say that the father
> Is not the prince, but is another
> Who to the King is secret;
> All is sufficiently known.[76]

Here the use of 'many say' ['multi dicunt'] alludes to the very public knowledge of Condé's cuckolding by a man of lower rank, and the verse's author appears to delight in this public shaming of such a high-profile figure.

International Scandal

The scandal would continue to grow on an international scale: in a dispatch on 11 April 1565 from France to the English court, it was claimed that 'The Prince of Condé has by a certain gentleman stolen Mademoiselle de Lymoel from Tournon, where she was kept, and has her with him'.[77] Similarly, Gaspar Barchino's dispatch of 15 March 1565 to the Spanish ambassador Alava quoted at the beginning of this chapter related how Condé had recently received a letter which ended with the words 'La demoiselle est arrivée' ['The lady has arrived'] and how he ordered that she be brought to him.[78] If these two dispatches are to be believed, Limeuil left – or escaped from – prison at some point around March 1565, 10 months after her arrest. As these exchanges between France, England, Italy and Spain demonstrate, the 'Limeuil affair' was a considerable matter on the European political scene: the leader of the Huguenots was seen to be wavering in his devotion to his faith because of his love for her, putting the entire cause of the French Reformation in jeopardy. When Calvin wrote to Condé back in September 1563 to warn him of 'distractions', Condé was still married to the staunchly Protestant Eléonore de Roye, but after her death in July 1564 he was free to marry a woman from either religion. Barchino was clearly delighted at the prospect of Condé's defection to Catholicism and discussed how the Spanish could capitalize on what he saw as Condé's 'weakness' for women by offering him 'a beautiful, rich and honoured woman like Monsieur de Guise's sister [Catherine-Marie de Lorraine]'.[79] Intriguingly, the letter reveals that although Catholics felt that providing Condé with a suitable woman was key to retaining his religious loyalty, the Catholic Limeuil was explicitly not a candidate. Barchino also revealed the extreme measures the Protestant leaders were prepared to take to convince Condé to give up 'la sua Limolia' ['his Limeuil']: in the first instance, the leading ministers would consult privately with him, urging him to forsake her for fear of the 'peril and personal infamy, and the scandal felt by the whole religion', and persuading him to take a wife; failing that, the 'principal gentlemen of the religion and his intimate friends' would present him with the same reproaches, threatening him with the ultimatum of being left deserted by his friends; finally, and most interestingly, they would 'excommunicate Limeuil, anathematise her, and declare her to be devoted to Satan's power'.[80] In this final option, we can see a conscious decision to portray Limeuil as diabolical, a traditional response to a woman whose sexual power was perceived as threatening – in this case, on an international scale.

Barchino then discussed Catherine's role in the matter:

> The Catholics say that she uses Limeuil to impede Condé's marriage to the niece of the cardinal of Lorraine. The Protestants say that by the same means she wants to tempt Condé and turn him into a papist, as was done to Vendôme [Condé's brother, Antoine de Navarre] stricken with love for la Rouet [Louise de La Beraudière, who had his child]. I am not of the opinion either of the one or the other, but I think that, if however she has a part in the Limeuil affair, it is to attract Condé to her own party and so that he depends on no one but her.[81]

Barchino's comments once again reveal that communication between elite men, in this case ambassadorial intelligence, could be nothing more than scurrilous rumour and unsubstantiated claims. The comments make it clear that contemporaries on both sides of the religious divide believed that Catherine was prepared to sacrifice the honour and reputation of her ladies-in-waiting to further her own political goals.

The Huguenot opposition to Condé's cohabitation with Limeuil was so strong, claimed Barchino, that the affair had caused a serious rupture in Condé's alliance with one of his most loyal friends, the cardinal de Châtillon, who had deserted him for Paris along with many of the other Protestant followers. Despite this, or perhaps because of it, Condé made a public display of his love for Limeuil by commissioning Ronsard to write further love sonnets in her honour. Ronsard's *Elégies, Mascarades et Bergeries* appeared sometime in July or August 1565, with several poems in honour of Condé and Limeuil.[82] While the imagery of the sonnet explicitly dedicated to Limeuil ('Douce beauté à qui je doy la vie'), particularly the reference to the woman's eyes as the vehicle for transmission of grace, is stock Petrarchan figurative style, it can also be interpreted as Ronsard's praise of the woman who appeared to be succeeding in converting Condé back to the Catholic faith. As it was, Condé would crush Catholic hopes and cement his status as Huguenot leader by his marriage to Françoise d'Orléans, duchesse de Longueville, daughter of the staunchly Protestant Rohan-Orléans family, on 8 November 1565. When it became clear that Limeuil had not been successful in converting Condé, Ronsard was keen to deny any personal involvement with the lady in the poem and resentful of the imposition placed on him by patrons such as Condé. In the editions published from 1567 to 1572, Ronsard included a prefatory comment to the sonnet by his friend Remy Belleau:

> The Poet told me several times that this sonnet was not made to represent his passion, but on behalf of someone who prayed him write it; he infinitely wished he were not sought out by such importunate people, who cause him more displeasure in telling him of their loves, than he has in singing his own.[83]

Thus, Limeuil found herself without a partner, exiled from court, discarded as a literary muse and with her reputation tarnished by an illegitimate birth and a stay in prison.

Management of Rumour

Limeuil's scandalous story of cuckoldry, illegitimate birth and imprisonment would go on to be recounted in almost every history of the Valois court; however, no historian mentioned the poisoning accusation until 1863, when a dossier belonging to L'Aubespine, one of the interrogating bishops, was transcribed and published.[84] According to that dossier, the final meeting with the bishops was a confrontation between Limeuil and Maulevrier on 18 July 1564, in which both parties stood by their original assertions. Despite Isabelle's pleas for justice to the queen mother, no other witnesses were ever interviewed, even those mentioned by name in Maulevrier's deposition. No further action was taken against either party, however, Limeuil remained in prison for a further eight months, all the while being moved to locations close to the itinerant court where de Saulx's letters show that Catherine was keeping her under observation. It would appear that Catherine suppressed the information within the dossier thereby keeping the accusation of poisoning a secret. Even Fresnes, in his privileged position as Catherine's secretary, seems to have been unaware of the poisoning accusation against Limeuil, never mentioning it in his letters to her. Such behaviour would indicate that an accusation of poisoning was potentially more damaging to one's reputation than an illegitimate birth. Catherine's decision to keep Limeuil imprisoned appears to show that, rather than – or as well as – punishing her, Catherine was trying to safeguard Limeuil's reputation by removing her from the gossip-fuelled environment of the court while allowing her contemporaries to assume that the red herring of illegitimate birth, rather than poison, was the cause of her disgrace.

That the case against Limeuil was not taken any further seems to indicate that Catherine believed the accusations of poisoning to be without substance, but was aware of the links, both metaphorical and literal, between rumour and poison in early modern France. In the same way that venom was thought to invisibly attack a healthy body, causing it to rot from inside, slanderous rumours and gossip were often portrayed as poisons that infiltrated society to critically injure a person's reputation. In his 1690 *Dictionnaire universel*, Antoine Furetière defined 'venom' in its figurative sense as 'speeches of slander, of the hatred one keeps in one's heart, which would cause one to hurt one's enemy as much as possible'.[85] Moreover, when it comes to the term *bruit*, the illustrative example given by Furetière speaks volumes about the supposed links between gossip and poison: 'The Chamber established to try the poisoners [the *Chambre Ardente* of the Affaire des Poisons] was much talked about [*a fait grand bruit*], made a big impact in France'.[86] Aware of the destructive power of the poison accusation, Catherine successfully suppressed the venomous denunciation of her lady-in-waiting and let the *bruit* of the scandalous pregnancy circulate instead.

'Poison', as Normand reminds us, 'was associated with displacement – its perpetrators were often those who simply did not belong'.[87] If the accusation of poisoning had been an attempt to exclude Limeuil because of the threat her behaviour presented to the status quo, it was Catherine's responsibility as her guardian to limit the damage to the reputation of her *fille damoiselle* by removing her until the controversial relationship with Condé had run its course. Having achieved that, she invited Limeuil to return to court two years later, paving the way for her wedding, on 20 January 1569, less than four years after she was released from prison, to the wealthy Italian financier Scipion Sardini with whom she would go on to have five children.[88] The widely-held theory, therefore, that Catherine manipulated Limeuil for her own political ends and then cruelly abandoned her because of her failure to keep Condé on the side of the crown is unfounded. Instead, the evidence shows her to have been concerned about the reputation of her household, discreet when scandal broke, and pro-active when it came to rehabilitating someone's honour. What has been described for centuries as an abuse of monarchical power can be interpreted instead as effective housekeeping.

Early modern stereotypes of women as frail, irrational and prone to gossip are belied by the examination of Limeuil's case, in which the men involved appear to favour rumour and gossip over the transmission of factual and reliable information. While the men in this case sent each other verse that only told half the story and boasted to each other of fictitious sexual exploits, Limeuil befriended information-bearers from both religions who relayed vital intelligence both to and from her cell. Meanwhile, Catherine controlled the flow of information about Limeuil, concealing it from even her most trusted secretaries, in order to protect her lady's reputation. If we can argue in this case for a 'gendering' of information management, we also witness a gendering of accusations: while poisoning was seen as a particularly 'female' crime, the shaming epithet of cuckold was a damaging attack on a man's reputation. That both could be based purely on scurrilous rumour highlights the arbitrary and fraught nature of creating and defending personal honour and reputation in the early modern period. But not only personal honour was at stake in this case. If Condé had abandoned the Protestant cause to wed the Catholic Limeuil, the ramifications for French Protestantism – and European history – would have been enormous. One can only speculate about whether the taunting of Condé about cuckoldry was a significant factor in his decision to relinquish Limeuil, but were it so, it would demonstrate the power of gossip and rumour on a long-term, international scale. The traditional view of gossip as petty and trivial, concerned 'only' with details of interpersonal relationships, therefore needs re-evaluation, especially when those relationships are between politically influential actors.

The case of Isabelle de Limeuil also helps to delineate the hierarchy of scandal in the early modern period: while an illegitimate birth was generally deemed scandalous by contemporary observers, circumstances such as the legitimation of the bastard could mitigate the scandal to the extent that the mother could go on to make a later lucrative marriage. What was clearly more permanently damaging to a noblewoman's reputation was the accusation of poisoning, its reliance on rumour and gossip rather than hard evidence making it difficult to refute. It is a danger of which Catherine seems to have been aware, successfully concealing the accusation against Limeuil by the diversionary tactic of imprisonment. The exclusion of troublesome noblewomen by placing them in convents appears to have been an oft-used tactic in this period, but the letters that travelled between Limeuil's cell and the court reveal the peculiarly porous conditions of such an imprisonment, with a seemingly constant stream of information and material goods being transmitted to and from the prisoner. Those letters demonstrate the importance of agency: how a resourceful woman such as Limeuil could mobilise prestigious noble connections to rehabilitate her reputation and effect her escape.

Limeuil's story also gives us a sense of the very literary manner in which controversy in the early modern period was explored and discussed: the Latin verses sent from the travelling court back to Paris demonstrate how news of the court could be quickly transmitted to a wider audience, even when the court was on tour. Their depiction of Catherine as interfering in the personal relationships of her ladies-in-waiting for her own political ends reveals that the literary trope of the flying squadron had begun contemporaneously with Catherine's time in power. That the news was written in such a style – Latin rhyming couplets – reveals that, for the intellectual fraternity, the transmission of news was as concerned (if not more concerned) with entertainment as with the relaying of facts. Their participation in the public rumours of Condé's cuckolding by a man of lesser rank highlights what was arguably the most scandalous aspect of the story for contemporary observers. This phenomenon in which politically significant information was expressed in poetic form could also operate in reverse: Ronsard's love poetry written in praise of Limeuil took on a political aspect when Protestant writers saw his pursuit of Condé's patronage as a politically-charged act, reminding us again how the religious disputes continually overlapped into every facet of life in sixteenth-century France. It was the religious aspect that made the Limeuil affair an international scandal: the concern in the Vatican, Madrid, London and Paris as to whom Condé might remarry reveals the centrality of successful marriage negotiations among aristocratic society, and the pressures put on those negotiations by the religious dispute. The interweaving of the confessional struggle with aristocratic marriage structures is also discussed in the following chapter, which observes the fall-out throughout the extended family network when those structures broke down irrevocably.

Notes

1 Randle Cotgrave, *A Dictionarie of the French and English Tongues* (London: Adam Islip, 1611).
2 *Archivo Documental Español: Negociaciones con Francia*, 11 vols (Madrid: Real Academia de la Historia, 1953), VII, 186, Gaspar Barchino to Frances de Alava, 15 March 1565: 'che la Limolia si dovesse scomunicare, anatemizare et dare in potere di Satanasso'. The letter is also cited, with French translation, in Henri d'Orléans, duc d'Aumale, *Histoire des princes de Condé pendant les XVIe et XVIIe siècles* (Paris: Michel Lévy, 1863), 553. The proposal is ambiguously worded, although were it to be taken literally it would imply a surprising amount of complicity between Huguenot leaders and the Papacy who, one assumes, would be responsible for excommunicating the Catholic Limeuil.
3 The documents concerning Limeuil's story can be found in Henri d'Orléans, duc d'Aumale, 'Information contre Isabelle de Limeuil (mai-août, 1564)', *Miscellanies of the Philobiblon Society*, VII (London: Whittingham and Wilkins, 1862–3). The story is situated within its historical context in La Ferrière, *Trois amoureuses au XVIe siècle*. The case and its historiography is also discussed in Pierre Bayle, *The Dictionary Historical and Critical of Mr Peter Bayle* (London: Knapton et al., 1734–1738), III, 832–5: 'Limeuil'.
4 A study that argues for the term 'talk' rather than the pejorative term 'gossip' is *Fama: The Politics of Talk and Reputation in Medieval Europe*. For studies of slander and seditious speech see Gowing, *Domestic Dangers*, and David Cressy, *Dangerous Talk: Scandalous, Seditious, and Treasonable Speech in Pre-Modern England* (Oxford: Oxford University Press, 2010). For studies of rumour, see *Rumor Mills*, eds. Gary Alan Fine, Véronique Campion-Vincent, & Chip Heath (New Brunswick, NJ: Transaction, 2005); Hans-Joachim Neubauer, *The Rumour: A Cultural History*, trans. Christian Braun (London: Free Association Books, 1999).

5 Agrippa d'Aubigné, *Histoire universelle*, 10 vols, ed. André Thierry (Genève: Droz, 1982), II, 205: 'Si telles plaintes alloyent jusques au prince de Condé, les caresses de la roine et les amours de Limeuil employoyent tout son esprit'. D'Aubigné, who was seven at the time of the events, wrote the *Histoire* in 1616–18, over 50 years later.
6 Stuart Carroll, *Blood and Violence in Early Modern France* (Oxford: Oxford University Press, 2006), 237.
7 *Lettres de Jean Calvin*, ed. Jules Bonnet (Paris: Meyrueis, 1854), 537–9, Jean Calvin and Théodore de Bèze to Louis de Bourbon, 17 September 1563: 'Vous ne doubtez pas, Monseigneur, que nous n'aimions vostre honneur, comme nous désirons vostre salut. Or nous serions traistres en vous dissimulant les bruits qui courent. Nous n'estimons pas qu'il y ait du mal où Dieu soit directement offensé, mais quand on nous a dict que vous faites l'amour aux dames, cela est pour déroger beaucoup à vostre authorité et réputation. Les bonnes gens en seront offensez, les malins en feront leur risée. Il y a la distraction qui vous empesche et retarde à vaquer à vostre devoir'.
8 Castelnau, I, 859, Jeanne d'Albret to Henri de Navarre: 'ce ne sont pas les hommes ici qui prient les femmes, ce sont les femmes qui prient les hommes'.
9 *Discours merveilleux*, 166: 'le Prince de Condé estoit dès lors amoureux de la damoiselle Limeuil, une de ses filles, qu'elle luy avoit baillée pour le debaucher, comme elle se servoit tousjours de fort honnestes moyens pour parvenir à ses desseins'.
10 Jacques-Auguste de Thou, *Histoire universelle de Jacques-Auguste de Thou depuis 1543 jusqu'en 1607, traduite sur l'édition latine de Londres . . .*, 16 vols (Londres [i.e. Paris], 1734), IV, 537: 'Car la Reine s'étant apperçûë qu'il jettoit souvent les yeux sur une de ses filles d'honneur, qui étoit sa parente, elle conseilla à cette fille, pour pénétrer dans ses secrets, & pour l'enchaîner à la Cour, de répondre à son amour, & de ne rien omettre pour augmenter de plus en plus son ardente passion'.
11 The sonnet sequence appears in Brantôme, 752–768.
12 Ronsard, XII, 25–6: 'Chanson en faveur de Madamoiselle de Limeuil'; 163–70: 'Quand ce beau printemps je voy'.
13 Fernand Desonay, *Ronsard poète de l'amour*, 3 vols. (Brussels: Palais des Académies, 1952–59), II, 201–10.
14 Ronsard, XI, 61–107: 'Remonstrance au peuple de France'.
15 Ibid., 109–179: 'Responce de de Ronsard . . . aux injures et calomnies de je ne sçay quels Predicans & Ministres de Genève, sur son Discours & Continuation des Miseres de ce Temps', 174, lines 1148–9: 'ce magnanime Prince,/Ce Seigneur de Condé'.
16 Fernand Desonay, *Ronsard, poète de l'amour*, 3 vols. (Brussels: Palais des Académies, 1952–59), II, 203:

> Ainsique tu pensois qu'en faveur de Limeuil
> Tu recevrois de lui un plus gracieux oeil:
> Mais tu t'es bien trompé: une telle querelle
> Ne se doit apaiser par une damoiselle.

17 Jean Boutier, Alain Dewerpe and Daniel Nordman, *Un tour de France royal: Le voyage de Charles IX (1564–1566)* (Paris: Aubier Montaigne, 1984); Victor E. Graham and W. McAllister Johnson, *The Royal Tour of France by Charles IX and Catherine de' Medici – Festivals and Entries 1564–6* (Toronto: University of Toronto Press, 1979).
18 Aumale, 'Information contre Isabelle de Limeuil', 63: 'Il me souviendra, cependant, du malheureux lieu de Danetal et Fescamp, de Can et de la Chambrolle, lors de la pouvre dame qui n'en sçavoit rien: et diray bien heureux celuy qui en tous ses lieulx a receu tant de contentement'.
19 Ibid., 7.
20 Castelnau, II, 371:

> Contra hoc tamen regina
> Se ostendit tantum plena
> Cholera, ac si nescisset

> Hoc quod puella fecisset,
> Et dedit illi custodes
> Superbos nimis et rudes,
> Mittens in monasterium
> Quærere refrigerium.
> Sed certe pro tam levi re
> Sic non debebat tractare,
> At excusare modicum
> Tempus, personam et locum.
> Aliis non sit taliter
> Quæ faciunt similiter.

21 Brantôme, 64: 'elles eussent de la sagesse et de l'habileté et sçavoir, pour engarder l'enflure du ventre'. Brantôme's comments, however, must always be considered in the context of his intended male-only audience; see LaGuardia, *Intertextual Masculinity*, 181–5.

22 *Mémoires et lettres de Marguerite de Valois*, ed. Guessard: 'Je la feis promptement oster de la chambre des filles et la mis en une chambre escartée, avec mon medecin et des femmes pour la servir, et la feis tres-bien secourir... Estant delivrée, on la porta en la chambre des filles, où, bien que l'on apportast toute la discretion que l'on pouvoit, on ne peust empescher que ce bruict ne fust semé par tout le chasteau. Le Roy mon mary, estant revenu de la chasse, la va voir comme il avoit accoustumé. Elle le prie de faire que je l'allasse voir, comme j'avois accoustumé d'aller voir toutes mes filles, quand elles estoient malades, pensant par ce moyen oster le bruict qui couroit'.

23 La Ferrière, *Trois amoureuses*, 86: 'pareil malheur était arrivé à mademoiselle de Vitry; mais, accouchée le matin, elle avait eu la force et le courage de se traîner au bal donné au Louvre'. Louise de l'Hospital, damoiselle de Vitry, a *dame d'honneur* to Catherine de Medici, and wife of Jean de Symier, master of the wardrobe for the duc d'Anjou.

24 Brantôme, 468: 'Qu'y sçaurois-je faire? il ne m'en faut point blasmer, ny ma faute, ny la poincte de ma chair, mais ma trop lante prévoyance: car, si je fusse estée bien fine et bien advisée, comme la pluspart de mes compaignes, qu'y ont fait autant que moy, voire pis, mais qui très-bien ont sceu rémédier à leurs groisses, et à leurs couches, je ne fusse pas maintenant en ceste peine, et n'y eust-on rien cogneu'.

25 Matthew Gerber, *Bastards: Politics, Family, and Law in Early Modern France* (Oxford: Oxford University Press, 2012), 5.

26 Brantôme, 634: 'J'ay fait tant que j'ay pu, que, à Dieu mercy, je suis enceinte du roy, dont je m'en sens très-honnorée et très-heureuse; et si je veux dire que le sang royal a je ne sçay quoy de plus suave et friande liqueur que l'autre, tant je m'en trouve bien'.

27 For the very different situation in Italy, where bastardy among ruling families was much more common, see Helen S. Ettlinger, 'Visibilis et Invisibilis: The Mistress in Italian Renaissance Court Society', *Renaissance Quarterly* 47, no. 4 (Winter, 1994): 770–92.

28 Castelnau, II, 371:

> Puella illa nobilis,
> Quæ erat tam amabilis,
> Commisit adulterium
> Et nuper fecit filium.
> Sed dicunt matrem reginam
> Illi fuisse Lucinam;
> Et quod hoc patiebatur
> Ut principem lucraretur.

29 Brantôme, 468: 'renvoyée hors de la troupe par sa maistresse, qu'on disoit pourtant que sadite maistresse luy avoyt commandé d'obéir aux volluntez dudit prince; car ell'avoit affaire de luy et le gaigner'.

30 A short biography of la Roche-sur-Yon is given in Brantôme, *Oeuvres complètes*, 11 vols, ed. Ludovic Lalanne (Paris: Renouard, 1869), V, 26–29.
31 Ibid., III, 193: 'ayme fort à rire, passer son temps, dire le mot et goguenarder'. A short biography of Maulevrier is given in M. Carnoy, 'La Marck', in *Dictionnaire de biographie française*, eds. J. Balteau, M. Prevost and J.-P. Lobies (Paris: Letouzey et Ané, 2001), XIX, 467.
32 This preliminary investigation of both parties, conducted in secret, was known as an *apprise*. As we shall see, Limeuil was then interrogated by two officers of the king's household. Since no further legal action was taken against Limeuil, it can be assumed that the bishops, the officers and/or Catherine deemed the accusations baseless. See F.R. Akehurst, 'Good Name, Reputation, and Notoriety in French Customary Law', Fenster and Smail, eds. *Fama: The Politics of Talk*, 75–94, 83, 87.
33 Aumale, 'Information contre Isabelle de Limeuil', 11. In July 1560, Maulevrier had accidentally killed the prince's only son, the marquis de Beaupréau, while hunting, and the bereft father had been so intent on avenging his son's death that the queen mother had ordered him to subsist on the condition that Maulevrier avoid him completely.
34 Ibid., 34: 'ladite princess, à la sussitation dudit sieur prince son mari, oultre les peines quelle donnoit à toutes les filles de la Royne, sembloit en vouloir à elle plus particulièrement et rechercholt de vérifier quelle fut grosse, la faisant souvent tourmenter par la Royne sur ce faict et aultres'.
35 Ibid., 34–5: 'entreprins faire tout le pis qu'il pourroit aux filles de la Royne, comme il l'a bien dict luy mesme à monsieur le prince de Condé, et qu'il vouloit poursuivre la reffromation: luy demandant sy en foy, en conscience, il voudroit que l'on vesquist en sa maison de la sorte qu'on faysoit chez la Royne?'
36 Ibid., 14: 'il ne luy failloyt qu'ung bon repas'.
37 Ibid., 18: 'prist en sa bourse certaine pouldre blanche, laquelle estoyt dedans ung papier, et luy en bailla une partye dedans ung petit morceau de papier'.
38 Ibid., 14–15: 'il se trouvast mort en quelque coing de rue'
39 René La Bruyère, *L'affaire de Saint-Jean-d'Angély ou le mystère de la mort du Prince de Condé* (Paris: Le Croît Vif, 1995). Documents relating to the case are found in AN série O 800: 'Procedures, et autres actes intervenus en la poursuite criminelle contre Dame Charlotte Caterine de la Trimouille Princesse de Condé 1595–1596'. The case is also discussed in Aumale, *Histoire des princes de Condé*; L'Estoile, VI, 23–24.
40 La Bruyère suggests that Condé died from a ruptured stomach ulcer.
41 Silje Normand, 'Perceptions of Poison: Defining the Poisonous in Early Modern France' (unpublished doctoral thesis, University of Cambridge, 2005), 7. See also Normand's essay, 'Venomous Words and Political Poisons: Language(s) of Exclusion in Early Modern France' in *Exploring Cultural History: Essays in Honour of Peter Burke*, eds. Melissa Calaresu, Filippo de Vivo and Joan-Pau Rubiés (Farnham: Ashgate, 2010), 113–31; Lynn Wood Mollenauer, *Strange Revelations: Magic, Poison, and Sacrilege in Louis XIV's France* (University Park, PA: Pennsylvania State University Press, 2007).
42 Margaret Hallissy, *Venomous Woman: Fear of the Female in Literature* (New York: Greenwood Press, 1987).
43 Reginald Scot, *The Discoverie of Witchcraft, Wherein the Lewde Dealing of Witches and Witchmongers Is Notablie Detected* . . . (London: W. Brome, 1584), book VI, ch. III, 67.
44 Normand, 'Perceptions of Poison', 139.
45 Patricia Philippy, *Painting Women: Cosmetics, Canvases, and Early Modern Culture* (Baltimore: Johns Hopkins University Press, 2006).
46 Normand, 'Perceptions of Poison', 142–45.
47 Hallissy, *Venomous Woman*, xi.
48 Herrup, *A House in Gross Disorder*, 37. This theory of the exclusion of a disorderly subject, with sodomy as the accusation instead of poisoning, is also discussed in Alan

Stewart, 'Bribery, Buggery, and the Fall of Lord Chancellor Bacon', *Rhetoric and Law in Early Modern Europe*, eds. Lorna Hutson and Victoria Kahn, (New Haven: Yale University Press, 2001).

49 For a discussion of early modern French poison treatises, see Normand, 'Venomous Words'.
50 Dubost, *La France italienne*; Henry Heller, *Anti-Italianism in Sixteenth-Century France* (Toronto: University of Toronto Press, 2003).
51 Normand, 'Venomous Words', 123.
52 L'Estoile, IV, 71:

> Il est certain que toute medecine
> Prendre se doibt en son temps et saison,
> Selon le mal. Une grand' medecine
> Des Medicis est plaine de poison.

53 *Discours merveilleux*, 201: 'Pourtant a-elle recours à maistre René son empoisonneur à gages, qui en vendant des senteurs et colets perfumez à la Roine de navarre, trouva moyen de l'empoisonner de telle sorte que peu de jours apres elle en mourut, dont depuis il s'est osé vanter . . .'.
54 Hallissy, *Venomous Woman*, xii.
55 Neubauer, *The Rumour: A Cultural History*, 4.
56 Normand, 'Perceptions of Poison', 21.
57 Barbara B. Diefendorf, *From Penitence to Charity: Pious Women and the Catholic Reformation in Paris* (Oxford: Oxford University Press, 2004), 52.
58 Aumale, 'Information contre Isabelle de Limeuil', 58: 'Vous asseurant quelle n'a receue oncques nouvelles depuis le partement de messieurs du Puys et de Serlan, que est cause du grand desconfort quelle meyne, pensant estre délaissée de tous ceulx auxquels elle avoit espérance: et ne puys croyre quelle puisse vivre en cest estat longuement, sy une femme doibt mourir de mélancolie, car en voyant son visaige il semble quelle doibve incontinant mourir. Vous suppliant très humblement qui plaise à Votre Magesté la vouloir mectre ailleurs, ou bien d'avoir pitié d'elle'.
59 Ibid., 37: 'n'avoir jamais eu ni veu telles drogues, et souvent avoir désiré veoir du sublimé ou du blanc d'Espaigne, parce qu'elle oyoit dire qu'il y en avoit qui s'en fardoient'.
60 Ibid., 47: 'estoit notoirement tenu d'un chascun pour un fol et un yvroigne'.
61 Samuel Y. Edgerton, Jr., *Pictures and Punishment: Art and Criminal Prosecution during the Florentine Renaissance* (Ithaca: Cornell University Press, 1985), 60.
62 Jeffrey A. Bowman, 'Infamy and Proof in Medieval Spain', *Fama: The Politics of Talk*, eds. Fenster and Smail, 95–117, 96; Akehurst, 'Good Name, Reputation and Notoriety', 76–7, 83–5; A.H.J. Greenidge, *Infamia: Its Place in Roman Public and Private Law* (Oxford: Clarendon Press, 1864), 18–40. For a discussion of the complex legal systems operating concurrently in sixteenth-century France, see Frederic J. Baumgartner, *France in the Sixteenth Century* (New York: St. Martin's Press, 1995), 83–96.
63 For a discussion of the nuanced differences of the term 'notoire' in Roman, canon and customary law in France see Akehurst, 'Good Name, Reputation and Notoriety', 85.
64 Aumale, 'Information contre Isabelle de Limeuil', 54–5: 'Madame, après avoyr entandu par les syeurs Du Puy et Sarlan les causes qui avoyt meu Votre Maiesté les envoyer devers moy, sela m'a tellement aflygée que sans l'ayde de Dyeu et l'espéranse que j'ay en votre bonté quy ne resevra une telle cualongnye et fause acusasion, comme et sele sur quoy yls m'ont interroguée, je fuse entrée au plus grant despoyr que pauvre crature saroyt estre, n'estant sy oblyée de Dyeu d'avoir consu ny mys une telle meschanseté dans ma pansée. Mes puys qu'il a pleu à votre dicte Maiesté m'an avoir donné l'avertissemant, je la suplye très humblemant me vouloir fère sete grâse d'an voulloir savoyr la vérité; et où yl sera trouvé que j'aye pansé une sy meschante pensée, je vous suplye très humblemant en voulloyr fère une sy exsanplère justyse que l'on

saroyt fère de la plus malheureuse du monde; et quant il ara pleu à Dyeu vous fère congnoytre en sela mon inosanse, je vous suplye très humblement, pour l'honneur de seus à quy j'apartiens, fère fère une telle justice du faus aqusateur, come j'aroys méryteé, ayant conmys une telle faute. Vous suplyant très humblemant, Madame, de croyre que jamès je n'ay eu, ny n'avé voullonté que de vous fère très humble et fidelle servise'.

65 Ibid., 74: 'Comme aussi fais-je de vous prier de vous consoller et vous asseurer que (estre?) au lieu où vous estes vous servira de beaucoup. Aussy faut-il que vous y conduisiez saigement, car toutes ces choses là se font pour bonne occasion. Quant ce ne seroit qu'il vous a esté commandé par une si saige princesse, luy obéissant comme debvez, ne vous en peult advenir que bien, et jespère que vous aurez bien tost des nouvelles de vos bons parents et amys: parquoy ne vous ferai plus longue lettre, fors que me recommande bien humblement à votre bonne grâce, pryant Dieu vous donner la sienne'.

66 Ibid., 78: 'Je ne crains que une chose quest que, en la religion où elle est, les murailles y sont en d'aulcungs endroits fort basses, et qu'ayant gaigné toutes les Cordelières, ce quelle a faict, elle ne jecte des lettres pardessus ladite muraille ou que l'on luy en jette; . . . Ou bien que l'on luy donne la nuict quelqu'eschelle pour eschapper pardessus lesdites murailles, et après la receller en quelque maison de huguenot en ceste ville: je ne le dis pas sans cause, parce que j'en ay esté adverty par de mes soldars, que ledit basque a parlé à deux ou trois des plus apparans huguenots de ceste dite ville . . .'

67 Ibid., 92: Je vous escrips séte lêtre estant sur le chemin de Mâcon: mès delà je ne say où l'on me mennera. Mon conducteur est un valet de chambre de la Reyne nommé Gentil; vous le congnoysés byen'.

68 Ibid., 92, 94–5.

69 Ibid., 65–6: 'Monsieur du Fresne me mande prou souvant que luy etcryvés de voz nouvelles, mès moy je n'an puys savoir où vous estes menée. Je m'étonne fort, puys cavés le moien d'écryre à quelque ungs, que ne puys resevoyr de mesme de vos lestre, car vous savés quy n'y a home au monde quy tant sait faché de vos pènes que moy'.

70 Brantôme, 643: 'Par Dieu! j'en ay pris une douzaine en vingt-quatre heures sur la plus belle motte qui soit icy à l'entour, ny qui soit possible en France'. . . . 'car par là il apprit ce dont il se doutoit il y avoit longtemps; et d'autant qu'il estoit fort amoureux de cette princesse, fut fort mary de ce qu'il avoit si longuement chassé en cet endroit et n'avoit jamais rien pris, et l'autre avoit esté si heureux en rencontre et en sa prise'.

71 LaGuardia, *Intertextual Masculinity*, 183–184.

72 For discussions of early modern cuckoldry anxiety, see Ibid.; Mark Breitenberg, *Anxious Masculinity in Early Modern England* (Cambridge: Cambridge University Press, 1996); Valeria Finucci, *The Manly Masquerade: Masculinity, Paternity, and Castration in the Italian Renaissance* (Durham: Duke University Press, 2003); Coppélia Kahn, *Man's Estate: Masculine Identity in Shakespeare* (Berkeley: University of California Press, 1981), in particular ' "The Savage Yoke": Cuckoldry and Marriage', 119–50.

73 Aumale, 'Information contre Isabelle de Limeuil', 69–70: "Car je vous asurre, mon ceur, quy m'annuyrés bien grandemant que l'on pût prendre seur voz acsions seuget de dire: 'A quy èt sait enfant?' Come, sy deux y avèt passé'.

74 Ibid., 69.

75 Ibid., 32: 'estoit bien trompé s'il pensoit que si elle estoit grosse, ce fust de luy, et qu'aucunls n'y eussent part'.

76 Castlenau, II, 371:

> At multi dicunt quod pater
> Non est princeps, sed est alter
> Qui regis est à secretis,
> Omnibus est notus satis.

77 *CSPF*, VII, 331, 11 April 1565.

78 *Archivo Documental Español*, 186.

79 Ibid., 189; 'una moglie bella, ricca et honorata, come la sorella di Monsr. di Ghisa'.
80 Aumale, *Histoire des princes de Condé*, 554: 'il pericolo et infamia propria et il scandalo commune a tutta la relligione'; 'I primi gentilhuomini de la relligione et suoi particolari'; 'che la Limolia si dovesse scomunicare, anatematizare et dare in potere di Satanasso'.
81 *Archivo Documental Español*, 189: 'I catolici dicono che, per impedire il matrimonio di Condé con la nepote del cardinale di Lorena, si serve del mezo de la Limolia. Gl'ugonoti dicono che per il costei mezo vuole inescare Condé e farlo tornare papista, come fu fatto di Vandomo impazzito per li amori di Roet; jo non m'accordo col parere di questi, ne di quelli, anzi penso, se pur ha parte nel negotio de la Limolia, che sia per volere fare tutto suo Condé, e che non dipenda d'alcun altro che da lei'.
82 Ronsard, *Oeuvres complètes*, vol. XIII.
83 Desonay, II, 203: 'Le Poëte m'a quelquefois dit que ce sonnet n'est point fait pour représenter sa passion, mais pour quelque autre dont il fut prié, désirant infiniment n'estre point recherché de tels importuns, qui luy font plus de desplaisir en lui communiquant leurs amours, qu'il n'a de plaisir à chanter les siennes'.
84 Aumale, 'Information contre Isabelle de Limeuil'. This obscure publication, in a journal for nineteenth-century bibliophiles, has remained unknown to many historians of the Valois court.
85 Antoine Furetière, *Le Dictionnaire universel d'Antoine Furetière*, 3 vols (Paris: Le Robert, 1978), 'venim': 'des discours de medisance, des haines qu'on garde dans le coeur, qui sont causes qu'on fait à son ennemy tout le mal qu'on luy peut faire'.
86 Furetière, *Dictionnaire universel*, 'bruit': 'La Chambre establie contre les empoisonneurs a fait grand bruit, grand éclat dans la France'.
87 Normand, 'Perceptions of Poison', 167–8.
88 It was during this period of marital and familial stability that Limeuil and her husband would have their portraits drawn by Henri IV's court artist Benjamin Foulon (see Figure 4.1), Etienne Moreau-Nélaton, *Les Clouet et leurs émules*, 3 vols (Paris: Laurens, 1924), I, 217–23.

5 Word of Honour
Françoise de Rohan versus the Duke of Nemours

> Upon the fifth of May the obscene, withered,
> Putrid, worn-out harlot again seeks men for her marriage bed.
> Likewise he who marries her is wicked, treacherous, lawless,
> Bankrupt, adulterous, accursed, disloyal and worthy of torture.[1]

These charming lines were written in 1566 to commemorate the wedding of Anne d'Este, duchess of Guise, grand-daughter of Louis XII of France and lady-in-waiting to the queen mother Catherine de Medici, and her new husband, Jacques de Savoie, duke of Nemours, (Figure 5.1) the hero of the French campaigns in Italy. Once again, a woman of Catherine's household found herself the target of verse libels that attacked her sexual honour. That such vitriolic terms could be used to describe a granddaughter of France and the kingdom's arguably most successful warrior is an indication of the public resentment felt at the circumstances surrounding their wedding. For 10 years Nemours had been engaged in a bitter dispute with his former lover, Françoise de Rohan, also a lady-in-waiting to Catherine de Medici.[2] The duke's refusal to honour either an earlier secret, oral agreement of marriage with Rohan, or the child that was produced from their relationship, would become the matter of legal debate for over 20 years, causing a four-way jurisdictional battle between the Parlement of Paris, the King's private council, the Gallican Church and the Vatican Rota, and the familial feuds the case inflamed threatened to ignite further civil war.[3] If the previous case study explored the hierarchies of scandal and the ability of women to manage their reputation from their prison cell, this long-running scandal reveals other issues about honour and the reliability of words. While Limeuil's story demonstrates how a woman could be successfully rehabilitated after the shame of scurrilous accusations, the story of Françoise de Rohan offers a contrasting perspective: what happens when a woman makes a domestic dispute public, and the consequences for her own and her family's reputation.

In this period of heightened religious tension and bloody conflict that would divide families both peasant and noble, the perennial tale of the seduction and

Figure 5.1 François Clouet, *Jacques de Savoie, duc de Nemours*
Source: © The Trustees of the British Museum 1910,0212.61

betrayal of a naive woman may at first appear frivolous. However, the Rohan-Nemours story offers a fascinating case study of how orality played a central role in the construction of honour and reputation at the early modern court. The documents relating to the legal case allow us to recreate the oral and aural world within the court, and to explore the overlap and interweaving of orality and literacy in different genres of communication: how eavesdropping found its way into legal depositions and gossip into private correspondence. The role of rumour and gossip in this case is revelatory as to the structures, networks and divisions that characterised the court, and demonstrates how social class and, occasionally, gender could dictate how information was transmitted within the palace walls and disseminated beyond them into the public arena. The personal and political fallout from the dispute demonstrates the consequences for an elite woman's reputation, and that of her family, when she chose to make private domestic matters public. Furthermore, this chapter explores the legal and social context in which the scandal was based. As we have seen, the French legal system in the sixteenth century was in a state of flux, with the laws on marriage under constant debate and, moreover, with the precedence of oral testimony being gradually superseded by a new literate culture where the written word was considered more valuable.[4] These developments would affect, and be affected by, the high-profile case of Rohan vs. Nemours which exposed the tensions between oral, aural and written evidence.

Secret Agreements

Around 1553, the duke, a partisan of the pro-Catholic Guise faction, began an amorous relationship with Françoise de Rohan, first cousin to Jeanne d'Albret, the Huguenot queen of Navarre. While in Italy in 1555, however, he was involved in negotiations to marry Lucrezia d'Este, sister of the duke of Ferrara and the aforementioned Anne d'Este, but when rumours of the negotiations reached Rohan, Nemours vehemently denied them. In early 1556, Nemours allegedly agreed to a secret, oral marriage contract with Rohan and they soon thereafter began a sexual relationship. By June she was pregnant, but did not inform Nemours until after he had left on military campaigns in Italy in November. When the duke refused to honour the oral agreement by solemnizing their marriage in church, Rohan sued him for breach of promise. This decision to move the dispute from the private arena to the public law courts resulted in a wealth of written material in the form of depositions, material that, unlike the legal dossier relating to Limeuil's case, Catherine would be unable to control or conceal, and which would provide rich detail about daily life within the palace walls.

The written evidence of the case reveals the royal court to have been a porous environment where the control of sensitive information was rendered almost impossible by the gossip of ever-present servants who, despite their illiteracy – or perhaps because of it – could recall an extraordinary amount of detail about interpersonal transactions. As the suit involved the sacrament of marriage, it would – at least initially – be decided in the ecclesiastical courts. In March 1559, before the bishop of Paris's tribunal, Rohan produced 12 letters from Nemours in which he repeatedly professed his intentions to spend the rest of his life with her, but simultaneously implored her secrecy in the matter. She also called five of her domestic servants – her governess, her tailor, her page, her valet and her maid – as eyewitnesses to their secret vows, to their sexual activities and to his repeated claims to be Rohan's husband.[5]

Notwithstanding their potentially tendentious nature, the depositions nonetheless reveal a constant presence of servants around her, so ubiquitous as to sometimes go unnamed in the depositions, as if they were part of the furniture. Their quasi-invisibility resulted in their witnessing the most intimate details of her life, reading and keeping her letters, even watching her have sex. Rohan's tailor Fleury Barge described how, after falling asleep on a chest next to Rohan's bed one evening, he was woken by the couple having sex. He was able to describe their clothes in detail, including the petticoat Rohan was wearing which he himself had made.[6] Her page, Antoine de Coué, related another occasion when, dining with at least four other servants at a table near Rohan's bed, he 'heard the said lady cry out which made him turn his head towards the bed and saw the said lord de Nemours and the lady Rohan making the act of husband and wife'.[7] Her governess, Gabrielle de Binel, dame de Coué (no relation), described a similar incident which significantly confirmed both Nemours's verbal insistence upon their married status and the lack of privacy in the domestic environment of the court. She

> came into the room where she saw and found the said lord duke upright against the bed of the said lady and performing the actions of husband and wife. And as soon as the said lady Rohan noticed the said deponent enter she pulled away. And then the said lord duke seeing that the said lady Rohan pulled away out of shame said to her, in a voice that was bitter and deep and full of anger, these words, swearing: 'Mort dieu! What are you scared of? Am I not your husband? Are you not my wife?' To which the said lady replied, 'Yes, sir', which the said deponent heard clearly and assuredly, and in the room were the girls and ladies of the said lady Rohan . . .[8]

Binel's testimony evokes the densely-populated living quarters of the royal palace, where the unnamed 'girls and ladies of the said lady Rohan' were in the same room while the couple had sex, and where Rohan's servants could easily hear her private conversations.[9]

All of the servants were in agreement that Rohan and Nemours were a married couple. After all, they had not only witnessed their love-making, they had even heard them exchange marriage vows. Her chambermaid Perrine Legrand testified that, while doing some last-minute sewing before Rohan's planned trip to Brittany in 1556, she overheard the duke pleading with Rohan:

> 'I know well that when you are in Brittany that madame your mother wants to marry you. I beg you to not get married because you know well the agreement there is between us both'. And with these words the said deponent heard the said lord say to the said lady these words, 'I take you for my wife' and the

said lady said to the said lord, 'I take you for my husband'. And having done this they kissed each other.[10]

According to Binel, 'the common gossip of the whole household of the said lady and other non-domestic staff who frequented the said house was that the said lord duke was the true husband of the said lady and was regarded and reputed as such'.[11] The numerous references in the depositions to rumour and gossip ['*bruit*'] highlights the reliance on the spoken word by servants whose illiteracy meant that some were unable to even sign their own depositions. The details that Binel was able to recall about the nature of the sound of Nemours's voice ('bitter and deep and full of anger') demonstrate a familiarity with an oral culture that is difficult for a modern literate observer to fully appreciate.

This is combined with an early modern perception of time in which dates are described in terms of saints' holidays or major events at court. Fleury Barge recalled an incident taking place 'the court being at Fontainebleau, around the feast of St. Jean, when the queen had given birth to two children'.[12] Although they are generally unclear of their own age or birthdate (Antoine de Coué described himself as 'aged from 23 to 24 or thereabouts'[13]), the passing of time is precisely marked by aural signals: several witnesses distinctly remembered that Nemours would leave Rohan's chamber at 1 a.m. because they could hear the changing of the guard around the king's bedroom. Thus, despite their lack of literacy, the servants' depositions are full of precise, informative details about a world they experienced both orally and aurally.

This trust the servants placed in the spoken word was exploited by Nemours whenever he was challenged by Binel about his intentions concerning her mistress:

> To which the said lord duke made reply that he was a man of worth, swearing the name of the Lord like 'Mort-Dieu!' and other oaths, that he had promised marriage to the said lady Rohan, and would marry her, that she was assured of him and that she knew it well. And when the said deponent chided the said lord, 'Yes, my lord, but if you do not marry her look at the danger you will put us all in', then the said lord started swearing like before saying, 'I believe, Miss Coué, that you do not take me for a man of worth. I am neither so evil nor so wicked as to wish to deceive her'.[14]

In the early modern society where orality was paramount, where preachers' sermons were a powerful political weapon and where most people experienced books by listening to another person read them out loud, Rohan's claim that Nemours had reneged on his oral promises was a scandalous and troubling accusation. As a sacrament, marriage depended on the oral exchange of vows, not on public ceremony or written certificates. It was a society where, as Nemours himself claimed, a gentleman's honour was based on him keeping his word; if it could be shown that he had backed out on his promise, his own reputation was at risk. As Antoine de Bourbon, king of Navarre wrote to his wife, Rohan's cousin, Jeanne d'Albret, 'it seems to me that he cannot back out of it without damaging his honour'.[15] But it was not only Rohan and Nemours who stood to suffer from the fallout of the affair: Coué's comment about the 'danger you will put us all in' is a poignant reminder of how a noblewoman's dishonour could have repercussions for all those attached to her household.

The Scandal of Clandestine Marriage

For aristocratic families, an unarranged marriage was unthinkable, as a successful union was both a business transaction that benefitted a family in terms of landholdings, social status and financial assets, and, crucially, a public performance that displayed a family's ability to succeed in those areas.[16] A noble marriage, clandestine or not, had consequences not only for the couple but also for their unmarried siblings, who could benefit from a lucrative marriage in terms of the increased dowries and elevated status that a spouse from a more prestigious family could bring, or their own marriage plans could be thwarted by the shame and/or financial ruin brought upon the entire family by a *mésalliance*. *Romeo and Juliet* was not simply a story about star-crossed lovers: the perennial phenomenon of clandestine marriages in early modern France was a matter of such overwhelming concern to parents that every ordinance of the sixteenth century reinforced severe penalties for those found guilty of marrying in secret. Traditionally, the Catholic Church sanctioned marriage with only the consent of the couple, who had only to speak their intention (*verba de futuro*), followed either by more words declaring the mutual and present will of the couple (*verba de praesenti*) or by action: carnal union.[17] It would be this second option that Rohan would claim had occurred: intention (their secret vows) followed by action (sexual intercourse). However, in its 24th session, the Council of Trent attempted to introduce greater control of the Church in family matters by requiring the presence of a priest and two witnesses at the exchange of vows, although it still did not require the consent of parents. The Gallican Parlement's resentment of interference from Rome in its domestic matters, however, meant that it would never register the Council's decrees.

In practice, French law would nevertheless move towards the spirit of the Tridentine marriage regulations after the scandalous case in 1556 of François de Montmorency and Jeanne de Piennes. As we have seen, François's father, Anne de Montmorency, had arranged for his son to marry the king's daughter until François admitted to having already secretly married his lover, Jeanne de Piennes.[18] The enraged father encouraged Henri II to publish a royal edict that year that dramatically altered the laws.[19] The edict raised the age of consent for women to 25 and for men to 30, disinherited contractors of marriages made without parental consent, and required priests performing weddings to publish the banns of marriage before they took place, to ensure that there were four witnesses, rather than two, and to know the ages of the couple. It would appear that the new laws were not routinely enforced, however, as in 1576 the Estates General at Blois called for a stronger ban on clandestine marriages, complaining that 'clandestine marriages and in consequence bigamies and disastrous unions were ruining families and defying discipline'.[20] The resulting Ordinance of Blois in 1579 prescribed the keeping of registers of marriage, the public calling of the banns of marriage, a public celebration, and the necessary presence of the priest and four witnesses.[21] Priests were forbidden to perform marriage ceremonies for persons from outside their parishes in the expectation that this would reduce the opportunities for secret marriages. It also declared that those responsible for such a marriage, usually but not always the would-be husband, were guilty of the capital crime of *rapt* (either by seduction or abduction).[22] Given that clandestine marriages now incurred the penalties of disinheritance and capital punishment, the ordinance reflects the concern raised by secret marriages.[23] All these measures would come too late to affect the Rohan/Nemours case, but they highlight the perennial desire for couples to defy parental wishes regarding appropriate spouses and the shifting conditions and resulting confusion around clandestine marriage which repeated legislation was trying to erase. It is important to understand that at no time did Nemours claim that the marriage was invalid because it had been conducted clandestinely, for all were aware that Rohan's argument – that oral vows followed by sexual intercourse equalled binding marriage – was a valid one. Nemours's only defence was to claim that the vows had never taken place, and that Rohan's servants had therefore been bribed to give evidence against him.

Fortunately for Nemours, political events intervened. On 30 June 1559 Henri II was accidentally killed and the young François II and his Guise bride, Marie Stuart, ascended the throne. Her uncles, the Guise brothers, became *de facto* rulers of France, and Nemours found himself with powerful allies at court. Accordingly, in response to the eyewitness accounts given by mere servants, Nemours invoked the testimony of the most powerful nobles in the kingdom, including members of the royal family itself. The late king's sister, Marguerite de France; the cardinal of Lorraine; the late king's mistress, Diane de Poitiers; the royal surgeon, Ambroise Paré; and even Rohan's own mistress, Catherine de Medici, all gave testimony on Nemours's behalf.[24] Catherine, dismayed at the scandal caused to the reputation of her household by Rohan's pursuit of a high-profile legal case, gave a deposition on 1 August 1559 that was damning to her former lady-in-waiting. Catherine claimed that, when she confronted Rohan shortly before Nemours's departure for Italy, Rohan had denied being pregnant, blaming pregnancy rumours on the malicious gossip of other courtiers. Not convinced, Catherine claimed that the following day she commanded her own doctor Sallon not to agree to Rohan's request to bleed her foot – an action thought to redirect 'blocked' menstrual flow during missed periods – but Sallon admitted that he had already refused two such requests from Rohan because he was aware of the same rumours of pregnancy – testament to how widespread those rumours had become.[25] Interestingly, Catherine did not claim to have divulged any of this intimate information to Nemours before his departure.

Indeed, the hierarchy of transmission of pertinent information between less well-connected nobles such as Rohan and more powerful nobles such as Nemours can be seen in the deposition by Rohan's governess Binel, as she described hearing about Nemours's marriage negotiations with Lucrezia d'Este. She said

> that she had been warned by one of the Queen's ladies-in-waiting who had heard it being said to the signora Olivia, who said she had heard it being said

to Madame de Guise that the said Sr. de Nemours had promised Madame de Guise that he would marry one [of her] sisters.[26]

The tortuous path by which Binel received the information, relying on fourth-hand hearsay and gossip, stands in stark contrast to the deposition of the late king's mistress, Diane de Poitiers. While Diane mentioned that 'there was a rumour that the said duke of Nemours went to Italy to see madame Lucrezia, and that he might wed her', she also admitted that she 'did not know however if the damoiselle plaintiff [Rohan] knew anything about the said rumour of marriage'.[27] Evidently Diane did not feel it necessary to pass on the information herself. An anonymous letter in the Bibliothèque nationale de France which I have identified as Rohan's personally-written reply to one of Nemours's letters, refers to the marriage negotiations with Lucrezia d'Este, demonstrating how Rohan did know about the negotiations but claimed to trust Nemours over others to provide her with information about them (Figure 5.2): 'Regarding the marriage of the lady whom you know, I know as much from what you have told me about it that I am not afraid at all that she will do me this wrong . . .'[28]

The letter is not written in secretary hand, and uses phonetic spelling, which argues that it was most likely not dictated to a secretary but instead penned by Rohan herself. The gushing language and tone throughout gives the impression of a young and naïve lover desperate for concrete information. Although her sentiments may have been disingenuous, this long letter in which Rohan repeatedly enthused about her own faith in Nemours's honour demonstrates that she appeared to value Nemours's claims over those of her governess. Had Rohan consulted her mistress Catherine directly (which never seems to have happened) she would, however, have been given more relevant details about the matter.

But the impression given by the testimony of the leading nobles is of a wealth of information available only to a privileged few. Catherine, who as head of her female household, had a responsibility to her younger ladies to prepare them for the marriage market, never conveyed to Rohan the vital information that the Este negotiations were underway, nor Nemours's admission to the king's sister, Marguerite de France, that since his return from Italy he had had no intention of marrying Rohan. Instead, when Rohan's pregnancy was confirmed in January 1557, Catherine belatedly scolded the governess Binel for allowing Nemours into the room after she had forbidden it. Binel simply replied 'that she could not honestly refuse entry to such an honest prince'.[29] Catherine's testimony concurred with that of the other witnesses called by Nemours in painting Rohan as disobedient to her orders and as duplicitous in trying to hide the pregnancy. Her refusal to support her lady-in-waiting can be explained either by her new-found status as mere queen mother in the face of the powerful Guise faction (of which Nemours was an associate), and/or her dismay at the scandal caused by Rohan's pursuit of a legal case. Rohan had been invited by Catherine to return to court after the birth of her baby, implying that she had not been disgraced by the illegitimate birth. However, her decision to seek legal recognition of her bastard offspring drew unwelcome attention to Catherine's inability to effectively police her household, and gave

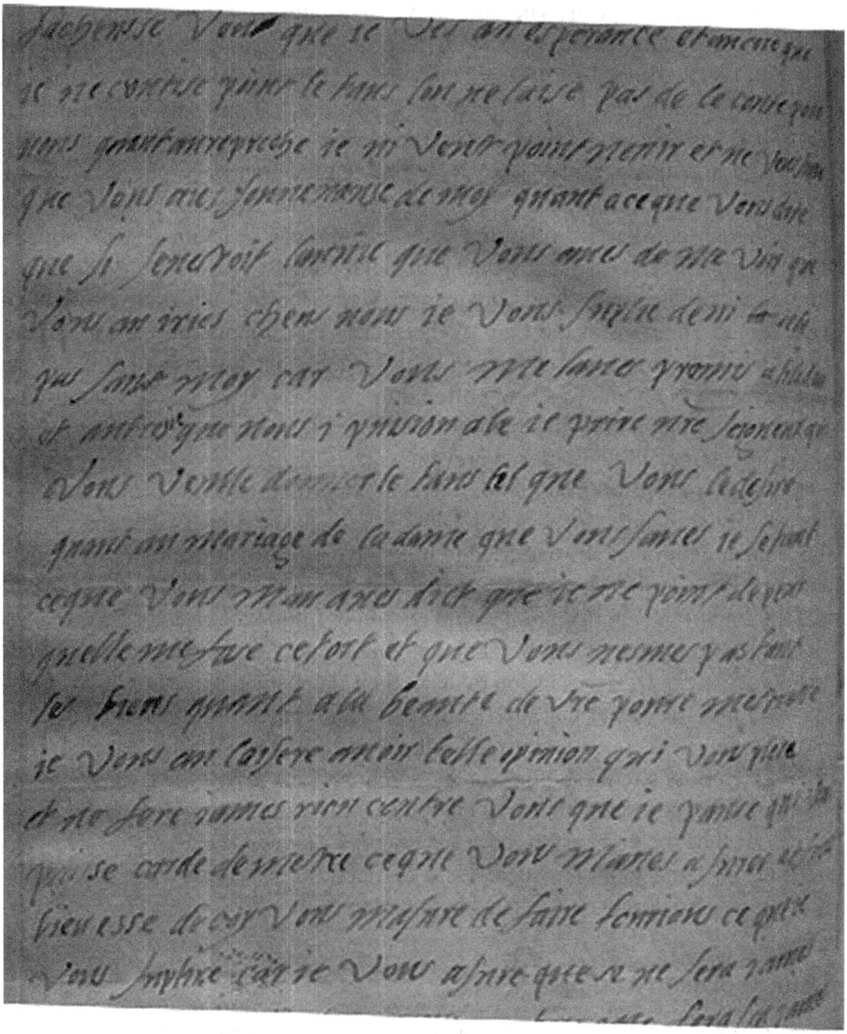

Figure 5.2 Autograph letter from Françoise de Rohan to Jacques de Savoie, duc de Nemours
Source: BnF MS Fr 3397, f. 70v. [author's own photo]

the court an unwanted reputation as a site of loose morality. Thus it was not the actual event which was scandalous, *per se*, but the fact that it moved from the elite network of court gossip to the more high-profile jurisdiction of the legal court.

To avoid more scandal, Catherine had sent Rohan to her cousin in Navarre, where she gave birth to a son, Henri, under Jeanne's roof in Pau on 24 March 1557. As we have seen, the birth of a child to an unmarried woman of the court was not necessarily irreparably damaging either to her career at court or to her future marriage prospects. The key to avoiding public disgrace was to have the child recognised by its father. As with the cases of two other ladies-in-waiting to Catherine, Isabelle de Limeuil and Louise de La Beraudière, known as 'la belle Rouet', who had illegitimate children by, respectively, Louis, prince of Condé in 1564, and his brother Antoine de Bourbon, king of Navarre in 1562, a woman could subsequently return to court and find another marriage partner. The difference in Rohan's case seems to be that while both Bourbon brothers offered to legitimate their bastard offspring and thereby reward them and their mothers, both in terms of status and subsequent financial income, Nemours initially denied any responsibility for Rohan's pregnancy. Significantly, both Bourbon brothers were already married at the time of their bastard children's births; for a single man such as Nemours, recognising the child would have meant marriage with the mother. Since Nemours was being offered far more lucrative matches than Rohan (including, at one point, Elizabeth I of England), it would appear that he refused to legitimate the child in order to prevent a *mésalliance*.

Nemours's assertion in the initial investigation that the child could have been fathered by someone else was a defamatory attack on Rohan's honour, and his subsequent claim that she had tried to hide the pregnancy and attempted to abort it by being bled was an accusation even graver than infanticide, as it was believed that the soul of the aborted child would remain in Limbo for eternity.[30] Such accusations left Rohan no option but to defend her reputation by exposing her lover's dishonesty in court. Her decision to make their domestic dispute public by pursuing a legal battle meant that, ironically, Rohan's reputation would also suffer. In an age when women were expected to be modest and submissive, her refusal to accept Nemours's requests for secrecy and, in effect, to call the renowned duke a liar, was already scandalous. To compound this with the testimony of Rohan's witnesses that she had performed 'carnal works' (*oeuvres charnelles*) while they were in the same room revealed her to be unchaste in an era when the onus of chastity was predominantly carried by the female.[31]

From Words to Actions

The honour of the female was, however, not simply an individual state; her entire family was subject to the rise and fall of the reputations of all its members, and they were responsible for doing what they could to ensure she retained her honour. Antoine de Navarre revealed how the apparently insignificant actions of Rohan's extended family could have an impact on her honour. Writing to his wife after hearing the news of Rohan's pregnancy, he said: 'Regarding her women, I have not followed your orders in returning them . . . for if I had expelled them, everyone would have believed that we knew that my cousin had been sold and that she had fault done against her honour'.[32]

Antoine realised the importance of keeping up appearances to avoid a slur on his cousin's reputation, and that dismissing her servants was tantamount to considering her guilty of premarital sex. Significantly, it was Antoine who became Rohan's protector as she was his wife's cousin. His letters to his wife are therefore enlightening as to the appropriate treatment of a woman in Rohan's situation, the likely outcome of such a case and, significantly, the ramifications for her extended family. He, for one, was convinced by Rohan's version of events, and knew it to be imperative that everyone behave as if the marriage had definitely occurred so that Nemours would be forced to act reciprocally:

> ... because of which we have decided to treat her as the wife of Monsieur de Nemours and to not look down on her, nor distance her from us until we have news from him, and we will do what we can for her; because he would do the same from his side, and the poor unhappy girl would be dishonoured and we would be in grave danger of having to avenge her.[33]

This threat of vengeance would become all too real as the political situation took a new turn. In December 1560, Catherine assumed the regency and began to attempt to introduce a measure of toleration for Protestants, a position implemented at the Estates General in Orléans a few weeks later. Capitalising on the new-found support for their religion at court, in February 1561 Rohan's brothers arrived at court with two hundred armed men to force Nemours to marry their sister. Their arrival, however, threatened to undo Catherine's efforts at reconciliation. The Florentine ambassador described the tensions that their presence caused:

> It seems that M. de Nemours has become suspicious, and so with the help of M. de Guise, has armed himself in his house, and outside still goes well accompanied ... This quarrel is not finished, but nevertheless it escalates, nor do there lack people who foment it ... And the Guise have had the worst of it, because they are universally hated, and everyone wishes they would go away, and shouts after them; and all of this is done so that they might be driven out.[34]

The ambassador's comments reveal the escalating animosity that the case was creating between the already-feuding Guises and Bourbons, and the damage it was causing to the reputations of the Guises as well as Nemours.

Although that particular crisis was averted, the bad blood between the two families because of the case would spill over, in February 1564, into a fatal battle in the streets:

> This night at Paris a gentleman of Bretagne, belonging to the Duke of Nemours, called Caharon, met M. De Fontenay, younger brother to M. De Rohan, riding in the street, and with his rapier thrust him through the left shoulder, thinking that he had slain him. De Fontenay alighted, and, with another captain, followed him, and hard at the house of Guise overtook him and slew him. The captain who was with Fontenay hurt another that was with Caharon in the head, so that he is like to die. The quarrel was for words Caharon should speak of Fontenay.[35]

These 'words' are what the French would have described as a *démenti*, the insulting words used to provoke a duel, and are an example of how, in this predominantly oral culture, the spoken word could be immediately transformed into physical acts of violence. The case of Rohan vs. Nemours both epitomised and antagonised the confessional tensions that had only recently plunged the country into civil war. The historian Jacques-Auguste de Thou would remember it thus: 'As the duke of Nemours had at that time more credit, and as there was much distancing from and hatred for the Protestant religion, to which Françoise de Rohan was attached, the suit was thrown out through the intervention of the Pope'.[36] For the Huguenots, the case came to represent everything against which they were struggling, and Nemours's alleged lies and promiscuity were depicted as the worst kind of Popish excess. It was not simply a matter of Protestant against Catholic; Rohan's argument was about honesty versus duplicity, about transparency over corruption. A 1566 poem addressed to the king after one of the verdicts in the protracted case went against Rohan claimed that the corruption in the church and the courts was inherently linked. Reform was needed in both 'the great Idolatry', meaning the Catholic Church, and 'the great Parlement', the country's leading law court.[37] The king's personal slogan of 'Mercy and Justice' was being made a mockery of, claimed the author, 'since your judges judge all to their guise', a pun that alluded to the pervasive and unfair influence the Guise family had in both institutions, influence that guaranteed an unfavourable verdict for Rohan. Antoine de Navarre's comments reveal how strictly the Huguenots viewed the situation: 'because I have hope that once he [Nemours] has considered everything well, that he can do no less than to go through with it; I mean either marriage or death'.[38]

Since 1560, Antoine's wife Jeanne d'Albret had openly declared herself a Calvinist along with leading noblewomen such as the Comtesse de Roye, her daughters Eléonore, princesse de Condé and Charlotte de La Rochefoucauld, and Charlotte de Laval, wife of Admiral Coligny. As the religious persecution escalated and the Protestant party eventually retreated to its stronghold of La Rochelle, Jeanne presided there over what Nancy Lyman Roelker called 'a brilliant assembly of Huguenot nobility'.[39] In effect, she offered a rival court to the Valois one where, as the Calvinists felt, 'women were superficially exalted but actually exploited as ornaments and as instruments of the power and pleasure of men'.[40] This rival court, with its powerful female leaders, would offer Rohan continual support in her battle against Nemours and his powerful alliances. It was not only moral support: Rohan also had the legal support from the 1570s of François Viète, the lawyer-mathematician who represented many of the leading Protestant families, in particular the Parthenay-Soubise.[41] After Antoine withdrew his support from Rohan in late February 1561, and then repudiated his own wife in early 1562, Jeanne became Rohan's most outspoken defender and viewed Rohan's treatment by Nemours and his allies as a personal affront. In her memoirs written in September 1568, she describes 'the injustice done to me at that time in the person of my cousin de Rohan ... this injurious injustice ... which I felt most deeply'.[42] Jeanne believed that the powerful Catholics at court operated in covert, corrupt and duplicitous fashion, a belief that was only strengthened by the repeated secretive actions of Nemours.

On 2 September 1562, Nemours wrote a secret letter to Rohan in which he offered to solemnise the marriage in Langey near Tours on 25 September, whereupon he would recognise her son as his legitimate heir on the grounds that she tell no one of their impending ceremony.[43] If this was a plot to murder Rohan in order to put an end to the lawsuit it failed, and the letter was presented by Rohan's legal team as further written evidence of Nemours's duplicity. We can only speculate as to why Nemours would continue with such secretive behaviour. It may have been because secrecy was considered to be a legitimate means of maintaining power in the hands of the elite. It was, claimed the French political theorist Jean Bodin, 'a princely virtue'.[44] In a similar fashion, the Estates General that met in Blois in 1576, 'swore, as was the custom, to preserve the secrecy of their deliberations and not to keep notes on what happened'.[45] In contrast with modern ideals of transparency within government, early modern rulers felt that good government was achieved through control of important information, information that could be dangerous in the hands of the non-elite. This tradition was a long-standing one. At the Estates General of 1484, the Third Estate, who represented non-noble magistrates and merchants, called for royal edicts to be published in every town in the realm, because one of the major problems in the legal system was that only a handful of influential people knew what the edicts were.[46] In his study of the Venetian senate, Filippo de Vivo has examined the obsessive concern with secrecy shown by the patriciate in regards to political debate within the Senate. 'It was', he says, 'a political system which made eloquence and command of information crucial tools of statecraft'.[47] Thus Nemours's attempts at secrecy, although foolishly committed to paper, were for him the natural actions of a nobleman.

This extraordinary development in the Rohan/Nemours case was soon followed by another. In February 1563 Nemours's close friend and ally, the duc de Guise, was assassinated and his widow Anne d'Este was now free to marry the man originally promised to her sister: Jacques de Savoie, duc de Nemours.[48] The only obstacle to their union was the tenaciously litigious Françoise de Rohan, who had launched endless appeals to have the case heard in the Parlement. Nemours thus began to fully exploit both his political and affective influence with the king and queen mother (to whom Este was not simply a lady-in-waiting but also a very close friend) to have the case moved from the Parisian tribunal to Lyon where Nemours was governor and where the Archbishop was a partisan. Although this blatant corruption caused a storm of protest (including both verses already mentioned), the Archbishop's verdict in May 1566 allowed the marriage of Nemours and Este to go ahead.

The protest did not only manifest itself in written libels: the marriage would cause a rift between Rohan's cousin and defender Jeanne d'Albret and her old friend Renée, duchess of Ferrara. While both women were leading Calvinists and allies for many years, Renée was Anne d'Este's mother, and could not forgive the uncomplimentary remarks that Jeanne had made about her daughter. In May 1566, the English ambassador Thomas Hoby noted that, 'Certain words of offence have passed between the Queen of Navarre and the old Duchess of Ferrara for the marriage of her daughter to M. De Nemours'.[49] The Ferrarese ambassador was more explicit: 'When [Jeanne] started to kiss her, as was her custom . . . Madama [refused] saying that she would never again allow lips as poisoned as [Jeanne's] to approach her'.[50] Similarly, the Spanish ambassador, Don Frances de Alava, described an argument between Jeanne d'Albret and Anne d'Este, in which he said they had 'dishonoured themselves by squabbling like washerwomen over the subject of the marriage of the latter, unafraid to exchange offensive remarks in the presence of the entire court and the queen'.[51] Orally uttered words could cause the breakdown of long-held alliances and networks. The oral transmission of information, the importance given to the spoken word, could backfire in a public and damaging way, reducing queens and duchesses to the status of 'washerwomen'. The ambassador's use of this term reveals how oral discussion of domestic disputes in public was freighted with ideas of social status and gender, with arguing about personal relationships reserved for the lowest class of female.

International Scandal

Moreover, as these examples make clear, ambassadors enjoyed a privileged, but ambiguous status at court: a semi-constant presence at sensitive and important moments, they were used as agents of information both by their host nation and by those who wished to send information abroad. Their accounts of the feuding at court made their way back to Spain, England and Italy, damaging the reputations of all involved. The ambassadors' unique status as the embodiment of the absent sovereign would present an acute problem at the occasion of the Nemours/Este wedding on 5 May 1566. The entire court had been invited to the wedding at the chapel of the Abbaye de la Roquette, in Saint-Maur-des-Fossés. However, to avoid any possible disruption by supporters of Rohan, the great hall of the château had been secretly prepared, and the wedding was celebrated there by the Cardinal of Lorraine with the foreign ambassadors in attendance, as they would have interpreted their exclusion from the real wedding as a diplomatic affront. But the attempts at secrecy were futile: as the Cardinal was about to pronounce the sacramental words, an officer of the Parlement, Vincent Petit, rose to his feet and proclaimed that he represented the 'dame de Rohan' and that she forbade the marriage to proceed. The Cardinal faltered for a moment, but the officer was quickly removed and the ceremony continued. The English ambassador, Thomas Hoby, credited Petit's appearance to Jeanne d'Albret and reported back to London that he 'was immediatlie committed to warde for a wholl day bicause he durst appeare in that place about such a matter without the kings speciall license which fact the Q of Navarr imputeth to want of iustice'.[52] The Spanish ambassador disclosed that the officer later continued his protest in front of the king's council, claiming that Nemours had raped Rohan and therefore

> following the laws of France, deserved to have his head cut off, because he had taken Mme de Rohan by force in the queen's chamber and made her pregnant. A great laugh took hold of Catherine de Medici, Charles IX and the whole council! The lawyer was removed.[53]

Petit's presence highlights the difficulties of keeping any information secret in the densely-populated court environment, and the reports by the ambassadors ensured that Jeanne's anger at the injustice reached an international audience. Hoby claimed that public sentiment was outraged at a marriage under such dubious legal circumstances and that Nemours's reputation would suffer as a result: 'This mariage, by commune reaport, is leeke to breed great trouble in fraunce, for all protestante and a nomber of papists are much against it and do not let to say that it shall cost him deere in the ende. He is a man universallie ill beloved, she generallie pitied'.[54] While the ambassador was a Protestant and therefore likely to be more sympathetic to Rohan, his reference to the 'commune reaport' alluded to the negative public perception of the secrecy used to facilitate the marriage.

The reputations of both parties rested on what the different witnesses claimed to have heard being spoken. Sixteenth-century French culture relied on the spoken word. Many letters between nobles contain little pertinent information except to recommend the bearer who will relay the information to the recipient orally. Kristen Neuschel explains that

> many of the most important messages between particularly intimate noble correspondents may have been wholly oral, wholly dependent on face-to-face encounters that left no documentary residue. . . . their letters reflect the habits of dictating, of listening, and of trusting personally conveyed information.[55]

The need to be able to trust the spoken word was the bedrock of the honour system. To be an *homme de bien*, 'a man of worth', demanded that a nobleman's actions correlated to his words. As Rohan, perhaps naively, expressed it in her letter to Nemours,

> I received the letter that you wrote me which was a really very great pleasure to know the truth; even though I was never in doubt that you were a man of worth, for had I been I would not have put as much faith in you as I have.[56]

That a leading noble such as Nemours – the 'flower of all chivalry', as Brantôme described him – elected to back out on an orally-agreed contract threatened the very stability of the honour code.[57] It was the most scandalous aspect of the case, more shocking than an illegitimate pregnancy or corruption of judges, and one of the key threats presented by clandestine marriages. However, while oral contracts were binding, once spoken they left no 'documentary residue' – unless there were witnesses who also heard the words being spoken. The memories of Rohan's servants, to whom Nemours had showed so little regard as to have sexual intercourse with Rohan while they were present in the room, were transformed into written depositions that incessantly challenged Nemours's own version of events. Combined with the letters that he had thoughtlessly written, they created a paper trail in which Nemours's own words would eventually come back to haunt him.

This phenomenon in which the written version of an event superseded in authority the oral version was at that very moment becoming enshrined in law.

The Ordinance of Moulins in 1566, the same year as the Nemours/Este wedding, decreed that in future, written proof took precedence over oral proof in legal cases involving over 100 *francs*. Previously, because so few people could read and write, oral proof was deemed more conclusive than written proof, and the accepted maxim was *témoins passent lettres* ('witnesses over letters'). After the ordinance the saying became *lettres passent témoins* ('letters over witnesses').[58] This major ideological shift in French legal culture reflected the newer privileging of written material, a cultural transformation that was problematic for those who continued to place a higher value in the oral transmission of information. Nemours's careless letter-writing in which, ironically, he asked for Rohan's silence and discretion exposed his traditional belief that it was the (un)spoken word that mattered rather than the written. However, now that his letters had become so imbued with value, it was fortunate for Nemours (some would say not coincidental) that when Rohan's home in La Garnache was sacked by Catholic forces during the second religious war in 1567, many of her papers relating to the case were stolen.

Nevertheless, Rohan continued her legal appeal to have her marriage and son recognised. It was not only in the courts that she continued her legal argument: in December 1575, almost ten years after Nemours had married Este, Henri III forbade Rohan to use the name of 'dame de Nemours, under pain of being declared recalcitrant and disobedient to decrees'.[59] Fashioning herself in public as well as in legal documents as Nemours's legitimate wife, Rohan had maintained a persona that as a result portrayed the duke as a liar, and thereby attacked his honour. She had not been alone in styling herself thus: Henri de Savoie, prince de Genevois, was the provocative title her son had given himself – provocative because it was the title given to the duke of Nemours's second son (also confusingly called Henri). The use of Nemours's name and coat-of-arms by the young Protestant warrior was a source of continuing antagonism for the duke, who was trying to raise his own family with Anne d'Este.

Surprisingly, it was Este herself, probably weary of being labelled an adulteress in every appeal by Rohan, who finally employed her superlative negotiating abilities to resolve the case (of which more in the following chapter). On 22 January 1580, after 21 years of ceaseless legal wrangling, Françoise de Rohan made a formal declaration, confirmed by letters patent of Henri III, that she and Jacques de Savoie had been secretly married, that their union had produced a son which he now recognised, and that because of his 'adultery and infidelity' they were now divorced.[60] Rohan, now known as the dame de la Garnache, was awarded the duchy of Loudun, in Vienne, with a revenue of 50,000 livres raised on the hôtel de ville in Paris, while her son would receive 20,000 livres in income from the abbey of Boulbonne in Languedoc, which had belonged to Anne d'Este's brother, the Cardinal of Ferrara. He would also, thanks to Anne d'Este's negotiations, be appointed to the post of Grand Prior of Auvergne on the condition that he would convert to Catholicism.

The long-awaited recognition of her son by Nemours would be a bittersweet victory: in October 1581, Henri was imprisoned for the kidnap and assault of a silversmith, and compounded his crime by resisting arrest by force of arms. In his account of the event, L'Estoile mentions how Henri's notorious behaviour since his supposed conversion to Catholicism had so enraged all those involved in the earlier negotiations that they wanted to 'either have him killed or to refuse him all of the aforesaid promises'.[61] The *Pasquil Courtizan* of 1581 is particularly vitriolic when it comes to Henri de 'La Garnache', likening him to a capon, a castrated cock fattened for eating, while also labelling him a sodomite:

> Is this not the handsome duke of Mayenne
> Born of the first love
> Of the noble duke of Nemours?
> I don't mean la Garnache,
> But I'll be damned if I don't spit
> To see that Lodunois capon
> Who, however, is not castrated
> So Fourquevaux assures me
> Who offers him his ass to ride.[62]

Henri did not simply suffer from a negative reputation that could be mocked in satirical libels; his crimes were enough to keep him imprisoned for years. At one point in July 1582, there was talk of the king's brother, the duc d'Alençon, known as 'Monsieur', having Henri 'practised out of prison, where he lies at Paris; so that he might be "raised up an opposite instrument" to the Duke of Savoy and those of the House of Nemours'.[63] Whether this plan was effected is unknown, but Henri continued to be involved in outrageous behaviour. In August 1583, he sent a messenger to Elizabeth I, claiming that he had been taken hostage in Brouage and begging 2,000 crowns in ransom money. Elizabeth was instantly suspicious because she remembered that during the last visit to England by the French commissioners 'it was given out that he did misbehave himself much, to the great discontentment of divers, both of the one religion and the other'.[64] In January 1585, Catherine de Medici wrote to Anne d'Este about Henri's visit to her, during which he claimed that he had been in prison for two years (although that may have been an understatement). He was concerned, said Catherine, that Anne d'Este 'no longer wanted to appoint him' (presumably to the post of Grand Prior of Auvergne) to which Catherine replied that she had not heard Este mention the matter 'since he had fulfilled nothing of which he had promised'. He claimed 'his mother's people had tricked him and had made him do things that ruined both him and her'.[65]

He was correct in that his actions had adversely affected his mother's reputation. The son for whose rights Rohan had fought for so long was considered such a reprobate that even she would no longer speak to him. Their soured relationship became even more serious when in February 1587, Protestant forces led by Henri invaded his mother's fortress of La Garnache, which she had kept in neutrality during the religious wars. Rohan appealed to the queen mother for aid. Catherine's icy response demonstrated to what depths her opinion of her former lady-in-waiting had sunk:

> To madame de la Garnache.
> My cousin, I received the letter which you wrote me by this bearer and have seen what you tell me of the violence that you say the seigneur de La Garnache your son has done to you, having seized your home in La Garnache,

where *you had ample means by which to prevent his entry, having a garrison there at the expense of the King my son*; [a garrison] which your said son writes me, on the other hand, that he would like to serve from now on, and that, what made him go to you was only to attend to matters between you and him. These are things that I am doubtful to believe; because what one reads in this for certain is that *the intelligence was not so bad between you and your said son*, and that *you yourself had had the amount of the King's tax raised again in these past few days*, to three hundred and five livres, for which you had sent your receiver to the king of Navarre to ask for receipt, who because of this retained and retains your said receiver still in prison in La Rochelle to have him punished, if he has not yet been so, for not handing over the said money. If this is so, *you cannot deny that you have behaved very badly in the service of the King my said Lord and son*; but, to resolve it, you must have the said place of La Garnache put into the hands of some man of worth, a Catholic gentleman, who will guard it for the service of the King my said Lord and son, and you must return to the hands of his tax receiver the said money that it is said that you had had raised. As regards the receiver Viette, since your said son says that he is completely devoted to the service of the King my said son, he can therefore have him freed. Praying God, etc.[66]

Catherine accused Rohan of feigning neutrality at the expense of the crown while secretly negotiating with her son to take over La Garnache in order to turn it over to the Protestant forces. She also accused her of stealing from the crown by raising unsanctioned taxes. As punishment, Catherine decided, she should turn over La Garnache to a crown-appointed governor, but instead Henri de Navarre, Jeanne d'Albret's son, leader of the Protestants and the future Henri IV, assumed control of the lands. Nevertheless, the relationship between the queen mother and her former lady-in-waiting had been irreparably damaged, Catherine making the implicit suggestion that if her son was a troublemaker, it was due to Rohan's influence. The expression 'you have behaved very badly in the service of the King' was a highly accusatory statement, and Rohan was lucky to not have suffered worse punishment. Catherine had regarded Rohan as an opponent for nearly three decades, ever since the death of Henri II in 1559, when Rohan's legal suit forced the newly-powerless queen mother to choose between her and the more powerful Guise faction. Catherine was also defensive of the reputation of her household, and had been angry that her lady-in-waiting had attracted negative attention on the moral discipline within that household.

Although Nemours was ultimately successful in forcing Rohan to relinquish the documents relating to the case, much like in the case of Limeuil's dossier, those documents lay in obscurity in the archives until they were published in the nineteenth century. Rohan's 1580 declaration detailed all the abuses and corruption of which she felt Nemours was guilty, and even attacked Catherine and her sons for their 'shows and signs of ill will' towards her and her son, but it is unclear how well that declaration was publicised.[67] Certainly, the case was so notorious that in the short term the facts of the story would have been common knowledge, but

Word of Honour 149

by the eighteenth century, when the duc de Saint-Simon was writing his memoirs of court life, his own prejudices concerning the contemporary descendants of the house of Rohan coupled with the lack of official documentation had transformed the determined and proud Rohan into little more than a depraved gold-digger:

> The good La Garnache was left abused, and, while waiting for the outcome of her marriage, made of her turpitude her cause célèbre and the reason for the cries of those who protected her. The end of it all is that she was left to her shame, and her protectors to their cries, and that M. de Nemours married Mme de Guise in 1566. Miss La Garnache disappeared and went to raise her little baby in obscurity, where he lived and died. After several years, as the tireless pursuit and the talent of knowing how to make a comeback is still a special trait of the house of Rohan, Miss La Garnache half showed her face again, and tried to get Mme de Nemours to have pity on her so as to obtain some compensation from her.[68]

Thus, while Rohan had concentrated on salvaging her reputation in the immediate sense, Nemours's tactics of secrecy and seizure of written documentation meant that he could control his reputation for posterity. While Jacques de Savoie would be lauded as a great military captain, and immortalised in romantic fiction as the hero of Madame de La Fayette's *La Princesse de Clèves*, Françoise de Rohan would always be known as the woman seduced and abandoned by the duke of Nemours.

Conclusion

Although early modern archival documents can appear on the surface to be dry and dusty, to the reader with an ear to orality they are alive with sound: the sounds of lovemaking, swearing, gossip, threats, insults and laughter. The written documents relating to the Rohan-Nemours case reveal a rich world of oral transactions, demonstrating the mostly unsuccessful attempts to create and maintain secrecy in the court environment. The centrality of marriage to the successful maintenance of the aristocratic society meant that details of the intimate romantic encounters of noble men and women were valuable intelligence, and this also explains the clandestine and duplicitous behaviour of both Rohan and Nemours. Her initial denial of the pregnancy, both to herself and others, can be explained by the stigma of illegitimate pregnancy, but her decision to reveal those intimate details in the courts was part of a strategy to defend herself by attacking Nemours's reputation as an honourable man. His seduction of Rohan, facilitated by his reputation as an '*homme de bien*', whilst he was secretly negotiating another marriage, was interpreted as an attack not just on her honour, but that of her entire family. The scandalous implication that he had gone back on his word as a gentleman was eventually confirmed by a legal ruling, but not after both parties had suffered grave slights on their reputations. Furthermore, the increasingly superior role of written testimony over oral testimony meant that Nemours could no longer rely simply on his own elevated status and that of his high-ranking witnesses to outrank and thereby dismiss the evidence of lowly, but eyewitness, servants. Valuing the spoken word over the written, it appears to have taken Nemours longer than Rohan to appreciate the legal significance of his letters and the servants' depositions, although his eventual realisation of the value of that written documentation resulted in his apparently successful attempts to control its wider publication. Rohan's accumulation of written evidence, letters and eyewitness testimonies had made her case resistant in the face of powerful opposition. The depositions, from both servant and noble alike, reveal a densely-populated court environment, where higher ranked nobles attempted to keep sensitive information within a privileged circle but where the ubiquity of servants and ambassadors resulted in their presence at the most intimate of moments. A fertile breeding-ground for rumour and gossip, the close quarters of the royal household provided ample material for scandal, and the Rohan-Nemours dispute demonstrates how the gossip of illiterate and generally ignored servants could escape the walls of the palace to reach an international audience. The next chapter will examine the life of a woman tied up in that dispute, Anne d'Este, and her efforts to control the flow of sensitive information about her personal affairs, demonstrating how the fortuitous accident of birth could give a noblewoman the agency she needed to avoid scandal.

Notes

1 National Archives UK (NA) SP 70/84, f. 356, 'In nuptias Ducis de Nemours':

> Subnonas Maias meretrix obscaena, vieta
> Putida, trita viris lectū repetit genialem.
> Ducit eā uxorĕ sceleratus, perfidus, exlex,
> Decoctor, moechus, sacer, impius et cruce dignus.[. . .]

The verse, along with a French verse discussed further in this essay ('Sonet sur la devise du Roy'), formed the contents of an ambassadorial dispatch from France to England; see *CSPF*, 8 May 1566, no. 440.

2 The case is thoroughly studied in Matthew A. Vester, *Jacques de Savoie-Nemours: L'apanage du Genevois au coeur de la puissance dynastique savoyarde au XVIe siècle* (Genève: Droz, 2008), 67–109. It was also studied in the nineteenth century by Alphonse, baron de Ruble, *Le duc de Nemours et Mademoiselle de Rohan (1531–1592)* (Paris, 1883); and La Ferrière, *Trois amoureuses au XVIè siècle*. Given that his work is a biography of Nemours, Vester points out the positive biases of both earlier accounts towards Rohan.

3 The Gallican Church refers to the Catholic Church in France and its assertion that the pope should have authority only over ecclesiastical matters, leaving temporal matters in the hands of the French monarch and bishops. This argument, eventually set out in the *Declaration of the Clergy of France* in 1682, was never accepted by the Holy See. The Rota is the highest appellate tribunal of the Roman Catholic Church.

4 For studies of the relationship between orality and literacy, see Walter J. Ong, *Orality and Literacy: The Technologizing of the Word* (London: Methuen, 1982); Jack Goody, *The Interface Between the Written and the Oral* (Cambridge: Cambridge University Press, 1987); *Literacy and Orality*, eds. David R. Olson and Nancy Torrance (Cambridge: Cambridge University Press, 1991).

5 BnF MS Fr 3169, f. 47: deposition of Fleury Barge; f. 54: deposition of Pasquier Boucher; f. 59: deposition of Gabrielle Binel; f. 73: deposition of Antoine de Coué.

6 BnF MS Fr 3169, f. 53, deposition of Fleury Barge.
7 BnF MS Fr 3169, f. 37, deposition of Antoine de Coué: 'ouit ladite dame s'escrier a raison de quoy tourna la teste du coste du lict et veit iceulx seigneur de nemours et dame de rohan faire acte de mary et femme'.
8 BnF MS Fr 3169, f. 32r, 32v, deposition of Gabrielle de Binel: 'ou elle veit et trouva ledit seigneur duc debout contre le lict de ladite dame et faisant les oeuvres de mary et femme | Et soudain que ladite dame de rohan appercent ladite depposant entrer se retira | Et lors ledit seigneur duc voiant que ladite dame de rohan se retiroit de honte luy deist d'un voix aspre et basse ressentant sa colere ces motz en jurant mort dieu que craignez vous ne suis je pas vostre mary n'estes vous pas ma femme Aquoy respondit ladite dame ouy Monsr Ainsi que ladite depposan ouit et entendit clairement et asseurement et estoient en ladite chambre les filles et damoiselles de ladite dame de rohan'.
9 For a detailed description of the logistics of life at court, including architectural plans of various royal châteaux, see Chatenet, *La cour de France au XVIe siècle*; also Chatenet, 'Les logis des femmes à la cour des derniers Valois', 175–92.
10 BnF MS Fr 3169, f. 41v, deposition of Perrine Legrand: 'Je scay bien quant vous serez en bretagne que madame vre mere vous vouldre marier. Je vous prie ne vous mariez point car vous scavez bien les propos quil y a entre nous deux | Et sur ces propos entendit ladite depposant que ledit signeur deist a ladite dame ces motz Je vous prendz pour ma femme Et ladite dame deist audit seigneur duc Je vous prendz pour mon mary Et en ce faisan se baiserent lun lautre'.
11 BnF MS Fr 3169, f.33r, deposition of Gabrielle de Binel: 'le commun bruict de toute la maison de ladite dame et autres non domesticques hantans en ladite maison estoit que ledit seigneur duc estoit le vray mary deladite dame et estoit tenu et reputé pour tel'.
12 BnF MS Fr 3169, f. 53, deposition of Fleury Barge: 'la court estant à Fontainebleau, environ la saint Jehan, au temps que la royne estoit accouchée de deux enfans'.
13 BnF MS Fr 3169, f. 37, deposition of Antoine de Coué: 'agé de vingtrois a vingtquatre ans ou environ'.
14 BnF MS Fr 3169, f. 29r, 29v, deposition of Gabrielle de Binel: 'A laquelle ledit Sr duc feist response qu'il estoit homme de bien jurant le nom de dieu comme la mort dieu et autres sermens qu'il avoit promis mariage a ladite dame de rohan et lespouser Qu'elle estoit asseuree de luy et qu'elle le scavoit bien Et quant ladite depposant remonstroit audit seigneur Ouy Monseigneur mais si vous ne lespousiez regardez le danger auquel vous nous mectoiez | Lors se meist a juer ledit Sr comme devant luy disant Je croy madamoiselle de coué que vous ne me pensez poinct homme de bien. je ne suis poinct si meschant ne si mallheureux que je la voulusse tromper'.
15 *Lettres d'Antoine de Bourbon et de Jehanne d'Albret* (Paris, 1877), 224, Antoine de Bourbon to Jeanne d'Albret, 1560: 'me semble que il ne sen peult dédire sans à son honneur fère tort'.
16 For the laws concerning clandestine marriage and public opinion surrounding it in early modern Europe, see Gerber, *Bastards*; Marian Rothstein, 'Clandestine Marriage and Amadis de Gaule: The Text, the World, and the Reader', *The Sixteenth Century Journal* 25, no. 4 (1994): 873–86; Cathleen M. Bauschatz, 'Rabelais and Marguerite de Navarre on Sixteenth-Century Views of Clandestine Marriage', *The Sixteenth Century Journal* 34, no. 2 (2003): 395–408; R. B. Outhwaite, *Clandestine Marriage in England, 1500–1850* (London, 1995).
17 Rothstein, 'Clandestine Marriage and Amadis de Gaule', 879.
18 Ruble, *François de Montmorency*.
19 In her seminal essay on royal legislation around marriage in early modern France, Sarah Hanley expresses doubt that the Montmorency affair could have played a part in the edict. Hanley, 'Engendering the State', 4–27. However, I disagree, arguing that François's age, then 26, was the reason for the extremely high age of consent for males (30).
20 Walter S. Johnson, *Chapters in the History of French Law* (Montreal, 1957), 250.
21 Johnson, *French Law*, 250. See also Gerber, *Bastards*, 38–9.

22 Jean Brissaud, *A History of French Private Law*, trans. Rapelje Howell (London, 1912), 116.
23 Frederic J. Baumgartner, *France in the Sixteenth Century* (New York, 1995), 285.
24 BnF MS Fr 3169, f.1: deposition of Catherine de Medici; f. 5: deposition of Cardinal de Lorraine; f.9: deposition of Constable Montmorency; f. 11: deposition of Marguerite de France; f. 14: deposition of Madeleine de Savoie; f.16: deposition of Diane de Poitiers; f. 20: deposition of Ambroise Paré.
25 For early modern beliefs around menstruation and pregnancy, see Cathy McClive, 'The Hidden Truths of the Belly: The Uncertainties of Pregnancy in Early Modern Europe', *Social History of Medicine* 15 no. 2 (2002): 209–227; McClive, 'Menstrual Knowledge and Medical Practice in France, c. 1555–1761', *Menstruation: A Cultural History*, eds. Gillian Howie and Andrew Shail (Basingstoke, 2005), 76–89.
26 BnF MS Fr 3169, f. 31r, deposition of Gabrielle de Binel: 'qu'elle avoit esté advertie par une des filles de la Royne qui avoit ouy dire a la seignora olivia qui disoit lavoir ouy dire a Madame de Guise que ledit Sr. de Nemours avoit promis a Madame de Guise deppouser une [illegible] seur'.
27 BnF MS Fr 3169, f. 16, deposition of Diane de Poitiers: 'que le bruict couroit que ledict duc de Nemours alloit en Italie pour veoir madame Lucresse, que peult estre il l'espouseroit. Ne sait toutefois si ladicte damoiselle demanderesse sçavoit rien dudict bruict de mariage'.
28 BnF MS Fr 3397, f. 70, Françoise de Rohan to Jacques de Savoie: 'quant au mariage de la dame que vous saves i.e. se tant ce que vous man aves dict que i.e. ne point de peur quelle me fase ce tort'.
29 BnF MS Fr 3169, f.1, deposition of Catherine de Medici: 'qu'elle ne pouvoit honnestement refuser l'entrée à ung si honneste prince'.
30 Vester, *Jacques de Savoie-Nemours*, 83.
31 Ian Maclean, *The Renaissance Notion of Woman: A Study in the Fortunes of Scholasticism and Medical Science in European Intellectual Life* (Cambridge: Cambridge University Press, 1980).
32 *Lettres d'Antoine de Bourbon et de Jehanne d'Albret*, ed. Rochambeau (Paris: Renouard, 1877), 224, Antoine de Bourbon to Jeanne d'Albret, 1560 [BnF MS Fr 8746, f. 97]: 'Quant à ses femmes, je ne les ay point suivant ce que me mandiez en n'envoier, car il nous semble pourmilleur avis de ne les envoier point, et les laisser avecques leur mestresse pour l'acompaigner vers vous; et puis après en ferés comme il vous plaira, car sy je les heussions chassee, tout le monde eust creu que nous eussions congnu que ma cousine eust esté vendue et quelle eust fait faulte contre son honneur'.
33 Ibid., 222, Antoine de Bourbon to Jeanne d'Albret, 1560 [BnF MS Fr 8746, f.77]: 'parquoy nous nous dellibérons de la tenir pour famme de Monsr de Nemours et ne la mespriser ne l'élongner de nous jusques à ce que nous aions nouvelles de luy, et fait ce que pourons pour elle; car il en feroit de mesmes de son cousté, et la pouvre malheureuze demeuroit désonorée et nous en peine grande de l'an venger'.
34 *Négociations diplomatiques de la France avec la Toscane*, 6 vols, eds. Giuseppe Canestrini, Abel Desjardins (Paris: Imprimerie nationale, 1859–1886), 3, 444, Niccolo Tornabuoni to Cosimo I, [translation by Rosa Salzberg]: 'pare che M. de Nemours sia insospettito, e così aiutato da M. de Guise, si sia armato in casa, e fuora ancora vadi bene accompagnato . . . Non è fornita questa lite, ma tuttavia va pullulando, nè manca chi accenda, come il Conestabile che non si sta. E Guisi n'hanno peggio, perchè hanno tutto l'odio dell' universale, e ciascuno vorria che se n'andassino, e gli gridono dietro; e tutto questo è fatto acciò diloggino'.
35 *CSPF*, 7, 27 Jan 1564, no. 109 (8) 'Occurrences in France'. It appears that 'Fontenay' (Françoise's brother, Jean de Rohan, baron de Frontenay) was simultaneously experiencing marital difficulties of his own; see Potter, David, 'Marriage and Cruelty among the Protestant Nobility in Sixteenth-Century France: Diane de Barbançon and Jean de Rohan, 1561–7', *European History Quarterly* 20 (1990): 5–38.

36 de Thou, *Histoire universelle de Jacques-Auguste de Thou*, 5, 185: 'Comme le duc de Nemours avoit alors plus de crédit, & qu'on avoit beaucoup d'éloignement & de haine pour la Religion Protestante, à laquelle Françoise de Rohan étoit attachée; ce procès fut vuidé par l'entremise du Pape, & le mariage du duc de Nemours avec Françoise de Rohan fut déclaré nul'. Jacques-Auguste's father, Christophe de Thou, was *premier président* of the Parlement of Paris while the case was under debate.
37 NA SP 70/84 f. 356, 'Sonet sur la devise du Roy'. See note 1.
38 *Lettres d'Antoine de Bourbon et de Jehanne d'Albret*, 222, Antoine de Bourbon to Jeanne d'Albret, 1560: 'car j'ay espérance que le tout bien considéré de luy, qu'il ne peult moins que de passer par là, j'entens de mariage ou de mort'.
39 Roelker, *Queen of Navarre*, 322.
40 Nancy Lyman Roelker, 'The Appeal of Calvinism to French Noblewomen in the Sixteenth Century', *Journal of Interdisciplinary History* 2, 4 Psychoanalysis and History (Spring 1972): 391–418, 412.
41 Viète was tutor to Catherine de Parthenay, and he would dedicate his most famous work, *In Artem Analycitem Isagoge*, a foundational work for modern algebra, to both Parthenay and her close friend Françoise de Rohan. François Viète, *In artem analyticem isagoge: seorsim excussa ab Opere restitutae mathematicae analyseos, seu Algebra nova / Francisci Vietae* (Tours: J. Mettayer, 1591).
42 *Mémoires de Jeanne d'Albret*, 39–42: 'l'injustice qui me fut faicte en ce temps-là en la personne de ma cousine de Rohan, ceste injurieuse injustice . . . c'est celle de quoy je me suis plus ressentie'.
43 BnF MS Fr 3215, f. 71.
44 Mark Greengrass, 'A Day in the Life of the Third Estate: Blois, 26th December 1576', *Politics, Ideology and the Law in Early Modern Europe: Essays in Honour of J.H.M. Salmon*, ed. Adrianna Bakos (New York: University of Rochester Press, 1994), 74.
45 Ibid., 75.
46 Baumgartner, *France in the Sixteenth Century*, 92.
47 de Vivo, *Information and Communication in Venice*, 4.
48 For the details of this marriage arrangement from Este's perspective, see Coester, *Schön wie Venus, mutig wie Mars*.
49 *CSPF*, 8, 21 May 1566, Hoby to Cecil.
50 Roelker, *Queen of Navarre*, 247.
51 Pierre Champion, *Catherine de Médicis présente à Charles IX son royaume 1564–1566* (Paris: Grasset, 1937), 431–2: 'Enfin, Mme de Vendôme et Mme de Guise s'étaient déshonorées en se chamaillant comme des blanchisseuses (lavacerias) au sujet du mariage de cette dernière, ne craignant pas d'échanger des paroles malsonnantes en présence de toute la cour, et de la reine'.
52 *CSPF*, 8, 16 May 1566, Hoby to Cecil.
53 Champion, *Catherine de Médicis*, 429: 'Mais le procureur avait continué son instance devant le conseil privé, affirmant que M. De Nemours, suivant les lois de France, méritait d'avoir la tête tranchée, car il avait pris de force Mme de Rohan dans la chambre de la reine et l'avait rendue enceinte. Un grand rire s'empara de Catherine de Médicis, de Charles IX et de tout le conseil! On fit sortir le procureur'.
54 *CSPF*, 8, 4 May 1566, Hoby to Cecil.
55 Neuschel, *Word of Honor*, 114.
56 BnF MS Fr 3397, f. 70, Françoise de Rohan to Jacques de Savoie: 'i.e. receu la laitre que vour maves escrite qui ma este ung bien fort grant plesir de savoir la verite ancore que i.e. ne fust point an doute que vous ne fusies homme de bien car si i.e. i euse este i.e. ne me fuse tant fiee an vous comme i.e. suis'.
57 Brantôme, 642: 'le parangon de toute chevallerie'.
58 Johnson, *French Law*, 250.
59 Ruble, *Le duc de Nemours*, 132: 'dame de Nemours, a peine d'estre declaree réfractaire et désobéissante aux arrêts'.

60 BnF MS Fr 3215, f. 13: 'pour cet effect nous declarons, comme autrefois, que depuis l'adultère et l'infidélité dudict sieur duc, nostre intention n'a esté ny n'est de jamais converser avecques lui et avons accepté et acceptons son divorce'.
61 L'Estoile, 163–4: 'ou de le faire mourir ou de le frustrer de toutes lesdites promesses'.
62 L'Estoile, 'Pasquil Courtizan', 176:

> N'est-ce pas ce beau duc de Maine
> Qui nasquit des premiers amours
> De ce noble duc de Nemours?
> Je n'entens pas de la Garnache,
> Mais à peine que je ne crache,
> De voir ce chappon Lodunois,
> Qui n'est pas chastré toutefois,
> Ainsi que Fourquevaux asseure
> Qui de son cul lui fait monture.

63 *CSPF*, July 12 1582, no. 152 Cobham to Walsingham.
64 *CSPF*, Aug 27 1583, no. 102 [Robert Beale] to Cobham.
65 *Lettres*, VIII, 232, 12 January 1585. (Aut. BnF MS Fr 3367, f. 4), Catherine de Medici to Anne d'Este [emphasis added].
66 Ibid., IX, 178, 19 February 1587, Catherine de Médicis to Françoise de Rohan. [emphasis added]
67 BnF MS Fr 3215, f. 13: 'leurs Majestez nous ayant fait toutes démonstrations et signe de malveillance'
68 Louis de Rouvroy, duc de Saint-Simon, *Mémoires complets et authentiques du duc de Saint-Simon sur le siècle de Louis XIV et la régence*, 21 vols, (Paris: A. Sautelet, 1829), II, 158: 'La bonne la Garnache demeurait abusée, et en attendant ce qui arriverait de son mariage, faisait de sa turpitude la principale pièce de son sac, et toute la force des cris de ceux qui la protégaient. La fin de tout cela fut qu'elle en fut pour sa honte, et ses protecteurs pour leurs cris, et que M. de Nemours épousa madame de Guise en 1566. Mademoiselle de la Garnache disparut et alla élever son poupon dans l'obscurité où il vécut et mourut. Après plusieurs années, comme la suite infatigable et le talent de savoir se retourner est encore un apanage spécial de la maison de Rohan, mademoiselle de la Garnache se remontra à demi, essaya de faire pitié à madame de Nemours, et d'obtenir quelque dédommagement par elle'.

6 The Triumph of the Matriarch
Anne d'Este, Duchesse de Guise, Duchesse de Nemours

On 25 November 1591, as Paris suffered under the militant Terror of 'the Sixteen', the increasingly powerful and ever more fanatical wing of the Catholic League, Pierre de L'Estoile made this entry in his journal:

> Today . . . madame de Nemours, astonished by the evil rumours that were circulating and the strange plots and proceedings of the Sixteen . . . dispatched towards her son a gentleman with letters and speeches of credit, by which she gave him knowledge of what was being done and what was happening, and how much his presence was needed here to rescue her and her daughter, and all the people of worth, from the tyranny and servitude to which they were reduced under the domination of these men of nothing. She gave orders to the said gentleman to say to the duc de Mayenne's face that he was to remember that she was his mother, and that it was she who had carried him who asked him to do this. These words touched greatly the heart of the duc de Mayenne, as it made things immediate, and they hastened his voyage and advanced his resolve.[1]

Exploiting her maternal ties, playing on her son's guilt at his absence, as well as appealing to his pride and sympathy in order to command the leader of the League forces to return home, Anne d'Este, duchesse de Guise and then duchesse de Nemours, (Figure 6.1) demonstrated in this single action the power that lay within the person of the Guise matriarch. In the words of Stuart Carroll, 'For an eldest son charged with the responsibility of family head, the righteous anger of one's mother can be the most chastening of experiences'.[2] Known as the 'Queen Mother' during the prominence of the League in Paris (1588–1594), Anne d'Este was very familiar with the strategies available to powerful women in the political arena, as she had been employing them throughout her life as a wife and mother within the influential Guise clan. While the two previous case studies have dealt with specific scandals as they affected the women involved, this chapter focuses on a woman whose familial ties, status and position at court meant that she was closely involved in all kinds of notorious events but who managed to emerge from them without substantial damage to her reputation. By examining three specific phases in her life when she was involved with scandal, it explores how she was able to effectively manipulate and control her self-representation, ending her days with a reputation for impeccable noble behaviour.

Figure 6.1 François Clouet, *Anne d'Este, duchesse de Guise, duchesse de Nemours*
Source: BnF Réserve NA-22 (19)-BTE

The agency Anne d'Este enjoyed was in distinct contrast to that of Limeuil and Rohan and came about through a series of very fortunate circumstances. The daughter of Renée de France, daughter of Louis XII of France, and Ercole II d'Este, duke of Ferrara, Anne d'Este was given an exemplary humanist education at the court of Ferrara alongside Olympia Morata, the acclaimed classical scholar.[3] In 1548, at the age of 16, she came to France to marry François, duc d'Aumale, shortly to become the second duc de Guise. Her beauty, learning and willingness to assimilate to her new family and country won her many admirers from the start. Her first marriage allied her to one of the most powerful and active families of the French nobility while her ancestry was that of the royal family itself. She became lady-in-waiting and a very close friend to Catherine de Medici, then the recently-crowned queen of France. Este would bear eight children with the duc de Guise before his assassination in 1563. As we have seen, three years later, she would marry an associate of the Guise family, the duc de Nemours, with whom she would have four children. In an age when beauty, fertility and powerful family connections were the most desirable qualities in a noblewoman, Anne d'Este excelled as a noble consort. Her prominent role would, however, bring her into conflict. First, the Guise family's position as the leaders of the Catholic campaign against the 'heretics' of the Reformed religion led to virulent polemic being written against them, in which Este would see her own sexual honour attacked. Second, as described in the previous chapter, her decision in 1566 to remarry with a man who was already involved in a protracted legal battle over an alleged clandestine marriage exposed her to charges of adultery. Finally, her campaign, in tandem with the other women of the Guise clan, to depose Henri III after his murder of her sons in 1588, and her subsequent role as head of the League left her similarly vulnerable to attacks by those opposed to the League and its often brutal tactics. The strategies employed by Anne d'Este throughout the events that threatened her reputation in her later life demonstrate how she fully exploited the agency she had been blessed with through her familial connections and status at court to avoid scandal. But her eventual success should not diminish the challenges that she faced in controlling her reputation.

The Scandal of Incest

One of the earliest examples of scandal attaching itself to Anne d'Este can be found in the notorious 1560 printed pamphlet, *Epistre envoiee au Tigre de la France* [*Letter Sent to the Tiger of France*], which, although anonymous, is attributed to François Hotman, the Protestant lawyer and author of the anti-monarchical 1573 treatise, *Franco-Gallia*.[4] The target of the *Tigre*'s vitriol is Anne's brother-in-law Charles, cardinal of Lorraine, who is attacked, among other things, for his incestuous relationship with his 'sister':

> The honour of your sister cannot be guaranteed with you. You leave your gown, you don the sword to go to see her. The husband cannot be so vigilant that you cannot deceive his wife.[5]
> ... a husband is more restrained with his wife than you are with your own female kin.[6]

Although Anne d'Este is never mentioned by name in the pamphlet, her public profile was such that no one was ever in doubt as to whom Hotman was referring. While she is portrayed as a passive recipient of her brother-in-law's unnatural sexual advances (themselves a by-product of his unnatural ambition), such an accusation would have been an attack on her sexual honour nonetheless, especially with reference to her cuckolded husband, the celebrated military hero, François, duc de Guise. The pamphlet thus participates in the tradition of cuckold literature we are now familiar with which portrays the cardinal as a sexually perverse 'other', the duke as the comic figure of the cuckold and Anne d'Este as the voracious female whose desires are so unlimited as to include her own brother-in-law.

The only account we have of the personal reactions of Anne and her brother-in-law to the libel comes from Brantôme, who reveals – through his shortening of the title to its more popular nickname, *Le Tigre* – the public notoriety of the pamphlet:

> There were many defamatory libels against those who then governed the kingdom, but none was sharper and more offensive than an invective entitled *The Tiger* (in imitation of Cicero's first invective against Catiline), because it mentioned the amorous relationship of a very great and beautiful lady and of a great man related to her. If the . . . author had been apprehended, even had he had a hundred thousand lives he would have lost them all; because the great man and the great lady were so nauseated by it that they were almost desperate.[7]

Two important points should be noted about Brantôme's account. First, the very mention of the pamphlet, moreover by its better-known shortened title, reveals that this libel in particular stood out from the countless anti-Guise libels circulating at the time, so much so that Brantôme can remember it when writing his memoirs at the end of his life.[8] Second, he does not remember it for the dominant themes of the pamphlet, the attacks on the cardinal's greed, ambition and murderous instincts, but rather he recalls it only for its mention of incest between the cardinal and his sister.

Incest was a trope often employed against ambitious clerics: in the collection of Huguenot libels by Rasse des Noeux at least five describe the cardinal de Lorraine as incestuous. As Jean-Claude Ternaux explains, 'When it is a matter of an ecclesiastic it is only fair to denounce his lack of chastity and to aggravate the count of indictment by imputing incest to him'.[9] Charles, cardinal de Lorraine's dual position as both a leading cleric in France and a senior member of one of the kingdom's most powerful families made him a target for critics eager to equate his desire for clerical benefices with other, more worldly lusts. In *Les Tragiques* d'Aubigné linked the scarlet of the cardinal's hat to his blood, which he claimed to be polluted through sexual intercourse with his own family:

> And then the scarlet again warns us
> That he has in his blood soaked his lewdness
> When in the same subject is created the monstrous
> Adulterer, lecher, sodomite and incestuous.[10]

Like the cardinal of Lorraine, Pierre d'Épinac, the archbishop of Lyon, was regularly accused of incestuous behaviour with his sister Grisolde. The satirical libel *The Library of Madame de Montpensier* contained the imaginary book title: *Singular Treatise of Incest, by M. the Archbishop of Lyon; Newly Printed and Dedicated to Madamoiselle de Grisolles, his Sister* [*Traicté singulier de l'Inceste, par M. l'archevesque de Lion; imprimé nouvellement et dedié à Madamoiselle de*

Grisolles, sa seur], and the *Satyre Ménippée* would later make the same accusation against him.

There exists only one original copy of the 1560 printed text of *Le Tigre*. The fact that so few copies of such a notorious libel survive points to a systematic – and mostly successful – effort to destroy all evidence of this particular pamphlet. The cardinal employed the councillor De Lyon to prosecute the author. Unable to locate him, De Lyon found a bookseller, Martin Lhommet, who had a few copies, and on 15 June 1560, hanged him in the Place Maubert. At the execution, the crowd of spectators was scolded for its bloodthirsty jeering by a passer-by, Robert Dehors, a Rouennais merchant who was promptly arrested and executed for 'said scandalous and blasphemous remarks . . . inducing . . . the people to sedition and public scandals'.[11] The strenuous attempts to silence this particular pamphlet point to deep-held anxieties about the accusations of incest it contained.

In his study of incest in Renaissance England, Bruce Thomas Boehrer claims that 'incest can easily be viewed as something close to an obsession within courtly circles in sixteenth- and seventeenth-century England'.[12] He points out that the nobility's concern to preserve their inheritances within their families led to increasingly endogamous marriage choices, which left them sensitive to concerns about incest. The most famous claims of incest in the early modern period were made by Henry VIII, who dissolved his first marriage to Catherine of Aragon on the grounds that it was incestuous because she had been married to his elder brother. The divorce left him free to marry Anne Boleyn, but the irony of Henry's behaviour was not lost on his contemporaries: the Catholic commentator Nicholas Harpsfield remarked that Henry 'laboured to the Pope to have a dispensation to marry that woman whose sister he had carnally known before', referring to Henry's previous mistress, Anne's sister Mary.[13] Henry would go on to have Anne executed for, among other things, alleged incestuous relations with her brother George. These accusations would have far-reaching repercussions: Anne d'Este's niece, Marie Stuart, Queen of Scots, would base her claim to the English throne on the varying beliefs that Elizabeth I was either the illegitimate product of incest between Anne and her brother, or that Anne was herself the product of Henry's relationship with Anne's own mother – an illogical claim given that Henry was only a few years older than Anne. Nevertheless, outrage at the execution of Marie Stuart found its expression in France through a 1587 libel, 'Sonnet to the English Jezabel', decrying Elizabeth I as the unnatural and beastly offspring of a mother who was also her sister:

> Bastard, incestuous and public whore
> Perfidious, disloyal and daughter of your sister,
> When your father and hers discovered his error,
> The cruel father and husband had the slut killed.[14]

The debates over the legitimacy of each of these claims produced a wealth of documentation on incest theory which point to a real concern with, and interest in, incest in the early modern period. According to Jean-Claude Arnould, incest was a constant theme in the popular literature of the period, finding expression in stories of the father's pursuit of his daughter.[15] Although French playwrights in the sixteenth century would not become as obsessed with the topic as their English counterparts (Boehrer counts nearly 50 dramas of the English Renaissance which have incest as their subject, not to mention other prose works), French literature does provide some evidence of the interest in this crime. Tale 30 of Marguerite de Navarre's *Héptameron* contains a particularly convoluted tale of double incest in which a woman commits incest with her unwitting son and conceives a daughter who then goes on to marry him, becoming in the process his daughter, sister and wife.[16] Tale 33 offers a different take: a priest and his sister are executed for trying to hide their sexual relationship and the resulting pregnancy. This diversity within the incest *topos* was mirrored in the actual news of the day. L'Estoile included two cases of incest in his journal which illustrate the variety of forms which the crime could take: the first case involved a respected Councillor in the Parlement, Scoreol, murdered by a servant of his stepdaughter's husband in July 1576 after the latter had discovered that his young wife had been abused by Scoreol to the extent that her secret letters to the stepfather repeatedly begged him to murder her, 'to tear her from the pain she was in, by poison or other means'. After his attack, Scoreol did not die for three days, giving him time to admit to his crime and seek absolution.[17] The second case was the execution in July 1585 of Vermondet, lieutenant general of Limoges, for incest committed with his sister, of which he maintained 'until his last breath' he was innocent.[18] These examples demonstrate how elastic the concept of incest could be: the parties involved could be parents and children, brothers and sisters, or even in-laws and stepchildren; the act could be forced, consensual or the result of trickery or ignorance; moreover, the parties could be guilty or innocent.

Incest was thus a highly malleable accusation: given the grey area around consanguinity laws and the resultant concept of 'degrees of consanguinity', almost anyone could be considered as a relative. For the nobility – especially the higher nobility – incest was a legitimate concern: maintaining a 'pure' blood line that did not risk diluting the family estate through exogamous marriages inevitably led to the risk of close alliances between relatives. As a result, although the use of an accusation of incest to discredit a public figure is so common in the sixteenth century that one would expect its emotive force to be diminished, instead one finds the accused nobles often seeking prosecution for those responsible for disseminating the allegation. The archbishop of Lyon, Pierre d'Épinac was, like the cardinal of Lorraine, so aggrieved by the accusations of incest in the satirical literature that he unsuccessfully petitioned Henri III to prosecute those responsible.[19] Indeed, the most famous duel of the sixteenth century, Jarnac vs. Châtaigneraye, was provoked by an accusation of incest. François de Vivonne, seigneur de La Châtaigneraye, a partisan of the dauphin Henri (later Henri II), confirmed publicly the dauphin's suggestion that Guy Chabot, baron de Jarnac maintained an incestuous relationship with his wealthy stepmother. Jarnac accused him of a blatant lie, and a year later, on 10 July 1547, the newly-crowned king offered them a field of combat with the entire court present to watch as the king's favourite was slain by the young and inexperienced Jarnac.[20] That nobles would fight to the death to save their honour from the slur of an incest accusation demonstrates how conscious they were of concerns of consanguinity.

An imputation of incest was, by its very nature, levelled not simply at one individual, but at that individual's family, and in particular, families whose overt ambition was seen as a threat to legitimate power. Thus the Howard family's rising status at Henry VIII's court was quashed by claims of incest between Anne Boleyn and her brother (as well as other members of their family). In the plays of the later Caroline era, Boehrer claims that 'incest consistently appears as a principle of disorder insinuated into the royal household by subjects who presumptuously seek to control the affairs of princes'.[21] This concern with overweening ambition is also found in early modern French libels that used the trope of incest to discredit public figures. For example, the 1581 *Pasquil Courtizan* accused Anne d'Este's nephew, Charles, duc d'Aumale, of committing incest with his daughter, and implied that it was a trait characteristic of his entire family:

> What will we say of the sieur d'Aumale?
> Does he not have the male grace
> To abuse his own good wife!
> And if he cannot excuse himself of it,
> Saying that he sleeps, out of good zeal,
> With his wife and daughter,
> All three sleeping in the same bed:
> Is that not committing a crime?
> All are but made out of cuckoldry,
> Witness he who wants his share
> In the house of this Guisard [22]

Similarly, the *Satyre Ménippée* satirises the leaders of the Catholic League which controlled Paris from 1588 to 1594, Anne d'Este and her children being the most prominent, by portraying them as incestuous.[23] Allusions are made to incest between her daughter, Catherine-Marie de Lorraine, duchesse de Montpensier and her nephew, the duc de Guise, and between the archbishop of Lyon, Pierre d'Épinac, and his sister Grisolde. The Catholic League was perceived by its opponents to be usurping power from the legitimate king, Henri IV, and the fact that its key figures came predominantly from the Guise household (its leader was Este's son, the duc de Mayenne) explains the numerous references to incest within the satire. Similarly, d'Aubigné's use of the word 'joyeux' in book two of *Les Tragiques* was an allusion to Henri III's highly-favoured *mignon* Anne de Joyeuse and their alleged homosexual relationship, a relationship that d'Aubigné also regarded as incestuous because Joyeuse had married the queen's sister: 'The sin of Sodom, and bloody incest / Are the joyous reproaches of our impure courts'.[24]

Joyeuse's rapid ascension to a position of unprecedented prominence made him a much-reviled figure, and led naturally to an accusation of incest which, in this case, would implicate the king as well. Thus, by accusing the cardinal of Lorraine of incestuous relations with his sister, Hotman directly implicated Anne d'Este in the Guise family's attempts to usurp authority. She had become a central figure in the Guise clan, a powerful matriarch in the style of her mother-in-law Antoinette de Bourbon. She was therefore linked to the bloody reprisals, overseen primarily by her brother-in-law, for the failed Huguenot conspiracy of Amboise in 1560. The scale of those executions, and the emotional repercussions they had within the Huguenot community, were a direct stimulus for the creation of *Le Tigre*.

This theme of the cardinal de Lorraine's incestuous relationship with his sister-in-law was continued by the author of the 1574 pamphlet *Le Réveille-Matin des François*, a fictional dialogue in which the cardinal is described as being tricked into accepting a portrait 'in which the Cardinal of Lorraine, the Queen his niece [Marie Stuart], the Queen Mother [Catherine de Medici] and the duchesse de Guise [Anne d'Este] were painted fully nude, having their arms around the necks, and the legs intertwined one with the other'.[25] This development of the image of the incestuous cardinal to include other members of the royal family (the Guises were related by marriage to the Valois since their niece Marie Stuart had married Catherine's son, François II) illustrates the fascination that this idea held for contemporary observers. Despite the attempts to erase all knowledge of *Le Tigre*, a second version in verse would appear in 1561, and successive versions, each with slight variations, suggest the popularity of the original and demonstrate the willingness of writers to risk prosecution by re-working the incestuous image, thereby reinforcing its impact and ensuring its continuity.

The accusation also reveals how common was the knowledge of Charles's particularly close relationship with his sister-in-law. His regular letters to her demonstrate his fondness for Este, and his pain at being separated from her: 'there is no remedy, I must see you'.[26] One of his letters hints at the intimacy of their relationship: 'you must go to Paris where I will find the queen, and you and I will not move from the table'.[27] In December 1561, Catherine de Medici wrote to her friend that 'your good husband and good brother and you are but one like the Trinity'.[28] The queen mother was not the only witness to the closeness of the Guise threesome. In the intimate environment of the court, which acted as both the private residence of the monarch's chosen entourage and the public venue of government, visitors on official government business, such as François Hotman, who at that time served as ambassador for Huguenot dignitaries, would have been witness to the domestic behaviour of high-profile nobles and could have used this knowledge to threaten public figures.[29] Ménager notes that Hotman's use of the first and second person singular ['*Quand je te diray* . . .'] makes the libel sound like a private discussion between him and the cardinal, in which Hotman threatens to blackmail the cardinal with the secrets to which he is privy. 'The author becomes', says Ménager, 'a man of good will who employs the information which he alone possesses in the service of the people'.[30] In other words, Hotman creates a fiction in which he not only claims to have witnessed incestuous relations between Anne and Charles, but also pretends to blackmail the cardinal with the knowledge. Hotman's fictional narrative of Anne d'Este's illicit relationship with her brother-in-law, which originated in rumour and gossip, was countered, however, by a very real prosecution, in which Guise censorship of the text led to the deaths of two men.

At the time of the libel's publication, Este was 29 years old, and married to a high-profile political figure, with four children under the age of 10. Her gender, marital and familial status probably played a part in her inability to order any direct action against the publisher. As the young mother of the future Guise inheritors, her role was a domestic one, limited to overseeing their upbringing at Joinville, thus making it unseemly for her to participate in legal proceedings that could attract further scandal. Furthermore, since the incestuous allegations were all included in pamphlets that were directed at her brother-in-law, it would have been deemed his responsibility rather than hers to control their distribution. We do not know of Este's reaction to the news of the executions, however, considering the strategies she employed later in life to deal with other scandals that were damaging to her reputation, it is unlikely that she would have approved of such an arbitrary execution of two men, one of whom was no more than an innocent bystander. Her documented horror at the massacre of Wassy, when her first husband's forces slew hundreds of Protestant worshippers, as well as her longstanding support for her mother's legal campaign to protect Huguenot writers and preachers, points to Este's rejection of violent or provocative measures that only served to inflame one's opponents, and a tolerant attitude towards writers and thinkers whose beliefs did not accord with her own.[31] Her lack of agency in this early, indirect attack on her reputation can be contrasted with her response to a later, more obvious slander concerning her second marriage. As a much-older widow who by this time had accumulated years of experience in dealing with protracted legal matters, when Este finally took control of matters, she demonstrated a savvy and efficient approach to dealing with scandalous accusations.

Marriage to Nemours

Shortly after her husband's assassination in 1563 negotiations began to enable Anne to marry her late husband's companion-at-arms, Jacques de Savoie, duc de Nemours. As we have seen in the previous chapter, Nemours had been involved since January 1559 in a bitter and protracted lawsuit with another of Catherine de Medici's ladies-in-waiting, Françoise de Rohan, who claimed that Nemours had promised to marry her and was the father of her child. Although there had been little progress in the case, once Anne d'Este became involved in the dispute her influence with the queen mother enabled the couple to achieve a verdict in Nemours's favour and they were married in May 1566, just over three years after her first husband's death. The controversy surrounding the speedy marriage after the death of the duc de Guise gave rise to much speculation and rumour about the possibility that Este and Nemours had been conducting a sexual relationship before her first husband's death, but since our best source of popular pamphlets, the journal of Pierre de L'Estoile, does not begin until 1574, it is unclear how much of this speculation made its way into libellous verse and commentary at the time. However, in 1581, the *Pasquil Courtizan* implied that the last child that

Anne had given birth to in the duc de Guise's lifetime, the later duc de Mayenne (or du Maine), had actually been fathered by Nemours: 'Is this not the handsome duc du Maine / Who was born of the first love / Of this noble duc de Nemours?'[32]

The claim that Mayenne was the son of the duc de Nemours, rather than the duc de Guise, made Este look like an adulteress, rather than the grieving widow she appeared to be after the death of the duc de Guise. The same theme would be carried on in the 1593 *Satyre Ménippée* where, in his address to the duc de Mayenne, the Recteur Roze refers to the rumours of his mother's adultery and 'true' father: 'I will not speak here of Monsieur de Nemours, your "uterine" brother (the Politiques say "adulterine")'.[33]

Whether true or not, the rumours of an extra-marital affair with Nemours before the death of her husband had survived, developed and had become entrenched. They were still fodder for satire over 20 years later when the Guises were felt to be overly dominant on the political scene, as during the League's control of Paris, when these last two pamphlets appeared.

The light-hearted satirical mockery of Anne's alleged adultery in pamphlets written 20 years after the fact would pale in comparison, however, with the violent attacks she suffered in 1566 because of her marriage to Nemours under the controversial circumstances of the Rohan case. Rohan's appeals repeatedly portrayed Anne as an adulteress, trying to marry another woman's husband. The case divided the court, and the Rohan family's status as leading Protestants resulted in an escalation of already-volatile religious and political tensions.[34] But there was already plenty of opposition to the marriage from within Anne's own family. While most of those opposed were concerned primarily with the effects on her children's inheritance should she remarry, Anne's mother, Renée de France, was more concerned with the possibility that her daughter would be labelled an adulteress. In a letter to Catherine de Medici a month before the wedding she wrote:

> I cannot nor should not be silent, while I know that your said majesty could resolve this and prevail, being fully certain that my said daughter has not the will to marry as much as she has to obey you, [. . .] I see that all the help and favours in the world will never take away from her the name which is to be most hated and avoided, and which I see will be given her if the marriage takes place.[35]

Renée's use of the word 'obey' reveals that she understood the relationship between Catherine and Este to still be one of mistress and servant, and that Catherine still had the power to force her ladies – no matter how rich or influential – to make marriage choices of which she approved. That Catherine ignored Renée's request and in fact used her own influence to encourage the wedding to Nemours is evidence that Catherine may have viewed Este more as a friend than as a servant, or that she simply was not concerned about potential ill effects on Este's reputation. As Renée had predicted, however, a poem in protest against the marriage appeared, *On the marriage of the Duke of Nemours*, which opened with a sordid portrait of the new duchesse de Nemours: 'Upon the fifth of May the obscene, withered, / Putrid, worn-out harlot again seeks men [for her] marriage bed'.[36]

The vocabulary of the libel paints the bride as sexually rapacious, the words '*viris . . . repetit*' ('again seeks men') transforming her decision to remarry into a greedy hunt for sex. This sexual greed has turned her into a '*meretrix . . . putida*', a rotten, putrid whore, an image that links the ideas of greed and corruption which are then developed further in the poem. Using both connotations of the word corruption, both as undue influence and as putrefaction, the author claims that the corruption which led to the unjust verdict against Rohan has begun to infect the kingdom, which now 'threatens to lie fallen in complete destruction and rot'. Anne d'Este's efforts to secure her second marriage are thus directly linked to the breakdown of morality on a national scale. Este's central role in such a politically-charged case resulted in her opponents feeling free to label her as a whore. But while she is criticised in terms of her sexual identity, her sexual degradation is linked to her corruptive power and influence at the heart of government, foreshadowing later criticisms of her central role within the Catholic League.

As we saw in the previous chapter, even the wedding itself was marred by the appearance of Vincent Petit, the representative of the Parlement who tried to have the ceremony stopped, and that story made its way to every court in Europe, thanks to the ambassadors present at the ceremony. Hoby credited Petit's appearance to Rohan's cousin and protector, Jeanne d'Albret, a claim corroborated by an anonymous, contemporary French chronicle which claimed Jeanne had planted the individual overnight in the room.[37] Jeanne's vigorous defence of her cousin's interests would cause a rift with her old friend Renée, duchess of Ferrara, Anne d'Este's mother, and would further result in Jeanne and Este 'squabbling like washerwomen over the subject of the marriage of the latter'.[38] Apparently the pressures of the controversy were taking their toll on the otherwise impeccably diplomatic duchesse de Nemours. The various ambassadors' accounts of the disputes at court and the verses sent to England that month describing Este as a harlot ensured that her involvement in the fiasco reached an international audience, and that her mother's concerns for her reputation had been legitimate.

Despite (or because of) the children that her second marriage produced, Este was continually referred to indirectly as an adulteress in the countless appeals that Rohan continued to make to the Parlement, the King's Council and the Vatican Rota long after the wedding. In her 1580 declaration, Rohan claimed that 'our said husband produced with the lady dowager of Guise two male children', continuing her legal narrative that depicted Este as a widow who was committing adultery with another woman's husband.[39] This fictional (at least from Este's viewpoint) narrative was sustained through the activities of Rohan's son, Henri, who had given himself the same title, 'Henri de Savoie, prince de Genevois', as Nemours's second son, and the young man's violent and dissolute reputation only added to the frustration felt by Anne d'Este and her husband and sons. Aware that her husband's aggressive and uncompromising legal tactics were not discouraging Rohan in her quest to clear her name, Anne d'Este endeavoured to resolve the dispute out of court.

In February 1579 she began a tireless campaign to appoint Henri to the post of Grand Prior of Auvergne, a ecclesiastical benefice within the Order of Malta worth 20,000 francs in revenue.[40] In return, Rohan would renounce all claims to the marriage between herself and Nemours, her son would cease to use Nemours's name and coats-of-arms and, significantly, he would convert to Catholicism after 21 years within the Protestant faith. Este's proposition was not a simple one: the title was already being disputed by both the king's choice of candidate, Louis de La Chambre, abbé de la Trinité de Vendôme, and the candidate put forward by the Order itself. She also had to convince the Pope to grant Henri absolution for his life spent as a heretic. But, as Ivan Cloulas remarks, 'The tenacity of the duchesse de Nemours overcame all obstacles'.[41] D'Este exploited her familial links to the papacy to override the objections of both the king and the Order. Worried in particular that Vendôme would secretly campaign in Rome to secure the post, she asked both the papal nuncio and her own brother, the cardinal Luigi d'Este, to intercede on her behalf with the pope. She also secured and sent to Rome the necessary paperwork for Henri's absolution.[42] Through her tenacity, all parties finally agreed to her choice, but in February 1581 the matter was still not finalised.[43] Her diplomatic efforts to resolve the dispute, however, had evidently resulted in other negotiations: in January 1580, after a 21-year legal battle, Françoise de Rohan made a formal declaration that she and Nemours had been married, that he recognised the son from the marriage and that they were now divorced.[44] Faced with the most defamatory attack on her honour in her lifetime, Anne d'Este responded with a thoughtful alternative to the endless litigation that had characterised this most public of scandals. Her combination of legal tenacity and negotiation skills resulted in a resolution so complete that only the next year Françoise de Rohan would write to the duchesse de Nemours expressing her 'will to do [her] very humble service'.[45]

Este's skills of negotiation and legal prowess that allowed her to mitigate scandal were developed over the years due to the distinctly awkward position she had been placed in because of her mother Renée de France's open profession of Calvinist faith and subsequent protection of Protestant preachers at her château of Montargis. Este found herself acting regularly as a mediator between her mother and her mistress Catherine, such as during the second religious war when Renée complained about Charles IX's desire to station a garrison of Catholic troops in Montargis. After writing to Catherine and the king to reassure them that her mother was 'a woman of her word' ('*femme de promesse*'), Este was able to spare her mother such an indignity.[46] She simultaneously worked to discourage her mother from being too rebellious: after the St. Bartholomew's Day Massacre, when Renée wrote to Catherine and Charles to ask to shelter Protestant preachers in her home, Catherine's icy response prompted Este to write to her mother, 'I am afraid for your servants and also that if they know that you have some minister with you that they will cause them pain. I beg you very humbly to think on this'.[47] Despite her status as the matriarch of the most prominent Catholic noble family in the kingdom, Este showed concern for the Protestants under her mother's protection and negotiated as much as possible to permit her mother's continued Protestant worship.

This potentially fraught relationship was made even more delicate when Este, in collaboration with Renée, began a legal suit in 1568 to recover her mother's Breton inheritance from the French crown. The duchy of Brittany had been passed by Renée's father Louis XII (against the wishes of his queen, Anne of Brittany) to her other sister Claude, because Claude's marriage to (the soon-to-be) François I would allow France to subsume the fiercely independent duchy. Although she was unsuccessful in securing her ambitious claims – the entire duchy of Brittany and half of the land of the house of Orléans – Este did come to an agreement with Charles IX: the duchy of Nemours was elevated to a peerage, as was the dominion of Montargis. In a letter to her now ex-husband the duke of Ferrara, Renée would praise their daughter's legal tenacity, urging him to admire

> the care and diligence which she has used to uncover titles and documents which had been unknown, and to employ the credit that she and her family have towards the lords near to Their Majesties and in their council, without which this contract would never have been passed.[48]

Although this suit pitted her against the French crown, Este clearly did not predict it to produce scandalous repercussions in the way the Rohan-Nemours case would. Her legal expertise, negotiation skills and tenacity in locating and securing valuable documentation that would strengthen her case made Este a formidable opponent when she sought to strengthen and defend her family and their fortunes, but she knew the appropriate balance between litigation and persuasion. This balance is evident in the manner in which she would seek justice for the deadly crimes committed against her husband and sons.

The Pursuit of Vengeance

As the years passed and Este not only survived the physical demands of motherhood but enjoyed increasing respect due to the glorious achievements of her children, she began to employ her public image of matriarch in a political sense. Her success in this can be gauged by comparing the public perception of her with that of her daughter by her first marriage, Catherine-Marie de Lorraine, duchesse de Montpensier (1551–1596), also a major political figure of the late sixteenth century. Unlike Este who was married twice, first to the young, powerful and very eligible François, duc d'Aumale (later duc de Guise) with whom she gave birth to eight children (four of whom reached adulthood), and second to 'the flower of all chivalry', the duc de Nemours, with whom she had three children (two of whom reached adulthood), Catherine-Marie was married at 18 to the 57-year-old Louis de Bourbon, duc de Montpensier. It was a childless marriage, and she would be widowed at 30, never to marry again. While her mother's beauty was the subject of much commentary throughout her life, Catherine-Marie's appearance was only mentioned in terms of the limp she had, earning her the nickname among her enemies of '*La Boiteuse*' ('The Limper').[49] Both were obviously acutely affected by the murders of François, duc de Guise in 1563 and by his sons, Henri, duc de

Guise and Louis, cardinal de Guise in 1588, as wife and mother in Anne d'Este's case, and as daughter and sister in Catherine-Marie's case. Their public reactions to these murders, however, reveal that mother and daughter took a fundamentally different approach to the pursuit of vengeance. Este's campaign of propaganda, both textual and performative, after the death of her husband was a careful display of feminine helplessness in keeping with contemporary expectations of female behaviour, subtly reinforced by the military strength of her powerful male Guise relatives. After the assassinations of her brothers in 1588, Montpensier, on the other hand, was criticised for her unrestrained fervour, her pro-active involvement in political matters and her lack of diplomacy. The different behaviour of each woman cannot be simply attributed to personality, however. As Dora Polachek remarks, 'it is not habitual for the women of the great nobility to display their most intimate emotions. All public spectacle of their pain is part of a very precise and well thought-out political objective'.[50] How Este and Montpensier chose to display their intimate emotions had major ramifications for their historical reputations.

In February 1563, Anne d'Este's husband, François duc de Guise, was assassinated by Jean Poltrot de Méré who, under torture, claimed that he had been hired to kill Guise by the Huguenot Admiral Coligny. Although Méré was executed, no pursuit was made of Coligny on the grounds that, given the already volatile confessional divisions within the kingdom, it might incite further religious tensions. In response, on 26 September 1563, the family of the deceased presented itself at the church of Meulan where the king Charles IX was attending vespers. In what has been described as 'a remarkable piece of political pageantry', the widow Anne d'Este and her bereaved mother-in-law Antoinette de Bourbon, 'dressed in great gowns with long flowing trains' and flanked by their children and grandchildren, fell to their knees in front of the king, 'supported by ladies-in-waiting veiled in black and filling the air with their moans'.[51] The women presented themselves to Charles IX as 'outraged and aggrieved widows and orphans' and petitioned for justice and the prosecution of those they held responsible for the murder of the duke, i.e., the Admiral Coligny.[52] Although the dukes of Montpensier, Nemours and Longueville along with other male members of the family were present, the demonstration was led by the women, whose masterful display of both strength and submission has been analysed by Jessica Munns and Penny Richards:

> In the specular economy of an aristocratic culture, the details of clothing, such as the 'grandes robes', presumably court dress, and the extravagantly trailing trains, juxtaposed against the gestural language of submission, present a complex emblem in which status and humility, grief and pride, were held in balance.[53]

The young king was moved to tears at the sight of the elite noblewomen and their children prostrate before him, and immediately promised to have the matter looked into.

The procession at Meulan was followed and reinforced by a vigorous legal process in which the family sought to have Coligny prosecuted. Four days later the same women, accompanied this time by approximately two hundred noblemen, filed into the Parlement of Paris to demand justice, the perceived frailty of the bereaved widow and mother belied by the military potential of the men who filled the chamber.[54] It was 'madame de Guise' along with her brother-in-law the cardinal of Lorraine who were the chief plaintiffs, and when in mid-October the king decided that the matter would be heard in his private council in order to ease the tensions caused in Paris by such a politically-charged case, Anne d'Este relentlessly campaigned against what she felt was an injustice. She made endless requests to the king for Coligny to appear in court, had copies made of important documents and acts, and even requested that the case be heard in another city's Parlement to avoid inflaming an already tense situation.[55] It was to be in vain: at the meeting of the King's Council on 29 January 1566, Coligny was declared 'purgé, deschargé et innocent' of the murder of the duc de Guise and all parties were sworn to 'silence perpetuel' on the matter.[56] Although ultimately unsuccessful in her quest for justice, Anne d'Este's relentless legal campaign and her public display of mourning, which was both couched within an acceptable register of female and noble grief and reinforced with a visible demonstration of the Guise family's military potential, made her appear as the noble widow, evoking the maximum amount of sympathy for her cause. In her analysis of the appearances of Este and her mother-in-law, Penny Richards says that they 'brilliantly *staged themselves*, that is, they used their gender, family and status to construct a political theatre following the assassination'.[57] This 'political theatre', restricted to the parameters of acceptable feminine behaviour of submission, impotence and controlled grief, can now be compared to Este's daughter's behaviour under similar circumstances.

On 23 and 24 December 1588, Este's sons Henri, duc de Guise, and his brother Louis, cardinal de Guise, were assassinated in the chateau of Blois by the 'Quarante-Cinq' ('Forty-Five'), Henri III's band of personal bodyguards. Their mother found herself under house arrest within the chateau, only finding out about her sons' deaths upon her release a few days later. Her daughter, Catherine-Marie de Lorraine, duchesse de Montpensier, wasted no time in seeking vengeance for the murders:

> And on hearing the news in Paris, instead of staying closed up in her room to mourn them, like other women would do, she left her hotel with the children of Monsieur her brother, taking them by the hands, trailing them around the city, making her lament to the people, animating them with tears, cries of pity and with speeches in which she told everyone to take up arms and to rise up in fury and perform acts of violence on the house and the portraits of the King [. . .] and to refuse him all loyalty, but instead to swear him total rebellion [. . .] after she had thus worked up the people of Paris with such animosity and insolences, she departed towards the Prince of Parma to ask him for aid in the vengeance.[58]

There are several similarities between Montpensier's behaviour and that of her mother's at Meulan 25 years earlier. Like her mother, she performed a public display of grief to evoke sympathy for herself and her family and, once again, was accompanied by the fatherless children of the murdered duke to increase that sympathy. Unlike her mother, however, who knelt (albeit dramatically) in front of the king in a gesture of submission, Montpensier moved around the city making speeches to the people, and calling for 'total rebellion'. As Polachek has noted, Montpensier carried out her own political theatre in three acts: first she evoked pity by 'animating them with tears, cries of pity'; next, once she was sure of their sympathy she transformed it into anger, calling on them to 'rise up in fury' and perform iconoclastic acts on the homes and pictures of the king; finally, she acted, riding out to the Prince of Parma, Alessandro Farnese, to seek his help in the overthrow of the king.[59] This pro-active approach, rejecting early modern ideals of femininity based on silence, submission and passivity, earned Montpensier many critics, particularly among the parlementaires, who called such behaviour 'impudente'.[60] Eliane Viennot points out that the active political role played by the women of leading aristocratic families, in which diplomacy and propaganda were their designated specialities, was recognised and accepted by the princely aristocracy but was unpalatable to the nobility of the robe and the bourgeoisie, who had a more reductive vision of how women should engage in political matters.[61]

Both mother and daughter participated after the murders in a campaign of propaganda that, as Polachek argues, had as its ultimate goal the death of the king. Este, however, would employ a strategy that was in complete conformity with accepted gender roles, openly lamenting the death of her sons, while her daughter engaged in a more public pursuit of vengeance. Observers at court remarked on Este's traditional form of mourning. The Italian historian Davila recounted that Anne d'Este 'abandoned herself to tears, the ordinary resources of women' while Catherine-Marie 'had all the audacity and the firmness that one could desire in a man'.[62] Brantôme recalled how Este, although

> she was naturally a lady of very gentle temperament and phlegmatic, and who only was only moved for good reason, she started to vomit a thousand insults against the king, and to cover him with as many curses and imprecations [...] not calling him King but always 'this tyrant'. Then after having regained herself she'd say, 'Alas! what am I saying, tyrant? No, no! I no longer want to call him that, but instead very good and merciful king, if he gives me death like my children, to remove me from the misery I am in, and to place me in the blessing of God'.[63]

Este thus did go so far as to regularly name Henri a tyrant, although she would immediately revoke the words, claiming a feminine, maternal weakness. Brantôme does not specify in what kind of environment or circumstances he heard Este make such claims, but it is perhaps interesting to compare her reaction with her daughter-in-law Catherine de Clèves, the widow of the assassinated duke. Clèves also employed vitriolic language to express her emotions, in particular using the language of vengeance in her letters, calling the king a 'evil, cruel, inhuman tyrant'[64] and claiming that 'since I am deprived of what I held most dear, nothing remains for me but vengeance'.[65] Significantly, however, this vitriol was expressed only in letters, addressed to a sympathetic audience: her parents and other family members, allies, and even the Pope, with whom it is clear the Guise family had a regular correspondence. As Brantôme remarked,

> Madame de Guise, Catherine de Clèves, . . . celebrated and celebrates in a very dignified way the eternal absence of Monsieur her husband. But then what kind of husband was he? He was without equal in the world; so she called him in some of her letters that she wrote to certain of her closest ladies as I saw her after her loss, demonstrating well by her mournful and sad words how much her soul had been injured.[66]

The words 'in a very dignified way' (*fort dignement*) reveal that there were acceptable modes for widows to mourn, and that letters and tears fit into this range of approved responses. But the death of the duke had not only left a widow; a few weeks after the assassination, Catherine de Clèves gave birth to the dead duke's son, at whose baptism on 7 February the role of godmother was played by the city of Paris itself. Such a choice of godparent attempted to elicit the maximum amount of sympathy for a bereaved widow and her fatherless children by making the people of Paris responsible for the spiritual welfare of the child. The Guise women thus regularly demonstrated their understanding of the emotive potential of a performance of feminine weakness.

Another acceptable means for women to demand justice was through the courts, and much like Este had done at the time of her own husband's murder, Catherine de Clèves requested that the Parlement of Paris launch an official inquest into the assassination of her husband.[67] Moreover, the four Guise duchesses – de Nemours, de Montpensier, de Guise and de Mayenne – together had power of attorney drawn up for Lazare Coqueley, a counsellor-clerk at the Parlement, and Jacques de Diou, ambassador for the duc de Mayenne in Rome, to appear before the Pope to prevent Henri III seeking absolution for the murders. This document, signed by all four Guise duchesses, has been described by Nicolas Le Roux as a 'sort of pact of vengeance', although it is also reminiscent of Anne d'Este's earlier efforts, during the negotiations over the award of the Grand Prior of Auvergne in 1579, to pre-empt her opponents undermining her actions with the Papacy.[68] It would appear that the strategies that she had learned through years of campaigning were being passed on to her female Guise successors. There may also have been an awareness of the delimited roles that each woman could play: for Clèves as devoted widow and Este as bereaved mother, their performance of marital and familial devotion and feminine weakness would garner the most sympathy, while for Montpensier, a childless widow who appeared unlikely to ever marry again, there was little to lose in terms of her reputation and honour. Instead, she chose to become the publicist of her mother's performance of grief.

The motif of maternal grief in almost all of the literature that describes Este in this period is a uniform one, and based upon real incidents: upon hearing of the murders of her sons, the duchesse de Nemours asked for their bodies to be returned to her for burial, only to discover that Henri III had already had the bodies decapitated, dismembered and burnt so as to prevent them from being used as relics or memorials. The literature – pamphlets, images and theatre – thus portrays Este as the bereaved mother, decrying the barbarity of the 'tyrant' and begging him to murder her as he has done her sons. One of the best-known pamphlets, the *Remonstrance faicte au roy par Madame de Nemours*, perhaps based on a real letter written by Este to Henri III, takes this line: 'I pray you, make me die with my children, for it is the thing I most desire'.[69] This theme would be repeated in a series of woodcuts produced during the campaign, one of which, *Comme les deux princes estans mis sur un table, avec la remonstrance de madame de Nemours* (Figure 3.1), featured Este standing beside Henri III over the corpses of her sons, in an image that would be clear even to its illiterate viewers (even if the reality of the incinerated corpses contradicted this image). The text repeated the anguish of the bereaved mother and her pleas for death:

> Madame de Nemours, seeing her two sons
> So evilly and perfidiously slain,
> Took to crying out, saying: O Evil One
> Barbarian, inhuman, is this the reward
> For those who allowed you to reign in France?
> Do the same to me then, I will lie with them![70]

Her repeated requests for the king to kill her as he has her children were perfectly conventional modes of mourning for a bereaved mother in a society that saw maternal grief as unbearable. It was therefore acceptable for Este to claim that it was impossible for her to live without her children. Furthermore, by asking the king to murder her along with them she not only reminded the reader/viewer of the king's guilt but also showed respect for church law forbidding suicide, thereby reinforcing both her anguish and her Catholic dogma, and evoking the maximum amount of sympathy.[71]

The role for her daughter in this propaganda campaign was far less socially acceptable, as Montpensier was credited (at least by L'Estoile) with masterminding the entire project and becoming, as he called her in 1587, 'the governess (*gouvernante*) of the League in Paris. He attributed to her what Polachek has called 'a patronage of murder': a systematic and sophisticated campaign involving literature, artwork, sermons and rumour that had as its goal the vilification and diabolisation of the king which would ultimately lead to his regicide.[72] First, she commissioned large numbers of polemic libels and pamphlets decrying the king's perverse relationships with his *mignons* and, as L'Estoile implied, paid colporteurs (or, as he called them 'portepaniers') to circulate them: 'This is witnessed by the common pictures and defamatory libels (of Henri III) cried publicly by the portepaniers of madame de Montpensier, printed with the privilege of the Holy League'.[73]

The various pamphlets that use the motif of Este's grief (*Les Regrets de madame de Nemours sur la mort de messeigneurs de Guyse ses enfans, Remonstrance faicte au roy par Madame de Nemours*, and the above series featuring *Comme les deux princes mis sur une table...*) were all part of this campaign.[74]

Montpensier was also held responsible for the infamous 'Tableau de madame de Montpensier', an exhibition in July 1587 in the cemetery of Saint-Séverin of six pictures from a book, the *Briefve Description des diverses cruautez que les Catholiques endurent en Angelterre pour la foy* [*Brief Description of the Diverse Cruelties that Catholics Endure in England for the Faith*] by Richard Verstegan, which depicted acts of barbarous cruelty performed on English Catholics by Protestants under Elizabeth I as a warning to the French what might happen were they to allow a heretic (Henri de Navarre) on the throne (Figure 6.2).[75] The English ambassador noted the enormous public appeal the event inspired:

> I never saw a thing done with fury nor with that danger of great emotion as that hath brought; for I see not so few as five thousand people a day come to see it, and some English knave priests that be there, they point with a rod and show everything; affirm it to be true and aggravate it.[76]

Perhaps the most significant and effective aspect of Montpensier's propaganda, however, were the preachers whom she paid to deliver sermons against the king and in praise of her brothers and their League forces. In 1587, L'Estoile bemoaned that 'most of the . . . preachers of Paris confessed themselves that they preached nothing but from the bulletins that madame de Montpensier sent them'.[77] He claimed that she

> does more by the mouth of her preachers (to whom she gives money to continually build their [her brothers'] reputation among the people, and to attribute to them all the good successes of the war to the discredit of the honour of the king) than they do with their maneouvres, weapons and armies combined: of which she boasts out loud, so impudent is she, that news of it reaches even the ears of the king.[78]

It was this final aspect, her overt pride in her achievements and consciously high-profile role as political leader, that drew the harshest criticism from her enemies. Unlike her mother, whose grief was expressed in a feminine inability to take action, provoking her to ask the king to take her life for her, Montpensier was visibly pro-active in her campaign.

Montpensier's flagrant flouting of conventional gender codes combined with her explicit calls for regicide may have appealed to the Parisian masses, but earned her few friends in the conservative, loyalist Parlement, and it was here that originated the satirical literature attacking her. We are by now familiar with the *Library of madame de Montpensier*, its very title revealing her primary role in the capital's politics. As we saw in Chapter 3, one version mocked her disability with the imaginary title *The Method of Working/Getting One's Leg Over With a Limp With All Comers, by Madame de Montpensier* (*Le Moien de besongner à clochepied à tous venans, par Madame de Montpensier*), which implied that she was sexually voracious, a theme common to the women throughout the oeuvre. This implicit attack on her sexual honour was made explicit, however, by the pamphlet *Letter*

Figure 6.2 'Le Tableau de Madame de Montpensier' or 'Briefue description des diverses cruautez que les catholiques endurent en Angleterre pour la foy' (Pierre de L'Estoile's own marginal notation can be seen at the top right)

Source: Pierre de L'Estoile, *Les Belles Figures et Drolleries de la Ligue . . .*, BnF Tolbiac Rés. LA25–6

from the clergy of Paris to the duke of Mayenne, which blamed Montpensier for the regicide of Henri III on 2 August 1589. The verses accused Montpensier of having used sexual favours to persuade the Jacobin monk, Jacques Clément, to carry out the murder of the king:

> She, who knew how
> Lovers often do it,
> In order to test the man
> And to not have an affront
> Said to him, of a modesty
> In keeping with her grandeur:
> 'Be strong, be jubilant,
> But show me the stiffness,
> Taking your mistress,
> With which you, in the heart
> Of Henry your scourge,
> Will stick the knife'.
>
> So the devout monk
> Redoubles his efforts,
> Resolved to the pain
> Of a thousand thousand deaths,
> Rather than fail
> To accomplish his wish.
> Right to the depths of the bowels/womb
> He pierces her,
> Shield, breastplate, scales
> Of his lance piercing;
> In her in quantity
> He spreads his deity.
>
> Madame Catherine,
> O blessed is the fruit
> Swelling your breast
> By the gift of the Holy Spirit!
> O how all the clergy
> Are obliged to you![79]

The excerpt begins with an extended metaphor likening the penetrative act of sex with the thrusting of the dagger into Henri III's body, a logical extension of the danger men saw in the public actions of prominent women such as Montpensier: women who transgressed the domestic norm of femininity were both oversexed and dangerous. Thus Montpensier's public actions that threaten the body politic are so dangerous that they literally threaten the physical body of the king. The final words of the excerpt echo the words of the 'Hail Mary', transforming Montpensier into a perverse Virgin Mother. It was a metaphor that may have consciously evoked her nickname at the time of '*La Sainte-Veuve*' ('the Holy

Virgin'), a name that mocked both her zealous Catholicism and her childless, widowed state.[80] That the fruit swelling within her is in her breast rather than in her womb is an attack on her pride in having orchestrated the king's death, an emotion that, in the eyes of the literary fraternity of the magistrature, appeared unseemly in a woman. It is perhaps unsurprising then, that the author of the *Letter from the clergy of Paris* that so slandered the honour of Anne d'Este's daughter was François Viète, the lawyer-mathematician who had represented Françoise de Rohan in her legal battle to prevent Este from marrying the duc de Nemours. A lawyer who built his professional reputation on his legal work for Huguenot families, and who therefore suffered the wrath of the League, would have derived even more enjoyment from the sacrilegious mockery of the Marian prayer.

While Viète's poem is obviously a fiction, that the mother and daughter worked together, albeit via different methods, on the project to depose the king is made clear by their joint reaction to the news of his assassination. L'Estoile described how Montpensier, upon hearing the news of the king's death,

> that instant having made her way to madame de Nemours her mother (who appeared no less content than she), both of them mounted in their carriages and made a tour of the city, where at all the crossroads and squares where they saw people assembled, cried out to them in a loud voice: 'Good news, my friends! Good news! The tyrant is dead! There is no more Henri de Valois in France!' Then, having headed to [the church of] the Cordeliers, madame de Nemours climbed up the steps of the great altar, and there, harangued the stupid people on the death of the tyrant, displaying in this act a great immodesty and impotence of woman, to continue to chew on a corpse. They also had bonfires put on everywhere, testifying by speeches, acts, dissolute clothing, liveries and feasts, the great joy they had from it.[81]

In these actions the two women demonstrated their innate understanding of the logistics of information transmission and news distribution by first making a tour of the city, broadcasting 'at all the crossroads and squares', much like a town crier or one of the many colporteurs whom Montpensier had employed in her campaign, and then heading to a major church to deliver a speech like one of the many sermons she had bribed the preachers to read out. Interestingly, here it was Anne d'Este who delivered the sermon from the steps of the great altar of the Cordeliers, a place reserved for ordained men, an action which drew her the opprobrium of L'Estoile who – in a rare example of direct criticism of Este – described it as 'a great immodesty and impotence of woman'. Although he credited his reaction to the fact that she continued 'to chew on a corpse', it is clear that this rare moment of 'masculine' behaviour by Este, which eschewed her former displays of submission and impotence, was what L'Estoile and his parlementaire brothers could not accept.

As with the collateral damage to her reputation that she suffered due to her close relationship with the controversial figure of the cardinal de Lorraine, Este was once again linked to a public figure who attracted polemical satire and saw her own reputation endure criticism as a result. On this occasion, however, she was able to create a discrete public role from her daughter which allowed her to avoid the more virulent attacks. Accordingly, the 1587 *Manifesto of the Ladies of the Court* would attack Este specifically for her alleged secret involvement in the affairs for which her husband and children were primarily to blame, and then for her alleged adultery before the death of her first husband:

> Madame de Nemours
> I confess, my Lord, in the presence of Neuchelles and of captain Jaques, and of Monsieur de Mandelot, that my sins are great, having given secret counsel and lent my hand to the iniquity of my last husband and of all my children. It is the reason why I have had so little contentment from them; but, at this point, Monsieur Du Maine learns of the lamentations of his mother, and says: 'But, Mother, since my brother de Nemours and I are both from one father and from you, why do you love him more than me?' – 'My son, when I made you, I conceived you in sin, and him in all the liberty of marriage, providing that Madame de Rohan does not oppose it'.[82]

As we have seen, the pamphlet cleverly targets Este's sexual honour, implying that her last son during her marriage to the duc de Guise, Mayenne (or Du Maine), was really fathered by Nemours, and by reminding the reader of the scandal of the Rohan affair. It also mocks Este's apparent favouritism of her son the duc de Nemours over Mayenne, and portrays her as receiving no satisfaction from any of her children. Significantly, she is satirised purely in terms of her role as wife and mother, and the tone of the entry is comic and relatively gentle. By contrast, Montpensier's flagrant contravention of normative gender roles resulted in the pamphlet's depiction of her in hyperbolic terms of sexual voracity, boundless depravity and devilish scheming:

> Madame de Montpensier.
> I have sinned so many times, so rudely, so publicly, so indiscreetly, so evilly, that I have completely spoiled, lowered, shamed and contaminated the principality of Bourbon and of Lorraine. My body has been given over to nothing but lechery and madness, and my spirit only to diabolical plots and all quarrels.[83]

With the terms 'lechery', 'madness' and 'diabolical plots', we can see the full range of negative tropes used to denigrate females whose behaviour transgressed social norms of acceptable feminine behaviour: unlimited sexual desire, insanity and witchcraft. By contrast, Este's ability to negotiate a public role that conformed to accepted notions of female and maternal behaviour prevented her reputation from suffering the most virulent attacks visited on her daughter.

Este's long-term reputation suffered little lasting damage from polemical attacks, and her political stature would continue to grow. After the death of her old friend Catherine de Medici in January 1589, Este was undeniably the most powerful woman in the kingdom. After Henri III was assassinated on 1 August 1589, and the League forces, under her son the duc de Mayenne, were trying to prevent the new king Henri IV from entering the capital, Este became the *de facto* leader of the League, and thus, the city. Known as the 'Queen Mother', Este was praised for her generosity during the siege of the city by L'Estoile, as well as for her negotiating skills which recognised when the battle was lost, and sought a rapprochement with Henri IV. Upon his entry to the city on 22 March 1594, the king immediately made his way to Este and Montpensier to assure them in person that he meant them no harm and to assure himself of their loyalty.[84]

Nevertheless, Anne d'Este's ability, even in her most prominent political phase, to avoid the most virulent polemic of the literary fraternity of the magistrature was grounded in more than simply knowing how to behave in public. An anecdote related by L'Estoile reveals both the origins of the reputation Este enjoyed among the magistrature and her own interest in that reputation:

> On Tuesday 3 this month of November (1592), *a secretary of the king, one of my friends*, told me that having gone to kiss the hands of madame de Nemours, and the said lady having asked him of news of the king and the court which was then at Saint-Denis, of M. the Chancellor, and all sorts of other particularities . . . Then she asked him *what they said of her, and what opinion they had of her*. Of you, madame? said the other, everyone says that if you had been seen once getting into your carriage to make some sort of good accord, that everyone would praise you and follow you. For the rest, *no one is unaware of your qualities, your merits and your rank: they recognise you as the daughter of a king*, and that you could do much to promote peace where your children are concerned.[85]

It is significant that this anecdote was told to L'Estoile by one of his friends, a secretary to the king, presumably (given that he went to 'kiss the hands of madame de Nemours') a secretary of state and thus holder of one of the highest ranks attainable by the robe nobility. The story is another example (if one were needed) of the exchange of stories about courtly women among this intellectual fraternity, and reveals how well-connected L'Estoile was to those who were assiduous in the corridors of power. Este is seen to be curious as to her reputation among the new king and his courtiers, to which the secretary claims she is held in such esteem that they are disappointed that she did not make more effort to bring about a peace accord. This reputation is based not only on her 'qualities' and 'merits', but also on her rank: 'they recognise you as the daughter of a king'. Este's royal lineage, as granddaughter of Louis XII, was a fortuitous aspect of her public image that was ever-present and unchanging, and which earned her respect in a society that saw royal status as a quality that manifested itself in natural leaders. Although Catherine de Medici also had royal lineage through her mother, Madeleine de La Tour d'Auvergne, it was not as close to the throne as Este's and was regularly overlooked by her critics, who chose to present her instead as an Italian usurper of French power.

Conclusion

Incest, adultery and corruption were all accusations which Anne d'Este had to deal with throughout her life. In so doing, she employed not only the agency she was blessed with through birth but also the legal tenacity and skills for negotiation she acquired as she became older to navigate through the scandalous circumstances and threats to her reputation that came with such a high-profile career. The accusations of incest that indirectly attacked her sexual honour can be understood in the context of a literary motif that was regularly used in the early modern period against noble families whose rise to power was resented by their rivals. The persecution of Huguenots by her brother-in-law found a retaliatory response in the form of verse libels and prose pamphlets that directly accused him of incestuous relationships with her, but his response – the arbitrary executions of innocent people – is unlikely to have satisfied a woman known for her tolerance of Protestant writers and her revulsion at the massacre of Huguenots at Wassy and after the Conspiracy of Amboise.[86] It is likely that, given her age and status as the mother of young children, Este was not in a position to seek retribution for scandalous accusations, and was forced to let her male kin deal with the repercussions of notorious libels at this point in her life.

However, the aggressive tactics employed by many of the men surrounding Este seem to have been at odds with her own preference for negotiation, demonstrated by her actions to bring about the end of the scandalous Françoise de Rohan lawsuit. Now a mature widow who had a wealth of experience with legal wrangling, both in the pursuit of justice for her murdered husband and in the delicate negotiations around her mother's estate that not only allowed her to defend her mother's protection of Protestant preachers but also to secure her mother's inheritance, Este could pro-actively work to defend herself against libellous accusations. Faced with the legal tenacity of Rohan, Este responded with her own tenacious pursuit of an ecclesiastical office for Rohan's son. Exploiting her familial ties with the Papacy, Este used a combination of correspondence and the personal appearances of her male relatives in Rome to negotiate on her behalf, thereby securing her objective through methods that were traditionally 'feminine' yet no less successful. Her diplomatic efforts on an international level thereby resolved a dispute that had troubled her reputation for years.

As we have seen, diplomacy and propaganda were responsibilities awarded to the female members of aristocratic houses, who could not perform on the battlefield. Este's pursuit of vengeance for the murders of her husband and sons conformed perfectly to early modern expectations of ideal feminine behaviour, presenting herself as an impotent, submissive widow and bereaved mother while subtly reinforcing her message with the military might of the powerful clan to which she belonged. And this combination of a performance of feminine weakness coupled with persistent legal campaigning seems to have been a strategy that she instilled in her daughters-in-law. Her own daughter's less subtle, more pro-active role in seeking vengeance for her brothers' deaths was as effective, one might argue, but her reputation, both in the short- and long-term, was irreparably damaged because of her refusal to moderate her behaviour to accepted gender codes. The literature that attacked them both for their role in the League thus vilified Montpensier as the epitome of female scandal, while Este was portrayed simply as an over-indulgent mother, a gentle comic parody of the matriarchal status she had worked so long to achieve.

At each juncture, the age, marital status, and familial status of the Guise women appear to have dictated how they were willing to perform in the public arena, by determining how much they were concerned about the effects of scandal on their individual reputations. Indeed, the model of behaviour by the Guise matriarch in the face of scandal bequeathed by Anne d'Este to her female descendants can be seen in the response by Catherine de Clèves in 1613, after her son François-Alexandre, chevalier de Guise, the baby born weeks after his father's death, was accused of murder. He had killed in a duel the baron de Luz, one of the Quarante-Cinq involved in the assassination of his father, the duc de Guise. Clèves successfully petitioned for her son's banishment rather than execution. As Jonathan Spangler notes, 'The Dowager Duchess Catherine de Clèves's comments are illuminating here on the role of the matriarch in dynastic honour, attesting that her son had been born ready to avenge his father's death ... and that if she had been a man 20 years ago she would have done it herself'.[87] Achieving a peaceful settlement through negotiation while defending the honour and martial power of her lineage, Clèves revealed herself to be the typical Guise matriarch, offering a performance of feminine strength learned from her mother-in-law, Anne d'Este.

Notes

1 L'Estoile, VI, 142: 'Ce jour, qui était le 25e novembre [1591], madame de Nemours, étonnée des mauvais bruits qui couraient et des étranges menées et procédures des Seize ... dépêcha vers son fils un gentilhomme avec lettres et paroles de créances, par lesquelles elle lui donnait avis de ce qui se faisait et passait, et combien sa présence était ici que pour la délivrer elle et sa fille, et tous les gens de bien, de la tyrannie et servitude où ils étaient réduits sous la domination de ces hommes de néant. Elle donna charge audit gentilhomme de dire de bouche au duc de Mayenne qu'il se souvînt qu'elle était sa mère, et que c'était celle qui l'avait porté qui l'en priait. Lesquelles paroles touchèrent fort le coeur du duc de Mayenne, comme il parut incontinent à ses yeux, hâtèrent son voyage et avancèrent sa résolution'.
2 Stuart Carroll, *Martyrs and Murderers: The Guise Family and the Making of Europe* (Oxford: Oxford University Press, 2009), 6. In this quote, Carroll is describing the relationship between Anne d'Este's husband, François de Guise, and his own mother, Antoinette de Bourbon.
3 All biographical material is taken from Coester, *Schön wie Venus, mutig wie Mars*.
4 Read, *Le Tigre de 1560*. For more on Hotman, see Donald R. Kelley, *François Hotman: A Revolutionary's Ordeal* (Princeton, N.J.: Princeton University Press, 1973).
5 Read, *Le Tigre*, 44: 'L'honneur de ta soeur ne se peut garantir d'avec toy. Tu laisses ta robe, tu prends l'épée pour l'aller voir. Le mari ne peut être si vigilant, que tu ne déçoives sa femme'.
6 Read, *Le Tigre*, 43: '... ung mari est plus continent avec sa femme que tu n'es avec tes propres parentes'.

7 Brantôme, 635–6: 'Il y eut force libelles diffamatoires contre ceux qui gouvernoyent alors le royaume; mais il n'y eut aucun qui piquast et offensât plus qu'une invective intitulée *le Tigre* (sur l'imitation de la première invective de Cicéron contre Catillina), d'autant qu'elle parloit des amours d'une très-grande et belle dame, et d'un grand son proche. Si le gallant auteur fust esté appréhendé, quand il eust eu cent mille vies il les eust toutes perdues; car et le grand et la grande en furent si estommaquez qu'ils en cuidèrent désespérer'.

8 The best collection of anti-Guise libels is found in the collection of Rasse des Noeux, the majority of which is published in Louis Hardouin Prosper Tarbé, *Recueil de poésies calvinistes, 1550–1566* (Reims, 1866).

9 Jean-Claude Ternaux, 'Les excès de la maison de Lorraine dans l'épître et la satire du *Tigre* (1560–1561)', *Le mécénat et l'influence des Guises (Actes du Colloque tenu à Joinville du 31 mai au 4 juin 1994)* (Paris: Honoré Champion, 1997), 387: 'Quand il est question d'un ecclésiastique il est de bonne guerre de dénoncer son manque de chasteté et d'aggraver le chef d'accusation en lui imputant l'inceste'.

10 Aubigné, *Les Tragiques*, I, 122, 'Livre I, Miseres', lines 1001–4:

> Et puis le cramoisy encores nous avise
> Qu'il a dedans son sang trempe sa paillardise,
> Quand en mesme subject se fit le monstrueux
> Adultere, paillard, bougre et incestueux.

11 Read, *Le Tigre*, 8–19: 'propos scandaleux et blasphêmes dicts . . . induisant . . . le peuple à sédition et scandales publics'.

12 Bruce Thomas Boehrer, *Monarchy and Incest in Renaissance England: Literature, Culture, Kinship, and Kingship* (Philadelphia: University of Pennsylvania Press, 1992), 12.

13 Ibid., 12.

14 L'Estoile, V, 273: 'Sonnet a la Jezabel Angloise'

> Bastarde, incestueuse et paillarde publique,
> Perfide, desloiale et fille de ta seur,
> Que ton pere et le sien descouvrant son erreur,
> Pere et mari cruel, fist mourir impudique.

15 Jean-Claude Arnould, 'Récits d'inceste (1516–1635)', *Studi francesi* 34, n° 102: 443–53.

16 Marguerite de Navarre, *Heptaméron*, ed. Renja Salminen (Helsinki: Suomalainen Tiedeakatemia, 1991).

17 L'Estoile, II, 39–40: 'elle conjuroit de la tirer de la peine où elle estoit, par poison ou autrement'.

18 L'Estoile, V, 39.

19 Read, *Le Tigre*.

20 François Billacois, *Le duel dans la société française des XVIe-XVIIe siècles: essai de psychosociologie historique*, Civilisations et sociétés 73 (Paris: Editions de l'Ecole des hautes études en sciences sociales, 1986).

21 Boehrer, 16.

22 L'Estoile, III, 176:

> Que dirons-nous du sieur d'Aumale?
> N'a-t'il pas bien la grâce male
> De sa bonne femme abuser!
> Et si ne s'en peut excuser,
> Disant qu'il couche, par bon zèle,
> Avec sa femme et demoiselle,
> Dormant tous trois en même lit:

> N'est-ce pas commettre un délit?
> Tous ne sont faits qu'en cocuage,
> Témoins cil qui veut son partage
> En la maison de ce Guisart

23 *Satyre Ménippée*, 27, 37, 53.
24 Aubigné, *Les Tragiques*, I, 233, 'Livre II, Princes', lines 1056–7:

> Le peché de Sodome, et le sanglant inceste
> Sont reproches joyeux de noz impures cours.

25 *Le Réveille-Matin des François et de leurs voisins, composé par Eusèbe Philadelphe, cosmopolite, en forme de dialogues*, 2 vols (Edinburgh: Jaques James, 1574), 12: 'où le Cardinal de Lorraine, la Royne sa niece, la Royne mere, et la duchesse de Guyse estoyent peints au vif nuds, ayans les bras au col, et les jambes entrelacees l'un avec l'autre'.
26 BnF MS Fr 3232, f. 5, Charles, cardinal of Lorraine to Anne d'Este:'il n'i a remede, il fault que je vous voye'.
27 BnF MS Fr 3232, f. 48, Charles, cardinal of Lorraine to Anne d'Este: 'il vous fault aller a paris ou je yray trouver la royne et ne bougerons vous et moy de table'.
28 *Lettres*, I, 259, December 1561, Catherine de Medici to Anne d'Este: 'vostre bon mari et bon frère et vous n'este que heun come la Trinité'.
29 Hotman was, ironically, based in Strasbourg when he wrote *Le Tigre*.
30 Daniel Ménager, 'Le *Tigre* et la mission du pamphlétaire', *Le Pamphlet en France au XVIe siècle* (Paris: Cahiers V.L. Saulnier, 1983), 23–34, 31: 'L'auteur est ici un homme de bonne volonté qui met au service du peuple des informations qu'il est seul à posseder'.
31 For Este's horror at the massacre of Wassy, see Carroll, *Martyrs and Murderers*; on Este's support for her mother's legal battle to protect Protestants, see Coester, *Schön wie Venus, mutig wie Mars*.
32 L'Estoile, III, 176:

> N'est-ce pas ce beau duc du Maine
> Qui naquit des premiers amours
> De ce noble duc de Nemours?

33 *Satyre Ménippée*, 156: 'Je ne parleray point icy de Monsieur de Nemours, vostre frere *uterin* (les Politiques disent *adulterin*)'.
34 Vester, *Jacques de Savoie-Nemours*; Ruble, *Le duc de Nemours*.
35 BnF MS Fr 3002, f. 81r, Renée de France to Catherine de Medici (April 1566): 'Je ne puis ny doibs taire, tandis que je congnoys que votredite majesté y peut remedier et pourvoir, estant bien certaine que madite fille n'a pas la volunté de ce marier comme elle a de vous obeyr, [. . .] je voy que toutes les aydes et faveurs du monde ne luy leveront jamais le nom qui est trop à hayr et fuir, et voy qu'on luy donnera si le mariage se faict'.
36 NA SP 70/84 f. 356, *In nuptias ducis de Nemours*.
37 BnF MS Fr 12795, f. 485r, 'Chronique anonyme'.
38 Champion, 431–2.
39 BnF MS Fr 3215, f. 13, Declaration of Françoise de Rohan: 'nostre dit sieur mary a suscité de dame douairière de Guise deux enfants masles'.
40 *Acta Nuntiaturae Gallicae, 8: Correspondance du Nonce en France Anselmo Dandino (1578–1581)*, ed. Ivan Cloulas (Paris: E. de Boccard, 1970), 102.
41 Ibid., 8, 102.
42 Ibid., 8, 662: Dandino to Cardinal de Côme, Paris, 12 May 1580.
43 Ibid., 8, 430: Cardinal de Côme to Dandino, Rome, 20 February 1581.
44 BnF MS Fr 3215, f. 13.

45 BnF MS Fr 3346, f. 50; also in Ruble, *Le duc de Nemours*, 139, Françoise de Rohan to Anne d'Este: 'la volonté de vous faire tres humble service'.
46 Coester, *Schön wie Venus, mutig wie Mars*, 206.
47 Ibid., 206–7.
48 Ibid., 207–10: 'le soin et diligence dont elle a use a recouvrer les tittres et papiers qui nous estoient incongneuz et emploie le credit quelle et les siens avoient envers les Seigneurs estans pres leurs Magestez et en leur conseil sans lesquelles choses jamais ce contract ne fut passe'.
49 Henri III called her 'la boiteuse' in a letter to his secretary of state Villeroy: BnF Ms Champion 5083, 1587, Henri III to Nicolas de Neufville, seigneur de Villeroy.
50 Dora E. Polachek, 'Le mécénat meurtrier, l'iconoclasme et les limites de l'acceptable: Anne d'Este, Catherine-Marie de Lorraine et l'anéantissment d'Henri III' in *Patronnes et mécènes en France à la Renaissance*, ed. Kathleen Wilson-Chevalier with Eugénie Pascal (Saint-Étienne: Publications de l'Université de Saint-Étienne, 2007), 433–454, 438: 'il n'est pas d'usage que les femmes de la grande noblesse fassent étalage de leurs émotions les plus intimes. Tout spectacle public de leur douleur répond à un objectif politique bien précis et mûrement réfléchi'.
51 Gabriel de Pimodan, *La mère des Guises: Antoinette de Bourbon (1494–1583)* (Paris: Honoré Champion, 1889), 217: 'vetues de grandes robes a queues trainantes ... soutenues par des femmes de service voilees de noir et remplissant l'air de leurs gemissements'.
52 Ibid., 218: 'Vefves et pupilles oultragiés et affligez'.
53 Jessica Munns and Penny Richards, 'Exploiting and Destabilizing Gender Roles: Anne d'Este', *French History* 6, 2 (1992): 206–15.
54 Coester, *Schön wie Venus, mutig wie Mars*, 194.
55 Ibid., 195.
56 BnF MS Fr 6610, f. 161.
57 Penny Richards, 'The Guise Women: Politics, War and Peace', *Gender, Power and Privilege in Early Modern Europe*, eds. Jessica Munns and Penny Richards (Harlow: Pearson, 2003), 159–70, 165.
58 Brantôme, 703–4: 'Et en ayant sceu les nouvelles dans Paris, sans se tenir recluse en sa chambre à en faire les regrets, à mode d'autres femmes, sort de son hostel avec les enfants de Monsieur son frere, les tenant par les mains, les pourmeine par la ville, fait sa deploration devant le peuple, l'animant de pleurs, de cris de pitié et de paroles qu'elle fit à tous de prendre les armes et s'eslever en furie et faire les insolences sur la maison et tableau du Roy [. . .] et à luy denier toute fidelité, ains au contraire de luy jurer toute rebellion [. . .] qu'après qu'elle eut ainsi bien mis le peuple de Paris en besogne de tels animositez et insolences, elle partit vers le Prince de Parme à lui demander secours de vengeance'.
59 Polachek, 'Le mécénat meurtrier', 446.
60 L'Estoile, VI, 504.
61 Viennot, 'Des 'femmes d'Etat' au XVIe siècle, 87–88.
62 Arrigo Caterino Davila, *Histoire des guerres civiles de France*, trans. l'abbé Mallet (Amsterdam, 1737), II, book X, 413: 's'estoit abandonnée aux larmes, ressources ordinaires des femmes'; 'avoit toute l'audace & la fermeté qu'on eût pu désirer dans un homme'.
63 Brantôme, 704–5: 'que de son naturel elle est dame de fort douce humeur et froide, et qui ne s'esmeut que bien à propos, elle vint à débagouller mille injures contre le roy, et luy jetter autant de malédictions et d'exécrations [. . .] jusques à ne nommer le roy autrement et tousjours que *ce tyran*. Puis après estant à soy revenue, elle dit: "Las! que dis-je, tyran? Non, non! je ne le veux plus appeler tel, mais roy très-bon et clément, s'il me donne la mort comme à mes enfans, pour m'oster de la misère où je suis, et me colloque en la béatitude de Dieu"'.
64 BnF MS Fr 3363, f. 207, the duchesse de Guise to the duc de Nevers, Paris, January 1589: 'malheureus creuel tirant hinneumin'

65 Ibid., f. 132, the duchesse de Guise to the duchesse de Nevers, Paris, January 1589: 'etant privée de se que j'avés de pleus cher, il ne me resete que la vangense'
66 Brantôme, 531: 'Madame de Guyse, Catherine de Cleves, ... a cellebré et celebre tous les jours fort dignement l'absence eternelle de Monsieur son mary: mais aussi quel mary estoit-ce? C'estoit le nomper du monde; ainsi l'appeloit-elle en quelques-unes de ses lettres qu'elle escrivoit à aucunes Dames de ses plus famillieres que après son malheur j'ay veu, leur bien manniffestant par ses funestes et tristes parolles desquelz regretz son ame estoit blessée'.
67 *Requeste présentée à Messieurs de la Court de Parlement de Paris, Par Madame la Duchesse de Guyse. Pour informer du massacre et assassinat commis en la personne de feu Monseigneur de Guyse* (Paris: Chez Rolin Thierry, 1589).
68 Nicolas Le Roux, '"Justice, justice, justice, au nom de Jésus-Christ": Les princesses de la Ligue, le devoir de vengeance et l'honneur de la maison de Guise', *Femmes de pouvoir et pouvoir des femmes dans l'Occident médiéval et moderne*, eds. Armel Nayt-Dubois and Emmanuelle Santinelli-Foltz (Valenciennes: Presses Universitaires de Valenciennes, 2009), 439–457, 444.
69 *Remonstrance faicte au Roy par Madame de Nemours, sur le massacre de ses enfans* (Paris, 1589): 'je te prie, fay moy mourir avec mes enfans, car c'est ce que le plus je desire'. For the argument that the pamphlet is based on a real letter written by Este, see Richard Cooper, 'The Aftermath of the Blois Assassination of 1588: Documents in the Vatican', *French History* 3, no. 4 (December 1, 1989): 404–26.
70 L'Estoile, *Les belles figures et drolleries de la Ligue*:

> 'Madame de Nemours voyant ses deux fils
> Si malheureusement & perfidement occis
> Se print à escrier O malheureux,
> Barbare inhumain, est-ce la recompense
> De ceux qui te maintenoient possible en France
> Fais m'en donc autant, je gise avec eux!'

71 It is unknown how Este's friendship with Catherine was affected by the fact that the son of one was responsible for the deaths of the sons of the other, but it is perhaps telling that within days of hearing about the murder of Este's sons Catherine was dead. After her death on 5 January 1589, L'Estoile wrote, 'Those close to her believed that her life had been shortened by displeasure over her son's deed'. L'Estoile, V, 130.
72 Polachek, 'Le mécénat meurtrier'.
73 L'Estoile, VI, 610–11: 'De quoi rendent suffisant témoignage les vilaines figures et libelles diffamatoires (de Henri III) criés publiquement par les portepaniers de madame de Montpensier, imprimés avec privilège de la Sainte-Union'.
74 *Les Regrets de Madame de Nemours sur la Mort de Messeigneurs de Guyse ses enfans* (Paris: H. Velu, 1589); *Remonstrance faicte au roy par Madame de Nemours* (Paris, 1589); L'Estoile, *Les belles figures et drolleries de la Ligue*.
75 Richard Verstegan, *Theatrum Crudelitatum Haereticorum nostri temporis* (Antwerp: Huberti, 1587).
76 CSPF, July 1587.
77 L'Estoile, VI, 502: 'la plupart des autres prédicateurs de Paris confessaient eux-mêmes qu'ils ne prêchaient plus que sur les bulletins que leur envoyait madame de Montpensier'.
78 Ibid., 504: 'Cependant madame de Montpensier est la gouvernante de la Ligue à Paris, qui entretient ses frères aux bonnes grâces des Parisiens et achète du taffetas pou faire faire des enseignes pour les trophées du duc de Guise son frère, et fait plus par la bouche de ses prédicateurs (auxquels elle donne de l'argent pour toujours accroître envers le peuple leur réputation, et leur attribuer tous les bons succès de la guerre aux dépens de l'honneur du roi) qu'ils ne font tous ensemble avec toutes leurs pratiques, armes et armées: de quoi elle se vante tout haut, tant elle est impudente, jusques là que le bruit même en vient jusques aux oreilles du roi'.

79 Viète, 'Prose du clergé de Paris':

> 'Elle, qui savoit comme
> Souvent amoureux font,
> Afin d'esprouver l'homme
> Et n'avoir un affront,
> Luy dist, d'une pudeur
> Seante à sa grandeur:
> «Soit fait, prenez liesse,
> Maismonstrez la roideur,
> Prenant vostre maistresse,
> Dont vous dedans le coeur
> De Henry, vostre fleau,
> Ficherez le cousteau.»
>
> Doncques le devot moine
> Redouble ses efforts,
> Resolu à la peine
> De mille et mille morts,
> Ainçois que de faillir
> De son veu accomplir.
> Jusqu'au fond des entrailles
> Il va l'entreperçant,
> Pavois, plastrons, ecailles
> De sa lance faussant;
> Dans elle en quantité
> Espand sa deité.
>
> Madame Catherine,
> O bienheureux le fruit
> Enflant vostre poitrine
> Par don du Sainct-Esprit!
> O que tout le clergé
> Est à vous obligé!'

80 L'Estoile, VI, 156.
81 L'Estoile, *JHIV*, I, 19: 'Et à l'instant s'étant acheminée vers madame de Nemours sa mère (qui ne s'en montra moins contente qu'elle), étant toutes deux montées en leurs carrosses et se faisant promener par la ville, en tous les carrefours et place où elles voyaient du peuple assemblé, lui criaient à haute voix: 'Bonnes nouvelles, mes amis! Bonnes nouvelles! Le tyran est mort! Il n'y a plus de Henri de Valois en France!' Puis s'en étant allées aux Cordeliers, madame de Nemours monta sur les degrés du grand autel, et là, harangua ce sot peuple sur la mort du tyran, montrant en cet acte une grande immodestie et impuissance de femme, de mordre encore sur un mort. Elles firent faire aussi des feux de joie partout, témoignant par paroles, gestes, accoutrements dissolus, livrées et festins, la grande joie qu'elles en avaient'.
82 L'Estoile, V, 346: 'Je confesse, mon Dieu, en presence de Neuchelles et du capitaine Jaques, et de Monsieur de Mandelot, que mes pecchés sont grands, aiant donné conseil secret et presté la main à l'iniquité de mon dernier mari et à tous mes enfans. C'est la cause pourquoi j'en ai reçeu si peu de contentement; mais, à ce faict, Monsieur Du Maine vient à sçavoir les lamentations de sa mere, et dit: Mais, Madame, puisque mon frere de Nemours et moi sommes tous d'un pere et de vous, pourquoi l'aimez vous plus que moi? – Mon fils, quand je vous fis, je vous conçeus en pecché, et lui avec toute liberté de mariage, pourveu que Madame de Rohan ne s'y oppose pas'.
83 Ibid., 346–7: 'J'ai pecché tant de fois, si vilainement, si publiquement, si indiscrettement, si meschamment, que j'ay tout gasté, vilené, honni et contaminé la principauté

de Bourbon et de Lorraine. Mon corps ne s'est jamais adonné qu'à lubricité et à folie, et mon esprit qu'à menées diaboliques et toutes brouilleries'.
84 L'Estoile, *JHIV*, I, 390–396.
85 L'Estoile, I, 193: 'Le mardi 3e dudit mois de novembre [1592], un secrétaire du roi, de mes amis, me conta qu'étant allé baiser les mains à madame de Nemours, et lui ayant ladite dame demandé des nouvelles du roi et de la cours qui lors était à Saint-Denis, de M. le Chancelier, et tout plein d'autres particularités [. . .] Puis lui demanda que c'est qu'ils disaient d'elle, et quelle opinion qu'ils en avaient. "De vous, madame? dit l'autre, chacun dit que si on vous avait vu une fois monter en votre carrosse pour faire quelque bon accord, que tout le monde vous bénirait et vous suivrait. Au reste, on n'ignore point de par delà vos qualités, vos mérites et vos grades: ils vous reconnaissent pour fille de roi, et qui pouvez beaucoup pour une bonne paix à l'endroit de vos enfants"'. [emphasis added]
86 Carroll, *Martyrs and Murderers*, 19 and 118.
87 Jonathan Spangler, 'Mother Knows Best: The Dowager Duchess of Guise, a Son's Ambitions, and the Regencies of Marie de Medici and Anne of Austria' in *Aspiration, Representation and Memory: The Guise in Europe, 1506–1688*, eds. Jessica Munns, Penny Richards, Jonathan Spangler (Farnham: Ashgate, 2015), 125–146, 133.

7 Conclusion
A Re-assessment of Scandal

The three case studies of Isabelle de Limeuil, Françoise de Rohan and Anne d'Este illustrate the palimpsest of scandalous accusations that could circulate in early modern France: adultery, illegitimacy, incest, infanticide and poisoning were all mixed with claims of sexual deviancy and voracity. As the religious and political conflicts worsened, so too did the language used to attack the reputation of the Queen and her ladies, and specific women in her entourage, such as Charlotte de Beaune, dame de Sauve, Claude-Catherine Clermont, maréchale de Retz, and Catherine de Lorraine, duchesse de Montpensier, repeatedly found themselves the victims of slanderous attacks in verse. But reputation was not an individual matter; it was a collective issue. As the sixteenth century progressed, French authorities, both secular and religious, became increasingly concerned with attempting to control both the formation of the family and the moral behaviour of its members, through laws governing marriage, birth and inheritance. Their efforts had a corollary effect on the lifestyles of women, whose rights were steadily diminished by the patriarchal influence of the ever more powerful legists of the Parlements. As these men registered new laws limiting the personal freedoms of women, they simultaneously produced literature that denigrated those women whom they felt to be transgressing the boundaries of acceptable female behaviour. That this trend occurred contemporaneously with the *de facto* rule of a woman, Catherine de Medici, a rule that those same legists had ruled inadmissible through the invention of a fraudulent Salic Law, resulted in the ridicule of Catherine and her female entourage through the means of misogynistic literature which portrayed her ladies as sexually promiscuous, and Catherine as a Machiavellian schemer, using sex, poison and murder as her preferred methods of rule rather than as the ceaseless negotiator for peace that the historical record shows her to have been.

In this study I have tried to demonstrate how that literature both helped to construct a myth of the female court as scandalous, and how such literature about the court reached the public outside the palace walls. Verse libels, printed pamphlets, songs and preachers' sermons were all vehicles for dissemination of scandal, but as the case studies show, there were means of controlling and manipulating all these media. In this nascent news culture, before the introduction of formally recognised newspapers, and without even the newsletters seen abroad, such as the Italian *avvisi* or German *zeitungen*, information about the court was largely produced and disseminated by men in a privileged position of access to knowledge.

Primarily destined only for the eyes of their colleagues, commentary about the court, written predominantly in verse and reflecting a common viewpoint, served several overlapping functions. It could operate as the straightforward transmission of newsworthy events, while simultaneously offering editorial commentary on the known facts, such as the verses sent to Paris detailing the story of Isabelle de Limeuil's scandalous birth, or the verses sent to England as evidence of the public opinion surrounding the notorious wedding of Anne d'Este to the duc de Nemours. That the news was delivered in verse, however, points to another crucial function of this literature: to entertain and impress their male colleagues. Accuracy of information could therefore be sacrificed to the demands of poetic form or musical metre, and elements could be imagined or exaggerated for the sake of humour. Satire often demands the caricaturisation of its targets and information about the women of the court, whether about real events or imagined ones, was usually distorted and unrepresentative of reality.

Satire was a key weapon in this literature which also functioned to shame those who transgressed social boundaries or who threatened the status quo. In this sense, the accusations of incest against Este ridiculed not only her but the ambitions of the entire Guise clan. Similarly, the verses on the murder of Françoise de La Marck served to shame not only her husband, who had lost control of the morality of his household, but also the women of the court in general, portraying them as licentious and as prostitutes. The group of women that found new prominence as a result of their mistress's primary political role were ridiculed by the increasingly powerful parlementaires, who attempted to shame these women into a more passive domesticity by attacking their sexual honour. In her analysis of the libellous literature that criticised Marie-Antoinette, Lynn Hunt notes that for the republicans, 'male virtue meant participation in the public world of politics; female virtue meant withdrawal into the private world of the family'.[1] While Hunt and other Revolutionary scholars have traditionally located the beginnings of a misogynist, pornographic literature attacking the queen and other 'public women' in the late eighteenth century, this study has shown its origins 200 years earlier, but stimulated by much the same sort of patriarchal anxieties, and using many of the same sorts of literary tropes and motifs. In the same way that Marie-Antoinette and her close female officers were reputed to engage in orgies at Versailles, so was the late Valois court depicted as a locus of sexual deviance; as she was accused in her trial of committing incest, so we find allegations of incest against female members of Catherine's household.[2] While Catherine's self-presentation of black-clad widow and devoted mother made it problematic for critics to portray her as a sexualised virago, they had no problem displacing that sexual deviance onto her female officers. The *Library of Madame de Montpensier* and the *Manifesto of the Ladies of the Court* likewise depict them collectively as whores, listing their promiscuities and sexual deviances. This compulsion to catalogue women, to list them along with their vices or virtues, reduces them to mere members of a group, rather than individuals. Even when such lists are of women's virtues, Alison Booth asks, 'do the model lists not reinforce rather than alter the differential norms?'[3] To group women together as representative of a certain kind of behaviour forces a collective reputation on them that erases all sense of their individuality and personal agency. However, the women in the case studies demonstrated a keen awareness of their own agency, even when faced with what seemed like insurmountable odds, and fought – sometimes for years, in the cases of Rohan and La Trémoille – to recover their honour and protect their reputation.

If the literature about courtly women is thus viewed as having a shaming function, it problematizes the idea that it is somehow representative of life at court. To read L'Estoile's journal as an accurate description of sixteenth-century Parisian society is to forget that the majority of verse libels he includes were penned by a group of elite men whose priorities were to entertain and impress their (predominantly male) readers, rather than to accurately transmit information. If we add to these intentions of entertainment and performance the intention to dishonour, it gives a very different perspective to the concept of early modern 'news' transmission. Rather than aim for an objective viewpoint, early modern writers, operating in a milieu that rejected medieval notions of politically and publicly involved noblewomen, wrote literature for their colleagues that would entertain them with salacious content, dazzle them with linguistic and literary skill, and shame the women about whom they wrote into a more submissive role. The portrayal of courtly women in obscene situations could perform all of these functions simultaneously, titillating its reader while ridiculing its subject.

Legal and Social Nature of Scandal

Every scandal investigated in this study involved a crime, either actual or potential, and therefore came into contact with the legal system of the Ancien Régime. What becomes repeatedly evident as we look at each case is the confusing, complex and ambiguous nature of the law in early modern France. Until the Code Civil was enshrined in 1804, French law was an amalgamation of Roman law, canon law and customary law, where attempts to synthesise regional variants were undermined by individual cases setting new precedents. Because of the endless litigation around cases involving families, inheritance, sexuality and reproduction, as Matthew Gerber explains in his study of early modern bastardy and illegitimacy, 'far from determining social practice, early modern French law was shaped by it'.[4] Although two edicts relevant to these issues were proclaimed during the timeframe of this study, the Edict Against Clandestine Marriage (1557) and the Edict Against Concealed Pregnancy (1557), neither directly affected the cases we have looked at. What antagonised many of the legal disputes covered in this book was, in fact, the absence of a clear written statute applicable to the issue under dispute.

To add to this confusion were the battles over jurisdiction that could be fought between the civil and ecclesiastical courts, particularly in the case of the scandals under discussion here, given their concern with sexuality and morality. Church law ostensibly had precedence wherever issues related to sacraments were involved, which is why the lawsuit brought by Françoise de Rohan against the duc de Nemours over his refusal to honour their secret marriage was initially heard before the official of the bishop of Paris. However, and as the Rohan-Nemours case amply demonstrates, appeals could be launched against their decisions to the appellate courts, which in this case involved the Parlement of Paris. It is no wonder, then, that the men of the Parlement, with their intimate knowledge of the ins and outs of these cases, were so prompt in their commentary upon them. At times the writers of satirical literature about women of the court were in fact personally involved in the cases, such as François Viète and Nicolas Rapin, lawyers who worked for or against women of Catherine's household in their legal suits, and who also have literary works attributed to them that viciously attack women of the court.

Thankfully, the peculiar and endlessly debated status of the law in the period has left a paper trail of documentation, evidence which allows us to examine the intersections between crime and custom, between the letter of the law and social practice, in particular as these related to the nobility. The particular status of ladies-in-waiting as the richest and most elite group of women in the kingdom, meant that while they were not necessarily able to operate outside the law, they could afford to pursue costly legal cases, and to buy influence at the highest level. Este's relentless and lifelong litigation, both in her own causes and her mother's, was only possible because of her status. What is clear is that connections to those more powerful, endlessly cultivated through the clientage system that was the framework of aristocratic life, was often the single most important factor in the ability of these women to successfully mitigate the damage, both legal and social, of the scandals in which they were involved. A study of noble scandal therefore allows us to examine how elites viewed themselves in a legal sense. But the influence that the aristocracy held made their legal status more ambiguous, in a sense more fluid: ultimately the monarch retained the power to judge all cases at his discretion, and the repeated occasions when the Rohan-Nemours case found itself being judged in the King's Private Council, or the fact that Limeuil could be imprisoned without conviction for 10 months, highlight how arbitrary this discretion could be. It meant that effectively the king – or Catherine – could operate in what appeared to be an extra-legal sense, controlling, suppressing or destroying key documents and evidence with impunity. A revelatory excerpt of one of the countless documents within the Rohan-Nemours case, a declaration by the crown, states that 'all minutes evidence and acts agreeing with the fact of the marriage of the said lady . . . are to be placed and deposed in the hands of the queen mother of the king . . . for her to do with according to her good pleasure and will'.[5] Although in that specific instance Catherine was unable to force the handover, the crown would eventually seize control of the documents. Needless to say, this subjective discretion could be viewed negatively: Catherine's apparently arbitrary decision to imprison Isabelle de Limeuil after her illegitimate birth was viewed by most contemporary commentators as a draconian measure against an all-too-common mistake.

Changing Traditions and Cultural Anxieties

The scandalous case studies explored in this book offer an insight into the unwritten codes of moral conduct in the early modern period, at least as they affected noble women and men. The letters of Antoine, king of Navarre, are especially revealing here: if Rohan's extended family members were to treat her as a married woman – and crucially, not send away her personal maidservants – Nemours, he felt, would be compelled to recognise the marriage. To do otherwise would imply a sense of guilt on Rohan's part. While we have documentation relating to the legal framework that in theory governed sexual and moral crimes, the responses to the events by the families of the women in this study, by their mistress Catherine and by impartial observers, reveal where their anxieties around moral and sexual conduct were located in a socio-cultural sense. Some anxieties, such as those around clandestine marriage, were based in obvious and legitimate concerns: uncontrolled marital arrangements threatened the patriarchal social model with potentially widespread ramifications for many families' patrilineal plans. This could have severely negative consequences for women, even for those of a noble status, as seen in the arbitrary imprisonment of Jeanne de Piennes. Indeed, arbitrary imprisonment of noblewomen was not uncommon, as we have seen not only in the case of Piennes but also of Limeuil and La Trémoille, the latter placed under house arrest for seven years without any form of trial. In all of these cases, it was the petitions to the monarch by other nobles (or possibly in Limeuil's case, the illegal actions of Condé) that allowed them freedom, evidence that the connections a noble made within the clientage system were the most important factors in her ability to protect herself.

The conflicts between a traditional way of life and the imposition of new laws, and between the Vatican with its Tridentine decrees and the French authorities who resented its interference, exploded in the scandalous case of Rohan vs. Nemours. Witness testimony revealed the problems around oral agreements in the early modern period, when the only eye-witnesses in this case were mere servants whose word, Nemours argued, could not be trusted. His own word as a gentleman, however, was challenged by the written evidence of his own letters, and it was here that the real scandal of the case was located: if a gentleman's word of honour could not be trusted, then what was to happen to the oral culture on which society was based? The answer could be found in the new ordinance from 1566 that gave precedence to written testimony over oral testimony. The growing bureaucratic class of legists, in their attempt to control family formation, promulgated edicts that not only outlawed marriage without witnesses but also imbued the written word with greater value, appropriate to a fraternity that was defined, and defined itself, by its superior literacy.

The problems of illegitimate births threw up similar problems for an increasingly patriarchal society. In Françoise de Rohan's case, her demand to have her son recognised as the rightful heir to the duc de Nemours had enormous consequences for the Savoie, Rohan and Este family inheritances. In a reverse but equally revealing situation, Louis de Condé's willingness to marry the mother of his bastard son threw the entire French Reformation into jeopardy, albeit only temporarily. Although both of these cases involved an illegitimate birth, what propelled them into truly scandalous territory were the disputes over religious belief: Roelker argues that it was Jeanne d'Albret's Calvinist beliefs that made her urge her cousin Françoise to pursue her case against the odds, and we have seen the turmoil felt in capitals across Europe at the prospect of Condé marrying 'la sua Limolia'. Significantly, the moral implications of illegitimate birth, i.e., the Church decrees against extra-marital sex and the possible damage to a woman's sexual honour, appear to have concerned contemporary commentators less than the possible patrilineal ramifications. Numerous examples of illegitimate births show that, at least for women of noble birth, honour was a fluid entity that could be protected and rehabilitated on a remarkably regular basis.

Other anxieties, such as those around poison and incest, were the product of deeper-seated fears that were often based on rumour and hearsay. The discourse of poison was used to exclude any group felt to be strange or foreign, such as Jews and, particularly in the case of France, Italians. Women who transgressed acceptable norms of behaviour could also find themselves excluded without any evidence, such as the case of La Trémoille, convicted for the poisoning of her husband on the basis of alleged adultery. The role of rumour is integral to the spread of the anxiety around poison: the fear of poison, and the lack of knowledge surrounding it, created a vacuum in which rumour and gossip could operate, making the accusation virtually impossible to refute. Thus, simply linking a person's name with poison (much like labelling someone a terrorist today) effectively made that person unacceptable, and transformed her into a 'foreign body': Isabelle de Limeuil, who troubled the 'body politic' with her controversial relationship with the leader of the Protestant forces, found herself excluded from court on such a basis. Similarly, the regular accusations of incest that one finds directed at members of the court were often based on no more than scurrilous rumour, but noble anxieties around incest arising from their preference for endogamous marriages meant that such accusations were taken very seriously and prosecution was often sought. The charges of incest against her brother-in-law that implicated her was the one scandalous moment in Anne d'Este's life where she seems to have had almost no agency to protect her reputation: an accusation that requires no evidence is difficult to refute. It is unsurprising, then, to learn that when Marie-Antoinette was accused in her trial of having incestuous relations with her son she simply refused to respond to 'such a charge made against a mother'.[6] The multiplicity of accusations that attached themselves to the women in this study – incest, poisoning, sexual promiscuity – needed no evidence, only the willingness of others to engage in the dissemination of the rumours.

Another accusation that needs little, if any, evidence, and which operated on perhaps the greatest anxiety of the literary fraternity (at least if one gauges their anxiety through their literary production) was cuckoldry. The cuckold's horns, omnipresent in poetry, theatre and visual productions, were an obsession in the literature of the period because, for a literary fraternity that was deeply concerned with patriarchal control, the cuckold figure represented the 'other' to the heteronormative figure of the man in control of his wife and household. Although traditionally it was those men who did not conform to the patriarchal model who were the primary target of ridicule, sixteenth-century French literature featuring the cuckold developed a strand in which adulterous courtly women began to become the target of satire. The imaginary book titles in the *Library of Madame de Montpensier* depict the women of Catherine's court almost exclusively as licentious adulterers, their sexual appetites out of control. Similarly, the scandal of Françoise de la Marck allowed the writers' imaginations to run riot, depicting the court as a notorious site of prostitution, where foolish men were cuckolded by their own king.

This anxiety around cuckoldry that moves its focus from the male figure to the female is based, I argue, on a deeper concern: that of the growing public and political involvement of aristocratic women under the rule of Catherine de Medici and subsequently under the League. Noble women were often inherently involved in politics due to their status as heads of families and estates during times of their husbands' absence, but their public role was not welcomed by legists who were attempting to construct and reinforce greater patriarchal control over family and state. The satirical literature written by the same men thus ridiculed women who refused to conform to their model of acceptable female behaviour by depicting them as sexually deviant. Discipline for both men and women was enforced through the ridicule of those felt to not be conforming to normative modes of behaviour for their gender. The ridicule of courtly women defamed them as individuals in the short term and developed into the reputation of the licentious French court that still exists today.

Reputation, therefore, is a slippery notion. It can exist both in the short and long term; it can be both individual and collective, it can evolve over time. It is tied up with ideas of honour, shame and disgrace, terms that are themselves difficult to define and historically contingent. In a collective environment such as the queen's household did exclusion from court equal disgrace? Or, as I have argued for Isabelle de Limeuil, could it serve as protection of one's long-term reputation? Self-exclusion from court, as in Rohan's case, seems to have been about finding a more supportive environment among the Huguenot aristocracy at La Rochelle. Her disgrace was not in becoming pregnant but resulted from her pursuit of a case that threatened the collective reputation of the household and thus of Catherine de Medici herself. Throughout her time in power, and especially when scandal threatened the reputations of the women at her court, Catherine appears to have been acutely aware of the potency of the accusations against her ladies, supporting some women, excluding others and always with the collective reputation of her household as a top priority.

Dissemination of Scandal

That these accusations could and did appear in the form of verse is a phenomenon that results in this study being an examination of a specific period in literary history as well as a study of scandal itself. I have tried to show how scandal was created via literary production, how the negative collective portrayal of a group of women which has endured for centuries is a literary construct that can tell us more about the men who were doing the writing than about the women they were describing. The intertextual exchange among an all-male enclave of misogynistic verses, stories, images, songs and other new genres of satire (such as imaginary libraries) recounted women's sexual offences that supported their own desires for greater patriarchal control. If Joan DeJean's study identifies the emergence of obscenity as a literary issue in the early seventeenth century centred around the rise of print culture, then this study examines the volatile period just prior to that moment.[7] The verse libels I have looked at were often in manuscript, created and circulated by an elite male audience, as they had been for centuries. These were men who had access to the new printing, and who exploited it when it suited their purpose, but the nature of much of the satirical material I have examined – its ability to be amended, reworked and added to, as well as its libellous content – meant that manuscript circulation was more appropriate.

Perhaps it is unsurprising then, that it was a woman, the duchesse de Montpensier, who recognised the potential of the printing press and invested the mighty resources of the Spanish-backed Catholic League in a successful propaganda campaign to depose the king. Her actions won her the support of the Parisian masses but parlementaires, who were repulsed by such an empowered stance in a woman, smeared her reputation – in manuscript verse – through the depiction of her as sexually deviant, evil and insane. My argument is therefore a response to Joan Kelly's famous question, 'Did women have a Renaissance?'.[8] The ridicule or diabolisation of politically prominent or socially active noblewomen by male writers who thereby increased their own literary reputation confirms Kelly's argument that bourgeois and aristocratic women of the sixteenth century saw their public role weakened by men who had ironically assumed the label of 'humanists'. The individual reputations of the robe nobility were enhanced by the diminishment of the collective reputation of the queen's entourage. The question remains, however, how much of their material left this elite male audience?

The main primary sources I have used, the journals of Pierre de L'Estoile with their unrivalled collection of verse libels and pamphlets, allow us to get a sense of the dissemination of news and information transmission in early modern Paris. But given that he did not publish his journals in his lifetime, entrusting them instead to close friends within the magistrature, how much of the handwritten material he collected made it out of the hands of his colleagues and into the public arena? How much did it represent the views of those outside of the legal fraternity?[9] While we can track the active circulation and discussion of this material among the elite of the Palais thanks to L'Estoile's marginal commentary, gauging the accessibility of much of the handwritten material for the general populace is more difficult. If the song about the scandal of Jeanne de Piennes and François de Montmorency was so popular as to lend its name to many other songs, we can say with some certainty that the story was well known. When graffiti was written, and obscene pictures drawn, on the walls and gates of the city of Paris, we can be confident that they were widely viewed. It is harder to make statements with such certainty about manuscript verse, and we must rely on L'Estoile's repeated claims that libels were 'dispersed in the streets of Paris' and 'thrown under doors'. Certainly he incessantly refers to libels and *ramas* as being 'stuck up and dispersed in the streets'.[10] Even verses in Latin, such as the epigram mocking Catherine de Medici's fears related to a comet in 1577, were, claimed L'Estoile, 'published everywhere'.[11]

Such a claim problematises the notion that satirical literature can be exclusively linked with either a 'popular' or an 'elite' audience. The verse libels and other satirical material that targeted the women of the French court in the late sixteenth century were based in both a courtly tradition and the culture of the street song, and reveal the crossover between the humanistic revival of classical traditions and the obscene, corporeal, Rabelaisian tradition of the late medieval period.

A key strand of DeJean's argument about obscenity's 'reinvention' in its modern form rests on the premise that print culture allowed sexually explicit material to move beyond the elite, all-male, intellectual circles within which it had previously circulated to reach the average citizen. The predominance of phallic imagery and its related homosexual themes that had been permitted within these circles was now deemed unacceptable and liable to be censored. Thus, literature underwent a change in focus to a heterosexual view of desire and a subsequent shift to the female genitalia as the almost exclusive locus of sexual arousal, a view of obscenity which is more familiar to a modern audience. With their personal lives the target of sexually explicit mockery by a literature that was beginning to find its way from the hands of its male-only creators into the new print culture, it could be argued that the women of Catherine de Medici's court permitted this paradigm shift in literature and society to take place. Their unprecedented role at the forefront of public life resulted in their depiction in pamphlet literature as scandalous, a collective representation that would be a model for the portrayal of other women in public life. Certainly, all of the themes employed against Marie-Antoinette in the vitriolic and pornographic pamphlet literature that helped to bring down the monarchy can be seen repeatedly in the verse libels of the sixteenth century. Traditionally, women have only succeeded in entering the historical record because they were holy or because they were scandalous; this study will hopefully create a suspicion of these labels, and encourage others to investigate the sources that offer such a reductive vision of women both in the past and the present. It is our responsibility as historians to interrogate our sources in order to distinguish bias, to understand when and how opinion becomes historiography, and, in the words of Natalie Zemon Davis, to find the 'fiction in the archives'.[12]

Notes

1 Hunt, 'The Many Bodies of Marie-Antoinette', 133.
2 Marie-Antoinette was regularly portrayed, both in literature and at her trial, as having inherited the same malicious traits as her predecessor Catherine. For an imagined dialogue between the two queens, a common early modern literary device in which two infamous villains discuss their evil (usually in Hell), see *Catherine de Médicis dans le cabinet de Marie-Antoinette à Saint-Cloud* (Paris: Imprimerie Royale, 1790).
3 Booth, 'The Lessons of the Medusa', 258.
4 Gerber, *Bastards*, 14.
5 BnF MS Fr 3215, f. 22v: 'Que toutes mynuttes grosses et actes convenans le faict du mariage de ladicte dame ... soyent mises et deppossees entre les mains de la royne mere du roy ... pour en faire selon son bon plaisir et volunté'.
6 Hunt, 'The Many Bodies of Marie-Antoinette', 123.
7 DeJean, *The Reinvention of Obscenity*.

8 Joan Kelly, 'Did Women Have a Renaissance?', *Becoming Visible: Women in European History*, 3rd edn (Boston: Houghton Mifflin, 1998).
9 The same questions are raised by Henri-Jean Martin in his preface to Florence Greffe and José Lothe, 'La vie, les livres et les lectures de Pierre de l'Estoile: nouvelles recherches', *Pages d'archives*, 2004.
10 L'Estoile, II, 52: 'affichés et semés par les rues'.
11 Ibid., 147.
12 Natalie Zemon Davis, *Fiction in the Archives: Pardon Tales and Their Tellers* (Stanford: Stanford University Press, 1987).

Bibliography

Archival Sources

AN série O 800
BnF MS Anciens petits fonds français, 22560–22565
BnF MS Fr 3002
BnF MS Fr 3169
BnF MS Fr 3215
BnF MS Fr 3232
BnF MS Fr 3336
BnF MS Fr 3346
BnF MS Fr 3363
BnF MS Fr 3397
BnF MS Fr 6610
BnF MS Fr 12795
BnF MS Fr 15499
BnF MS Fr 15592
BnF MS Fr 25455
BnF Ms Champion 5083
National Archives UK (NA) SP 70/84

Primary Sources

A Checklist of French Political Pamphlets 1560–1644 in the Newberry Library, ed. Doris Varner Welsh (Chicago: The Newberry Library, 1950).
Acta Nuntiaturae Gallicae, 8: Correspondance du Nonce en France Anselmo Dandino (1578–1581), ed. Ivan Cloulas (Paris: E. de Boccard, 1970).
Les amours de Henri IV. Roy de France, avec ses lettres galantes & les réponses de ses Maîtresses (Cologne: n.p., 1695).
Ample recueil des chansons tant amoureuses, rustiques, musicales que autres, cŏposees par plusieurs Autheurs. Ausquelles sont adioustés plusieurs Chansons nouvelles, qui n'ont encores esté imprimées. (Lyon: Benoit Rigaud, 1582).
Antoinette d'Autriche, ou dialogue entre Catherine de Médicis et Frédégonde, Reines de France, aux enfers, etc. (Londres [Paris?], 1789).
Archivo Documental Español: Negociaciones con Francia, 11 vols (Madrid: Real Academia de la Historia, 1953).
Aubigné, Théodore Agrippa d', *Les Tragiques*, Textes de la Renaissance 6 (Paris: H. Champion, 1995).

———, *Oeuvres complètes*, ed. Reaume et Caussade (Genève: Slatkine, 1967).
———, *Histoire universelle*, 10 vols, ed. André Thierry (Genève: Droz, 1982).
Beaune, Renaud de, *Oraison funebre faicte aux obseques de la Royne mere du Roy* (Bloys: I. Mettayer, 1589).
BnF Rés. f. La 25.6
———, *Journal de L'Estoile pour le règne de Henri IV*, 2 vols (Paris: Gallimard, 1948).
———, *Journal de Henri III., Roy de France et de Pologne: ou, Mémoires pour servir à l'histoire de France*, ed. Lenglet du Fresnoy, 5 vols (Paris: La Haye, 1744).
———, *Registre-Journal du règne de Henri III*, eds. Madeleine Lazard and Gilbert Schrenck, 6 vols (Genève: Droz, 1992).
Bonnaffé, Edmond, *Inventaire des meubles de Catherine de Médicis en 1589: mobilier, tableaux, objets d'art, manuscrits* (Paris: Aubry, 1874).
Brantôme, Pierre de Bourdeille, abbé de, *Recueil des dames, poésies et tombeaux*, ed. Etienne Vaucheret (Paris: Gallimard, 1991).
———, *Oeuvres complètes*, 11 vols, ed. Ludovic Lalanne (Paris: Renouard, 1869).
Calendar of State Papers, Foreign Series, of the reign of Elizabeth, ed. Joseph Stevenson (London: Longman & Co., 1870).
Calendar of State Papers Relating to English Affairs in the Archives of Venice, ed. Rawdon Brown and G. Cavendish Bentinck (London: Her Majesty's Stationery Office, 1890).
Castelnau, Michel de, *Les mémoires de messire Michel de Castelnau, seigneur de Mauvissiere; illustrez et augmentez de plusieurs commentaires & manuscrits, tant lettres, instructions, traittez, qu'autres pieces secrettes & originalles, servans à donner la verité de l'histoire des regnes de François II., Charles IX & Henry III. & de la regence & du gouvernement de Catherine de Médicis; avec les eloges des rois, reynes, princes & autres personnes illustres de l'une & de l'autre réligion sous ces trois regnes . . . par J. Le Laboureur.* (Paris: Pierre Lamy, 1659).
Castiglione, Baldassare, *The Book of the Courtier*, trans. Thomas Hoby (London: Dent, 1974).
Catherine de Médicis dans le cabinet de Marie-Antoinette à Saint-Cloud (Paris: Imprimerie Royale, 1790).
Chevalier, Casimir, *Archives royales de Chenonceau. Debtes et créanciers de la Royne mère Catherine de Médicis, 1589–1606* (Paris, 1862).
'Compte de dépenses de Catherine de Médicis', *Archives curieuses de l'histoire de France*, eds Cimber and Danjou (Paris: Beauvais, 1836), series 1, vol 9, 115–9.
Cotgrave, Randle, *A Dictionarie of the French and English Tongues* (London: Adam Islip, 1611).
Courval, Thomas Sonnet de, *Satyre contre les Charlatans, et Pseudo-medecins Empyriques. En laquelle sont amplement descouuertes les ruses & tromperies de tous Theriacleurs, Alchimistes, Chimistes, Paracelsistes, Fondeurs d'or potable, Maistres de l'Elixir et telle pernicieuse engeance d'imposteurs. En laquelle sont refutees les erreurs, abus, et impietez des Iatromages, ou Medecins Magiciens, etc* (Paris: J. Milot, 1610).
Dépêches diplomatiques de M. de Longlée: résident de France en Espagne, 1582–1590 (Paris: Plon-Nourrit, 1912).
Dépêches de M. de Fourquevaux: ambassadeur du roi Charles IX en Espagne, 1565–1572, ed. Raimond Fourquevaux (Paris: E. Leroux, 1896).
Despatches of Michele Suriano and Marc'Antonio Barbaro, Venetian Ambassadors at the Court of France, 1560–1563 (Lymington: Huguenot Society of London, 1891).

de Thou, Jacques-Auguste, *Histoire universelle de Jacques-Auguste de Thou depuis 1543 jusqu'en 1607, traduite sur l'édition latine de Londres* ..., 16 vols (Londres [i.e. Paris], 1734).

Discours merveilleux de la vie, actions et deportements de Catherine de Médicis, royne-mère, ed. Nicole Cazauran (Genève: Droz, 1995).

Du Bellay, Joachim, *Les antiquitez de Rome; Les regrets*, GF-Flammarion 245 (Paris: Flammarion, 1994).

La fleur des chansons nouvelles. Traittans, partie de l'amour, partie de la guerre, selon les occurrences du temps present. Composees sur chants modernes fort recreatifs (Lyon, 1580).

Furetière, Antoine, *Dictionnaire universel: contenant généralement tous les mots françois*, ed. Jean Baptiste Brutel de la Rivière (Hildesheim: Georg Olms, 1972).

Gassot, Jules, *Sommaire mémorial (Souvenirs) de Jules Gassot, secrétaire du roi (1555–1625)* (Paris: Pierre Champion, 1934).

Janequin, Clément, [*Voulez ouyr] Les cris de Paris[?]* (Paris: La cité des livres, 1928).

Jeanne d'Albret, *Mémoires et poésies* (Genève: Slatkine Reprints, 1970).

Juvenal, *The Satires*, trans. Niall Rudd, ed. William Barr (Oxford: Clarendon Press, 1991).

L'Estoile, Pierre de, *Les belles Figures et Drolleries de la Ligue, avec les peintures Placcars et Affiches iniurieuses et diffamatoires contre la memoire et honneur du feu Roy que les Oisons de la Ligue apeloient Henri de Valois, imprimées, criées, preschées et vendues publiquement à Paris par tous les endroits et quarrefours de la Ville l'an 1589. Desquelles la garde (qui autrement n'est bonne que pour le feu) tesmoingnera à la Postérité la mes-chanceté, Vanité, Folie, et Imposture de ceste ligue infernale, et de combien nous sommes obligés à nostre bon Roi qui nous a délivrés de la Servitute et Tirannie de ce Monstre.*

Lettres d'Antoine de Bourbon et de Jehanne d'Albret, ed. Achille Lacroix de Vimeur, marquis de Rochambeau (Paris: Renouard, 1877).

Lettres de Catherine de Médicis, 11 vols, eds. Hector de la Ferrière, G. Baguenault de la Puchesse (Paris: Imprimerie nationale, 1880–1909).

Lettres du cardinal Charles de Lorraine (1525–1574), ed. Daniel Cuisiat (Genève: Droz, 1998).

Lettres de Henri III, roi de France, 6 vols, eds. Pierre Champion, Michel François (Paris: C. Klincksieck, 1959–2012).

Lettres de Jean Calvin, ed. Jules Bonnet (Paris: Meyrueis, 1854).

Machiavelli, Niccolò, *The Prince*, ed. and trans. Peter Bondanella, Oxford World's Classics (Oxford: Oxford University Press, 2005).

Malingre, Claude, *Les Annales générales de la ville de Paris* (Paris: Pierre Rocolet, Cardin Besongne, Henry Le Gras, & La Vefve Nicolas Trabovilliet, 1640).

Marguerite de Navarre, *Heptaméron*, ed. Renja Salminen (Helsinki: Suomalainen Tiedeak-atemia, 1991).

Marguerite de Valois, *Correspondance 1569–1614*, ed. Eliane Viennot (Paris: Honoré Champion, 1998).

———, *Mémoires et autres écrits 1574–1614*, ed. Eliane Viennot (Paris: Honoré Champion, 1999).

Mémoires de Jeanne d'Albret, ed. Alphonse de Ruble (Paris: Paul, Huart et Guillemin, 1893).

Mémoires et lettres de Marguerite de Valois, ed. François Guessard (Paris: Renouard, 1842).

Négociations diplomatiques de la France avec la Toscane, 6 vols, eds. Giuseppe Canestrini, Abel Desjardins (Paris: Imprimerie nationale, 1859–86).

Les Négociations politiques et religieuses entre la Toscane et la France à l'époque de Cosme Ier et de Catherine de Médicis, 1544–1580, d'après les documents des archives de l'état à Florence et à Paris, ed. Eletto Palandri (Paris: Roulers, 1908).

Nouveau recueil de toutes les Chansons nouvelles, tant de l'amour que de la guerre non encores si devant imprimée (Lyon: Benoit Rigaud, n.d.).

Rapin, Nicolas *Œuvres*, eds. Jean Brunel and Emile Brethé (Genève: Droz, 1982).

———, *Oeuvres latines et françoises* (Paris: Olivier de Varennes, 1610).

Recueil des chansons amoureuses de ce Temps. Tant Pastorelles que Musicales, propres pour danser & ioüer sur toutes sortes d'instrumens. Augmenté de plusieurs Airs de Cour non encor veus ny Imprimez (Paris: Pierre Des-Hayes [rue de la Harpe, a l'Escu de France, proche la Roze Rouge]).

Recueil général des anciennes lois françaises, depuis l'an 420 jusqu'à la révolution de 1789, 29 vols, eds. Isambert et al. (Paris, 1822–23).

Les Regrets de Madame de Nemours sur la Mort de Messeigneurs de Guyse ses enfans (Paris: H. Velu, 1589).

Remonstrance faicte au Roy par Madame de Nemours, sur le massacre de ses enfans (Paris, 1589).

Requeste présentée à Messieurs de la Court de Parlement de Paris, Par Madame la Duchesse de Guyse. Pour informer du massacre et assassinat commis en la personne de feu Monseigneur de Guyse (Paris: Chez Rolin Thierry, 1589).

Retz, Catherine de Clermont, Maréchale de, *Album de poésies (Manuscrit français 24255 de la BnF)*, eds. Colette H. Winn and François Rouget (Paris: Honoré Champion, 2004).

Le Réveille-Matin des François et de leurs voisins, composé par Eusèbe Philadelphe, cosmopolite, en forme de dialogues (Edimbourg: Jaques James, 1574).

Ronsard, Pierre de, *Oeuvres complètes*, ed. Paul Laumonier, 20 vols (Paris: Marcel Didier, 1946).

Le rosier des chansons nouvelles. Tant de l'amour, que de la guerre, contenant la pluspart les heureuses victoires obtenues en Auvergne & ailleurs (Lyon, 1580).

Le Roux de Lincy, Adrien Jean Victor, *Recueil de chants historiques français, 2ᵉ série: XVIe siècle* (Paris: Charles Gosselin, 1842).

Saint-Simon, Louis de Rouvroy, duc de, *Mémoires complets et authentiques du duc de Saint-Simon sur le siècle de Louis XIV et la régence*, 21 vols (Paris: A. Sautelet, 1829).

Satyre Ménippée: de la vertu du catholicon d'Espagne et de la tenue des estats de Paris, ed. Martin Martial, Textes de la Renaissance 117 (Paris: Champion, 2007).

Scot, Reginald, *The Discoverie of Witchcraft, Wherein the Lewde Dealing of Witches and Witchmongers Is Notablie Detected ...* (London: W. Brome, 1584).

Tasso, Torquato, *The Liberation of Jerusalem (Gerusalemme Liberata)* (Oxford: Oxford University Press, 2009).

Le Tocsain, contre les massacreurs et auteurs des confusions en France. Par lequel la source et origine de tous les maux, qui de long temps travaillent la France, est descouverte, etc (Reims, 1577).

Verstegan, Richard, *Theatrum Crudelitatum Haereticorum nostri temporis* (Antwerp: Huberti, 1587).

Viète, François, *In artem analyticem isagoge: seorsim excussa ab Opere restitutae mathematicae analyseos, seu Algebra nova / Francisci Vietae* (Tours: J. Mettayer, 1591).

———, 'Prosa cleri Parisiensis ad ducem de Mena, post cædem regis Henrici III. (Prose du clergé de Paris... traduite en françois par Pighenat, etc.)', *Recueil de poésies françoises des XVe et XVIe siècles, morales, facétieuses, historiques*, ed. Anatole de Montaiglon (Paris: Jannet, 1855).

Secondary Sources

Akehurst, F.R., 'Good Name, Reputation, and Notoriety in French Customary Law', *Fama: The Politics of Talk and Reputation in Medieval Europe*, eds. Thelma Fenster and Daniel Lord Smail (Ithaca: Cornell University Press, 2003), 75–94.

Alexander, John T., *Catherine the Great: Life and Legend* (Oxford: Oxford University Press, 1989).

Archer, Jayne Elisabeth, Elizabeth Goldring and Sarah Knight, eds., *The Intellectual and Cultural Worlds of the Early Modern Inns of Court* (Manchester: Manchester University Press, 2011).

Arnould, Jean-Claude, 'Récits d'inceste (1516–1635)', *Studi francesi* 34, n° 102: 443–53.

Aubailly, Jean-Claude, *Le Monologue, le dialogue et la sottie: essai sur quelques genres dramatiques de la fin du moyen âge et du début du XVIe siècle* (Paris: Honoré Champion, 1976).

Aumale, Henri d'Orléans, duc d', 'Information contre Isabelle de Limeuil (mai-août, 1564)', *Miscellanies of the Philobiblon Society*, VII (London: Whittingham and Wilkins, 1862–3).

———, *Histoire des princes de Condé pendant les XVIe et XVIIe siècles* (Paris: Michel Lévy, 1863).

Babelon, Jean Pierre, 'Les Laudes et Complainctes de Petit Pont', *Mélanges offerts à Émile Picot*, 2 vols, (Paris: Damascène Morgand, 1913), I, 83–9.

———, *Paris au XVIe siècle*, Nouvelle histoire de Paris (Paris: Diffusion Hachette, 1986).

Baumgartner, Frederic J., *France in the Sixteenth Century* (New York: St. Martin's Press, 1995).

Bauschatz, Cathleen M., 'Rabelais and Marguerite de Navarre on Sixteenth-Century Views of Clandestine Marriage', *The Sixteenth Century Journal* 34, no. 2 (2003): 395–408.

Bayle, Pierre, *The Dictionary Historical and Critical of Mr Peter Bayle* (London: Knapton et al., 1734–1738), III, 832–35: 'Limeuil'.

Bazancourt, César de, *L'Escadron volant de la reine. 1560* (Paris, 1836).

Beam, Sara, *Laughing Matters: Farce and the Making of Absolutism in France* (Ithaca, N.Y: Cornell University Press, 2007).

———, 'The "Basoche" and the "Bourgeoisie Seconde": Careerists at the Parlement of Paris During the League', *French History* 17 (2003): 367–87.

Bellany, Alastair, 'Early Stuart Libels: An Edition of Poetry from Manuscript Sources', eds. Alastair Bellany and Andrew McRae, *Early Modern Literary Studies Text Series I* (2005) http://purl.oclc.org/emls/texts/libels/

———, 'Railing Rhymes Revisited: Libels, Scandals, and Early Stuart Politics,' *History Compass* 5, no. 4 (2007): 1136–79.

———, '"Railing Rhymes and Vaunting Verse": Libellous Politics in Early Stuart England, 1603–28', *Culture and Politics in Early Stuart England*, eds. Kevin Sharpe and Peter Lake (Basingstoke: Macmillan, 1994), 285–310.

———, *The Politics of Court Scandal in Early Modern England: News Culture and the Overbury Affair, 1603–1660* (Cambridge: Cambridge University Press, 2002).

Bertière, Simone, *Les Reines de France au temps des Valois 2. 'Les années sanglantes'* (Paris: Fallois, 1994).

Billacois, François, *Le duel dans la société française des XVIe-XVIIe siècles: essai de psychosociologie historique*, Civilisations et sociétés 73 (Paris: Editions de l'Ecole des hautes études en sciences sociales, 1986).

Boehrer, Bruce Thomas, *Monarchy and Incest in Renaissance England: Literature, Culture, Kinship, and Kingship* (Philadelphia: University of Pennsylvania Press, 1992).

Booth, Alison, 'The Lessons of the Medusa: Anna Jameson and Collective Biographies of Women', *Victorian Studies* 42, no. 2 (Winter, 1999–Winter 2000): 257–88.

Boucher, Jacqueline, *La cour de Henri III* (Rennes: Ouest-France, 1986).

———, *Société et mentalités autour de Henri III*, 4 vols (Paris: Honoré Champion, 1981).

Boutier, Jean, Alain Dewerpe and Daniel Nordman, *Un tour de France royal: Le voyage de Charles IX (1564–1566)* (Paris: Aubier Montaigne, 1984).

Bowman, Jeffrey A., 'Infamy and Proof in Medieval Spain', *Fama: The Politics of Talk and Reputation in Medieval Europe*, eds. Thelma Fenster and Daniel Lord Smail (Ithaca: Cornell University Press, 2003), 95–117.

Braund, Susanna H., 'Juvenal – Misogynist or Misogamist?', *The Journal of Roman Studies*, 82 (1992), 71–86.

Breitenberg, Mark, *Anxious Masculinity in Early Modern England* (Cambridge: Cambridge University Press, 1996).

Brissaud, Jean, *A History of French Private Law*, trans. Rapelje Howell (Boston: Little, Brown, 1912).

Brochon, Pierre, *Le livre de colportage en France depuis le XVI siècle: Sa littérature, ses lecteurs* (Paris: Librairie Gründ, 1954).

Brockliss, Laurence, and Colin Jones, *The Medical World of Early Modern France* (Oxford: Clarendon Press, 1997).

Broomhall, Susan, *Women and the Book Trade in Sixteenth-Century France* (Aldershot: Ashgate, 2002).

———, ' "My daughter, my dear": the Correspondence of Catherine de Médicis and Elisabeth de Valois', *Women's History Review* 24/4 (2015): 548–69.

Brunel, Jean, *Un Poitevin poète, humaniste et soldat à l'époque des guerres de religion: Nicolas Rapin (1539–1608): la carrière, les milieux, l'oeuvre* (Paris: H. Champion, 2002).

Brunet, Gustave, 'Essai sur les bibliothèques imaginaires', *Catalogue de la bibliothèque de l'abbaye de Saint-Victor au seizième siècle*, ed. Le Bibliophile Jacob (Paris: Techener, 1862), 297–390.

Burrows, Simon, *Blackmail, Scandal and Revolution: London's French Libellistes, 1758–1792* (Manchester University Press, 2006).

Burt, Ronald, 'Gossip and Reputation', *Management et réseaux sociaux: ressources pour l'action ou outil de gestion?*, eds. Marc Lecoutre and Lievre Pascal (Paris: Hermès sciences publications, 2008), 27–42.

Butterworth, Emily, *Poisoned Words: Slander and Satire in Early Modern France* (London: Modern Humanities Research Association and Maney Publishing, 2006).

Cambridge Modern History, ed. A. W. Ward (Cambridge: University of Cambridge Press, 1904).

Cameron, Keith, *Henri III: A Maligned or Malignant King? (Aspects of the Satirical Iconography of Henri de Valois)* (Exeter: University of Exeter Press, 1978).

Carroll, Stuart, *Blood and Violence in Early Modern France* (Oxford: Oxford University Press, 2006).

———, *Martyrs and Murderers: The Guise Family and the Making of Europe* (Oxford: Oxford University Press, 2009).

———, *Noble Power During the French Wars of Religion* (Cambridge: Cambridge University Press, 1998).

Catalogue de la Bibliothèque de l'Abbaye de Saint-Victor au seizième siècle rédigé par François Rabelais, commenté par le Bibliophile Jacob [i.e. Paul Lacroix] et suivi d'un essai sur les bibliothèques imaginaires par G. Brunet, ed. Paul L. Jacob (Paris, 1862).

Champion, Pierre, *Catherine de Médicis présente à Charles IX son royaume 1564–1566* (Paris: Grasset, 1937).
Charpentier, Françoise, 'Formes de l'esprit pamphlétaire: quelques questions autour du manuscrit Rasse des Nœux', *Traditions Polémiques* (Paris: ENS Jeunes Filles, 1985).
Charrier, Charlotte, *Héloïse dans l'histoire et dans la légende* (Genève: Slatkine Reprints, 1977).
Chatenet, Monique, *La cour de France au XVIe siècle: Vie sociale et architecture* (Paris: Picard, 2002).
———, Les logis des femmes à la cour des derniers Valois' in *Das Frauenzimmer. Die Frau bei Hofe in Spätmittelalter und früher Neuzeit. 6. Symposium der Residenzen-Kommission der Akademie der Wissenschaften in Göttingen*, eds. Jan Hirschbiegel, Werner Paravicini (Stuttgart: Thorbecke, 2000), 175–92.
Cloulas, Ivan, *Diane de Poitiers* (Paris: Fayard, 1997).
———, *Catherine de Medici* (Paris: Fayard, 1979).
Coester, Christiane, *Schön wie Venus, mutig wie Mars. Anna d'Este, Herzogin von Guise und von Nemours (1531–1607)*, (München: Oldenbourg, 2006).
Colportage et lecture populaire: imprimés de large circulation en Europe, XVIe–XIXe siècles: Actes du colloque des 21–24 Avril 1991, Wolfenbüttel, eds. Roger Chartier and Hans-Jürgen Lüsebrink, Collection 'In Octavo' (Paris: IMEC éditions, Institut mémoires de l'édition contemporaine, 1996).
Cooper, Richard, 'The Aftermath of the Blois Assassination of 1588: Documents in the Vatican', *French History* 3, no. 4 (December 1, 1989): 404–26.
Crawford, Katherine B., 'Love, Sodomy, and Scandal: Controlling the Sexual Reputation of Henry III', *Journal of the History of Sexuality* 12 (2003): 513–42.
———, Catherine de Medici and the Performance of Political Motherhood', *Sixteenth Century Journal* 31, no. 3. (Autumn, 2000): 643–73.
———, *Perilous Performances: Gender and Regency in Early Modern France* (Cambridge, MA: Harvard University Press, 2004).
Cressy, David, *Dangerous Talk: Scandalous, Seditious, and Treasonable Speech in Pre-Modern England* (Oxford: Oxford University Press, 2010).
Crouzet, Denis 'Catherine de Médicis actrice d'une mutation dans l'imaginaire politique (1578–1579)', *Chrétiens et sociétés. Documents et mémoires* 9 (2009): 17–50, Special Issue: 'La coexistence confessionnelle à l'épreuve. Etudes sur les relations entre protestants et catholiques dans la France moderne'.
———, *Le haut coeur de Catherine de Médicis: une raison politique aux temps de la Saint-Barthélemy* (Paris: Albin Michel, 2005).
———, *Les Guerriers de Dieu. La violence au temps des troubles de religion (vers 1525–vers 1610)*, 2 vols, (Seyssel: Champ Vallon, 1990).
Cust, Richard, 'Honour and Politics in Early Stuart England: The Case of Beaumont v Hastings', *Past and Present* 149 (November 1995): 57–94.
Darnton, Robert, *The Forbidden Best-Sellers of Pre-Revolutionary France* (London: Harper Collins, 1996).
———, *The Literary Underground of the Old Regime* (Cambridge, MA: Harvard University Press, 1982).
Daubresse, Sylvie, *Le Parlement de Paris ou la voix de raison* (Genève: Droz, 2005).
———, with Bertrand Haan, *Actes du Parlement de Paris et documents du temps de la Ligue (1588–1594)* (Paris: Champion, 2012).
Davila, Arrigo Caterino, *Histoire des guerres civiles de France*, trans. l'abbé Mallet (Amsterdam, 1737).

204 Bibliography

de Vivo, Filippo, *Information and Communication in Venice: Rethinking Early Modern Politics* (Oxford: Oxford University Press, 2007).

Debbagi Baranova, Tatiana, 'Poésie officielle, poésie partisane pendant les guerres de Religion', *Terrain* 41 | 2003, URL: http://terrain.revues.org/1610; DOI: 10.4000/terrain.1610, accessed 17/05/2013

———, *À coups de libelles: une culture politique au temps des guerres de religion (1562–1598)* (Genève: Droz, 2012).

Defrance, Eugène, *Catherine de Médicis, ses astrologues et ses magiciens-envoûteurs: documents inédits sur la diplomatie et les sciences occultes du XVIe siècle* (Paris: Mercure de France, 1911).

DeJean, Joan E., *The Reinvention of Obscenity: Sex, Lies, and Tabloids in Early Modern France* (Chicago: University of Chicago Press, 2002).

Desonay, Fernand, *Ronsard, poète de l'amour*, 3 vols (Brussels: Palais des Académies, 1952–59).

Dictionnaire de biographie française, eds. J. Balteau, M. Prevost and J.-P. Lobies (Paris: Letouzey et Ané, 2001).

Dictionnaire des lettres françaises, ed. Georges Grente (Paris: Fayard, 1964).

Diefendorf, Barbara, *Beneath the Cross: Catholics and Huguenots in Sixteenth-Century Paris* (Oxford: Oxford University Press, 1991).

———, *From Penitence to Charity: Pious Women and the Catholic Reformation in Paris* (Oxford: Oxford University Press, 2004).

Dubost, Jean-François, *La France italienne, XVIe–XVIIe siècle* (Paris: Aubier, 1997).

Duindam, Jeroen, 'Rival Courts in Dynastic Europe: Vienna and Versailles 1550–1790', *The Court Historian*, vol 7, no. 2 (December 2002), 75–92.

Dumas, Alexandre, *La Reine Margot* (Oxford: Oxford University Press, 1997).

Edgerton, Jr., Samuel Y., *Pictures and Punishment: Art and Criminal Prosecution during the Florentine Renaissance* (Ithaca: Cornell University Press, 1985).

Ettlinger, Helen S., 'Visibilis et Invisibilis: The Mistress in Italian Renaissance Court Society', *Renaissance Quarterly* 47, no. 4 (Winter, 1994): 770–92.

Études sur la Satyre Ménippée, eds. Franck Lestringant and Daniel Ménager (Genève: Droz, 1987).

Fairs, Markets and the Itinerant Book Trade, eds. Robin Myers, Michael Harris and Giles Mandelbrote (New Castle, DE: Oak Knoll Press, 2007).

Fama: The Politics of Talk and Reputation in Medieval Europe, eds. Thelma Fenster and Daniel Lord Smail (Ithaca: Cornell University Press, 2003).

Femmes et pouvoir politique: les princesses d'Europe XVe–XVIIIe siècle, eds. Isabelle Poutrin and Marie-Karine Schaub (Rosny-sur-Bois: Bréal, 2007).

Ferguson, Gary, *Queer (Re)Readings in the French Renaissance: Homosexuality, Gender, Culture (*Aldershot: Ashgate, 2008).

ffolliott, Sheila, 'Casting a Rival into the Shade: Catherine de' Medici and Diane de Poitiers', *Art Journal* 48 (1989): 138–43.

———, 'Catherine de' Medici as Artemisia: Figuring the Powerful Widow', *Rewriting the Renaissance: The Discourses of Sexual Difference in Early Modern Europe*, eds. M. Ferguson, M. Quilligan, and N. Vickers (Chicago: University of Chicago Press, 1986), 227–41.

———, 'Portraying Queens: The International Language of Court Portraiture in the Sixteenth Century,' *Elizabeth I: Then and Now*, ed. Georgianna Ziegler (Washington, DC: The Folger Shakespeare Library, 2003), 164–75.

———, 'The Ideal Queenly Patron of the Renaissance: Catherine de' Medici Defining Herself or Defined by Others?', *Women and Art in Early Modern Europe: Patrons,*

Collectors, and Connoisseurs, ed. Cynthia Lawrence (Penn State University Press: 1997), 99–109.

———, 'The Italian "Training" of Catherine de Medici: Portraits as Dynastic Narrative', *The Court Historian* 10/1 (October 2005), special issue: *Queens and the Transmission of Political Culture: The Case of Early Modern France*, eds. Melinda Gough and Malcolm Smuts: 37–54.

Finucci, Valeria, *The Manly Masquerade: Masculinity, Paternity, and Castration in the Italian Renaissance* (Durham: Duke University Press, 2003).

Fletcher, A.J., 'Honour, Reputation and Local Officeholding in Elizabethan and Stuart England', *Order and Disorder in Early Modern England*, eds. Anthony Fletcher and John Stevenson (Cambridge: Cambridge University Press, 1985), 92–115.

Fontaine, Laurence, *Histoire du colportage en Europe: XVe–XIXe siècle* (Paris: A. Michel, 1993).

Fournel, Victor, *Les cris de Paris: Types et physionomies d'autrefois* (Paris: Les Editions de Paris, 2003).

François Viète: un mathématicien sous la Renaissance, eds. E. Barbin, Anne Boyé, and Laurence Augereau (Paris: Vuibert, 2005).

Franko, Mark, *Dance as Text: Ideologies of the Baroque Body* (Cambridge: Cambridge University Press, 1993).

Fraser, Antonia, *Marie Antoinette: The Journey* (New York: Doubleday, 2001).

Fumaroli, Marc, *L'Age de l'éloquence: rhétorique et 'res literaria', de la Renaissance au seuil de l'époque classique* (Genève: Droz, 1980).

Garrisson, Janine, *Catherine de Médicis: l'impossible harmonie* (Paris: Payot, 2002).

Gerber, Matthew, *Bastards: Politics, Family, and Law in Early Modern France* (Oxford: Oxford University Press, 2012).

Gluckman, Max, 'Papers in Honor of Melville J. Herskovits: Gossip and Scandal', *Current Anthropology* 4 (1963): 307–16.

Goddard, Victoria, 'Honour and Shame: The Control of Women's Sexuality and Group Identity in Naples', *The Cultural Construction of Sexuality*, ed. Pat Caplan (London: Tavistock, 1987), 166–92.

Goody, Jack, *The Interface Between the Written and the Oral* (Cambridge: Cambridge University Press, 1987).

Gowing, Laura, 'Language, Power, and the Law: Women's Slander Litigation in Early Modern England', *Women, Crime and the Courts in Early Modern England*, eds. Jenny Kermode and Garthine Walker (London: University College Press Ltd., 1994), 26–47.

———, *Domestic Dangers: Women, Words and Sex in Early Modern London* (Oxford: Clarendon Press, 1996).

Graham, Victor E., and W. McAllister Johnson, *The Royal Tour of France by Charles IX and Catherine de' Medici – Festivals and Entries 1564–6* (Toronto: University of Toronto Press, 1979).

Greengrass, Mark, 'A Day in the Life of the Third Estate: Blois, 26th December 1576', *Politics, Ideology and the Law in Early Modern Europe: Essays in Honour of J.H.M. Salmon*, ed. Adrianna Bakos (New York: University of Rochester Press, 1994), 73–90.

———, *Governing Passions: Peace and Reform in the French Kingdom, 1576–1585* (Oxford: Oxford University Press, 2007).

Greenidge, A. H. J., *Infamia: Its Place in Roman Public and Private Law* (Oxford: Clarendon Press, 1864).

Greffe, Florence, and José Lothe, *La vie, les livres et les lectures de Pierre de l'Estoile: nouvelles recherches* (Paris: H. Champion, 2004).

Bibliography

Guerzoni, Guido, and Guido Alfani, 'Court History and Career Analysis: A Prosopographic Approach to the Court of Renaissance Ferrara', *The Court Historian* 12, 1 (June 2007), 1–34.

Halasz, Alexandra, *The Marketplace of Print: Pamphlets and the Public Sphere in Early Modern England* (Cambridge: Cambridge University Press, 1997).

Hallissy, Margaret, *Venomous Woman: Fear of the Female in Literature* (New York: Greenwood Press, 1987).

Hammer, Paul, 'Sex and the Virgin Queen: Aristocratic Concupiscence and the Court of Elizabeth I', *Sixteenth Century Journal* 31, no. 1, *Special Edition: Gender in Early Modern Europe* (Spring 2000): 77–97.

Hanley, Sarah, 'Engendering the State: Family Formation and State Building in Early Modern France', *French Historical Studies* 16, no. 1 (Spring 1989): 4–27.

Hardwick, Julie, *Practice of Patriarchy: Gender and the Politics of Household Authority in Early Modern France* (University Park, PA: Penn State University Press, 1998).

Harris, Barbara, 'Sisterhood, Friendship and the Power of English Aristocratic Women, 1450–1550', *Women and Politics in Early Modern England*, ed. James Daybell (Aldershot: Ashgate, 2004).

Heller, Henry, *Anti-Italianism in Sixteenth-Century France* (Toronto: University of Toronto Press, 2003).

Henke, Robert, *Performance and Literature in the Commedia dell'arte* (Cambridge: Cambridge University Press, 2002).

Héritier, Jean, *Catherine de Medici* (London: George Allen & Unwin, 1963).

Herrup, Cynthia, *A House in Gross Disorder: Sex, Law, and the 2nd Earl of Castlehaven* (Oxford: Oxford University Press, 1999).

———, To Pluck Bright Honour from the Pale Faced Moon: Gender and Honour in the Castlehaven Story', *Transactions of the Royal Historical Society*, Sixth Series, 6 (1996): 137–59.

Histoire générale de la presse française, I: Des origines à 1814, ed. Claude Bellanger (Paris: Presses Universitaires de France, 1969).

Holt, Mack, 'Patterns of Clientele and Economic Opportunity at Court during the Wars of Religion: The Household of François, Duke of Anjou', *French Historical Studies* 13, no. 3 (Spring, 1984), 305–22.

———, *The French Wars of Religion, 1562–1629* (Cambridge: Cambridge University Press, 1995; 2nd ed. 2005).

Horodowich, Elizabeth, 'The gossiping tongue: oral networks, public life and political culture in early modern Venice', *Renaissance Studies* 19 (2005): 22–45.

———, *Language and Statecraft in Early Modern Venice* (Cambridge: Cambridge University Press, 2008).

Houllemare, Marie, *Politiques de la parole, le parlement de Paris au XVIe siècle* (Genève: Droz, 2011).

Hunt, Lynn, 'The Many Bodies of Marie-Antoinette: Political Pornography and the Problem of the Feminine in the French Revolution', *Marie-Antoinette: Writings on the Body of a Queen*, ed. Dena Goodman (New York: Routledge, 2003).

Hunter, David, *Understanding French Verse: A Guide for Singers* (New York: Oxford University Press, 2005).

Ives, Eric, *The Life and Death of Anne Boleyn* (Oxford: Blackwell, 2004).

Johnson, Walter S., *Chapters in the History of French Law* (Montreal: n.p., 1957).

Jones, Colin, *Paris: Biography of a City* (London: Penguin, 2006).

Jouanna, Arlette, Jacqueline Boucher, Dominique Biloghi, Guy Thiec, *Histoire et dictionnaire des Guerres de religion* (Paris: Laffont, 1998).
Kahn, Coppélia, *Man's Estate: Masculine Identity in Shakespeare* (Berkeley: University of California Press, 1981).
Kaplan, M. Lindsay, *The Culture of Slander in Early Modern England* (Cambridge: Cambridge University Press, 1997).
Kastner, Georges, *Les voix de Paris: Essai d'une histoire littéraire et musicale* (Paris: Brandus, Dufour et Co., 1857).
Kelley, Donald R., *The Beginning of Ideology: Consciousness and Society in the French Reformation* (Cambridge: Cambridge University Press, 1981).
———, *François Hotman: A Revolutionary's Ordeal* (Princeton, N.J.: Princeton University Press, 1973).
Kelly, Joan, 'Did Women Have a Renaissance?', *Becoming Visible: Women in European History*, 3rd edn (Boston: Houghton Mifflin, 1998).
Kettering, Sharon, 'Clientage During the French Wars of Religion', *The Sixteenth-Century Journal*, 20 (1989): 221–39.
———, 'Patronage in Early Modern France', *French Historical Studies* 20, no. 4 (1992): 839–62.
———, 'The Patronage Power of Early Modern French Noblewomen', *The Historical Journal* 32, no. 4 (Dec 1989): 817–41.
———, 'The Household Service of Early Modern French Noblewomen', *French Historical Studies*, 20, no. 1 (Winter 1997): 55–85.
Kinservik, Matthew J., *Sex, Scandal and Celebrity in Late Eighteenth-Century England* (New York: Palgrave Macmillan, 2007).
Knecht, Robert J., *Catherine de' Medici* (London: Longman, 1998).
Kruse, Elaine, 'The Blood-Stained Hands of Catherine de Medici', *Political Rhetoric, Power and Renaissance Women*, eds. Carole Levin, Patricia A. Sullivan (Albany: SUNY Press, 1995), 139–55.
La Bruyère, René, *L'affaire de Saint-Jean-d'Angély ou le mystère de la mort du Prince de Condé* (Paris: Le Croît Vif, 1995).
La Croix du Maine, François Grudé, sieur de, *Les bibliothéques françoises de La Croix du Maine et de Du Verdier* (Paris: Saillant & Noyon, 1773).
La Ferrière, Hector de, *Trois amoureuses au XVIe siècle: Françoise de Rohan, Isabelle de Limeuil, La reine Margot* (Paris: Calmann Levy, 1885).
La Reine Margot, dir. Patrice Chéreau (AMLF, 1994).
Labitte, Charles, *De la démocratie chez les prédicateurs de la Ligue* (Paris: Durand, 1865).
LaGuardia, David, *Intertextual Masculinity in French Renaissance Literature: Rabelais, Brantôme, and the Cent Nouvelles Nouvelles* (Aldershot: Ashgate, 2008).
Lazard, Madeleine, *Le théâtre en France au XVIe siècle* (Paris: Presses Universitaires de France, 1980).
Le pamphlet en France au 16e siècle (Paris: Centre National des Lettres, 1983).
Le Roux, Nicolas, '"Justice, justice, justice, au nom de Jésus-Christ": Les princesses de la Ligue, le devoir de vengeance et l'honneur de la maison de Guise', *Femmes de pouvoir et pouvoir des femmes dans l'Occident médiéval et moderne*, eds. Armel Nayt-Dubois and Emmanuelle Santinelli-Foltz (Valenciennes: Presses Universitaires de Valenciennes, 2009), 439–57.
———, *La faveur du roi: mignons et courtisans au temps des derniers Valois* (Seyssel: Champ Vallon, 2001).

208 Bibliography

Leferme-Falguières, Frédérique, *Les courtisans: une societe de spectacle sous l'Ancien Regime* (Paris: Presses Universitaires de France, 2007).

Lindley, David, *The Trials of Frances Howard: Fact and Fiction at the Court of King James* (London: Routledge, 1993).

Lindsay, Robert O., and John Neu, *French Political Pamphlets, 1547–1648: A Catalog of Major Collections in American Libraries* (Madison: University of Wisconsin Press, 1969).

Literacy and Orality, eds. David R. Olson and Nancy Torrance (Cambridge: Cambridge University Press, 1991).

Litolff, Henry Charles, Adolphe d'Ennery and Jules Brésil, *L'Escadron volant de la reine. Opera-comique en trois actes, etc* (Paris, Châtillon-sur-Seine, 1888).

Lloyd-Jones, Hugh, *Females of the Species: Semonides on Women* (London: Duckworth, 1975).

Maclean, Ian, *The Renaissance Notion of Woman: A Study in the Fortunes of Scholasticism and Medical Science in European Intellectual Life* (Cambridge: Cambridge University Press, 1980).

Mallick, Oliver, 'Clients and Friends: The Ladies-in-Waiting at the Court of Anne of Austria', *The Politics of Female Households: Ladies-in-Waiting Across Early Modern Europe*, eds. Nadine Akkerman and Birgit Houben (Leiden: Brill, 2014), 231–64.

Mariéjol, Jean-Hippolyte, *Catherine de Médicis 1519–1589* (Paris: Jules Tallandier, 1979, originally written 1920).

——, *Histoire de France, t. VI: La Reforme et la Ligue. L'edit de Nantes 1559–1598*, ed. Ernest Lavisse (Paris, 1904).

Marin, Fanny, 'La fortune éditoriale des *Registres journaux des règnes de Henri III et Henri IV* de Pierre de L'Estoile', *Nouvelle Revue du XVIe siècle* 20/2 (2002): 87–108.

Marotti, Arthur F., *Manuscript, Print, and the English Renaissance Lyric* (Ithaca, N.Y: Cornell University Press, 1995).

Marshall, Rosalind K., *Queen Mary's Women: Female Relatives, Servants, Friends and Enemies of Mary, Queen of Scots* (Edinburgh: John Donald, 2006).

Mattingly, Garrett, *Renaissance Diplomacy* (Baltimore: Penguin, 1964).

Maza, Sarah, *Private Lives and Public Affairs: The Causes Célèbres of Prerevolutionary France* (Berkeley: University of California Press, 1993).

McClive, Cathy, 'The Hidden Truths of the Belly: The Uncertainties of Pregnancy in Early Modern Europe', *Social History of Medicine* 15 no. 2 (2002): 209–27.

——, 'Menstrual Knowledge and Medical Practice in France, c. 1555–1761', *Menstruation: A Cultural History*, eds. Gillian Howie and Andrew Shail (Basingstoke: Palgrave Macmillan, 2005), 76–89.

McManus, Clare, *Women on the Renaissance Stage: Anna of Denmark and Female Masquing in the Stuart Court (1590–1619)* (Manchester: Manchester University Press, 2002).

Mears, Natalie, 'Politics in the Elizabethan Privy Chamber: Lady Mary Sidney and Kat Ashley', *Women and Politics in Early Modern England*, ed. James Daybell (Aldershot: Ashgate, 2004).

Ménager, Daniel, 'Le *Tigre* et la mission du pamphlétaire', *Le Pamphlet en France au XVIe siècle* (Paris: Cahiers V.L. Saulnier, 1983), 23–34.

Michelet, Jules, *Histoire de France* (Paris: Librairie Internationale, 1874).

Milstein, Joanna, *The Gondi: Family Strategy and Survival in Early Modern France* (Farnham: Ashgate, 2014).

Mollenauer, Lynn Wood, *Strange Revelations: Magic, Poison, and Sacrilege in Louis XIV's France* (University Park, PA: Pennsylvania State University Press, 2007).

Monteil, Amand-Alexis, *Histoire des Français des divers états aux cinq derniers siècles*, 5 vols (Paris, 1853).
Montesquieu, Charles de Secondat, *De l'esprit des lois* (Paris, 1834).
Munns, Jessica, and Penny Richards, 'Exploiting and Destabilizing Gender Roles: Anne d'Este', *French History* 6, 2 (1992): 206–15.
Murphy, Stephen, 'Catherine, Cybele, & Ronsard's Witnesses', *High Anxiety: Masculinity in Crisis in Early Modern France*, ed. Kathleen Long (Kirksville: Truman State University Press, 2002), 55–70.
Neubauer, Hans-Joachim, *The Rumour: A Cultural History*, trans. Christian Braun (London: Free Association Books, 1999).
Neuschel, Kristen B., *Word of Honor: Interpreting Noble Culture in Sixteenth-Century France* (Ithaca: Cornell University Press, 1989).
Nevitt, Marcus, *Women and the Pamphlet Culture of Revolutionary England, 1640–1660* (Aldershot: Ashgate, 2006).
Normand, Silje, 'Perceptions of Poison: Defining the Poisonous in Early Modern France' (unpublished doctoral thesis, University of Cambridge, 2005).
———, 'Venomous Words and Political Poisons: Language(s) of Exclusion in Early Modern France', *Exploring Cultural History: Essays in Honour of Peter Burke*, eds. Melissa Calaresu, Filippo de Vivo and Joan-Pau Rubiés (Farnham: Ashgate, 2010), 113–31.
Ong, Walter J., *Orality and Literacy: The Technologizing of the Word* (London: Methuen, 1982).
Outhwaite, R. B., *Clandestine Marriage in England, 1500–1850* (London: Hambledon Press, 1995).
Painted Ladies: Women at the Court of Charles II, eds. Catharine MacLeod and Julia Marciari Alexander (London: National Portrait Gallery, 2001).
Pallier, Denis, *Recherches sur l'imprimerie à Paris pendant la Ligue (1585–1594)* (Genève: Droz, 1975).
Parsons, Nicola, *Reading Gossip in Early Eighteenth-Century England* (Basingstoke: Palgrave Macmillan, 2009).
Patronnes et mécènes en France à la Renaissance, ed. Kathleen Wilson-Chevalier with Eugénie Pascal (Saint-Étienne: Publications de l'Université de Saint-Étienne, 2007).
Pettegree, Andrew, *The French Book and the European Book World* (Leiden: Brill, 2007).
Philippy, Patricia, *Painting Women: Cosmetics, Canvases, and Early Modern Culture* (Baltimore: Johns Hopkins University Press, 2006).
Pimodan, Gabriel de, *La mère des Guises: Antoinette de Bourbon (1494–1583)* (Paris: Honoré Champion, 1889).
Polachek, Dora, 'A la recherche du spirituel: l'Italie et les Dames galantes de Brantôme', *Romanic Review* 94, nos. 1–2 (2003): 227–43.
———, 'Le mécénat meurtrier, l'iconoclasme et les limites de l'acceptable: Anne d'Este, Catherine-Marie de Lorraine et l'anéantissement d'Henri III' in *Patronnes et mécènes en France à la Renaissance*, ed. Kathleen Wilson-Chevalier with Eugénie Pascal (Saint-Étienne: Publications de l'Université de Saint-Étienne, 2007), 433–54.
Politics, Transgression, and Representation at the Court of Charles II, eds. Catharine MacLeod and Julia Marciari Alexander (New Haven: Yale University Press, 2007).
Pommerol, Marie Henriette de, *Albert de Gondi, Maréchal de Retz* (Genève; Lyon printed, 1953).
Potter, David, 'Marriage and Cruelty among the Protestant Nobility in Sixteenth-Century France: Diane de Barbançon and Jean de Rohan, 1561–7', *European History Quarterly* 20 (1990): 5–38.

210 Bibliography

———, R. Roberts, 'An Englishman's View of the Court of Henri III, 1584–1585: Richard Cook's "Description of the Court of France"', *French History*, 2:3 (1988), 312–44.

Print, Manuscript, and Performance: The Changing Relations of the Media in Early Modern England, eds. Arthur F. Marotti and Michael D. Bristol, (Columbus: Ohio State University Press, 2000).

Quaintance, Courtney, 'Defaming the Courtesan: Satire and Invective in Sixteenth-Century Italy', *The Courtesan's Arts: Cross-Cultural Perspectives* (New York: Oxford University Press, 2006).

Racaut, Luc, *Hatred in Print: Catholic Propaganda and Protestant Identity during the French Wars of Religion* (Aldershot: Ashgate, 2002).

Raymond, Joad, *Pamphlets and Pamphleteering in Early Modern Britain* (Cambridge: Cambridge University Press, 2003).

Read, M. Charles, *Le Tigre de 1560* (Paris: Académie des Bibliophiles, 1875).

Reiss, Sheryl E., 'Widow, Mother, Patron of Art: Alfonsina Orsini de' Medici', *Beyond Isabella: Secular Women Patrons of Art in Renaissance Italy* (Kirksville: Truman State University Press, 2001), 125–8.

Richards, Penny, 'The Guise Women: Politics, War and Peace', *Gender, Power and Privilege in Early Modern Europe*, eds. Jessica Munns and Penny Richards (Harlow: Pearson, 2003), 159–70.

Richardson, Brian, *Manuscript Culture in Renaissance Italy* (Cambridge: Cambridge University Press, 2009).

Richmond, Hugh, 'Shakespeare's Navarre', *The Huntington Library Quarterly* 42, no. 3 (Summer, 1979).

Rickman, Johanna, *Love, Lust, and License in Early Modern England: Illicit Sex and the Nobility* (Aldershot: Ashgate, 2008).

Roberts, Penny, *Peace and Authority during the French Religious Wars c.1560–1600* (Basingstoke: Palgrave Macmillan, 2013).

Roberts, Yvonne, 'The Regency of 1574 in the Discours Merveilleux and in the Poems of Jean-Antoine de Baïf', *Bibliothèque d'Humanisme et Renaissance* 63, no. 2 (2001): 261–75.

Roelker, Nancy Lyman, 'The Appeal of Calvinism to French Noblewomen in the Sixteenth Century', *Journal of Interdisciplinary History* 2, 4 Psychoanalysis and History (Spring 1972): 391–418.

———, *Queen of Navarre: Jeanne d'Albret 1528–1572* (Cambridge MA: Harvard University Press, 1968).

Roller, Duane W., *Cleopatra: A Biography* (Oxford: Oxford University Press, 2010).

Rothstein, Marian, 'Clandestine Marriage and Amadis de Gaule: The Text, the World, and the Reader', *The Sixteenth Century Journal* 25, no. 4 (1994): 873–86.

Rubenhold, Hallie, *Lady Worsley's Whim: An Eighteenth-Century Tale of Sex, Scandal and Divorce* (London: Chatto & Windus, 2008).

Ruble, Alphonse, baron de, *François de Montmorency: Gouverneur de Paris et Lieutenant du Roi dans l'isle de France (1530–1579)* (Paris: Champion, 1880).

———, *Le duc de Nemours et Mademoiselle de Rohan (1531–1592)* (Paris: Labitte, 1883).

Rumor Mills, eds. Gary Alan Fine, Véronique Campion-Vincent and Chip Heath (New Brunswick, NJ: Transaction, 2005).

Salzberg, Rosa, 'In the Mouth of Charlatans: Street Performers and the Dissemination of Pamphlets in Renaissance Italy', *Renaissance Studies*, 24/5 (2010): 638–53.

———, *Ephemeral City: Cheap Print and Urban Culture in Renaissance Venice* (Manchester: Manchester University Press, 2014).

Sawyer, Jeffrey K., *Printed Poison: Pamphlet Propaganda, Faction Politics, and the Public Sphere in Early Seventeenth-Century France* (Berkeley: University of California Press, 1990).

Schrenck, Gilbert, 'Jeu et théorie du pamphlet dans le Journal du règne de Henri III (1574–1589) de Pierre de L'Estoile' in *Traditions Polémiques* (Paris: Cahiers V. L. Saulnier, 1984), 69–79.

——, and Chiara Lastraïoli, 'L'Estoile, Pierre de, 1546–1611' in *Dictionnaire des lettres françaises*, ed. Michel Simonin (Paris: Fayard, 2001), 739–41.

Scott-Warren, Jason, 'Reconstructing Manuscript Networks: The Textual Transactions of Sir Stephen Powle', *Communities in Early Modern England: Networks, Place, Rhetoric* (Manchester: Manchester University Press, 2000), 18–37.

Seguin, Jean Pierre, 'L'Information en France avant le périodique. 500 canards imprimés entre 1529 et 1631', *Arts et traditions populaires. année 11. no. 1–3/4* (1963).

Sharpe, Kevin, 'The Image of Virtue: The Court and Household of Charles I, 1625–1642)', *The English Court from the Wars of the Roses to the Civil War*, eds. Starkey et al. (Harlow: Addison Wesley Longman, 1987), 226–60.

Shennan, J.H., *The Parlement of Paris* (London: Eyre & Spottiswoode, 1968).

Smith, Pauline, *The Anti-Courtier Trend in Sixteenth-century French Literature* (Genève: Droz, 1966).

Solnon, Jean-François, *Catherine de Médicis* (Paris: Perrin, 2003).

Spacks, Patricia Meyer, *Gossip* (New York: Alfred A. Knopf, 1985).

Spangler, Jonathan, 'Mother Knows Best: The Dowager Duchess of Guise, a Son's Ambitions, and the Regencies of Marie de Medici and Anne of Austria', *Aspiration, Representation and Memory: The Guise in Europe, 1506–1688*, eds. Jessica Munns, Penny Richards, Jonathan Spangler (Farnham: Ashgate, 2015), 125–46.

Stewart, Alan, 'Bribery, Buggery, and the Fall of Lord Chancellor Bacon', *Rhetoric and Law in Early Modern Europe*, eds. Lorna Hutson and Victoria Kahn, (New Haven: Yale University Press, 2001).

Stombler, Mindy, ' "Buddies" or "Slutties": The Collective Sexual Reputation of Fraternity Little Sisters', *Gender and Society* 8, no. 3 (Sept. 1994): 297–323.

Stone, Bailey, *The French Parlements and the Crisis of the Old Regime* (Chapel Hill: UNC Press, 1986).

Stone, Lawrence, *The Crisis of the Aristocracy 1558–1641* (Oxford: Clarendon Press, 1979).

Sutherland, Nicola, 'Catherine de Medici: The Legend of the Wicked Italian Queen', *The Sixteenth Century Journal* 9, no. 2 (1978): 45–56.

Szabari, Antónia, *Less Rightly Said: Scandals and Readers in Sixteenth-Century France* (Stanford: Stanford University Press, 2010).

Tarbé, Louis Hardouin Prosper, *Recueil de poésies calvinistes* (Reims: P. Dubois, 1866).

Taylor, Larissa Juliet, 'Dangerous Vocations: Preaching in France in the Late Middle Ages and Reformations', *Preachers and People in the Reformations and Early Modern Period*, ed. Larissa Juliet Taylor (Leiden: Brill, 2001), 91–124.

Ternaux, Jean-Claude, 'Les excès de la maison de Lorraine dans l'épître et la satire du Tigre (1560–1561)', *Le mécénat et l'influence des Guises (Actes du Colloque tenu à Joinville du 31 mai au 4 juin 1994)* (Paris: Honoré Champion, 1997), 381–403.

The Court Historian 10/1 (October 2005), Special issue: *Queens and the Transmission of Political Culture: The Case of Early Modern France*, eds. Melinda Gough and Malcolm Smuts.

The Politics of Female Households: Ladies-in-Waiting Across Early Modern Europe, eds. Nadine Akkerman and Birgit Houben (Leiden: Brill, 2014).

212 Bibliography

Thickett, Dorothy, *Estienne Pasquier (1529–1615) The Versatile Barrister of Sixteenth-Century France* (London: Regency Press, 1979).
Thierry, Adrien, *Diane de Poitiers* (Paris: La Palatine, 1955).
Traditions Polémiques, ed. Nicole Cazauran (Paris: ENS Jeunes Filles, 1985).
Transnational Exchange in Early Modern Theater, eds. Robert Henke and Eric Nicholson (Aldershot: Ashgate, 2008).
van der Essen, Léon, *Alexandre Farnèse, prince de Parme, gouverneur général des Pays-Bas* (Bruxelles: Librairie nationale d'art et d'histoire, 1934), 2 (1578–1582).
van Orden, Kate, *Music, Discipline and Arms in Early Modern France* (Chicago: University of Chicago Press, 2005).
———, 'Cheap Print and Street Song Following the Saint Bartholomew's Massacres of 1572', *Music and the Cultures of Print*, ed. Kate van Orden (New York: Garland, 2000), 271–323.
———, 'Female "*Complaintes*": Laments of Venus, Queens, and City Women in Late Sixteenth-Century France', *Renaissance Quarterly* 54, 3 (Autumn, 2001): 801–45.
Vester, Matthew A., *Jacques de Savoie-Nemours: L'apanage du Genevois au coeur de la puissance dynastique savoyarde au XVIe siècle*, trans. Eléonore Mazel and Déborah Engel, (Genève: Droz, 2008).
Veyrin-Forrer, Jeanne, 'Un collectioneur peu connu, François Rasse Des Neux [sic], chirurgien parisien', *La Lettre et le Texte* (Paris: ENS Jeunes Filles, 1987), 423–77.
———, François Rasse des Neux [sic] et ses tombeaux poétiques' in *Le poète et son oeuvre de la composition à la publication: actes du colloque de Valenciennes (20–21 mai 1999)*, ed. Jean-Eudes Girot (Genève: Droz, 2004), 37–46.
Viennot, Eliane, 'Des "femmes d'Etat" au XVIe siècle: Les princesses de la Ligue et l'écriture de l'histoire', *Femmes et pouvoirs sous l'Ancien Régime*, eds. Danielle Hasse-Dubosc and Eliane Viennot (Paris: Rivages, 1991), 77–97.
———, 'Les femmes dans les "troubles" du XVIe siècle', *Clio. Histoire, femmes et sociétés* 5 (1997), accessed 13 July 2015, doi: 10.4000/clio.409
———, 'Marguerite de Valois et le Divorce satyrique', *Albineana – Cahiers d'Aubigné* 7 (1996): 111–29.
Voss, Paul J., *Elizabethan News Pamphlets: Shakespeare, Spenser, Marlowe and the Birth of Journalism* (Pittsburgh: Duquesne University Press, 2001).
Waele, Michel de, 'La fin des guerres de Religion et l'exclusion des femmes de la vie politique française', *French Historical Studies* 29, no. 2 (Spring 2006): 199–230.
Wanegffelen, Thierry, *Catherine de Médicis: le pouvoir au féminin* (Paris: Payot, 2005).
Warner, Lyndan, *The Ideas of Man and Woman in Renaissance France* (Farnham: Ashgate, 2011).
Welch, Evelyn, *Shopping in the Renaissance* (London: Yale University Press, 2005).
Wellman, Kathleen, *Queens and Mistresses of Renaissance France* (New Haven: Yale University Press, 2013).
Wickham, Chris, 'Gossip and Resistance among the Medieval Peasantry', *Past & Present* 160 (1998): 3–24.
Wolfson, Sara J., 'The Female Bedchamber of Queen Henrietta Maria: Politics, Familial Networks and Policy, 1626–40', *The Politics of Female Households: Ladies-in-Waiting Across Early Modern Europe*, eds. Nadine Akkerman and Birgit Houben (Leiden: Brill, 2014), 311–41.
Woman Defamed and Woman Defended: An Anthology of Medieval Texts, ed. Alcuin Blamires, with Karen Pratt and C. W. Marx (Oxford: Clarendon Press, 2002).

Women in Power: Caterina and Maria de' Medici: The Return to Florence of Two Queens of France, ed. Clarice Innocenti (Firenze: Mandragora, 2008).

Women, Crime and the Courts in Early Modern England, eds. Jenny Kermode and Garthine Walker (London: University College Press Ltd., 1994).

Woudhuysen, H.R., *Sir Philip Sidney and the Circulation of Manuscripts, 1558–1640* (Oxford: Clarendon Press, 1996).

Wright, Pam, 'A Change in Direction: The Ramifications of a Female Household, 1558–1603)', *The English Court from the Wars of the Roses to the Civil War*, eds. Starkey et al. (Harlow: Addison Wesley Longman, 1987), 147–72.

Zemon Davis, Natalie, *Fiction in the Archives: Pardon Tales and Their Tellers* (Stanford: Stanford University Press, 1987).

———, 'Printing and the People', *Society and Culture in Early Modern France: Eight Essays* (Cambridge: Polity, 1987).

Zum Kolk, Caroline, 'The Household of the Queen of France in the Sixteenth Century', *The Court Historian* 14, no. 1, (June 2009): 3–22.

———, 'Catherine de Médicis et sa maison. La fonction politique de l'hôtel de la reine au XVIe siècle' (unpublished doctoral thesis, Université Paris VIII, 2006).

Zvereva, Alexandra, *Les Clouet de Catherine de Médicis: chefs-d'oeuvre graphiques du musée Condé* (Paris: Somogy, 2002).

———, *Portraits dessinés de la cour de Valois: Les Clouet de Catherine de Médicis* (Paris: Arthena, 2011).

Index

Académie française 38
accusations, gendering of 5, 123
Adjacet, Ludovic 66
adultery 1–3, 14, 26, 41, 47, 49, 53, 61, 63, 64, 66, 80, 83, 85, 100n112, 102, 104–107, 110–111, 113, 114, 121, 146, 157, 164, 165, 177, 179, 187, 192
Affaire des Poisons 113, 122
agency 7, 25, 93, 104, 117, 123, 150, 155–157, 163, 179, 189, 192
Alava, Don Frances de 102, 120, 124n2, 144
Alençon, François, duc d' 15–17, 54, 64, 84, 147
ambassadors, diplomats 9, 13, 21, 29n33, 38, 48, 49, 50, 52, 56n12, 65, 69, 102, 120–121, 141, 143–145, 150, 162, 165, 171, 173
ambassadors, visit of Polish 13, 38, 52
ambition, Catherine de Medici's unnatural 3, 10, 12, 18, 55, 106
ambition, others' 46, 64, 116, 157, 158, 161, 167, 188
anagrams 62–63
anger, rage 36, 51, 71, 89, 107, 108, 115, 119, 134, 135, 136, 145, 146, 148, 155, 159, 168–171
animalistic imagery 85, 92, 119, 147
Anne de Beaujeu 37, 38
Anne de Bretagne, queen of France 13, 37, 44, 167
anonymity 12, 40, 41, 42, 48, 67, 80–82, 87, 138, 157, 165
Antwerp 114
appeals (legal) 23–24, 143, 146, 164, 165, 190
apport Baudoyer 73, 74
apport de Paris 73, 74
arbitrariness of judgments 116, 163, 179, 190, 191

Arnould, Jean-Claude 160–161
artwork, paintings 19, 20, 162
artwork, pencil drawings 20
Audebert, Nicolas 84
Aumale, Charles, duc d' 161
aurality 21, 77, 91, 132–136
Auxonne 102, 108, 115, 118

Baïf, Jean-Antoine de 38
Balet comique de la royne 13
baptism 171
Baranova, Tatiana Debaggi 22
Barbizi, seigneur 1–2
Barchino, Gaspar 9, 102, 120–121
Barge, Fleury 134, 135
Barnaud, Nicolas 80
barrenness 46
Basoche, clercs de la 79–80
bastards, bastardy 50, 110–111, 123, 138, 140, 159, 189, 191
bastards, recognition of 111, 123, 138, 140
Bayonne 52
Beaujoyeulx, Balthasar 13
beauty 2, 12–13, 18–20, 24, 53, 54, 68, 82, 87–88, 119, 120, 121, 157, 158, 167
Bellany, Alastair 5, 22, 64, 91
Belleau, Remy 121
Bellièvre, Pomponne de 54
Beraudière, Louise de la 47, 63–64, 111, 120, 140
Bertière, Simone 18
Bèze, Théodore de 106
Bible 21
Birague, Françoise de 50
blackmail 162
Bodin, Jean 75, 143
Boehrer, Bruce Thomas 159,
Boleyn, Anne, queen of England 5, 159, 161
Boleyn, Mary 159–161

Boni, Jean Baptiste 49
Boni, Marie 49
booksellers 70, 74, 159
Booth, Alison 14, 188
Bourbon, Antoine de, king of Navarre 47, 48, 63, 104, 111, 120, 135, 140–141, 142, 190–191
Bourbon, Charles, cardinal de 111
Bourbon, Henri de, prince de Condé 112–113
Bourbon, Louis de, prince de Condé 47, 50, 88, 100n112, 102, 104–108, 111, 112, 120, 121, 140
Bourdeille, Jeanne de 86–87
Bourdillon, Imbert de la Platière, maréchal de 118
Brantôme, Pierre de Bourdeille, abbé de 12, 13, 15, 36, 44, 45, 81, 107, 109, 110, 111, 112, 118–119, 145, 158, 170, 171
Brezé, Françoise de 46, 48
Brezé, Louise de 46
Brisson, Barnabé 75
Brittany 13, 37, 44, 50, 110, 134, 141, 167
Broomhall, Susan 37
Brouage 147
bruit 102, 106, 122, 135
Burt, Ronald 20

Calvinism 3, 22, 29, 106, 142, 143, 166, 191
Calvin, Jean 106, 120
canards 77, 88
capon 147
Carroll, Stuart 155
Castiglione, Baldessare 6
Castlehaven, earl of 5
catalogue of women 14, 84–87, 188
Catherine de Medici, queen of France, as head of household 2, 3, 4, 7, 8, 15–20, 21, 24, 25, 26, 36, 37, 38, 43–55, 109–110, 112, 115, 122–123, 131, 137, 138, 148, 188, 190, 193
Catherine de Medici, queen of France, as negotiator 3, 14, 17, 18, 19, 26, 33n77, 48, 50, 52, 54, 104, 106, 187
Catherine de Medici, queen of France, criticism of 2–4, 9–12, 15–19, 36, 43, 45, 48, 53–54, 55, 68, 102, 104, 108–109, 111, 178, 188
Catherine de Medici, queen of France, early life of 45–46
Catherine of Aragon, queen of England 159
Catherine the Great, queen of Russia 5
Catholic League 4, 25, 29n26, 40, 51, 54, 63, 69–70, 71, 79, 81, 83, 84, 87, 96n38, 96n44, 155, 157, 161, 164, 165, 172, 173, 176, 178, 180, 193, 194
Catiline 158
Catin 17, 32n69
Chambre Ardente 122
Chancellerie 21, 22, 74
Chapelle des Battus 71
Chardavoine, Jehan 88, 107
charlatans 62, 74, 76–80, 92
Charles I, king of England 5, 93n2
Charles II, king of England 19–20
Charles IX, king of France 3, 11, 18, 22, 38, 45, 47, 48, 52, 53, 54, 66, 80, 81, 108, 111, 144, 166, 167, 168
Charles VIII, king of France 37
Chastel, Anne du 50
chastity 7, 53, 82, 83, 85, 86, 140, 158
Châteauvillain, Antoinette, comtesse de 61
Chatenet, Monique 13, 44
Chenonceaux 53
childbirth, illegitimate 3, 5, 20, 24, 25, 63, 65, 66, 102, 104, 108–111, 121, 122, 123, 138, 139, 140, 188, 190, 191, 192
childbirth, reproduction 8, 46, 111, 113, 115, 116, 119, 135, 150, 164, 167, 171, 187
Chrestien, Florent 81, 82, 83, 107–108
Christine of Lorraine, grand duchess of Tuscany 49
Cicero 75, 158
Circe 18, 63, 68, 113
clandestine marriage 23, 51, 89–91, 115, 136–140, 145, 157, 189, 191
classical learning 6, 14, 38, 66, 68–69, 89, 91, 156, 195
Clement VII, pope 46
Clément, Jacques 83, 175
Cleopatra 5
clergy 21, 29n26, 75, 80, 83, 135, 150n3, 163, 166, 173, 175–176, 179, 187
Clermont, Louise de Bretagne-Avaugour 50
Clèves, Catherine de, duchesse de Guise 170–171, 180
clientage 6, 50, 51, 82, 190, 191
Clouet, François 20
Cloulas, Ivan 54, 166
Coester, Christiane 52
Coligny, Gaspard de, seigneur de Châtillon, admiral of France 142, 168–169
Coligny, Odet de, cardinal de Châtillon 121
colporteurs 62, 74, 76–79, 92, 172, 176
Combaut, Robert 63–64, 86
commedia dell'arte 79–80
complainte 89–91

Concordat of Bologna 23
consanguinity, degrees of 160–161
Conspiracy of Amboise (1560) 47, 162, 179
contrafactum 63, 88–92, 107
convent, imprisonment in 25, 73 (map), 89–91, 102, 104, 108–109, 111, 115–118, 121–123, 190, 191
Cook, Richard 45
Coqueley, Lazare 171
Cordeliers, church of the 176
Cornouailles 63–64
corruption 2, 3, 67, 68, 142, 143, 145, 148, 165, 179
Coryate, Thomas 79
cosmetics 113, 116
Coué, Antoine de 134, 135
Coué, Gabrielle de Binel, dame de 134, 135, 136, 137–138
Council of Trent 23, 75, 136, 191
courtesans 57n20, 83
courts, ecclesiastical 23, 132, 189
Crawford, Katherine 10
cris de Paris 77–78
Crouzet, Denis 19, 52
Crussol, Antoine de 49
cuckoldry 4, 5, 9, 14, 15, 21–22, 24, 25, 41, 42–43, 63, 68, 80, 85–87, 92, 94n22, 104, 114, 118–119, 123, 124, 158, 161, 192–193
Cureton, Charlotte de Vienne, dame de 117

dame d'honneur 46, 48, 112, 126n23
dames (as household officers) 46
dance 13, 19, 53, 77, 92
D'Aubigné, Agrippa 40, 41, 104, 158, 161
decorum 54, 110, 115
defamation 6, 22, 25, 70, 77, 140, 158, 166, 172, 193
Dehors, Robert 159
DeJean, Joan 194, 195
démenti 142
demoiselles 46, 49, 50, 51
depositions 21, 112, 116, 122, 132–136, 137–138, 145, 150
des Noeux, Rasse 22, 158
Desportes, Philippe 38, 40, 87
de Thou, Jacques-Auguste 106, 142
de Vivo, Filippo 9, 143
Diane de France 50, 51, 89, 116
Dijon 65, 102, 108
Diou, Jacques de 171
diplomacy 9, 17, 38, 50, 144, 165, 166, 168, 170, 179

discipline 48–49, 112, 136, 148, 193
Discours merveilleux 10, 11, 47, 62, 106, 114
disgrace 102, 116, 122, 138, 140, 193
disinheritance 136, 137
distribution of news 9, 21, 62, 70–74, 79, 80, 84, 163, 176
domesticity 2, 7, 37, 40, 80, 92, 113, 131, 132–136, 140, 144, 162, 163, 175, 188
Dorat, Jean 40
dressmakers, tailors 7, 134
duel 142, 160–161, 180
Duindam, Jeroen 27n2, 44, 51
Dumas, Alexandre 11, 17
duplicity 104, 113, 115, 138, 142, 143, 149
Durant, Gilles 81

Edict Against Clandestine Marriage (1557) 189
Edict Against Concealed Pregnancy (1557) 189
Edict of Moulins 70
Edict of Romorantin 70
edicts, pronouncements of 72–74, 143, 189
elegy 66
Elisabeth d'Autriche, queen of France 52
Elisabeth de Valois, queen of Spain 49–50
Elizabeth I, queen of England 10, 31n64, 50–51, 52, 140, 147, 159, 173
encomiastic verse 38–40, 81–82, 89
Enfants-sans-Souci 80
engravings 77
entourage 4, 7, 9, 11, 13, 14–20, 24, 36, 43–54, 63, 114, 115, 162, 187, 194
Entraguet, Charles de Balzac, baron d' 40–41, 85
enumeration (of women) 6, 14, 41, 53–54, 84–87, 92, 193–194
Épinac, Grisolde d' 158–159, 161
Épinac, Pierre d', archbishop of Lyon 158–159, 160, 161
Epistre envoiee au Tigre de la France 62, 157–159, 162
epitaphs 2, 34n95, 41–43, 62, 94n22
escadron volant *see* flying squadron
Estates General 47, 136, 141, 143
Este, Anne d', duchesse de Guise, as negotiator 26, 146–147, 163, 166–167, 171, 178, 179
Este, Anne d', duchesse de Guise, campaigns for justice by 167–172
Este, Anne d', duchesse de Guise, criticisms of 131, 143–144, 146, 157–158, 161–162, 163–165, 176–177

Este, Ercole II d', duke of Ferrara 156, 167
Este, Lucrezia d', duchess of Urbino 132, 137–138, 143
Este, Luigi d', cardinal of Ferrara 146, 166
Estrées family 54, 94n22
états de maison de la reine 24, 44, 45, 46, 48
exclusion 26, 67, 104, 115, 117, 122, 123, 127n48, 144, 192, 193
execution (death penalty) 5, 74, 75, 77, 97n57, 113, 137, 159, 160, 162, 163, 168, 179, 180

fama 116
fanaticism 81, 155
Farnese, Alessandro, prince of Parma 30n48, 169–170
Ferrara 68, 132, 143, 146, 156, 165, 167
Filles-Dieu convent 73, 89, 115–116
Flanders 114
Fleming, Lady 110–111
Florence 11, 29n35, 45–46, 49
Florentine exiles 11, 30n46
flying squadron 1, 3, 4, 9, 12–20, 30n48, 52, 54, 82, 102, 104, 111, 114–115, 124
Fontainebleau 52, 92, 135
Foulon, Benjamin 130n88
Franco-Gallia 157
François I, king of France 23, 38, 44, 45, 46, 74, 137, 167
François II, king of France 3, 47, 48, 49, 137, 162
French Revolution 22–23, 188
Fresnes, Florimond Robertet, seigneur de 104, 108, 118–119, 122
Fronde 38, 93n5
Fumaroli, Marc 8
Furetière, Antoine 122

Gallicanism 10, 23, 131, 136, 150n3
Garnier, Robert 75
gender 5, 8, 9, 15, 26, 41, 53, 83, 104, 123, 132, 144, 163, 169, 170, 173, 177, 180, 193
Geneva 3, 10, 105
genitalia 195
gentilshommes de la chambre 53
geography 8, 24, 62, 71–79, 84
Gerber, Matthew 110, 189
Gondi-Retz, Albert, maréchal de 40–41, 51, 85
Gonzague, Louis de, duc de Nevers 50, 80
gossip 1, 8, 11, 20–21, 34n89, 50, 65, 66, 76, 92, 104, 109–110, 118–119, 122–123, 124n4, 132, 135, 137–139, 149–150, 162, 192
gouvernante of France 38, 44, 50, 55
gouvernantes (household) 46 50
graffiti 9, 70–71, 194
Guillaume, fool of Henri IV, 87
guilt (legal) 5, 42, 70, 136, 137, 140, 148, 160, 172, 191
Guise family 22, 25, 51, 52, 142, 155, 157, 162, 169, 171, 188
Guise, Charles, duc de 161
Guise, François-Alexandre, chevalier de 180
Guise, François, duc de 3, 143, 156–157, 158, 163–164, 167–169, 177
Guise, Henri, duc de 61, 84, 167–168, 169, 180
Guise, Louis, cardinal de 168, 169

Hallissy, Margaret 113, 114
Hammer, Paul 51
Hanley, Sarah 29n27, 30n38, 36–37, 151n19
harangères 76
Harpsfield, Nicholas 159
Harris, Barbara 51–52
Henri II, king of France 3, 15, 19, 44, 46, 47, 48, 49, 51, 89, 110, 115, 136, 137, 148, 160
Henri III, king of France 1, 38, 42, 43, 52, 54, 63, 75, 80, 83, 84, 112, 146, 157, 160, 169, 171–172, 175, 178, 183
Henri III, king of France, and *mignons* 3–4, 17, 22, 27n9, 41, 43, 53–54, 64, 82–83, 161
Henri III, king of France, criticism of 3–4, 22, 23, 29n26, 53–54, 56n12, 70, 71, 80, 81, 82–83, 172–173
Henri IV, king of France (also Henri de Navarre) 4, 12, 13, 15, 17, 18, 33n77, 54, 62, 70, 77, 84, 87, 94n22, 106, 114, 130n88, 148, 161, 173, 178
Henry VIII, king of England 159, 161
Héptameron 160
heresy 4, 70, 74, 82, 97n57, 104, 157, 166, 173
Héritier, Jean 18
Herrup, Cynthia 5, 43, 113
Hieronimo di Bolonia 77
Hoby, Sir Thomas 65, 143, 144–145, 165
homosexuality 4, 53, 82–83, 161, 195
homosociality 14, 119
honour 6–7, 22, 42–43, 44, 45, 50, 53, 64, 106, 110, 115, 116, 117, 120, 121, 123,

131–132, 135–136, 138, 140–141, 144, 145, 146, 149, 157, 161, 166, 171, 173, 176, 177, 179, 180, 188, 189, 191, 192, 193
honour killing 1, 41–43
Hotman, François 157, 162
Houllemare, Marie 24, 37, 66, 75
house arrest 17, 113, 169, 191
household appointments 44, 45, 46, 48–50, 54, 61
Huguenots 2, 3, 4, 10, 18, 19, 22, 25, 40, 52, 55, 80, 82, 83, 84, 102, 104, 106, 107–108, 114, 118, 120–121, 123, 124n2, 132, 141–142, 145, 146, 147, 148, 157, 158, 162, 163, 164, 166, 168, 173, 176, 179, 192, 193
humanism 8, 38, 46, 68, 107, 156, 194, 195
Hunt, Lynn 188
hunting 46, 109, 119, 127n33
hypocrisy 82, 111

I Gelosi 80
île de la Cité 71, 74, 75
île-de-France 8
illness 47, 51, 109, 114
imaginary libraries 49, 63, 84–87, 112, 158, 173, 192–194
imprisonment 51, 113, 146, 147
incest 3, 11, 25, 157–163, 179, 187, 188, 192
infamia 116
infanticide 140, 187
infidelity see adultery
information management, gendering of 123
information transmission/circulation 2, 7–9, 20–25, 65, 74–76, 79, 80, 91, 92–93, 102, 104, 109, 115–118, 122, 123–124, 132, 137–138, 143, 144–146, 150, 162, 176, 187–188, 189, 194
In nuptias Ducis de Nemours 67, 131, 164–165
insults 77, 142, 149, 170
intelligence 9, 115–118, 121, 123, 148, 149
Isabeau de Bavière, queen of France 10
Italian financiers 66–67, 122
Italophobia 2, 3, 11–12, 45, 82–83, 114, 178, 192
itinerant vendors 62, 75, 76–79, 97n69

James I, king of England 5
Janequin, Clément 77
Jarnac, Guy Chabot, baron de 160–161

jealousy 2, 48, 51, 54, 118–119
Jeanne d'Albret, queen of Navarre 22, 38, 100n112, 106, 114, 132, 135, 139, 142, 143–145, 148, 165, 191
Joan of Arc 86
Joinville 51, 163
Jones, Colin 79
Joyeuse, Anne de Batarnay, duc de 4, 49, 85, 161
Julian law 42
Juvenal 14, 68

Kelly, Joan 194
Kernevenoy, Mme de 54
Kettering, Sharon 6, 43
King's Council 37, 74, 131, 144, 165, 167, 169, 190
Knecht, Robert 19

L'Altissimo 79
L'Escadron volant de la reine (comic-opera) 17
L'Escadron volant de la reine (novel) 17
L'Estoile, Pierre de 1–2, 4, 9, 21–22, 36, 40, 41, 53, 61, 62, 63, 64, 65, 66, 68, 69–71, 74, 76, 77, 80, 81, 82, 84–85, 87, 146, 155, 160, 163, 172–175, 176, 178, 189, 194
La Beraudière, Louise de 47, 63–64, 111, 120, 140
La Bourdaisière, Françoise Babou de 64–65
La Bourdaisière, Françoise Robertet de 94n22
La Bourdaisière, Georges Babou de 64–65
La Chambre, Louis de, abbé de la Trinité de Vendôme 166
La Châtaigneraye, François de Vivonne, seigneur de 160–161
La Croix du Maine, François Grudé, sieur de 40
La Ferrière, Hector de 17, 110
La Garnache 146, 147–148
La Garnache, Henri de 146–148
LaGuardia, David 8, 12, 13–14, 15, 84, 85, 86, 119
Laissez la verde couleur 89–91
La Marck, Françoise de 1–2, 14, 24, 40, 41–43, 54, 69, 83–84, 114, 115, 188, 193
Langey 143
La Princesse de Clèves 149
La Reine Margot (film) 11
La Reine Margot (novel) 11, 17

La Rochefoucauld, Charlotte de 142
La Rochelle 142, 148, 193
La Roche-sur-Yon, Charles de Bourbon, prince de 103–104, 111–112, 116, 119
La Roche-sur-Yon, Philippe de Montespedon, princesse de 48, 112
Latin 2, 9, 14, 24, 37, 38, 42, 61, 65–69, 71, 81, 83, 92, 95n26, 108–109, 111, 119, 123, 124, 194
La Trémoille, Charlotte-Catherine de 112–113, 114, 189, 191, 192
laundry, laundresses 7, 53
Laval, Charlotte de 142
law, canon 23, 110, 128n63, 132, 172, 189
law, customary 23, 110, 116, 127n32, 128n63, 189
law, Roman 23, 42, 110, 116, 128n63, 189
Left Bank 71–74, 79
legal court(s) 7, 8, 23–24, 25, 62, 76, 84, 132, 139, 142, 189
Le Guast, Louis Béranger 17, 64
Le Laboureur, Jean 65
Leo X, Pope 45
Le Roux, Nicolas 43, 53, 69, 171
les Halles 73 (map) 74
Les Tragiques 41, 158, 161
Letter of the clergy of Paris to the duke of Mayenne 83, 173–176
letters (correspondence) 1, 2, 45, 49, 50, 51, 52, 66, 69, 81, 83, 91, 106, 108, 116–118, 120, 122, 123, 132–134, 138–139, 140, 143, 145, 146, 147–148, 150, 155, 157, 160, 162, 164, 167, 170–171, 172, 173–176, 183n49, 184n69, 190, 191
letters patent 146
Lhommet, Martin 159
libraries 8, 75, 87, 98n70
Library of madame de Montpensier 14, 49, 63, 84–87, 112, 158, 173, 188, 192
library of Saint-Victor 63, 84
Limeuil, Isabelle de 11, 25, 48, 65–66, 77, 82, 87–89, 100n112, 104–130, 131, 132, 140, 148, 156, 187, 188, 190, 191, 192, 193
lineage 20, 47, 116, 178, 180
literacy 71, 76, 88, 91, 132, 135, 191
Loire valley 8
Lorraine, Charles, cardinal de 62, 120, 137, 144, 157–163, 169, 176
Loudun, duchy of 146
Louis XII, king of France 37, 45, 131, 156, 178
Louis XIII, king of France 87

Louis XIV, king of France 58n47, 87, 113
Louise de Lorraine, queen of France 52
Louise de Savoie 38
Louvre 8, 19, 44, 70, 73 (map), 75, 79, 81, 110
Lucina 66, 111
Lyon 88, 91, 95n24, 118, 143, 158, 160, 161

Machiavelli 3, 15, 17, 27n6, 49, 187
Mâcon 118
Madeleine de La Tour d'Auvergne 11, 45, 178
Madrid 124
Malcontents 19
Manifesto of Peronne 63
Manifesto of the Ladies of the Court 14, 40, 48–49, 63, 177, 188
manuscript circulation 9, 22, 23, 61–62, 66–67, 69–70, 79, 84–85, 87, 92–93, 93n4, 96n37, 194
Margaret of Austria 38
Marguerite de France, duchesse de Savoie 46, 118, 137, 138
Marguerite de Navarre 160
Marguerite de Valois, queen of France, queen of Navarre 15–17, 18, 38, 54, 56n19, 109
Marie-Antoinette, queen of France 5, 22, 26, 188, 192, 195, 195n2
Marie de Medici, queen of France 13, 29n35, 58n47
Mariéjol, Jean-Hippolyte 17
Marie Stuart, queen of France, queen of Scots 47, 48, 49, 110, 137, 159, 162
marriage, age of consent 136, 151n19
Martin, Henri-Jean 75
masculinity 8, 10, 13–15, 67–68, 84, 92–93, 119, 176
Maulevrier, Charles-Robert de La Marck, comte de 112, 115–116, 121–122, 127n 31, n33
Mayenne, duc de 83, 147, 155, 161, 164, 171, 175, 177, 178
Maza, Sarah 24
McManus, Clare 53
Mears, Natalie 52
Medea 68–69, 113
Medici family 11, 20, 27n6, 29n35, 45–46, 49, 69, 82–83, 114
Medici, Cosimo de, duke of Florence 49, 152n34
Medici, Lorenzo II de 27n6, 45
medicine, medical work 8, 22, 68–69, 77–79, 109, 110, 113, 114, 137

Index 221

menstruation 113, 137
Méré, Jean Poltrot de 168
Meulan 168, 169
Michelet, Jules 2
mignons 3–4, 17, 22, 41, 43, 53, 64, 82, 161, 172
military imagery 12–13, 17, 42
military power 7, 8, 51, 68, 92, 93, 107, 132, 141, 149, 158, 168, 169, 178, 179
misogyny 8, 9, 14, 22, 31n64, 56n19, 67–68, 83, 87, 114, 187, 188, 193
mistresses, royal 19, 46–47, 48, 51, 94n22, 109, 110–111, 113, 137, 138, 159
Montargis 166–167
Montespan, Françoise-Athénaïs, marquise de 113
Montmaur, Pierre de 87
Montmorency, Anne de 46, 89, 115, 136
Montmorency, François de 89–91, 115–116, 136, 151n19, 194
Montmorency-Fosseux, Françoise de 109
Montpensier, Catherine-Marie de Lorraine, duchesse de 14, 23, 26, 49, 54, 63, 71, 79, 83, 84–87, 112, 158, 161, 167–180, 187, 188, 192–193, 194
Montpensier, Jacqueline de Longwy, duchesse de 48
Montpensier, Louis de Bourbon, duc de 167
mont Saint-Genevieve 74
morality 3, 44, 53, 104, 112, 139, 165, 188, 189
Morata, Olympia 156
motherhood 3, 10–11, 15, 26, 46, 47, 48, 54, 64, 71, 82–83, 94n22, 123, 134, 139–140, 143–144, 147–148, 155, 159, 163, 164, 165, 166–167, 168–169, 170, 171–172, 175–176, 177, 178, 179–180, 188, 190, 191, 192
mountebanks see charlatans
mourning 47, 89, 169–172
Munns, Jessica 168
murder 1–2, 5, 14, 24, 41–43, 69, 71, 83, 112–113, 143, 157, 158, 160, 167–172, 175, 179, 180, 184n71, 187, 188
Muses 12–13, 82, 121
mythology (classical) 18, 63, 68–69, 84, 89–91, 94n22, 113

Navarre 139
negotiation 3, 14, 17, 18, 19, 26, 33n77, 38, 48, 50, 52, 54, 102, 104, 106, 124, 132, 137–138, 146–147, 148, 149, 163, 166–167, 171, 178, 179, 180, 187

Nemours, Jacques de Savoie, duc de 25, 50, 51, 65, 67, 83, 110, 131–150, 157, 163–167, 168, 176, 177, 188, 189, 190, 191
neo-Platonism 4, 52
Neuschel, Kristen 6, 145
Nevers, Henriette de Clèves, duchesse de 38, 50, 56n12, 85
news 2, 5, 7, 8, 20, 21, 24, 36, 61–62, 65–66, 72–80, 84, 87, 91, 92–93, 95n24, 108, 109, 116, 117, 118, 119, 123–124, 140, 141, 160, 163, 169, 173, 176, 178, 187–189, 194
noblesse d'épée 8
noblesse de robe 8, 36, 84, 178, 194
Normand, Silje 113, 114, 115, 122
Nostradamus 18
nudity 17, 53, 71, 162

obscenity 8, 64, 67, 82–83, 96n33, 131, 165, 189, 194, 195
occultism/sorcery 4, 18, 68, 113, 120, 177, 194
orality 20–21, 34n89, 36, 63, 72–74, 131–137, 142, 144, 145–146, 149–150, 150n4, 191
Order of Malta 146, 147, 166, 171
Ordinance of Blois (1579), 136
Ordinance of Moulins (1566), 146
Overbury, Thomas 5, 28n14

pageants 13, 52–53
Palais de Justice 8, 22, 24, 35n101, 61–62, 65, 70, 71, 73 (map), 74–77, 194
pamphlets 2, 5, 6, 10, 21, 22–23, 26, 36, 37, 47–48, 52, 55, 62–63, 69–82, 87, 91, 92, 93n5, 96n38, 106, 157–159, 162–163, 164, 172–174, 177, 179, 184n69, 187, 194, 195
Pantagruel 63, 84
papal nuncio 13, 71, 166
paradoxical behaviour 62, 83
Paré, Ambroise 137
Paris 1, 2, 8, 21, 24, 25, 36, 62, 65, 69–80
Parlement of Paris 8, 21, 24, 36–37
parlementaires 8–9, 22, 23, 29n27, 36–37, 38, 42, 61–62, 65–70, 74–76, 79, 80, 81–82, 83–84, 87, 92–93, 173, 176, 187, 188, 190, 194
parlementaires, as producers of literature 8–9, 22, 37, 42, 61–62, 65–70, 75–76, 81–82, 83–84, 87, 92–93, 173, 188, 190, 194
Parthenay-Soubise family 142, 153n41

Pasquier, Estienne 40, 42, 51, 65, 69, 83–84
Pasquil Courtizan 4, 53, 61, 63, 147, 161, 163–164
pasquils 21–22, 62, 68
Passerat, Jean 81
patriarchy 9, 29n30, 37, 42–43, 187, 188, 191–194
patronage 6, 8, 20, 41, 43–44, 47, 49, 53, 82, 83, 107, 121, 124, 172
Pau 139
Peace of Amboise 104, 107
Peace of Monsieur 54
Peace of the Ladies see Treaty of Cambrai
Petit Pont 73 (map), 74, 76, 79
Petit, Vincent 144–145, 165
Petrarchanism 12, 13, 40, 107, 121
Philip II, king of Spain 49, 71
Pibrac, Guy du Faur de 75
Piennes, Jeanne de Halluin de 77, 89–91, 115–116, 136, 191, 194
Pithou, Pierre 81, 96n44
Place Dauphine 77
place de Grève 73–74, 73 (map)
place Maubert 73–74, 97n57, 159
Platière, Imbert de la 50, 118
Pléiade 64
poison 1, 3, 5, 11–12, 20, 24, 25, 41, 63, 68–69, 102–105, 111–115, 116, 121, 122–123, 144, 160, 187, 192
Poitiers 1
Poitiers, Diane de 46–47, 48, 110, 137, 138
Polachek, Dora 168, 170, 172
polemic 2, 3, 4, 10, 21, 22, 41, 55, 56n12, 62, 81, 114, 157, 172, 176, 177, 178
Politics of Female Households, The 51
pollution 115, 158
Poncet, Maurice 81
pont Saint-Michel 73 (map), 74
pornography 15, 22–23, 26, 67, 188, 195
Porte Ste Antoine 71
Pragmatic Sanction of Bourges 23
preachers 21, 29n26, 75, 80, 135, 163, 166, 173, 176, 179, 187
pregnancy 1–2, 37, 46, 51, 109–111, 112, 113, 115, 119, 122, 132, 137, 138, 140, 144, 145, 149, 160, 189, 193
premier maître d'hôtel 63
prestige 7, 43, 46, 47, 52, 55
Prince of the Blood 47, 111, 112
printing 21, 22, 23, 26, 34n89, 37, 62, 69–79, 80, 87, 88, 89, 91, 92, 96n37, 97n57, 157, 158, 159, 172, 187, 194–195

privacy 7–8, 27n2, 79, 91, 115, 120, 132, 134, 162, 188
promiscuity 2, 5, 14, 15, 61, 64, 142, 187, 188, 192
propaganda 23, 38, 70, 168, 170–173, 179, 194
prosopography 19, 43–44
prostitution 1, 11, 14, 18, 21–22, 24, 36, 41–43, 85–87, 92, 112, 115, 188, 193
Protestants see Huguenots
publicity 21, 108
public opinion 1–2, 25, 65, 188
punishment 2, 22, 42–43, 51, 91, 102, 109, 116, 122, 137, 148; *see also* execution

Quaintance, Courtney 83
Quand ce beau printemps je voy 87–89, 107
Quarante-Cinq 169, 180
querelle des amyes 7
querelle des femmes 6

ramas 62, 70, 194
Rambouillet, Catherine de Vivonne, marquise de 38
Rapin, Nicolas 40, 75, 81–82, 83, 190
rapt 137
Recueil des dames 15
recueils de chansons 77, 79, 88, 89, 91
Reformation 3, 10, 38, 105–106, 107, 120, 157, 191
regency 2, 3, 10, 37–38, 44, 45, 47, 48, 49, 114, 141
regicide 23, 81, 172, 173, 175–176
remonstrances 72 (Figure 3.1), 75, 107, 172
Renée de France, duchess of Ferrara 143–144, 156, 164, 165, 166–167
Republic of Letters 8
reputation, collective 2, 3, 5, 6, 14, 19, 21, 26, 28n16, 41–42, 84, 92, 187, 188–189, 193, 194, 195
reputation, rehabilitation of 4, 7, 18, 102, 104, 122–123, 131, 192
Retz, Claude-Catherine de Clermont, maréchale de 12, 38–41, 51, 54, 56n12, 56n14, 62, 81–82, 83, 85, 187
Richards, Penny 168, 169
Richmond, Hugh 18
Rickman, Johanna 50–51
Robert, Anne 22, 37
Roelker, Nancy Lyman 142, 191
Rohan, Françoise de 23, 25, 50, 51, 83, 109, 131–154, 156, 163, 164–167, 176, 177, 179, 187, 189, 190–191, 193

Rohan, Jean de, baron de Frontenay 141, 152n35
Romeo and Juliet 136
Ronsard, Pierre de 13, 38, 82–83, 87–89, 107–108, 121, 124
royal court, absence from 51
royal household, numbers 44–45, 49, 52, 53, 55
royal tour of France (1564–1566) 108–109
Roye, Eléonore de, princesse de Condé 52, 104, 120, 142
Roye, Madeleine de Mailly, comtesse de 142
rue Saint-Denis 73 (map), 115
rue Saint-Jacques 73, 73 (map), 74, 79
Ruggieri, Cosimo 18
rumour 8, 11, 20–21, 25, 66, 91, 92, 102, 104, 105–106, 111, 114, 115, 117, 119, 121–124, 132, 135, 137, 138, 150, 155, 162, 163, 164, 172, 192

sacraments 23, 132, 135, 144, 189
Saint-André, Marguerite de Lustrac, maréchale de 46
Sainte-Chapelle 75
Saint-Gelais, Mellin de 89–91
Saint-Maur-des-Fossés 144
Saint-Séverin cemetery 173
Saint-Séverin crossroads 74
Saint-Simon, duc de 149
Salic law 10, 38, 47, 187
salons 12, 38–41, 62, 81–82, 83
Salzberg, Rosa 79
Sardini, Scipion 66, 122
satire 4, 6, 8, 14, 17, 19, 21–23, 24, 29n26, 36, 40–41, 49, 53, 61–101, 112, 147, 158, 160, 161, 164, 173, 176–177, 188, 190, 192, 193–194, 195
Satyre Ménippée 63, 79, 81, 107, 159, 161, 164
Saulx, Claude de, seigneur de Ventoux et de Torpes 115, 116, 117–118, 122
Sauve, Charlotte de Beaune, dame de 15–17, 18, 54, 61, 84, 187
Savoie, Jeanne de 50
Savoie, Madeleine de 46, 49, 51, 52
scandal, hierarchy of 5, 21, 25, 123
scandal, international knowledge of 9, 102, 104, 120–121, 123, 124, 144–145, 150, 165
Scoreol [councillor in Parlement] 160
Scot, Reginald 113
Scotland 110

Scott-Warren, Jason 85
secrecy 1, 8, 9, 11, 12, 17, 25, 40, 51, 62, 67, 69, 85, 89, 92, 106, 110, 113, 114, 115, 119, 122, 127n32, 131–140, 142–143, 144–145, 146, 148, 149, 160, 162, 166, 177, 189
secretary of state 108, 118, 119, 122, 178
seduction 3, 12, 15, 17, 19, 47, 61, 106, 131, 137, 149
Séguier, Pierre II 75
Semonides of Amorgos 14
sermons 29n26, 75, 135, 172, 173, 176, 187
servants 2, 6, 15, 21, 24, 41, 43, 44, 45, 46, 47, 48, 49–50, 51, 52, 53, 55, 61, 68, 80, 81, 85, 109, 113, 117, 118, 132, 134–136, 137–138, 140–141, 145, 148, 150, 160, 164, 166, 191
sexual deviance 3, 4, 5, 11, 12, 14, 26, 54, 65, 87, 187, 188, 193, 194
sexual intercourse 134, 136, 137, 145, 158
sexual voracity 14, 15, 24, 26, 61, 83, 84, 85, 158, 173, 177, 187
shame 5, 21, 22, 36, 42, 43, 91, 102, 110, 131, 134, 136, 149, 177, 188, 189, 193
Shennan, J. H. 74
sieges 12, 53, 71, 178
sixain 63–64
The Sixteen 155
sodomy 5, 41, 56n12, 61, 64, 65, 82–83, 113, 127n48, 147, 158, 161
Solnon, Jean-François 19, 44
songs 21, 62, 63, 77, 79, 80, 84, 87–92, 100n112, 101n124, 107, 187, 193, 194, 195
sonnet 13, 41, 62, 64, 82, 94n18, 107, 121, 159
sottie 80
soundscape 24, 62
St. Bartholomew Day's massacre 10, 166
Stombler, Mindy 6
Stone, Lawrence 6
submission 140, 168, 169, 170, 176, 179, 189
suicide 172
Sutherland, Nicola 9–10

Tabarin 77
Tableau de madame de Montpensier 173, 174 (Figure 6.2)
tabloid journalism 8
Tarbé, Prosper 22
taxes 67, 148
tenacity 7, 143, 166, 167, 179

224 *Index*

testimony 116, 132, 134, 137, 138, 140, 149, 191
torture 75, 86, 113, 131, 168
Touchet, Marie 111
treason 69, 80, 81, 92, 112, 113
Treaty d'Etaples 37
Treaty of Cambrai ('Ladies Peace'), 38
Tuscany 11, 49, 68
tyranny 11, 81, 155, 170, 172, 176

university education 9, 14, 36, 37, 40, 62, 65, 66, 67, 80, 109
University of Paris 70
Uzès, Louise de Clermont-Tonnerre, duchesse d' 49, 86

van Orden, Kate 13, 77, 89
Vatican 23, 89, 115, 124, 136, 166, 171, 179, 191
Vatican Rota 131, 165
Venice 69, 79, 80, 84
Vermondet, lieutenant general of Limoges 160
Versailles 43, 57n31, 188
verse libels 2, 6, 8, 14, 24, 41, 53, 63, 64, 65, 67, 70, 80, 83, 84, 131, 179, 187, 189, 194, 195
Vienne 118, 146
Viennot, Eliane 38, 170
Viète, François 83, 100n100, 142, 153n41, 176, 190

Villequier, René de 1, 41–43, 54, 114
Villon, François 76
Virgil 37, 40
virginity 31n64, 86–87, 175–176
virility 14, 119
Vitry, Louise de l'Hospital, damoiselle de 110, 126n23
vows, oral 134, 135, 136, 137

Waele, Michel de 38
warfare 12, 15
Wars of Religion 3, 6, 10, 13, 17, 22, 25, 38, 52, 88, 89, 131, 142, 146, 147, 166
Wassy, massacre 3, 163, 179
weddings 4, 51, 67, 80, 86, 114, 119, 122, 131, 136, 144–145, 146, 164, 165, 188
whoredom 1, 2, 17, 32n69, 41, 42, 49, 81, 83, 94n22, 159, 165, 188
widowhood 15, 26, 45, 47, 112, 143, 163, 164, 165, 167, 168–169, 170–171, 176, 179, 188
Windsor Beauties 19–20
witchcraft see occultism/sorcery
woodcuts 71, 172

xenophobia 3, 10, 11, 114

Zemon Davis, Natalie 91, 195
Zum Kolk, Caroline 10, 19, 44, 46, 48, 52, 53
Zvereva, Alexandra 20

9781472428219